Like a
Butterfly

1

Story and Art by
suu
Morishita

🦋 Contents 🦋

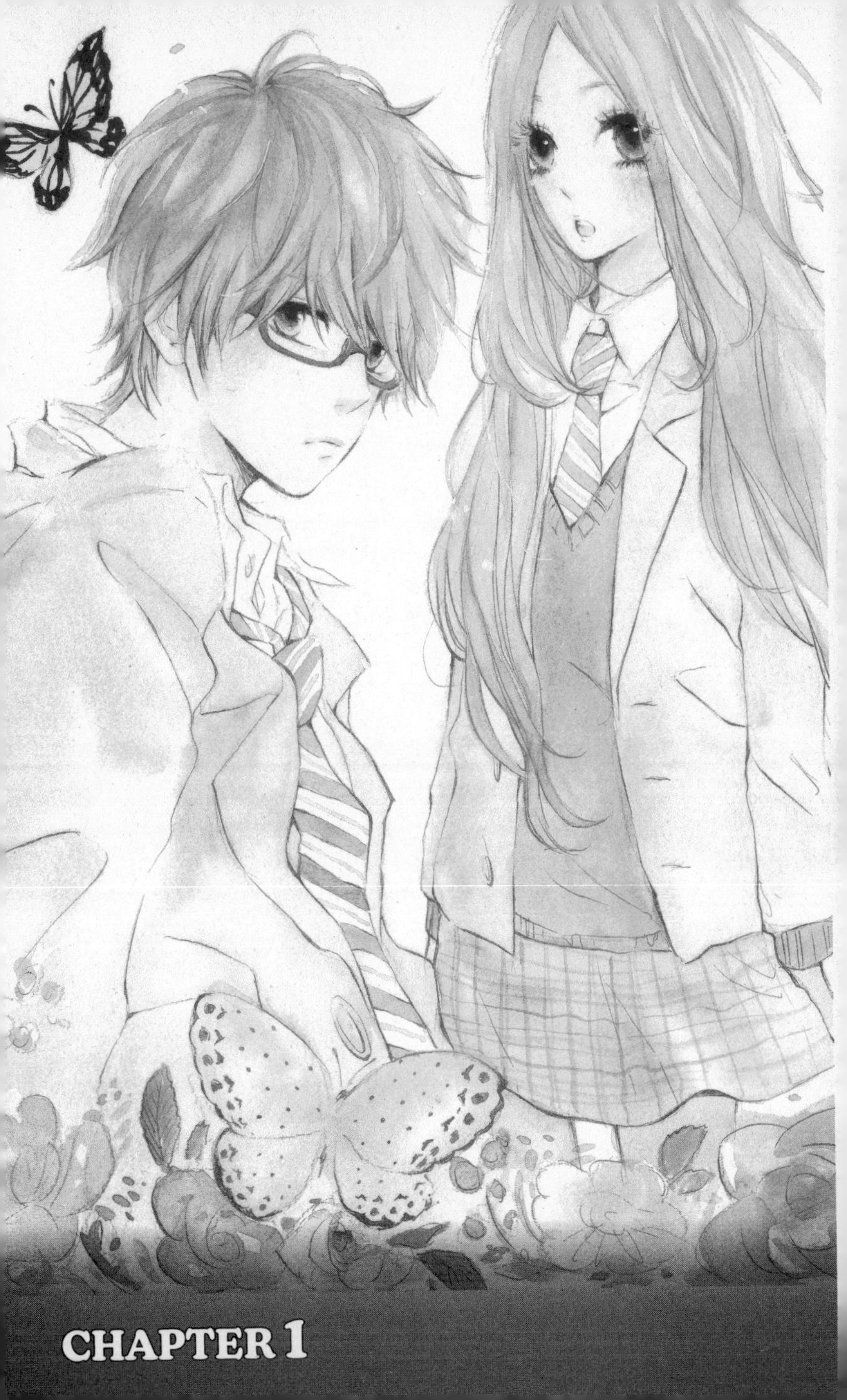

CHAPTER 1

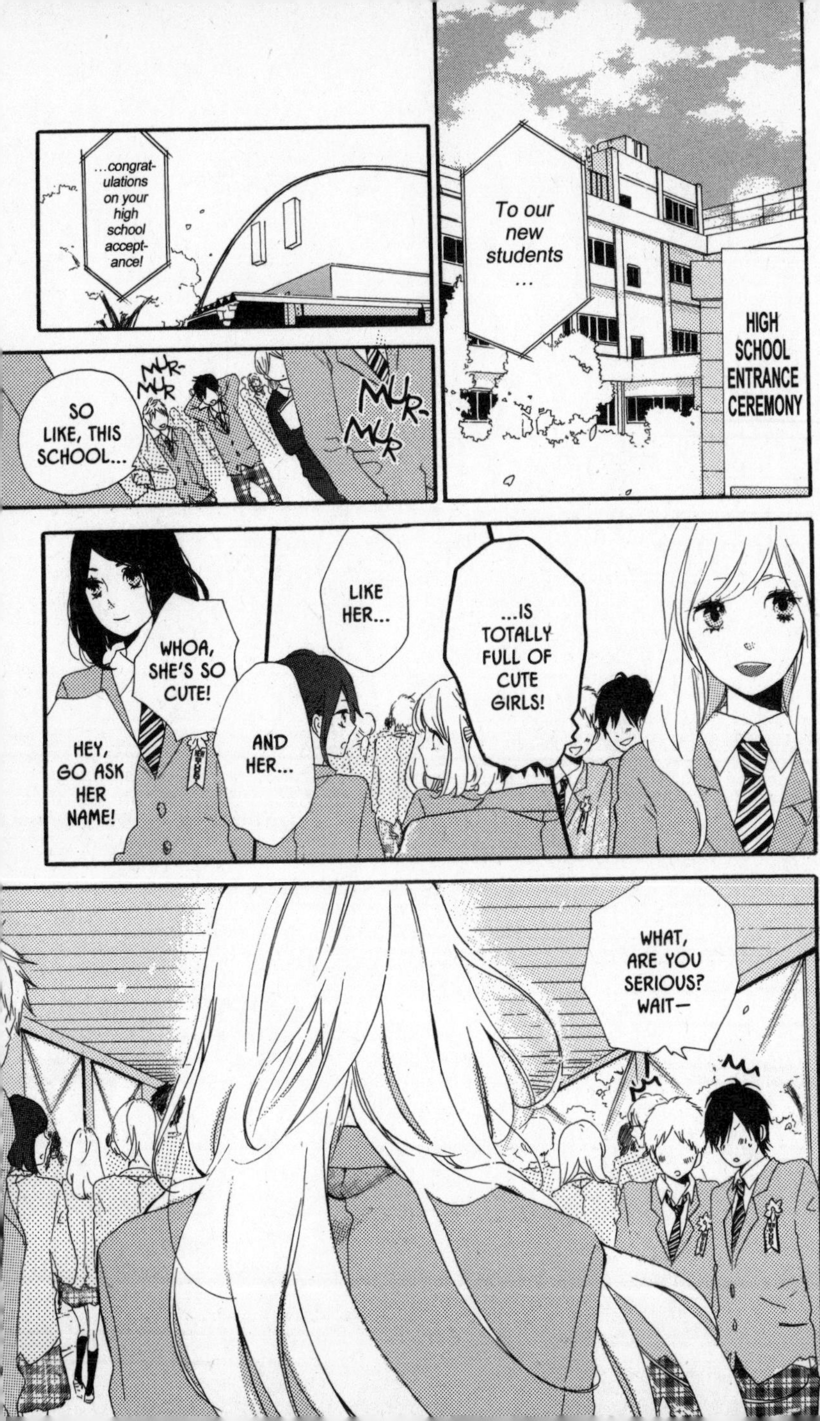
To our new students…
HIGH SCHOOL ENTRANCE CEREMONY
…congratulations on your high school acceptance!
MUR-MUR
MUR-MUR
SO LIKE, THIS SCHOOL…
…IS TOTALLY FULL OF CUTE GIRLS!
LIKE HER…
AND HER…
WHOA, SHE'S SO CUTE!
HEY, GO ASK HER NAME!
WHAT, ARE YOU SERIOUS? WAIT—

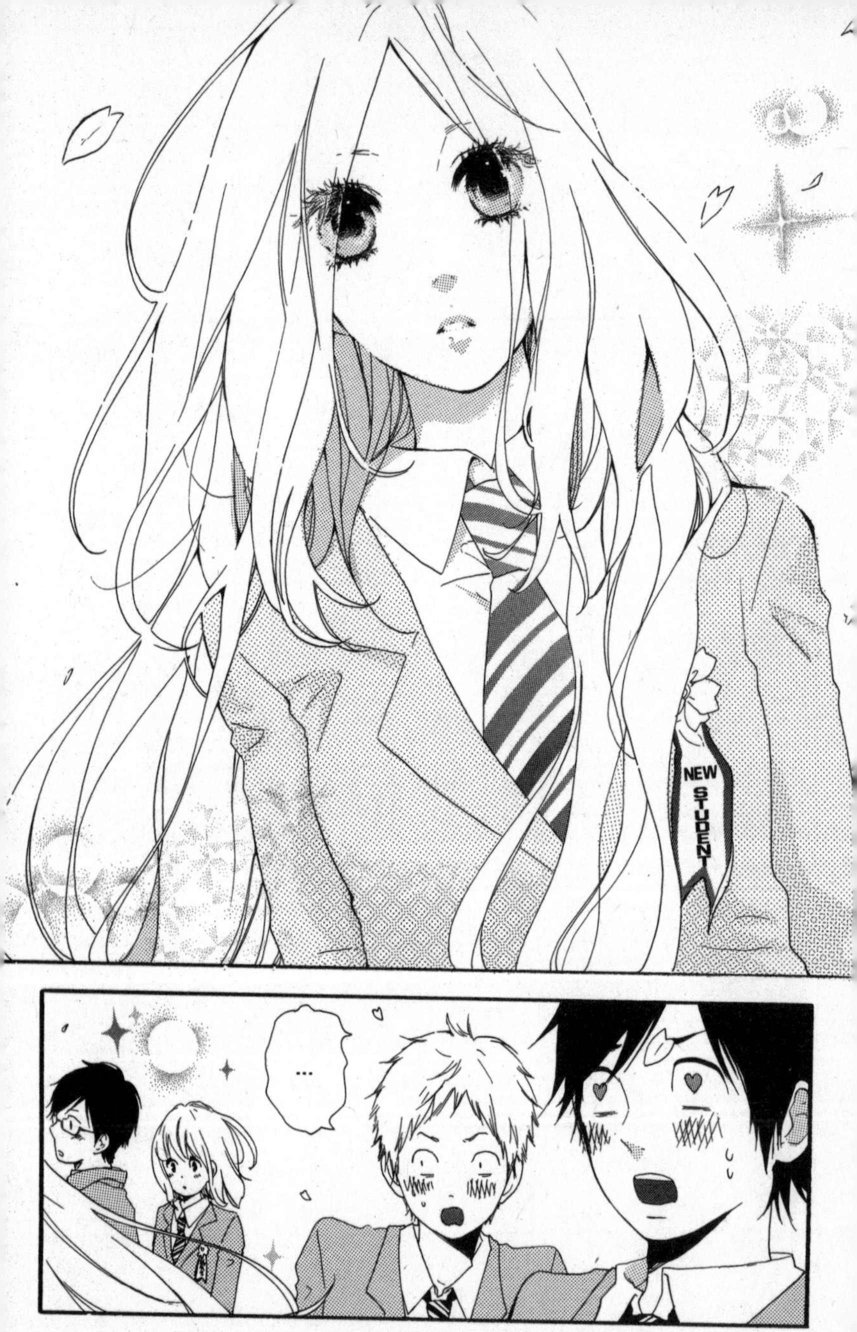
NEW STUDENT
...

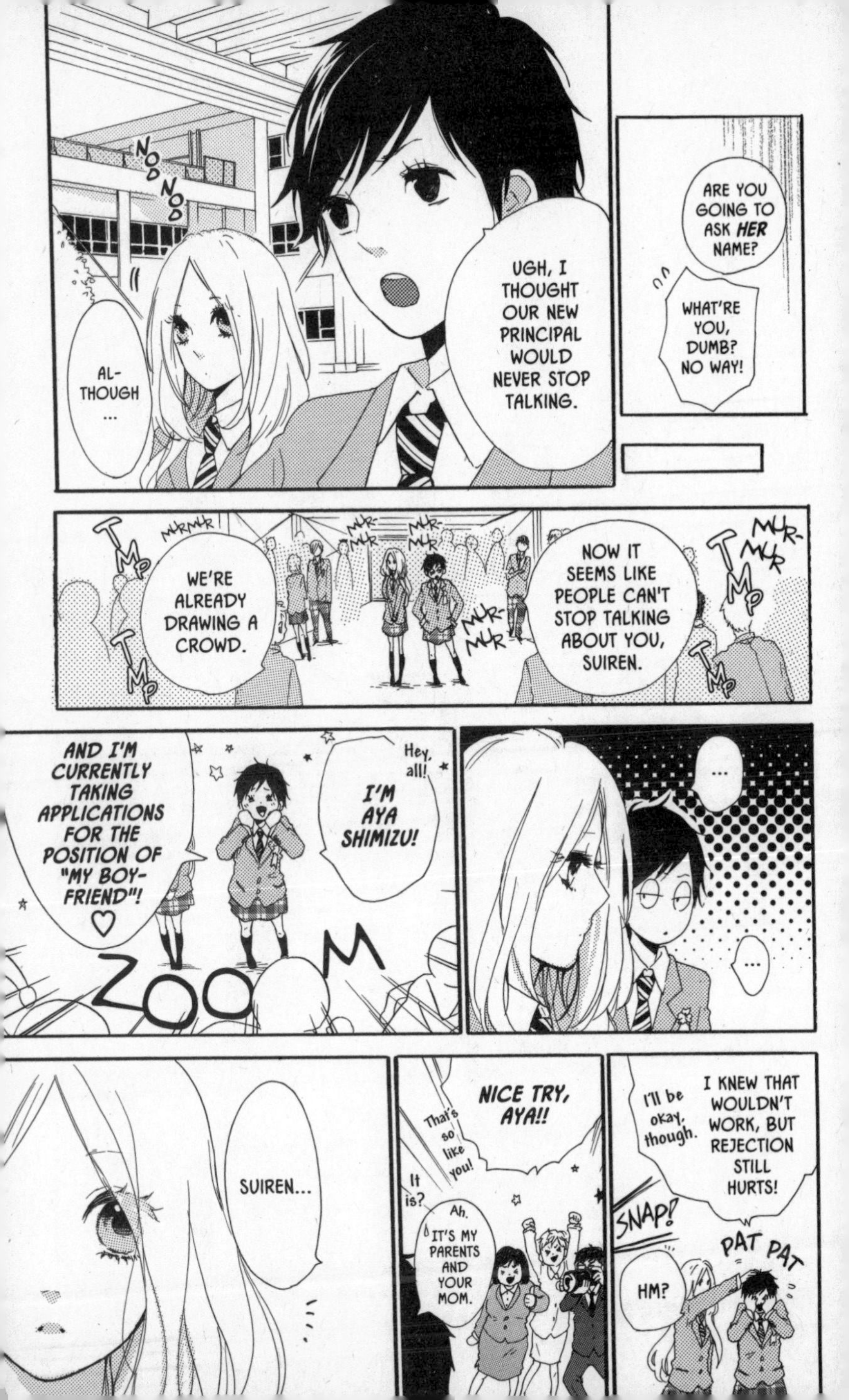
ARE YOU GOING TO ASK HER NAME?
WHAT'RE YOU, DUMB? NO WAY!
UGH, I THOUGHT OUR NEW PRINCIPAL WOULD NEVER STOP TALKING.
NOD NOD
AL-THOUGH ...
MUR-MUR
TMP
TMP
NOW IT SEEMS LIKE PEOPLE CAN'T STOP TALKING ABOUT YOU, SUIREN.
MUR-MUR
MUR-MUR
MURMUR
WE'RE ALREADY DRAWING A CROWD.
TMP
TMP
...
...
Hey, all!
I'M AYA SHIMIZU!
AND I'M CURRENTLY TAKING APPLICATIONS FOR THE POSITION OF "MY BOY-FRIEND"! ♡
ZOOOM
I KNEW THAT WOULDN'T WORK, BUT REJECTION STILL HURTS!
I'll be okay, though.
SNAP!
PAT PAT
HM?
NICE TRY, AYA!!
That's so like you!
It is?
Ah.
IT'S MY PARENTS AND YOUR MOM.
SUIREN...

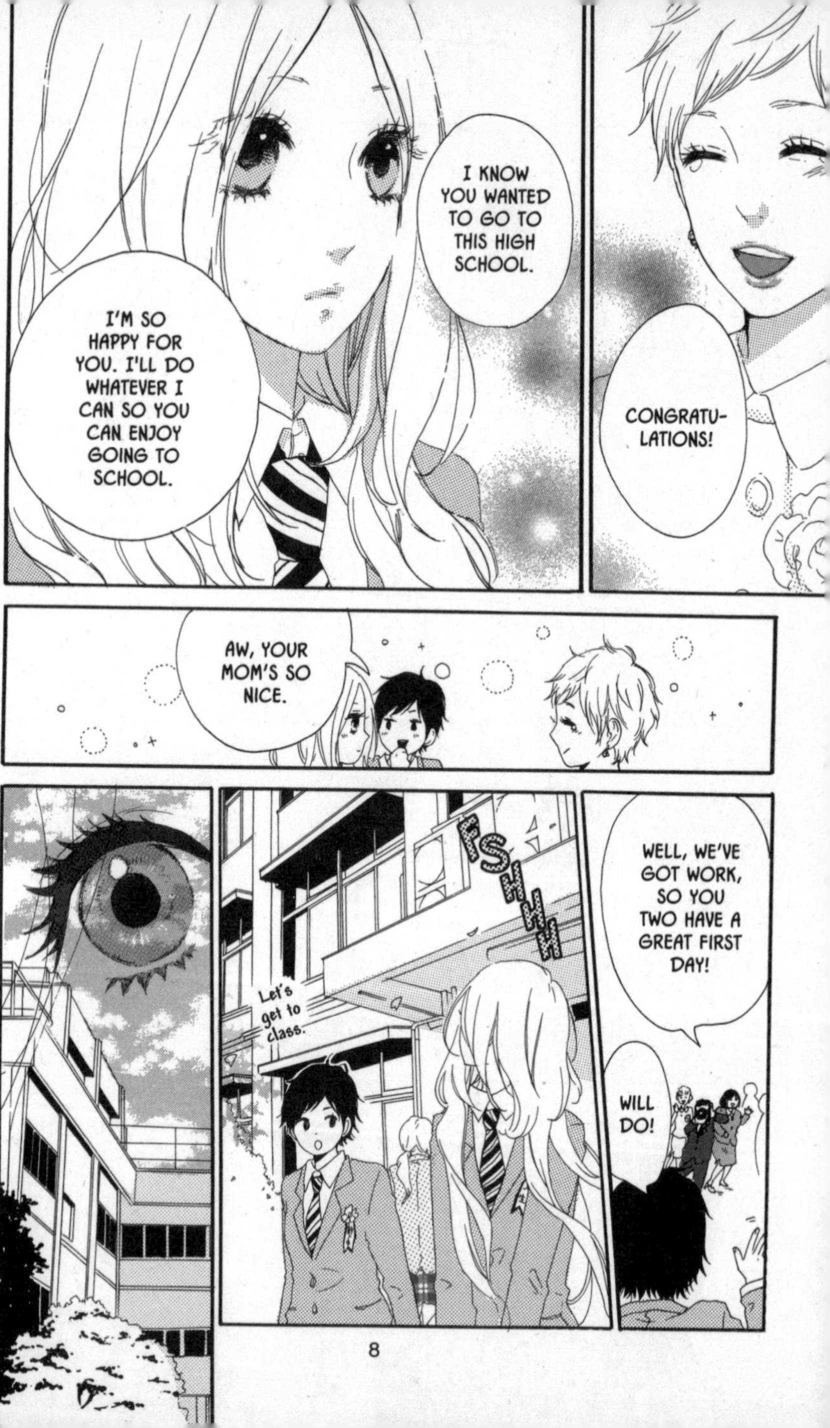
CONGRATU-LATIONS!
I KNOW YOU WANTED TO GO TO THIS HIGH SCHOOL.
I'M SO HAPPY FOR YOU. I'LL DO WHATEVER I CAN SO YOU CAN ENJOY GOING TO SCHOOL.
AW, YOUR MOM'S SO NICE.
WELL, WE'VE GOT WORK, SO YOU TWO HAVE A GREAT FIRST DAY!
WILL DO!
FSHHHH
Let's get to class.

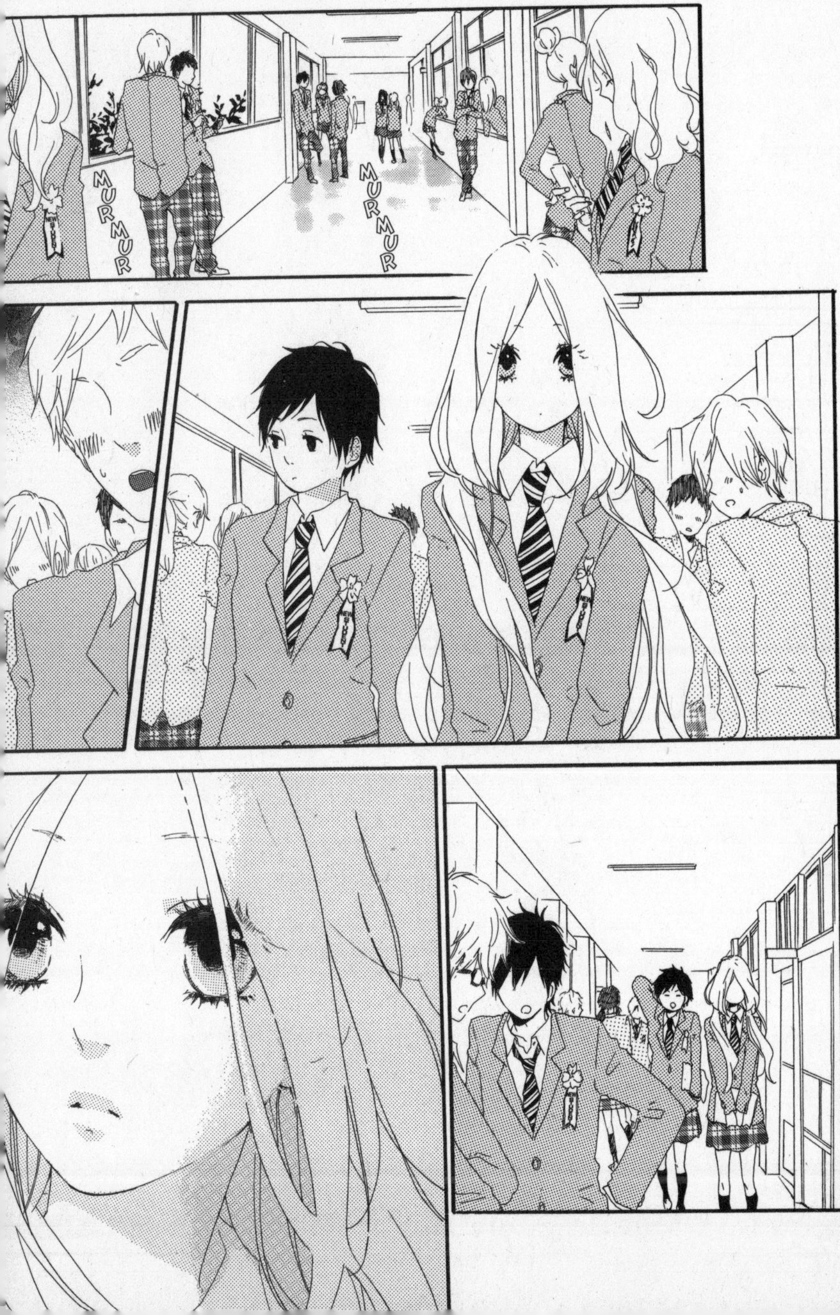
MURMUR
MURMUR

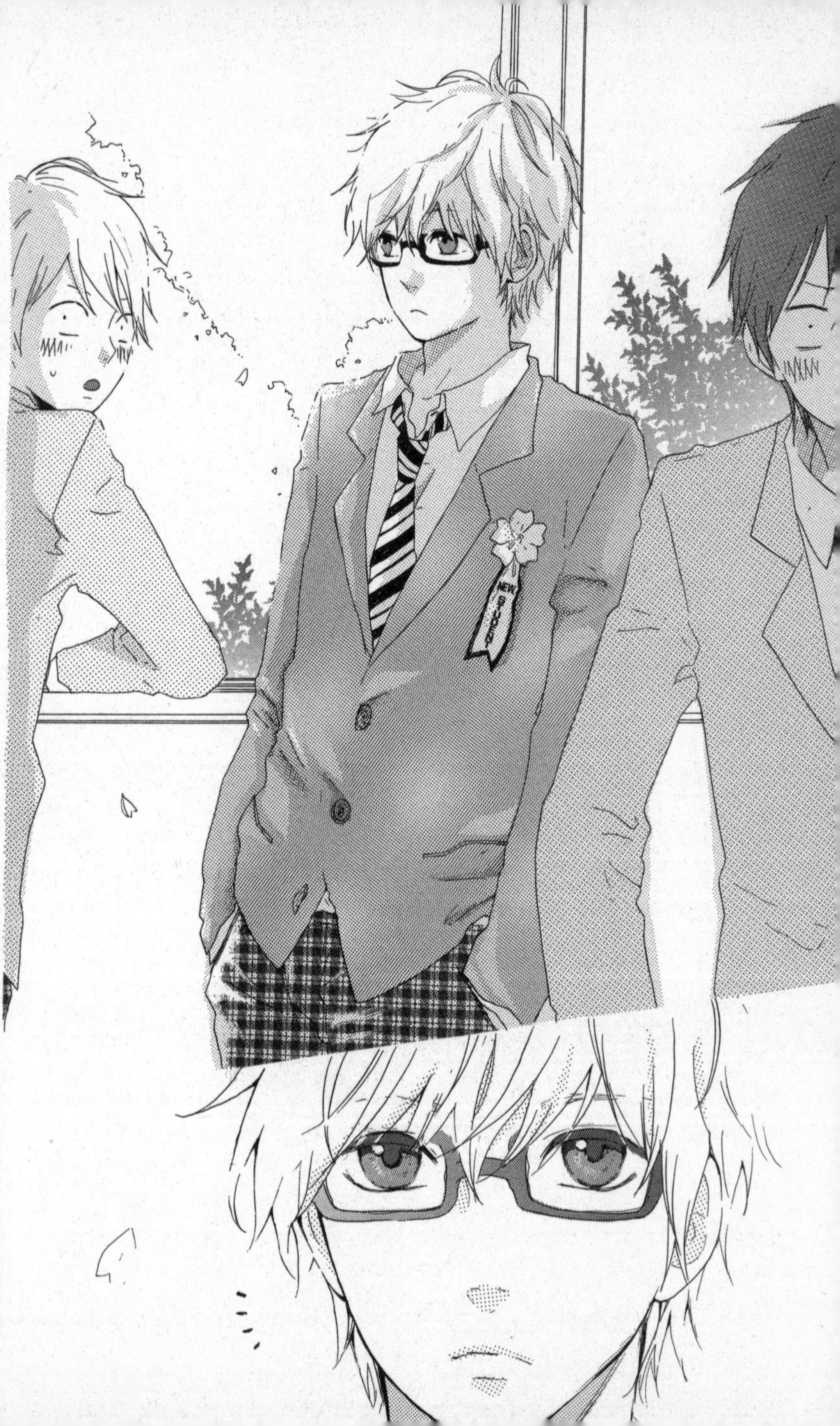
NEW STUDENT

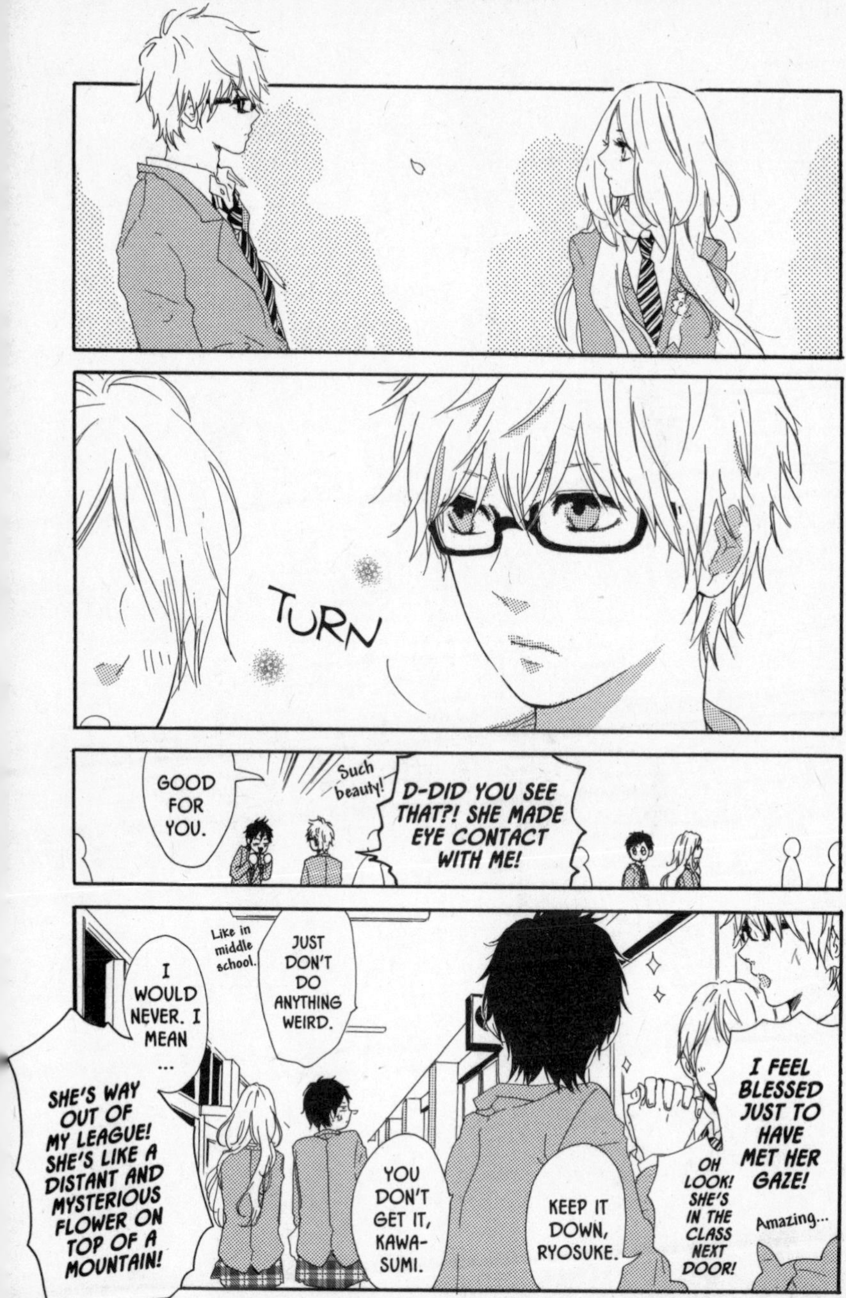
TURN
D-DID YOU SEE THAT?! SHE MADE EYE CONTACT WITH ME!
Such beauty!
GOOD FOR YOU.
I FEEL BLESSED JUST TO HAVE MET HER GAZE!
OH LOOK! SHE'S IN THE CLASS NEXT DOOR!
Amazing...
KEEP IT DOWN, RYOSUKE.
YOU DON'T GET IT, KAWA-SUMI.
JUST DON'T DO ANYTHING WEIRD.
Like in middle school.
I WOULD NEVER. I MEAN ...
SHE'S WAY OUT OF MY LEAGUE! SHE'S LIKE A DISTANT AND MYSTERIOUS FLOWER ON TOP OF A MOUNTAIN!

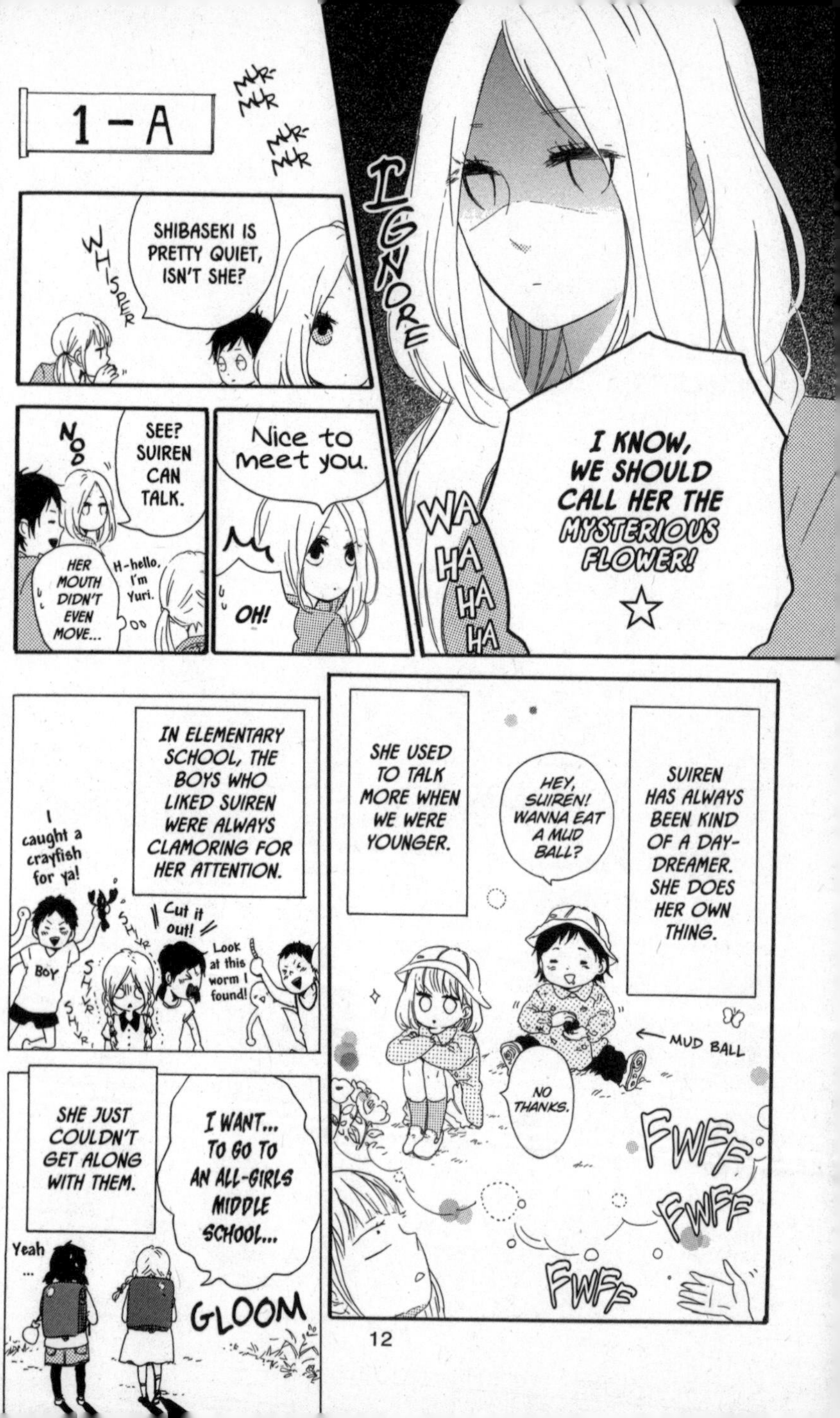
IGNORE
I KNOW, WE SHOULD CALL HER THE MYSTERIOUS FLOWER! ☆
WA HA HA HA HA
1-A
MUR-MUR
MUR-MUR
SHIBASEKI IS PRETTY QUIET, ISN'T SHE?
WHISPER
Nice to meet you.
OH!
SEE? SUIREN CAN TALK.
NOD
H-hello, I'm Yuri.
HER MOUTH DIDN'T EVEN MOVE...
SUIREN HAS ALWAYS BEEN KIND OF A DAY-DREAMER. SHE DOES HER OWN THING.
HEY, SUIREN! WANNA EAT A MUD BALL?
SHE USED TO TALK MORE WHEN WE WERE YOUNGER.
MUD BALL
NO THANKS.
FWFF
FWFF
FWFF
IN ELEMENTARY SCHOOL, THE BOYS WHO LIKED SUIREN WERE ALWAYS CLAMORING FOR HER ATTENTION.
Look at this worm I found!
Cut it out!
SHIVER
I caught a crayfish for ya!
BOY
I WANT... TO GO TO AN ALL-GIRLS MIDDLE SCHOOL...
SHE JUST COULDN'T GET ALONG WITH THEM.
GLOOM
Yeah...

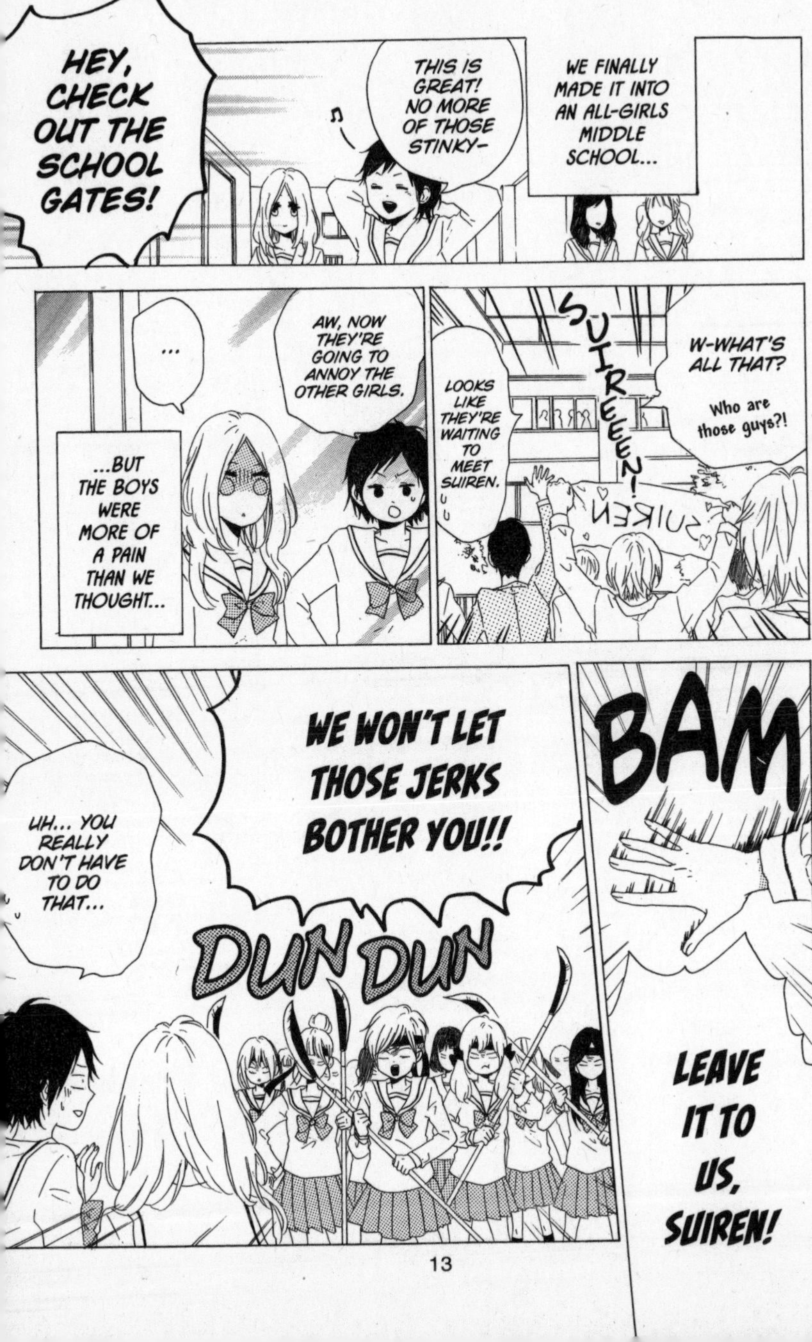
WE FINALLY MADE IT INTO AN ALL-GIRLS MIDDLE SCHOOL...
THIS IS GREAT! NO MORE OF THOSE STINKY-
HEY, CHECK OUT THE SCHOOL GATES!
SUIREEEN!
W-WHAT'S ALL THAT?
Who are those guys?!
LOOKS LIKE THEY'RE WAITING TO MEET SUIREN.
SUIREN
AW, NOW THEY'RE GOING TO ANNOY THE OTHER GIRLS.
...
...BUT THE BOYS WERE MORE OF A PAIN THAN WE THOUGHT...
BAM
LEAVE IT TO US, SUIREN!
WE WON'T LET THOSE JERKS BOTHER YOU!!
DUN DUN
UH... YOU REALLY DON'T HAVE TO DO THAT...

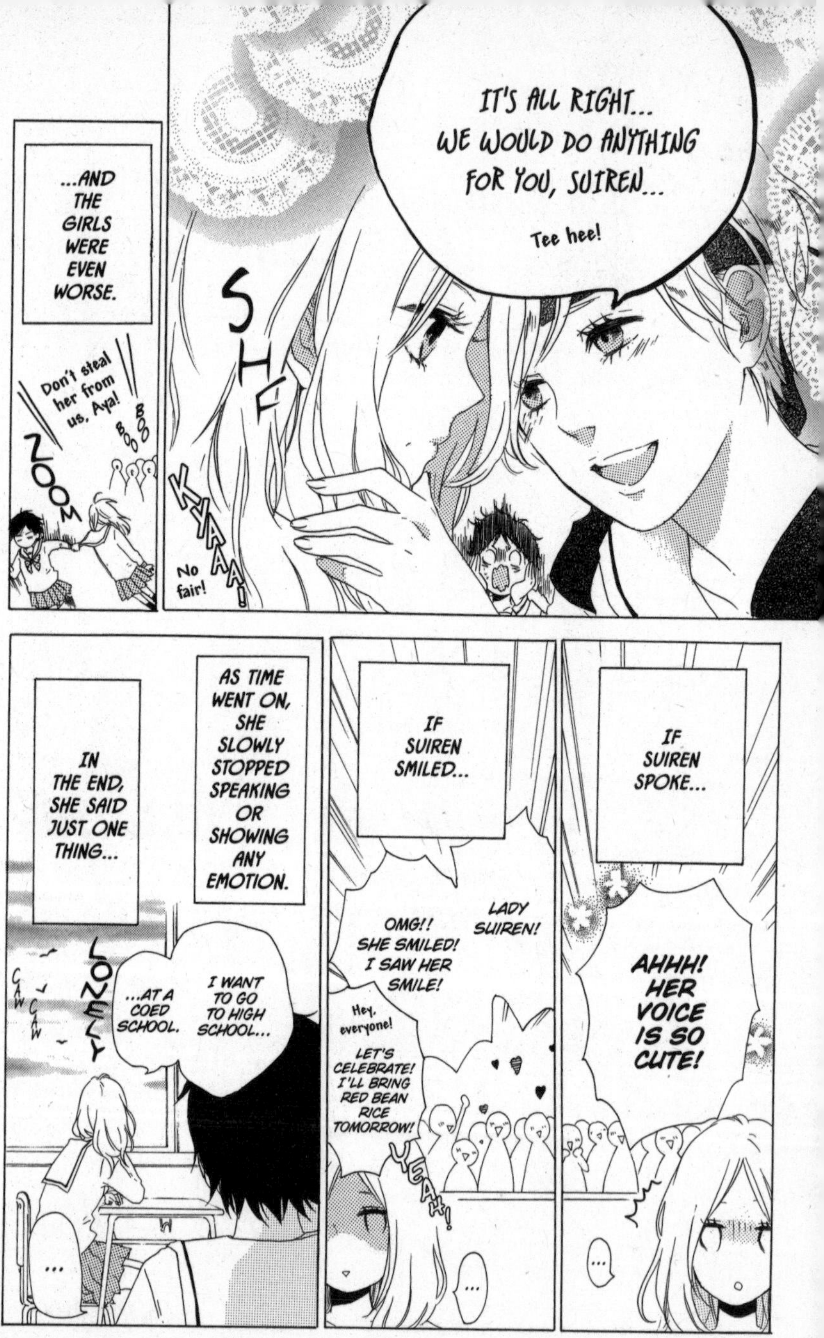
IT'S ALL RIGHT... WE WOULD DO ANYTHING FOR YOU, SUIREN...
Tee hee!
SHF
KYAAAA!
No fair!
...AND THE GIRLS WERE EVEN WORSE.
Don't steal her from us, Aya!
BOOO
ZOOM
IF SUIREN SPOKE...
AHHH! HER VOICE IS SO CUTE!
...
IF SUIREN SMILED...
LADY SUIREN!
OMG!! SHE SMILED! I SAW HER SMILE!
Hey, everyone!
LET'S CELEBRATE! I'LL BRING RED BEAN RICE TOMORROW!
YEAH!
...
AS TIME WENT ON, SHE SLOWLY STOPPED SPEAKING OR SHOWING ANY EMOTION.
IN THE END, SHE SAID JUST ONE THING...
I WANT TO GO TO HIGH SCHOOL...
...AT A COED SCHOOL.
LONELY
CAW CAW
...

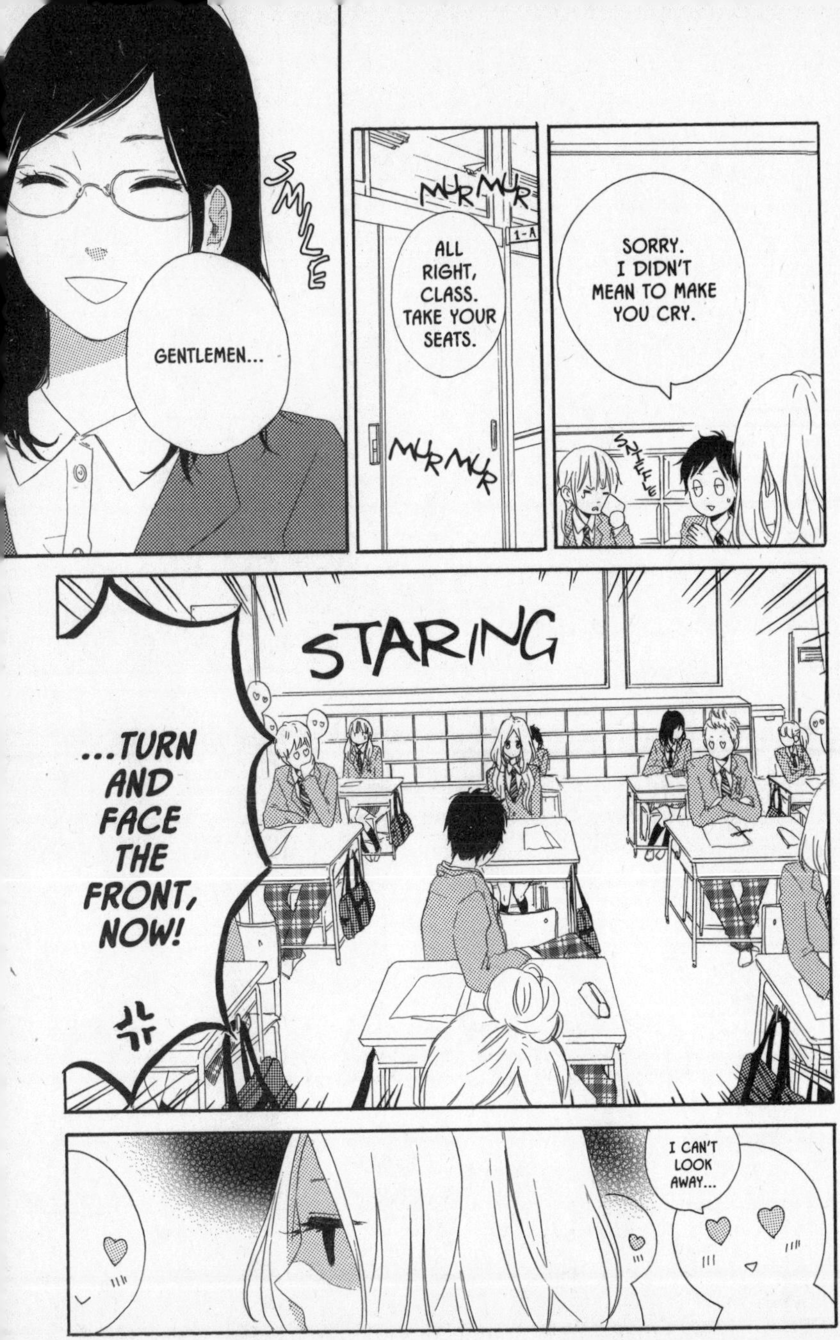
SORRY. I DIDN'T MEAN TO MAKE YOU CRY.
SNIFFLE
MURMUR
ALL RIGHT, CLASS. TAKE YOUR SEATS.
MURMUR
SMILE
GENTLEMEN...
STARING
...TURN AND FACE THE FRONT, NOW!
I CAN'T LOOK AWAY...

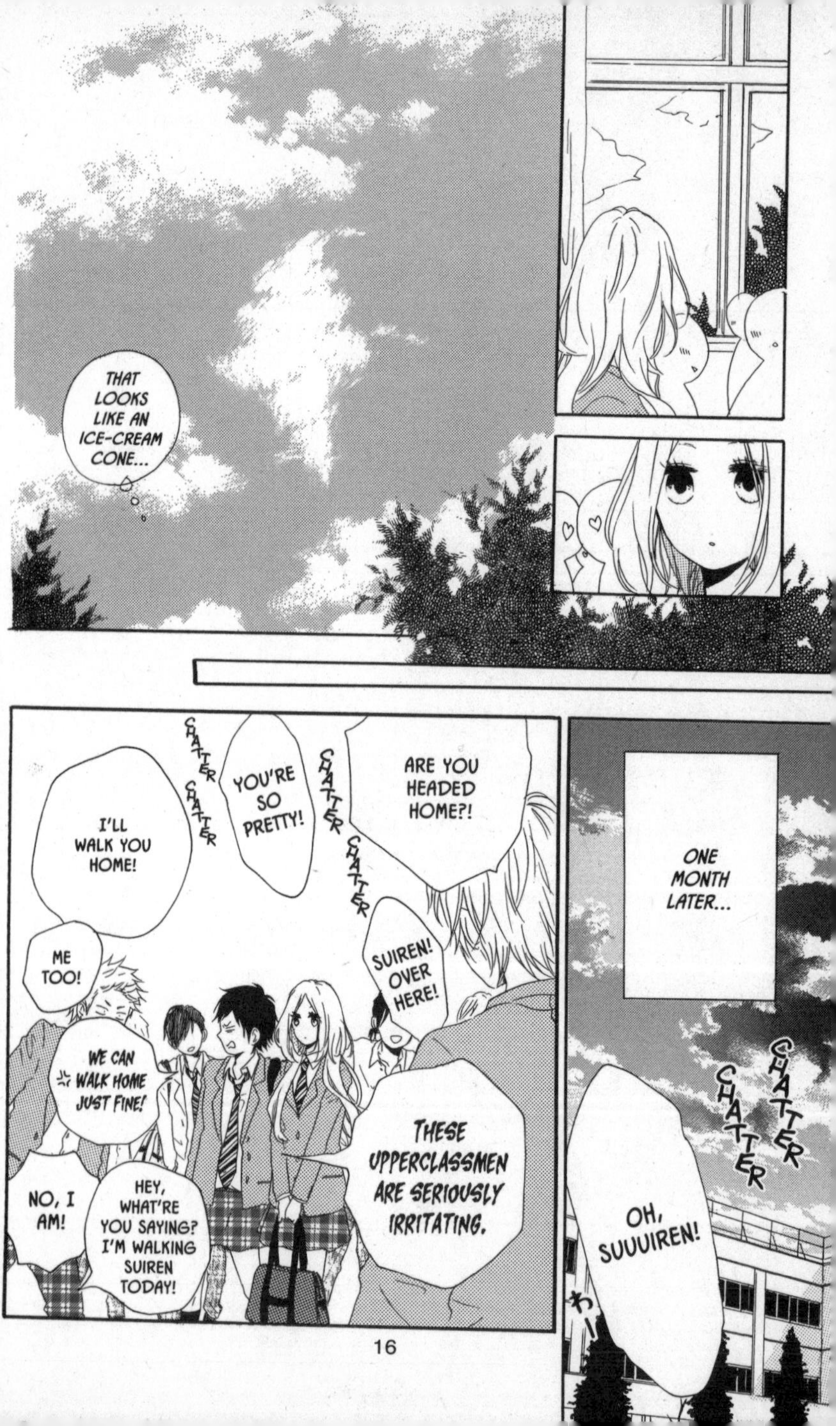
THAT LOOKS LIKE AN ICE-CREAM CONE...
ONE MONTH LATER...
CHATTER CHATTER
OH, SUUUIREN!
わー
ARE YOU HEADED HOME?!
CHATTER CHATTER
YOU'RE SO PRETTY!
CHATTER CHATTER
I'LL WALK YOU HOME!
SUIREN! OVER HERE!
ME TOO!
THESE UPPERCLASSMEN ARE SERIOUSLY IRRITATING.
WE CAN WALK HOME JUST FINE!
HEY, WHAT'RE YOU SAYING? I'M WALKING SUIREN TODAY!
NO, I AM!

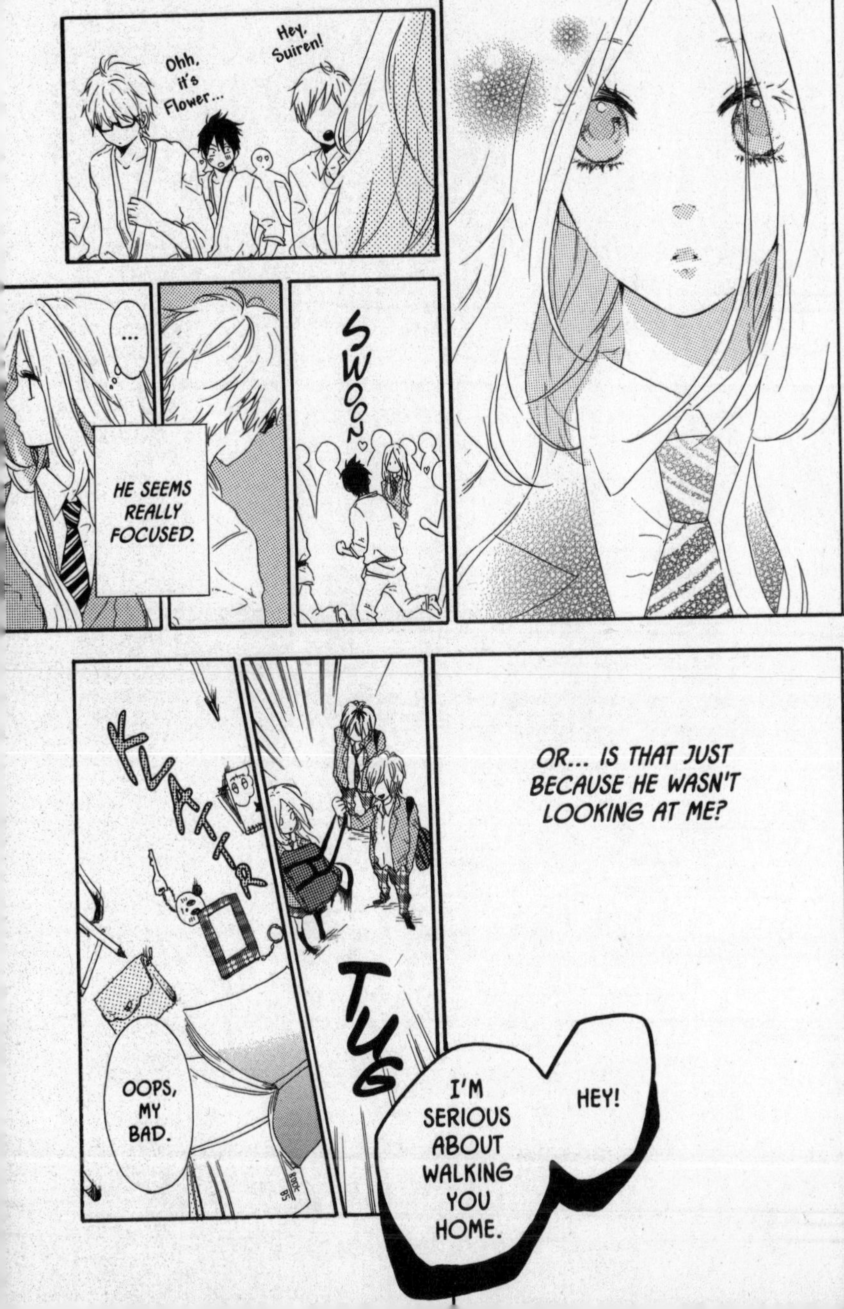
Hey, Suiren!
Ohh, it's Flower...
SWOON
...
HE SEEMS REALLY FOCUSED.
OR... IS THAT JUST BECAUSE HE WASN'T LOOKING AT ME?
HEY!
I'M SERIOUS ABOUT WALKING YOU HOME.
TUG
KLATTER
OOPS, MY BAD.

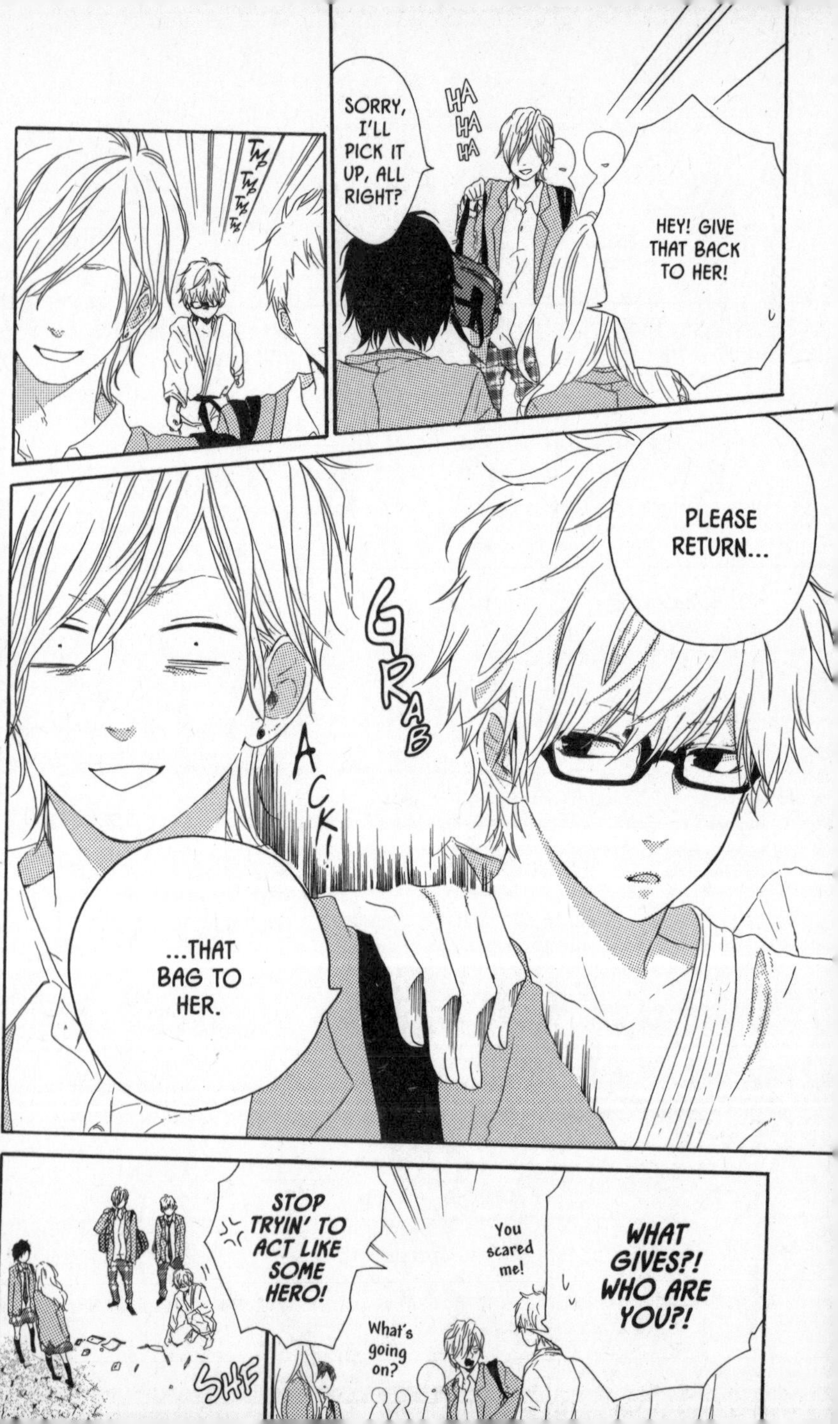
HEY! GIVE THAT BACK TO HER!
HA HA HA HA
SORRY, I'LL PICK IT UP, ALL RIGHT?
TMP TMP TMP TMP
PLEASE RETURN...
GRAB
ACK!
...THAT BAG TO HER.
WHAT GIVES?! WHO ARE YOU?!
You scared me!
What's going on?
STOP TRYIN' TO ACT LIKE SOME HERO!
SHF

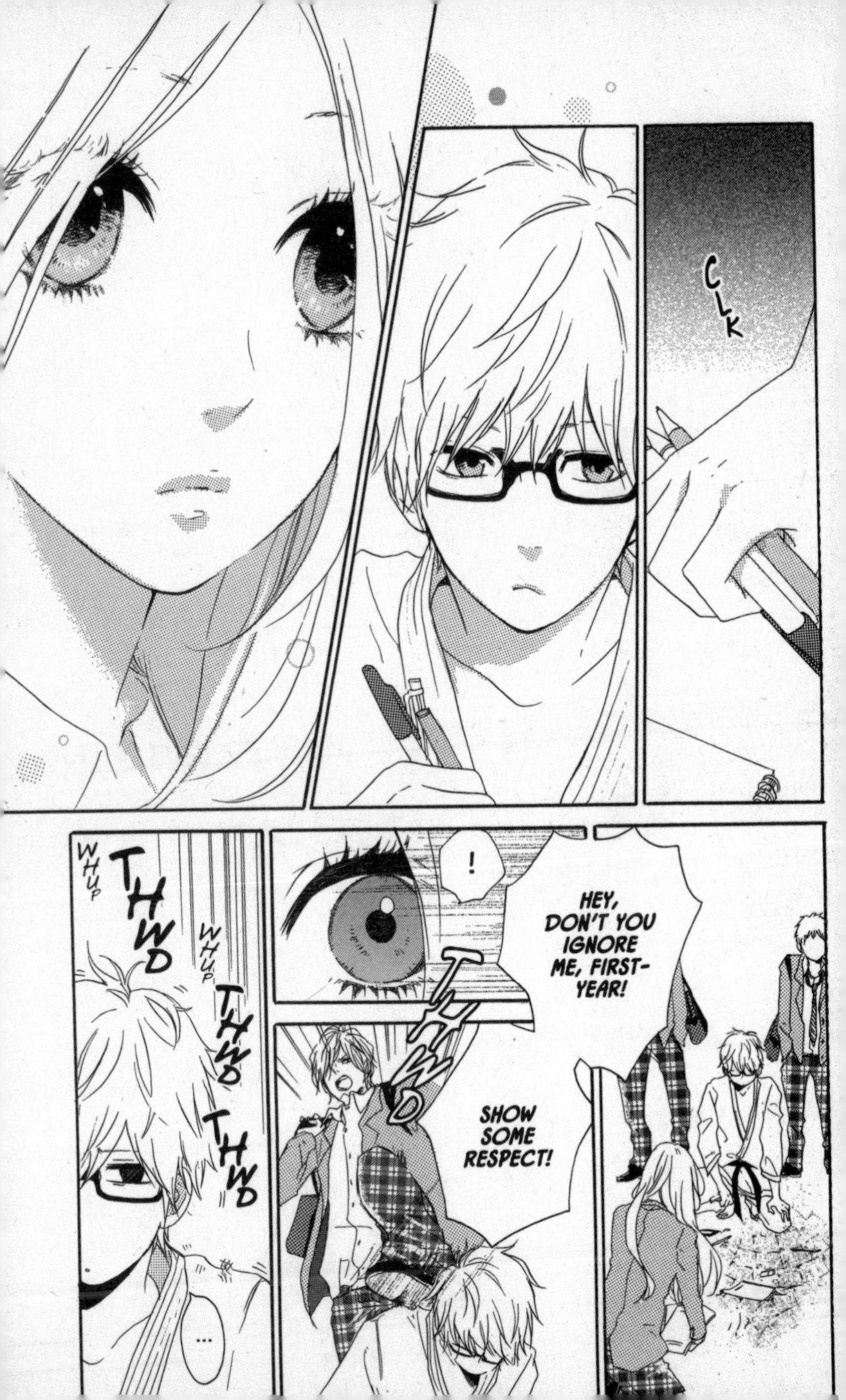
CLK
HEY, DON'T YOU IGNORE ME, FIRST-YEAR!
!
THWD
SHOW SOME RESPECT!
WHUP
THWD
WHUP
THWD
THWD
...

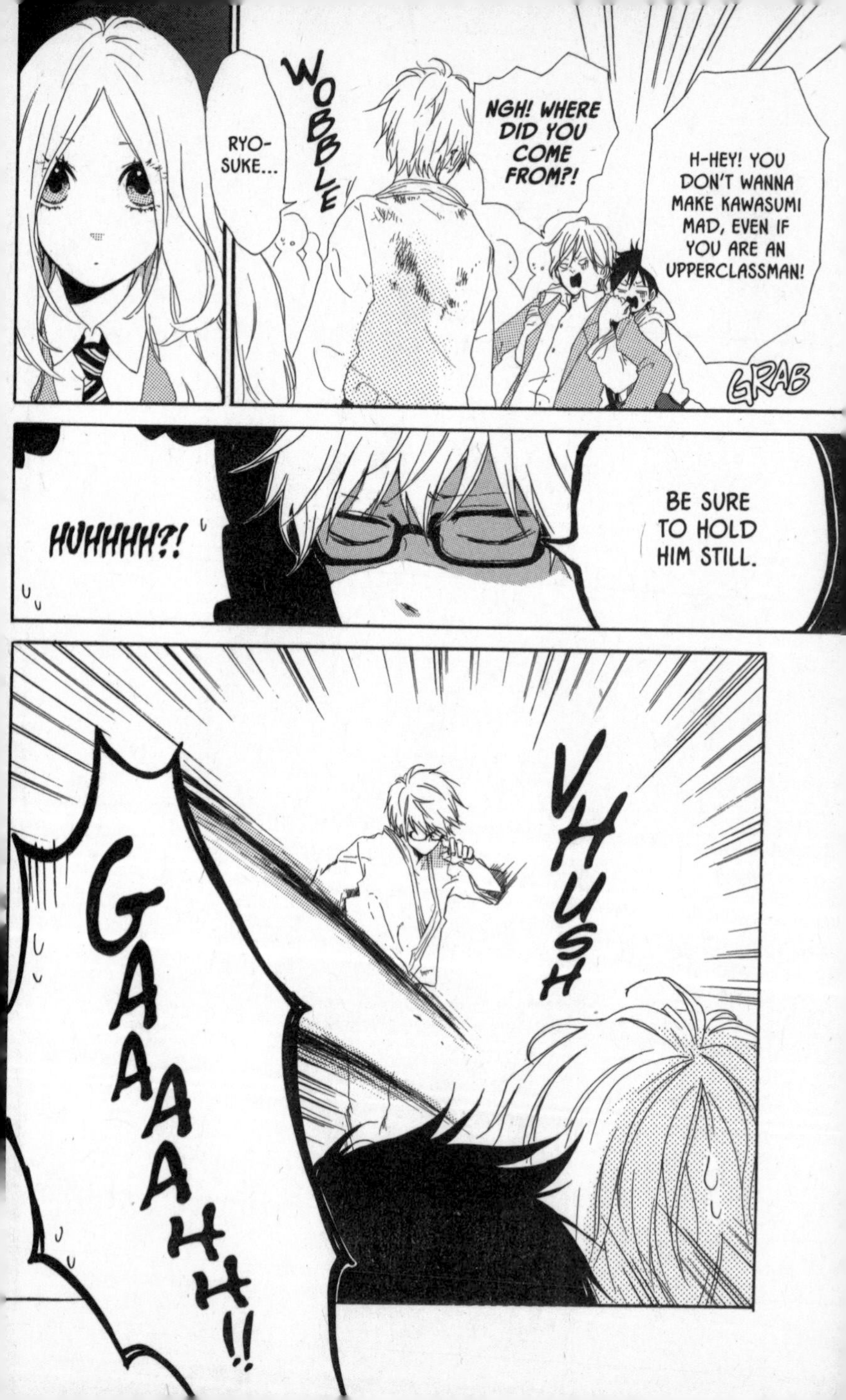
H-HEY! YOU DON'T WANNA MAKE KAWASUMI MAD, EVEN IF YOU ARE AN UPPERCLASSMAN!
GRAB
NGH! WHERE DID YOU COME FROM?!
WOBBLE
RYO-SUKE...
BE SURE TO HOLD HIM STILL.
HUHHHH?!
VHUSH
GAAAAAHH!!

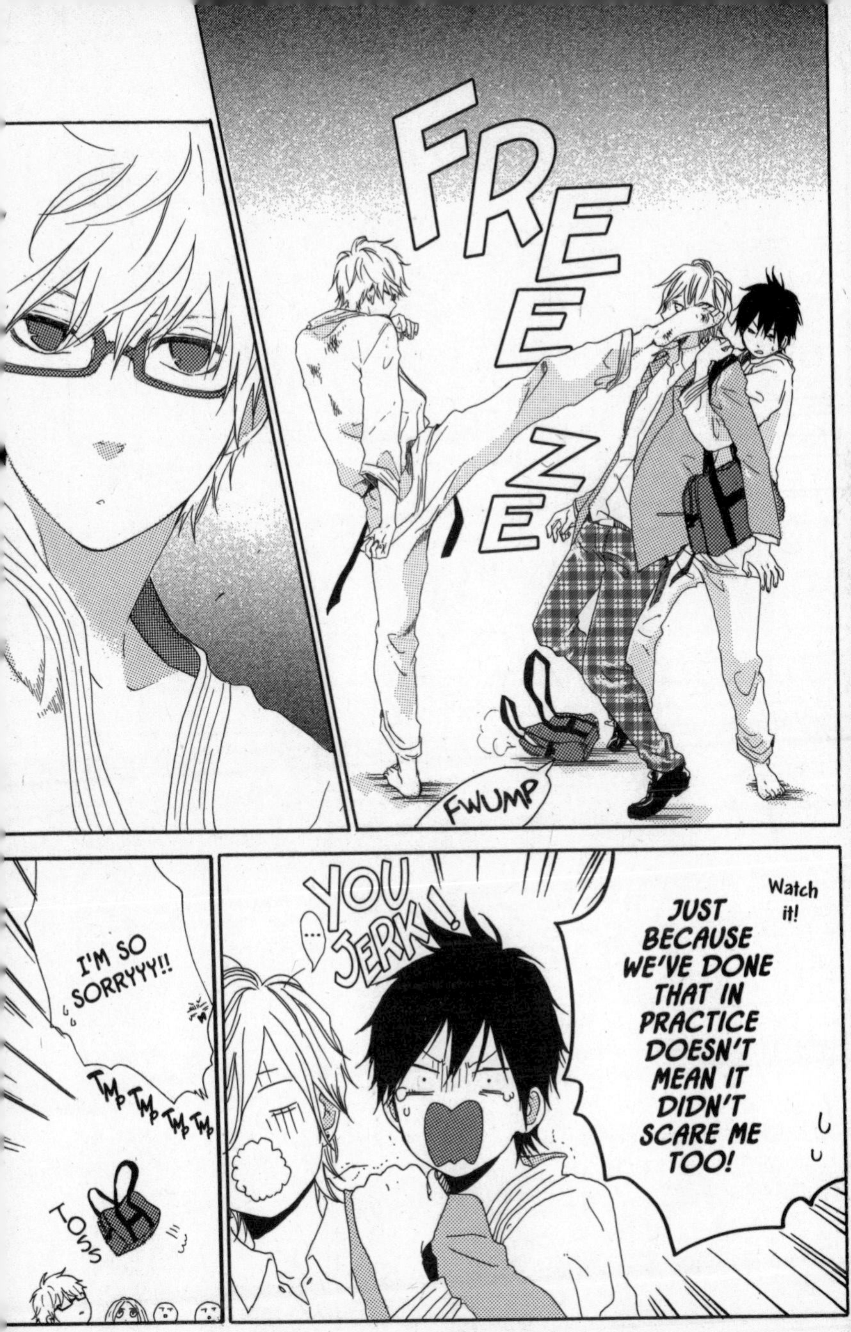
FREEZE
FWUMP
Watch it!
JUST BECAUSE WE'VE DONE THAT IN PRACTICE DOESN'T MEAN IT DIDN'T SCARE ME TOO!
YOU JERK!
...
I'M SO SORRYYY!!
TMP TMP TMP TMP
TOSS

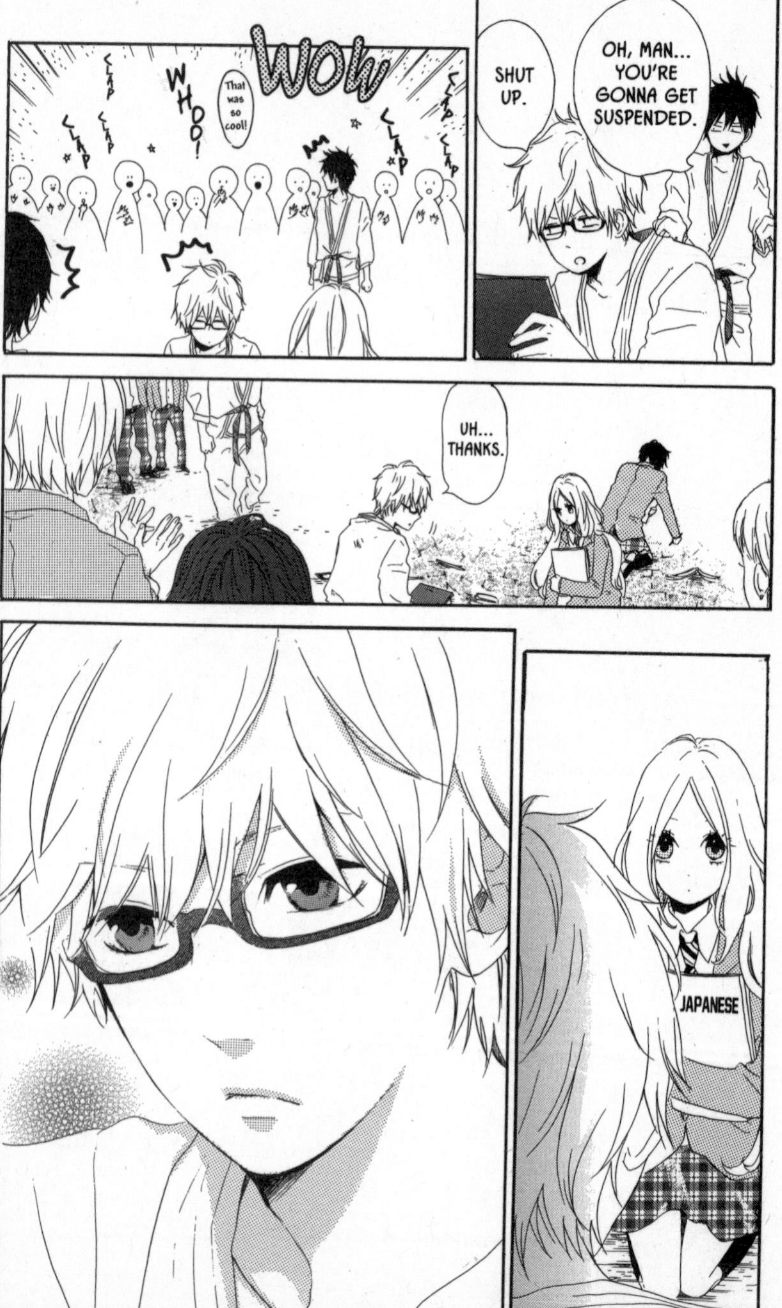
OH, MAN... YOU'RE GONNA GET SUSPENDED.
SHUT UP.
CLAP CLAP
WOW
CLAP
That was so cool!
WHOO!
CLAP CLAP
CLAP
UH... THANKS.
JAPANESE

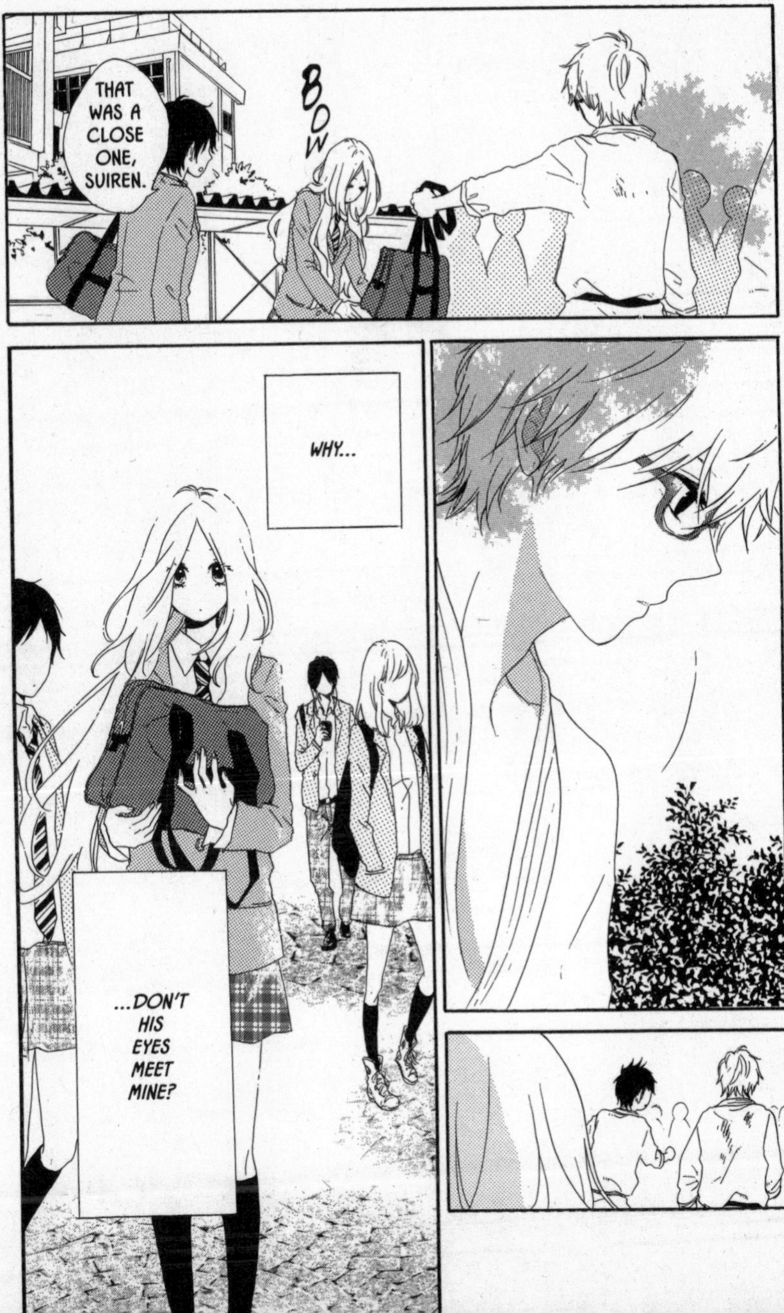
BOW
THAT WAS A CLOSE ONE, SUIREN.
WHY...
...DON'T HIS EYES MEET MINE?

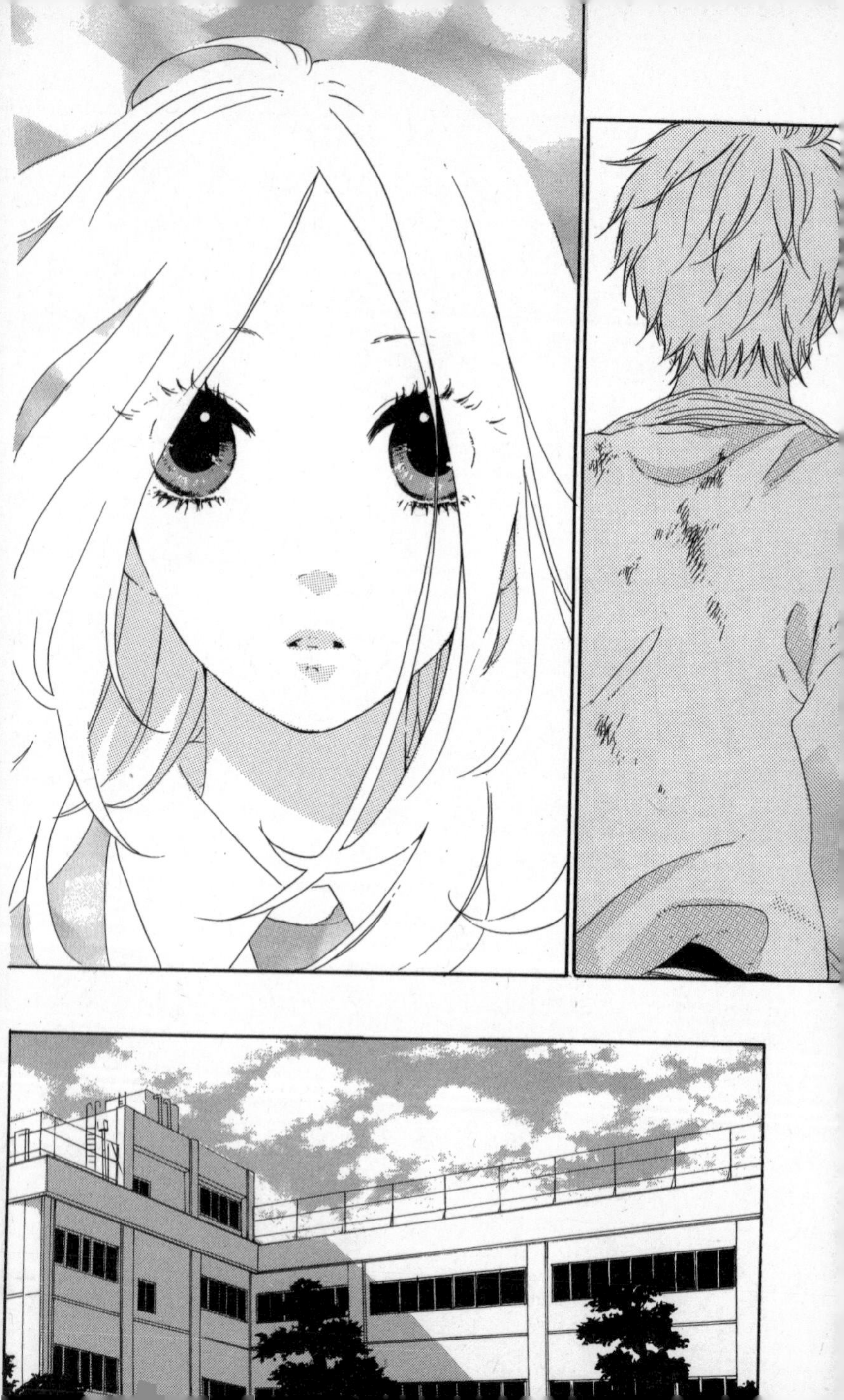

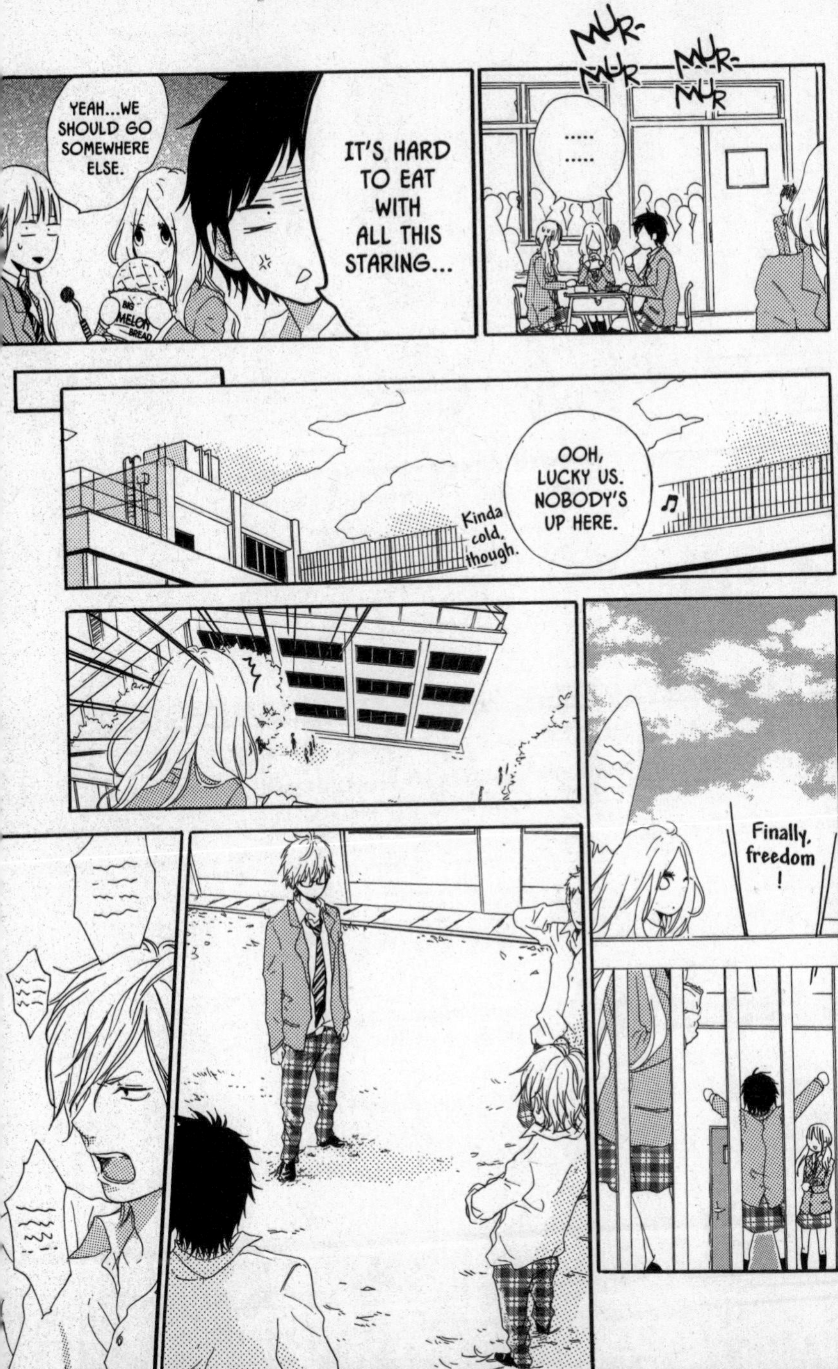

MUR-MUR
MUR-MUR
......
......
IT'S HARD TO EAT WITH ALL THIS STARING...
YEAH...WE SHOULD GO SOMEWHERE ELSE.
BIG MELON BREAD
OOH, LUCKY US. NOBODY'S UP HERE.
♫
Kinda cold, though.
Finally, freedom!

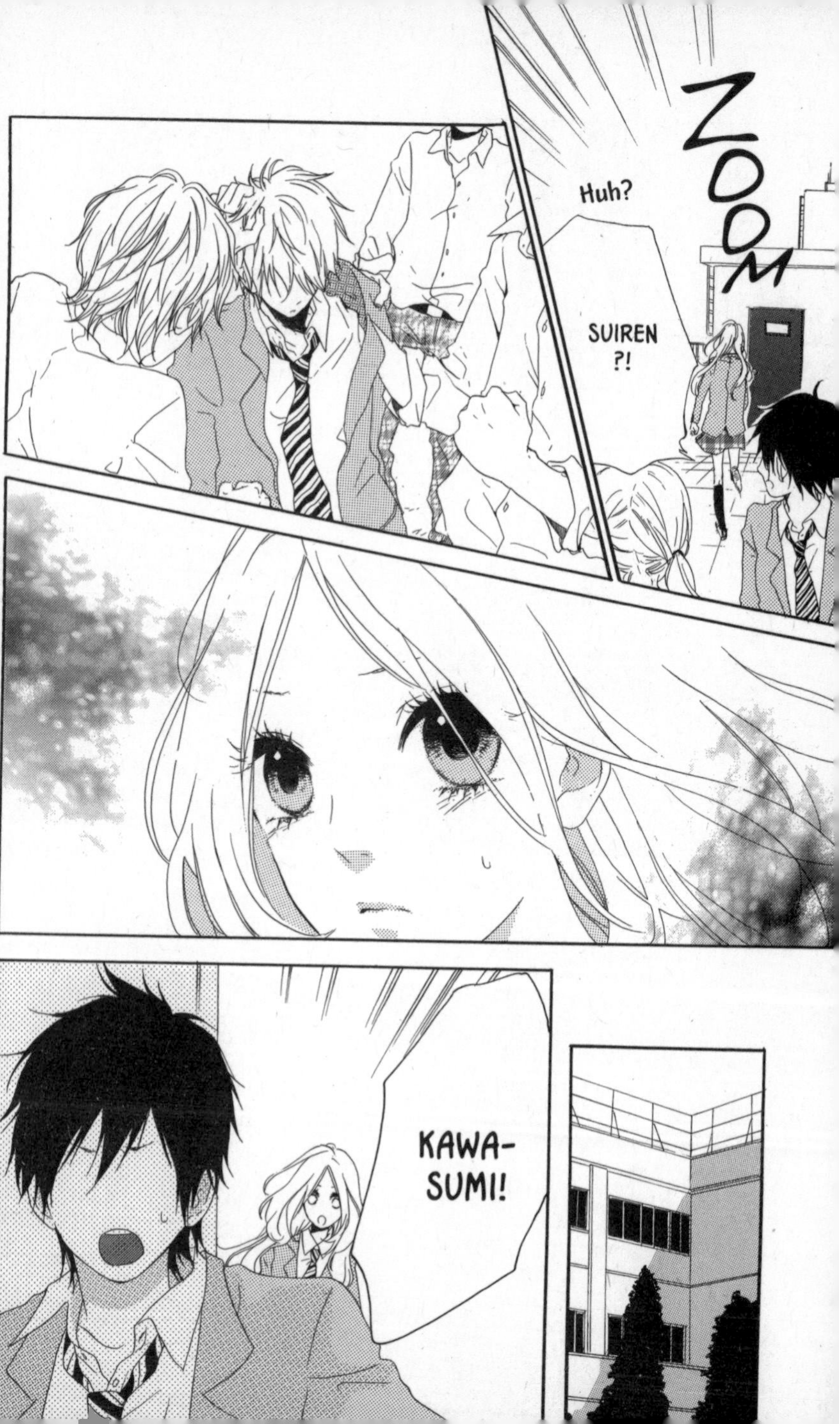
ZOOM
Huh?
SUIREN ?!
KAWA-SUMI!

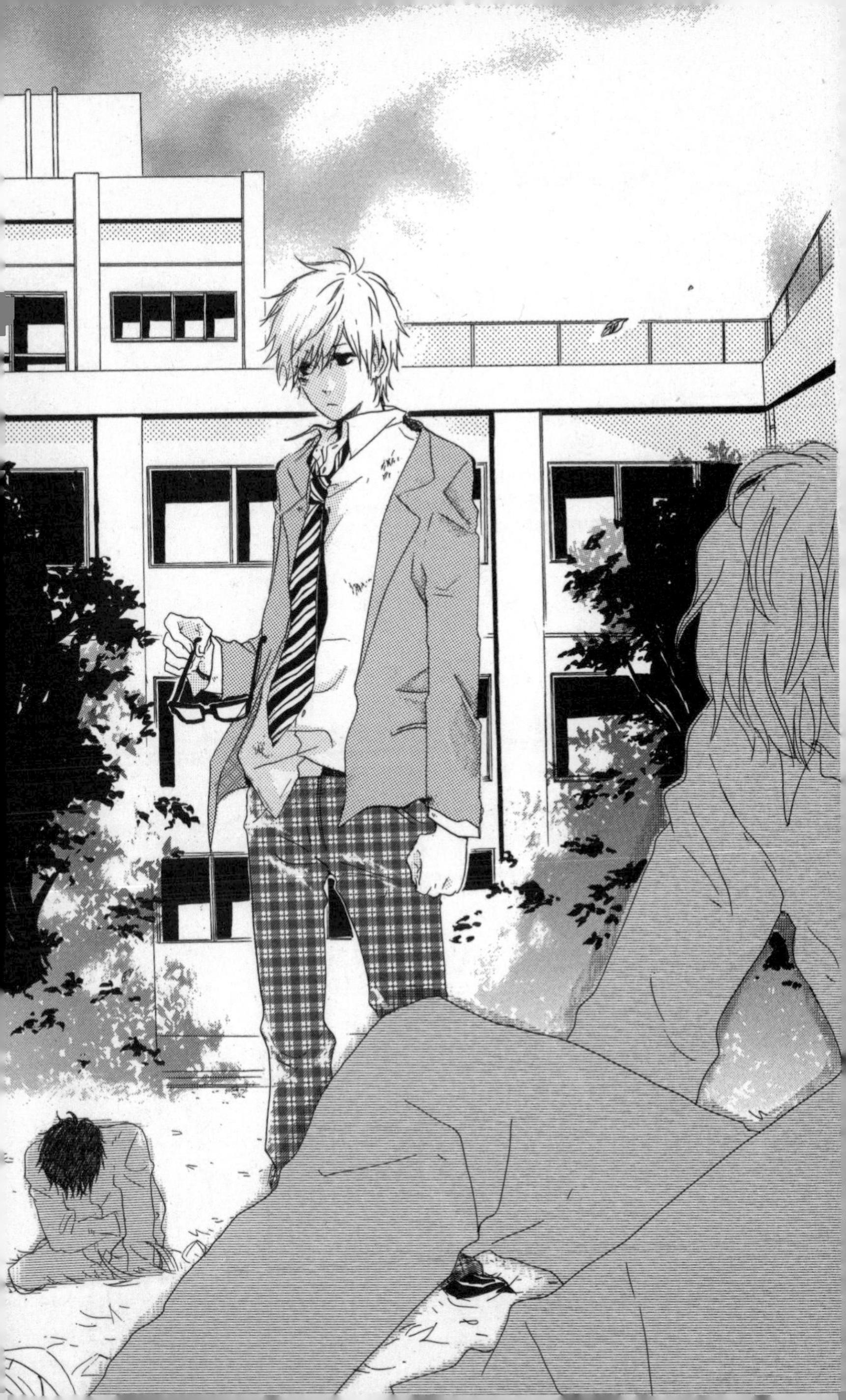

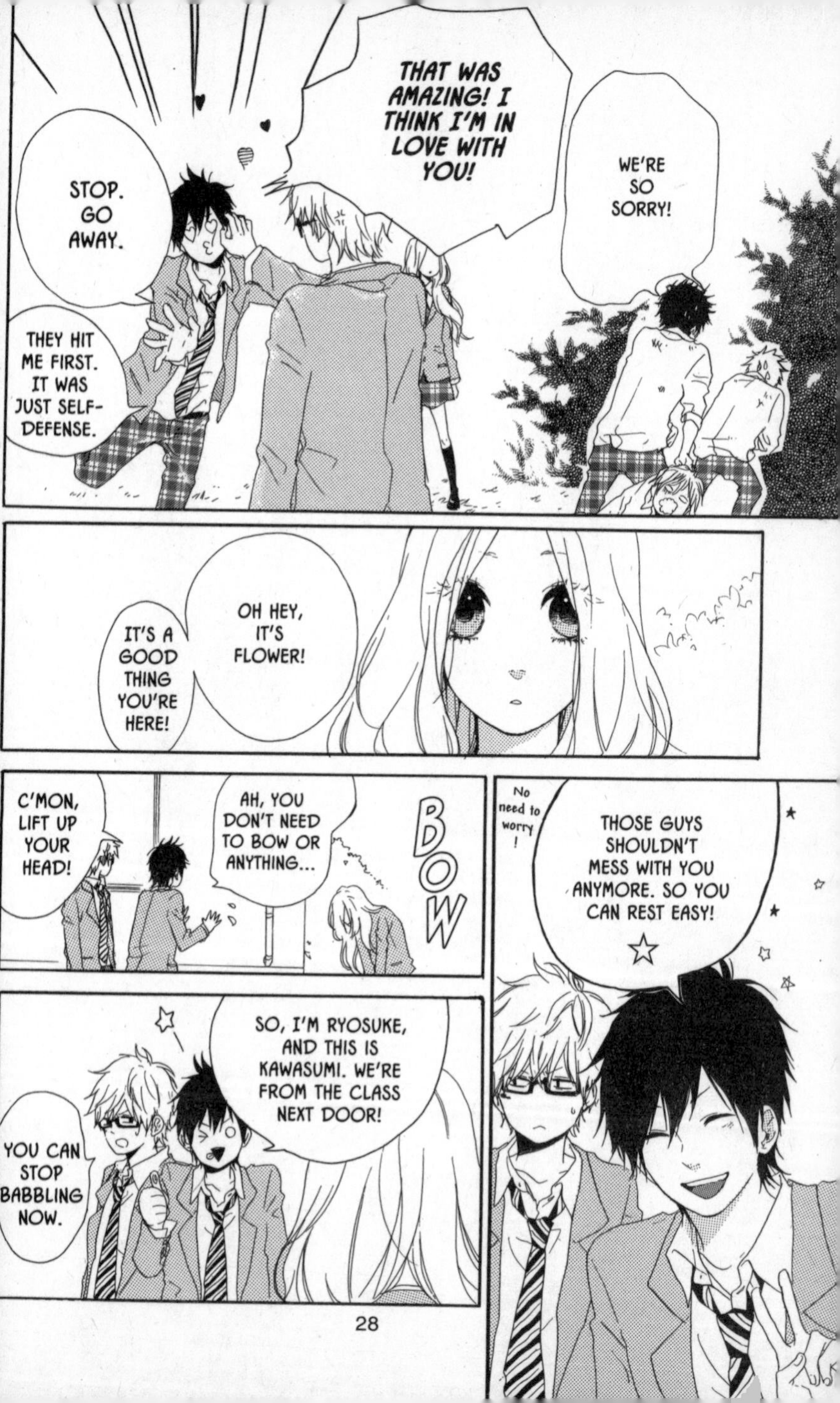
WE'RE SO SORRY!
THAT WAS AMAZING! I THINK I'M IN LOVE WITH YOU!
STOP. GO AWAY.
THEY HIT ME FIRST. IT WAS JUST SELF-DEFENSE.
OH HEY, IT'S FLOWER!
IT'S A GOOD THING YOU'RE HERE!
THOSE GUYS SHOULDN'T MESS WITH YOU ANYMORE. SO YOU CAN REST EASY!
No need to worry!
BOW
AH, YOU DON'T NEED TO BOW OR ANYTHING...
C'MON, LIFT UP YOUR HEAD!
SO, I'M RYOSUKE, AND THIS IS KAWASUMI. WE'RE FROM THE CLASS NEXT DOOR!
YOU CAN STOP BABBLING NOW.

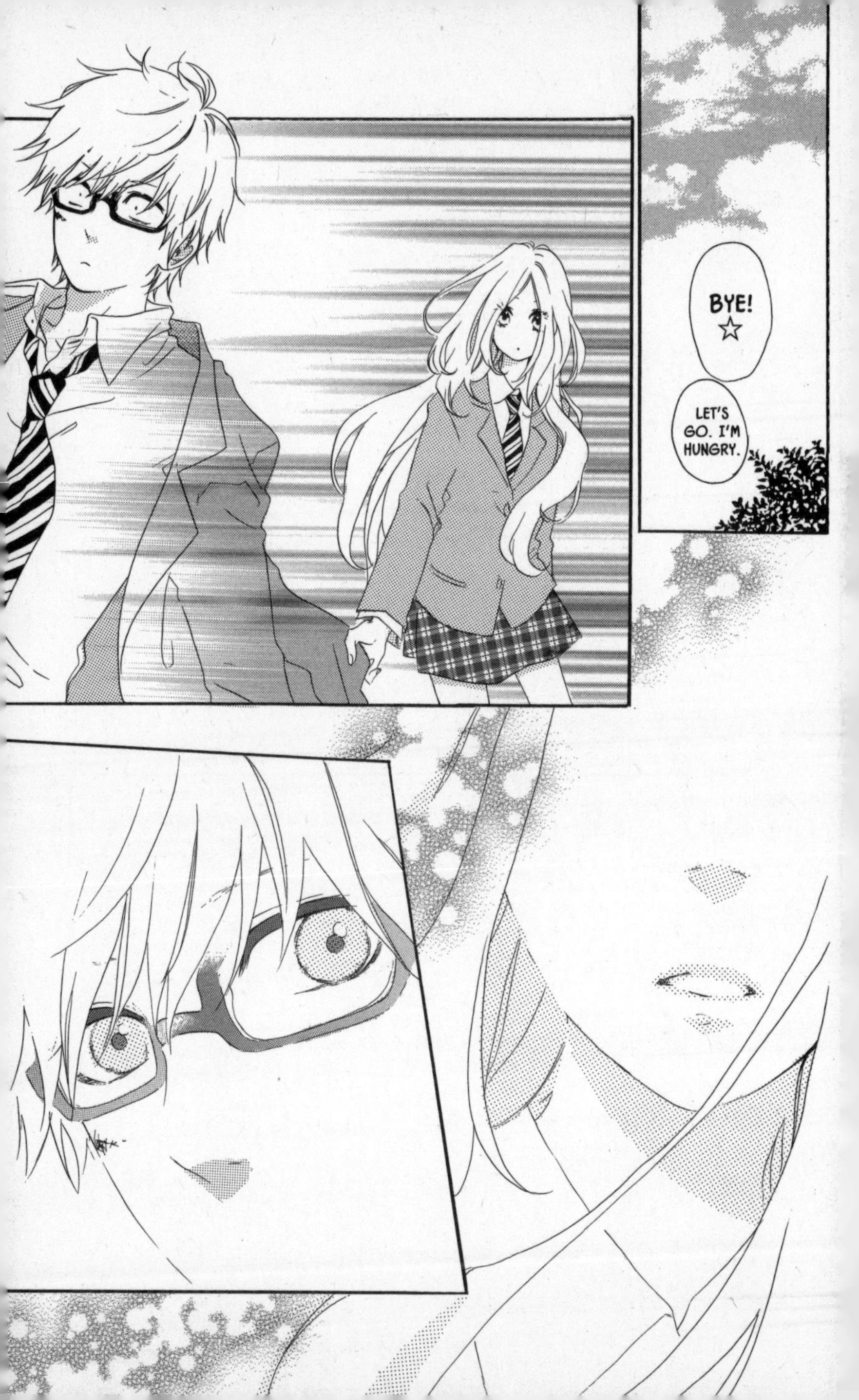
BYE! ☆
LET'S GO. I'M HUNGRY.

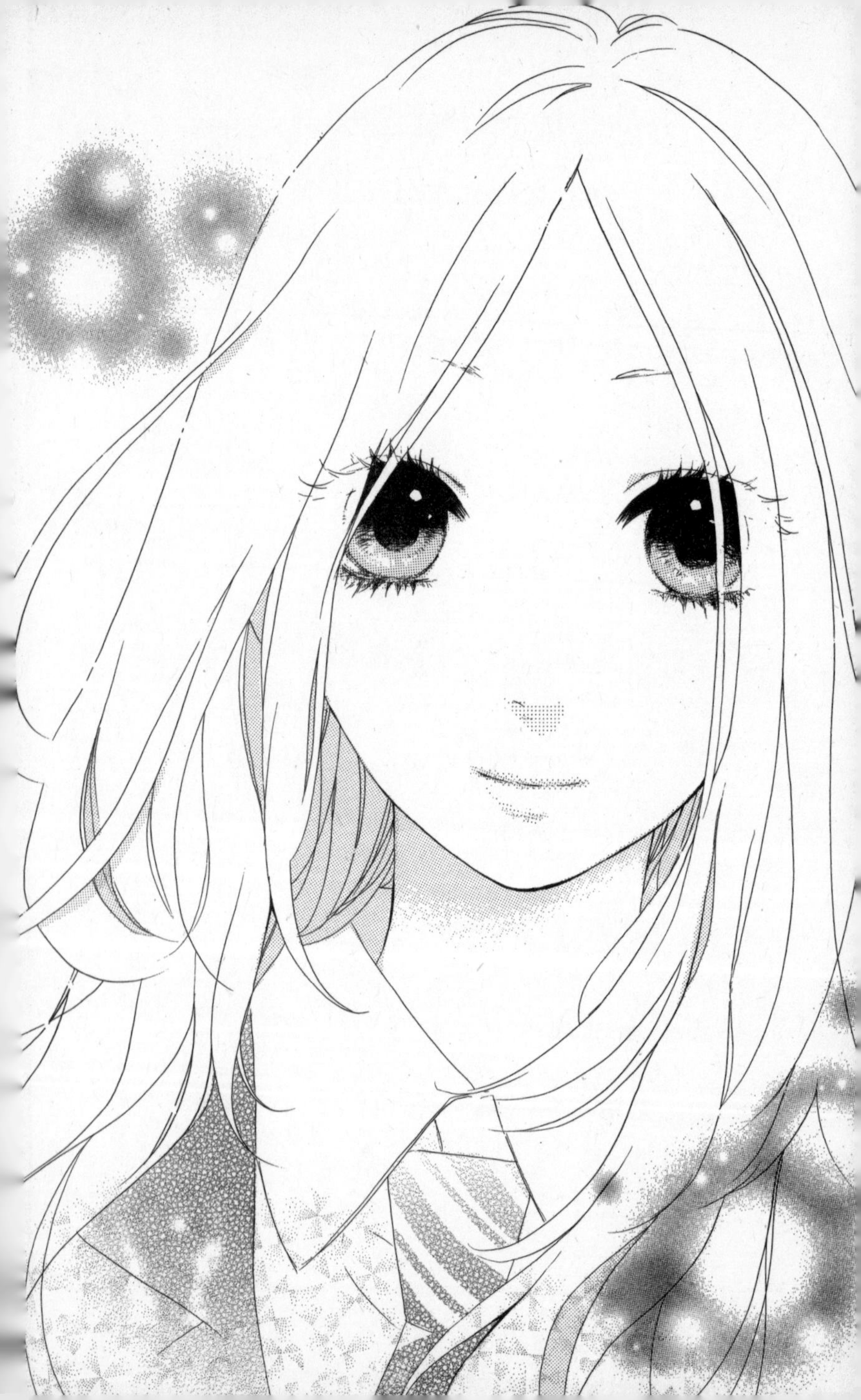

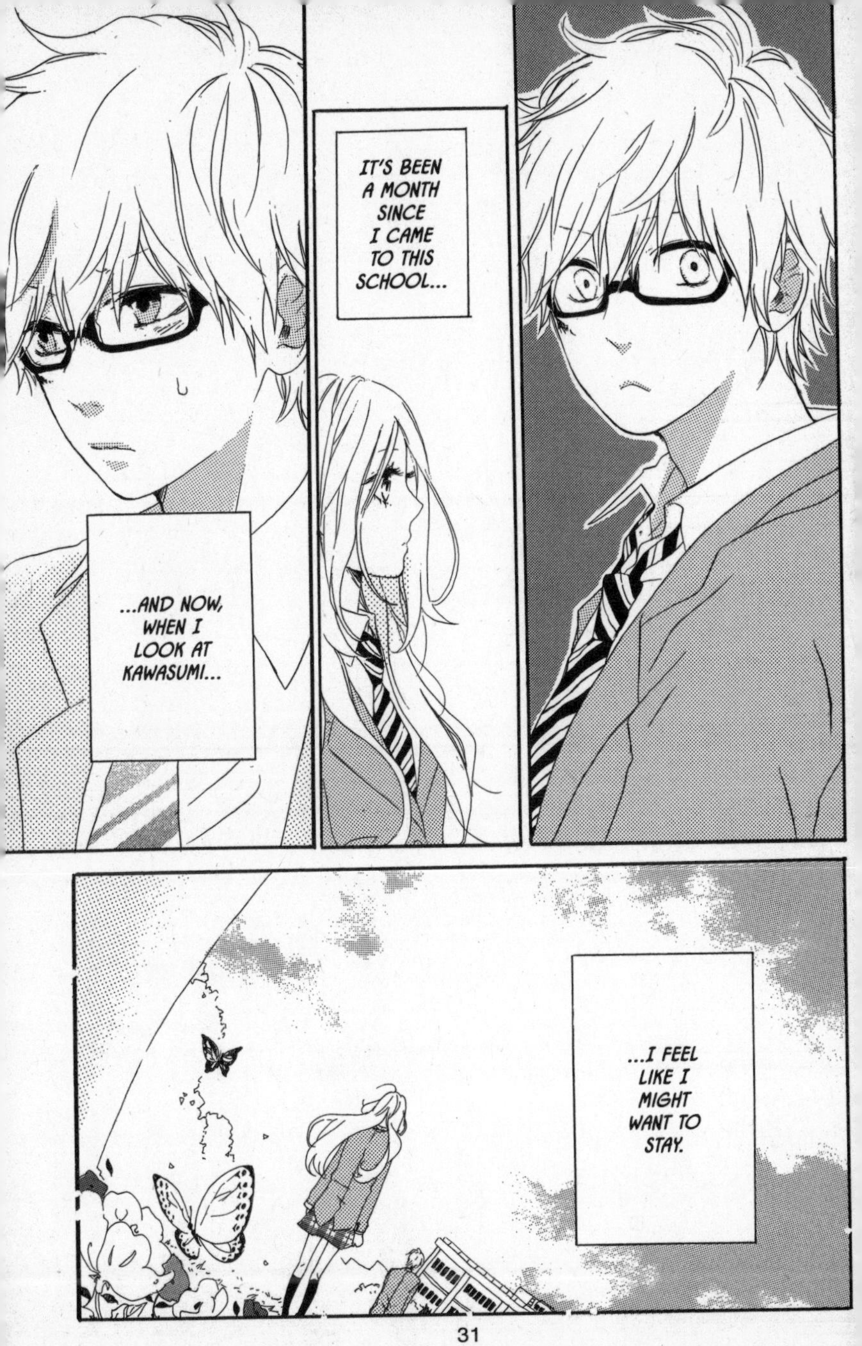
IT'S BEEN A MONTH SINCE I CAME TO THIS SCHOOL...
...AND NOW, WHEN I LOOK AT KAWASUMI...
...I FEEL LIKE I MIGHT WANT TO STAY.

CHAPTER 2

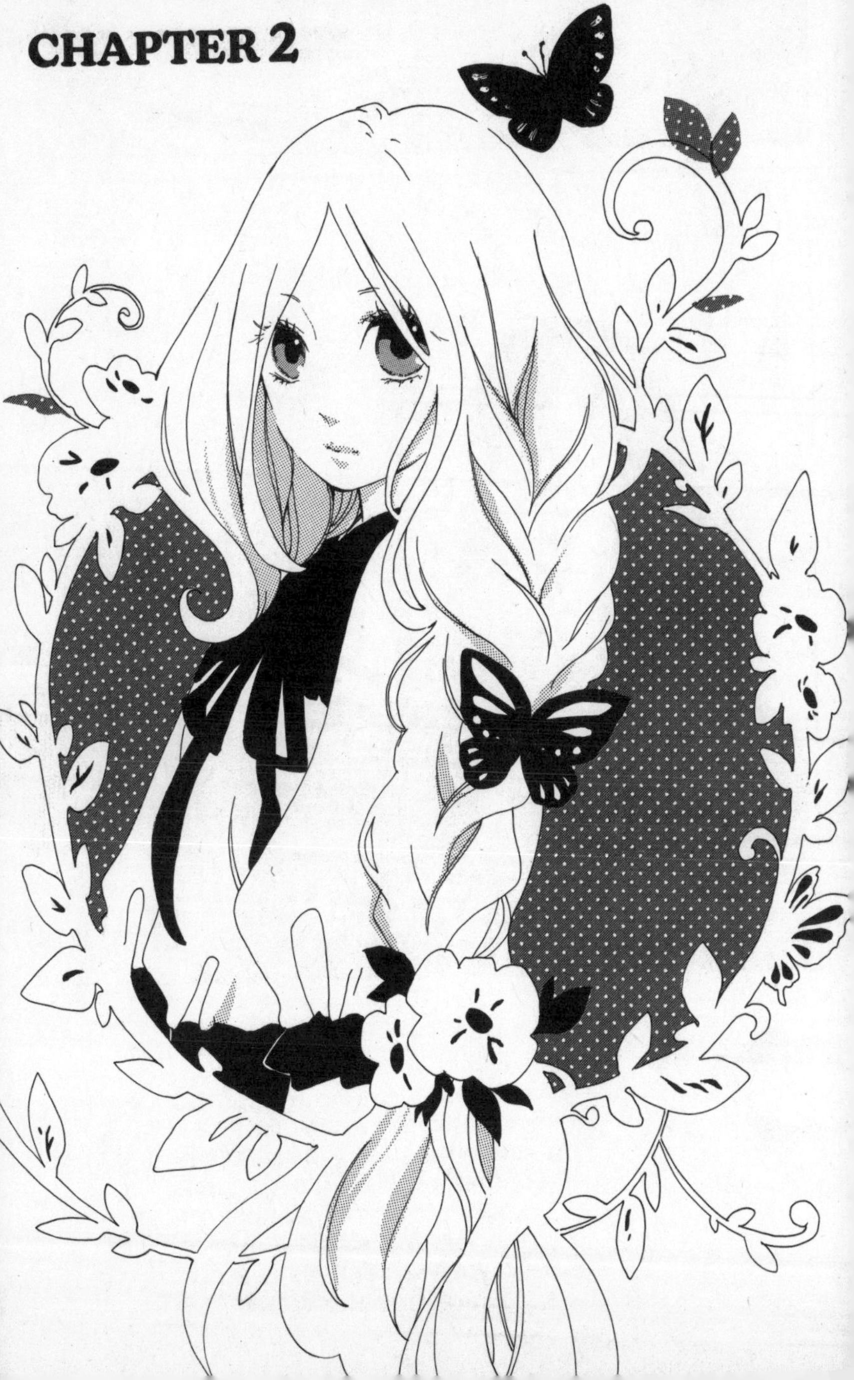

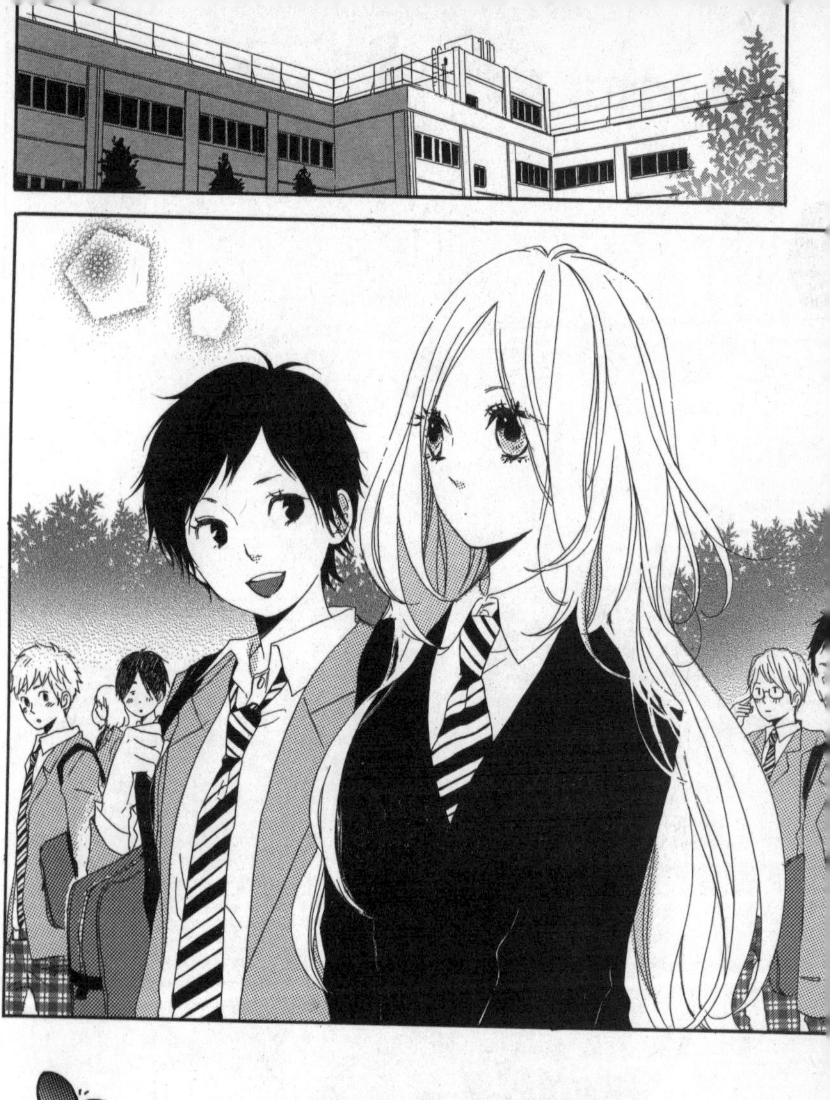

HELLO, NICE TO MEET YOU.
MY NAME IS SUU MORISHITA.
THANK YOU SO MUCH FOR
READING LIKE A BUTTERFLY
VOLUME 1. I'D LIKE TO SHARE
MORE ABOUT THE MAKING OF
THIS MANGA IN THESE NOTES,
SO PLEASE KEEP AN EYE OUT
FOR THE NEXT ONE!

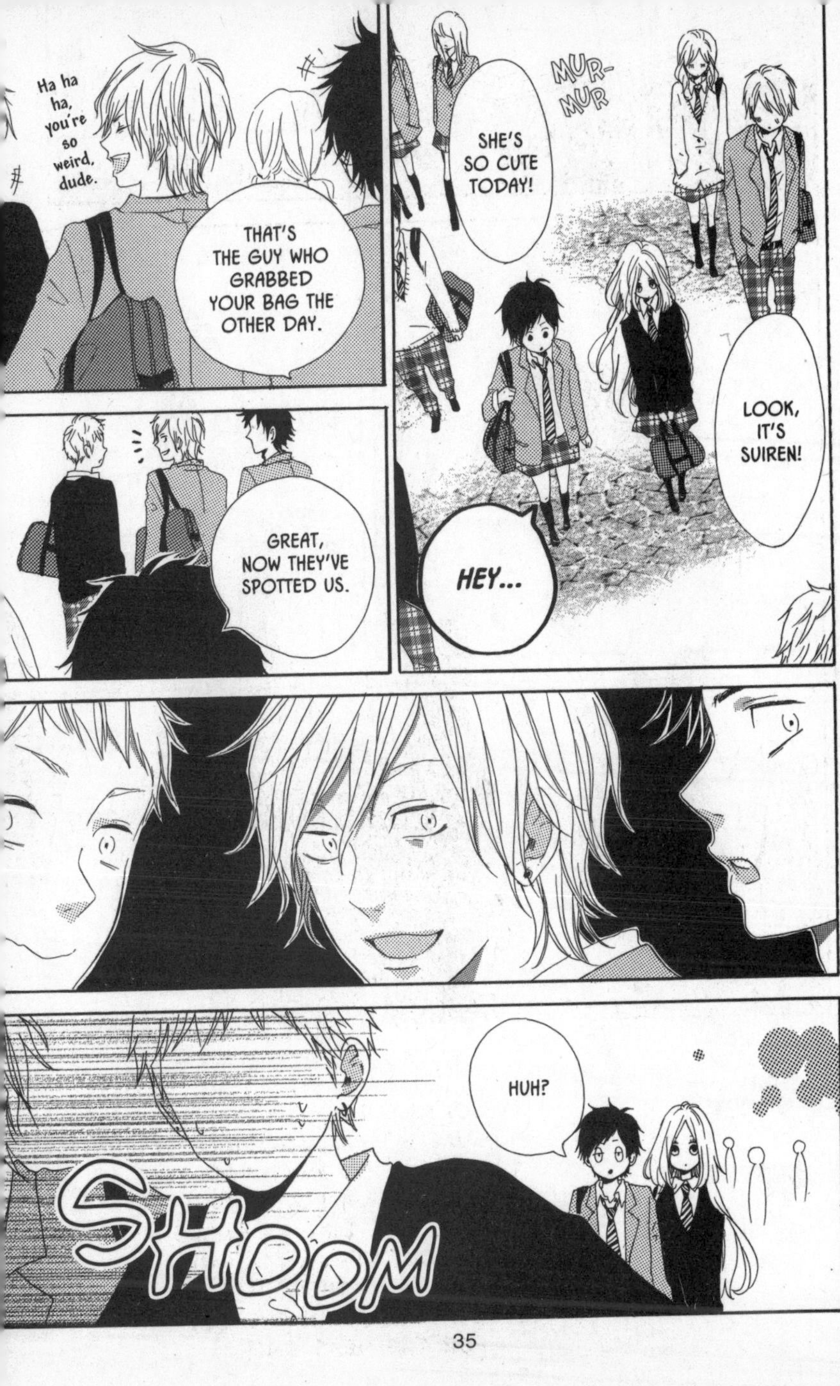
MUR-MUR
SHE'S SO CUTE TODAY!
LOOK, IT'S SUIREN!
HEY...
Ha ha ha, you're so weird, dude.
THAT'S THE GUY WHO GRABBED YOUR BAG THE OTHER DAY.
GREAT, NOW THEY'VE SPOTTED US.
HUH?
SHOOM

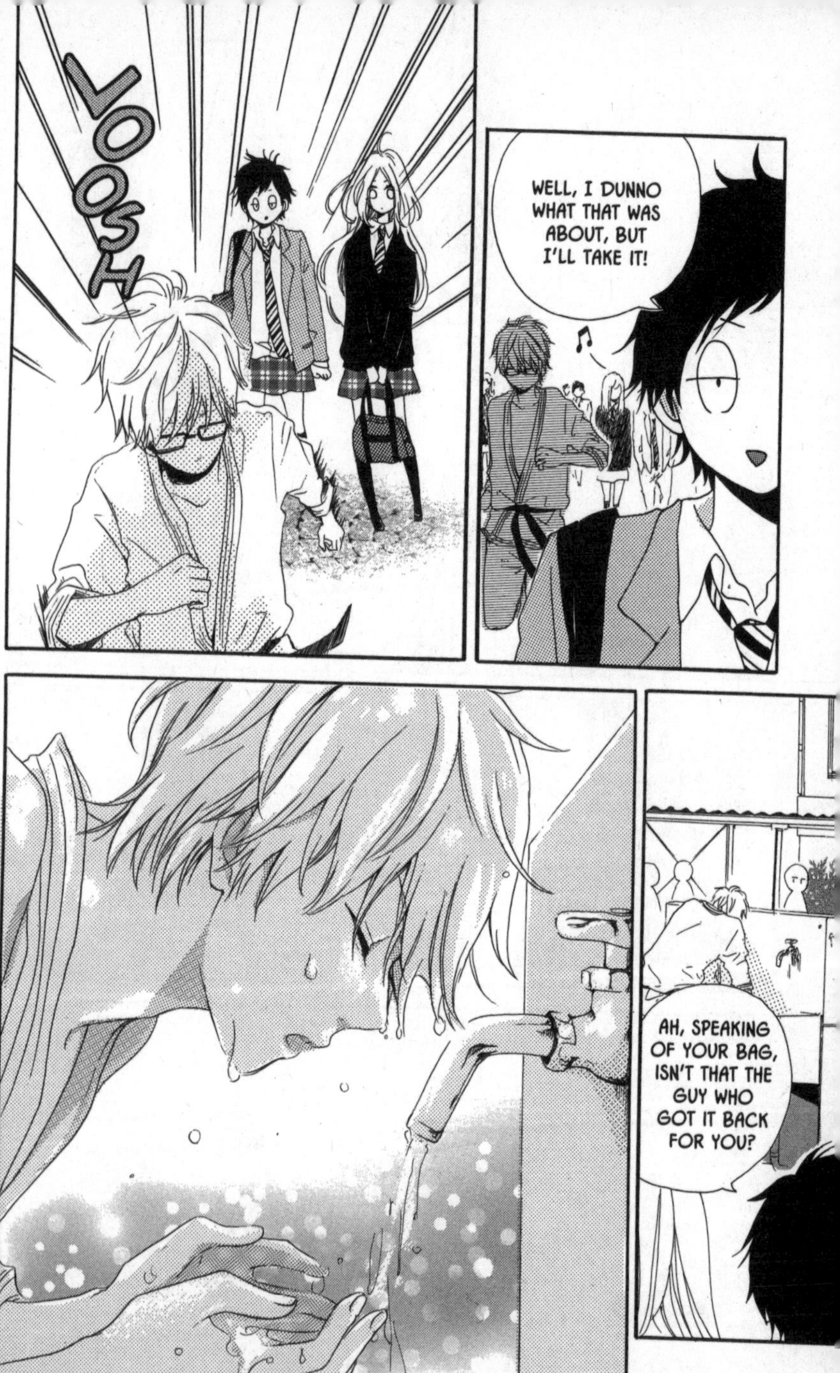
WELL, I DUNNO WHAT THAT WAS ABOUT, BUT I'LL TAKE IT!
VOOSH
AH, SPEAKING OF YOUR BAG, ISN'T THAT THE GUY WHO GOT IT BACK FOR YOU?

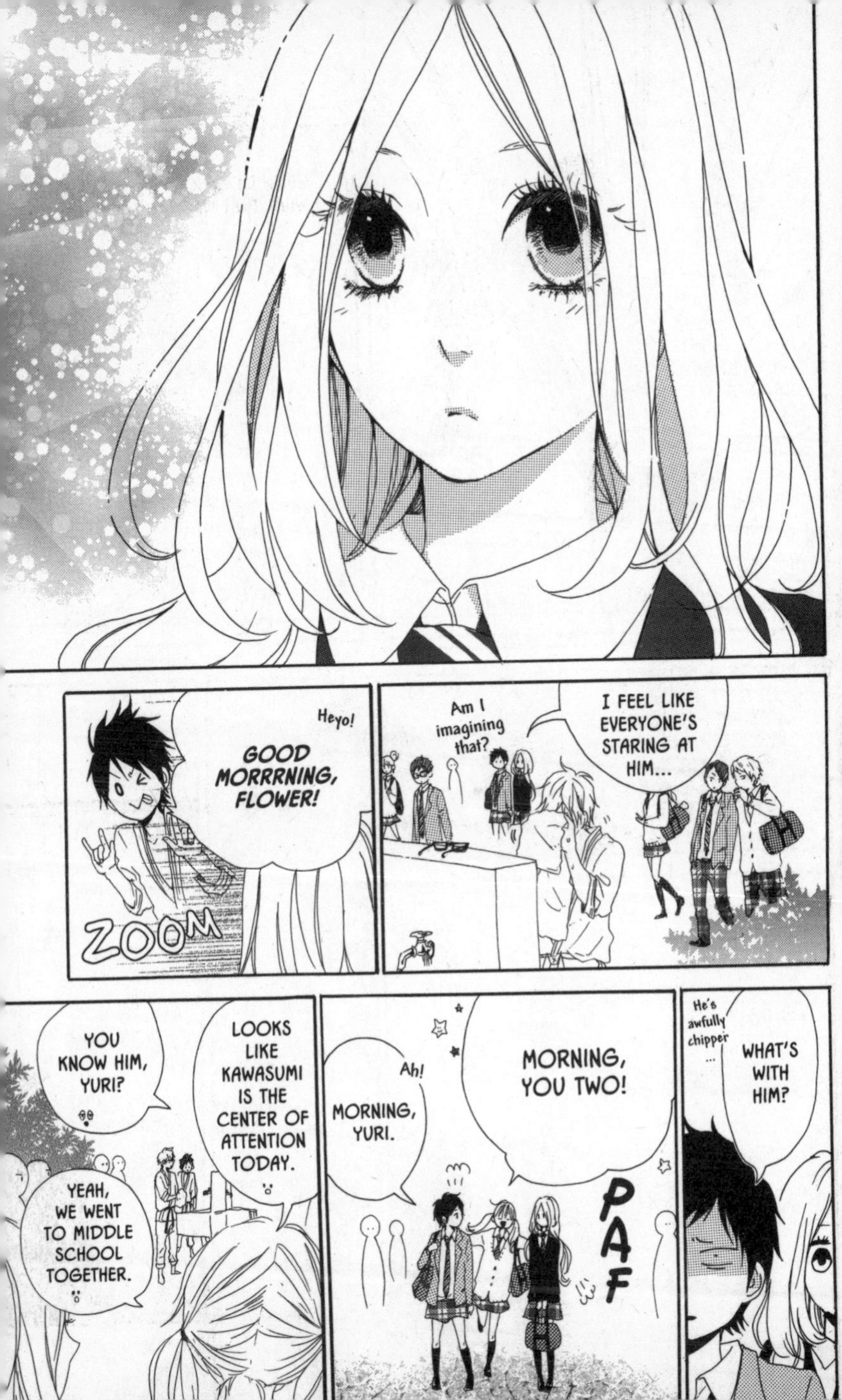
I FEEL LIKE EVERYONE'S STARING AT HIM...
Am I imagining that?
Heyo!
GOOD MORRRNING, FLOWER!
ZOOM
WHAT'S WITH HIM?
He's awfully chipper...
MORNING, YOU TWO!
PAF
Ah!
MORNING, YURI.
LOOKS LIKE KAWASUMI IS THE CENTER OF ATTENTION TODAY.
YOU KNOW HIM, YURI?
YEAH, WE WENT TO MIDDLE SCHOOL TOGETHER.

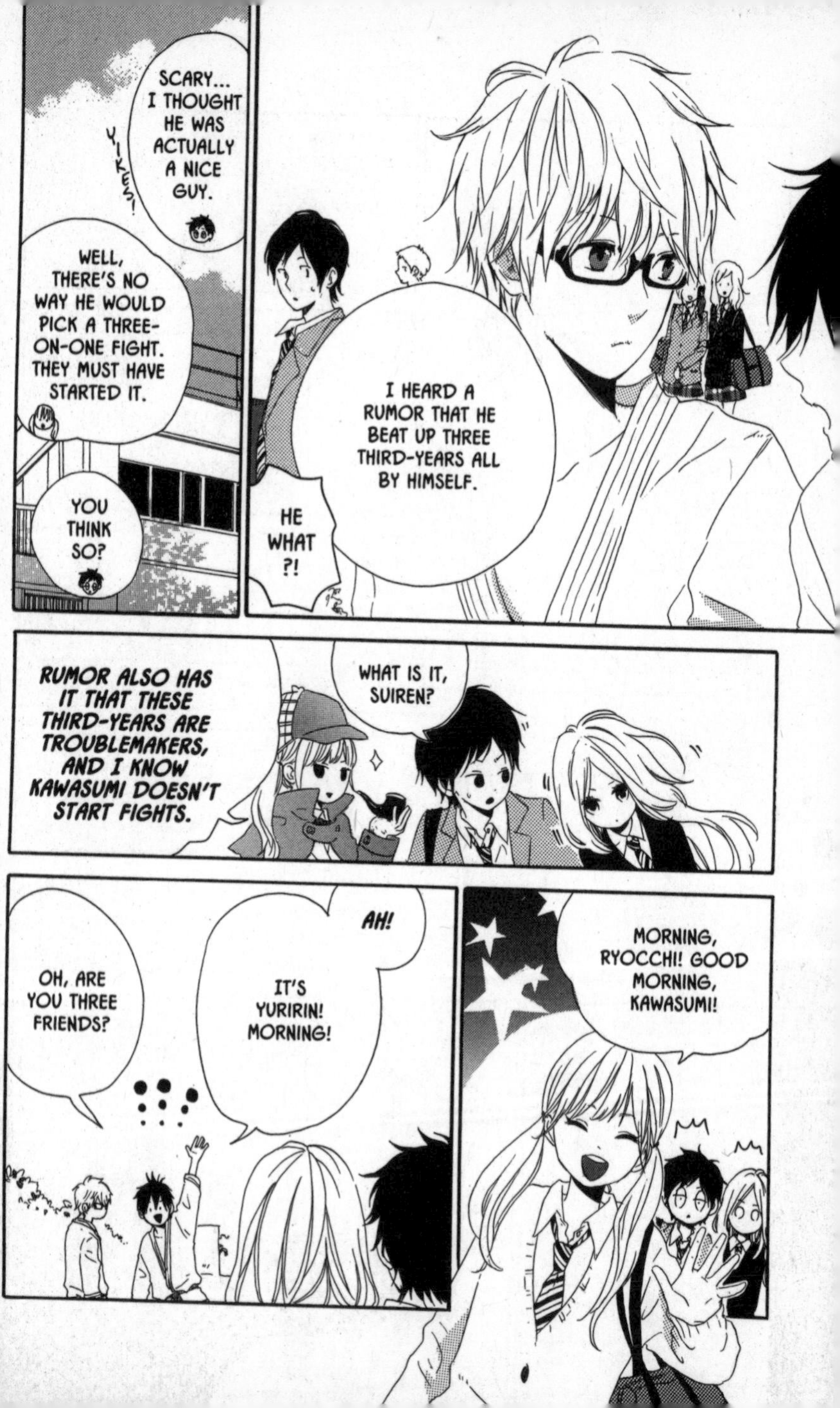
I HEARD A RUMOR THAT HE BEAT UP THREE THIRD-YEARS ALL BY HIMSELF.
HE WHAT?!
SCARY... I THOUGHT HE WAS ACTUALLY A NICE GUY.
YIKES!
WELL, THERE'S NO WAY HE WOULD PICK A THREE-ON-ONE FIGHT. THEY MUST HAVE STARTED IT.
YOU THINK SO?
WHAT IS IT, SUIREN?
RUMOR ALSO HAS IT THAT THESE THIRD-YEARS ARE TROUBLEMAKERS, AND I KNOW KAWASUMI DOESN'T START FIGHTS.
MORNING, RYOCCHI! GOOD MORNING, KAWASUMI!
AH!
IT'S YURIRIN! MORNING!
OH, ARE YOU THREE FRIENDS?

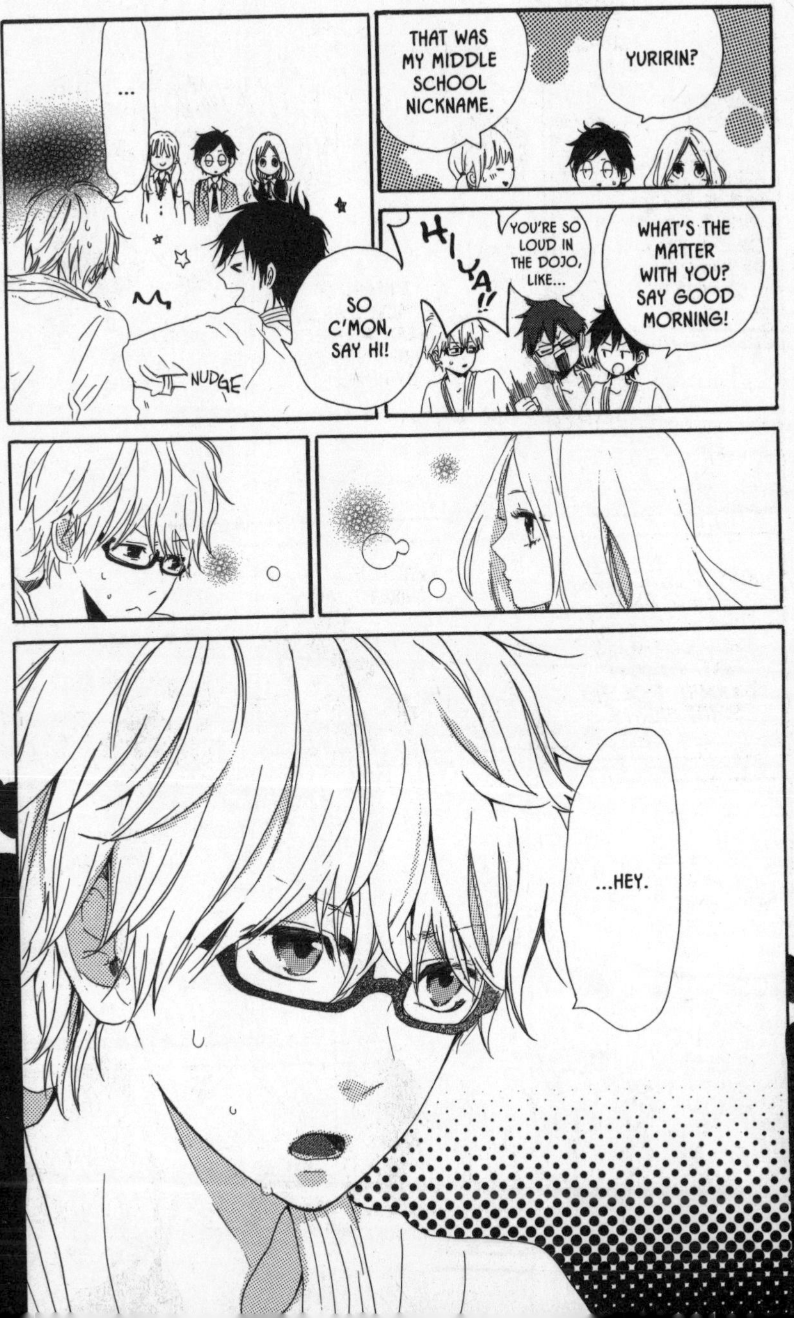
YURIRIN?
THAT WAS MY MIDDLE SCHOOL NICKNAME.
WHAT'S THE MATTER WITH YOU? SAY GOOD MORNING!
YOU'RE SO LOUD IN THE DOJO, LIKE...
HI YA!!
SO C'MON, SAY HI!
...
NUDGE
...HEY.

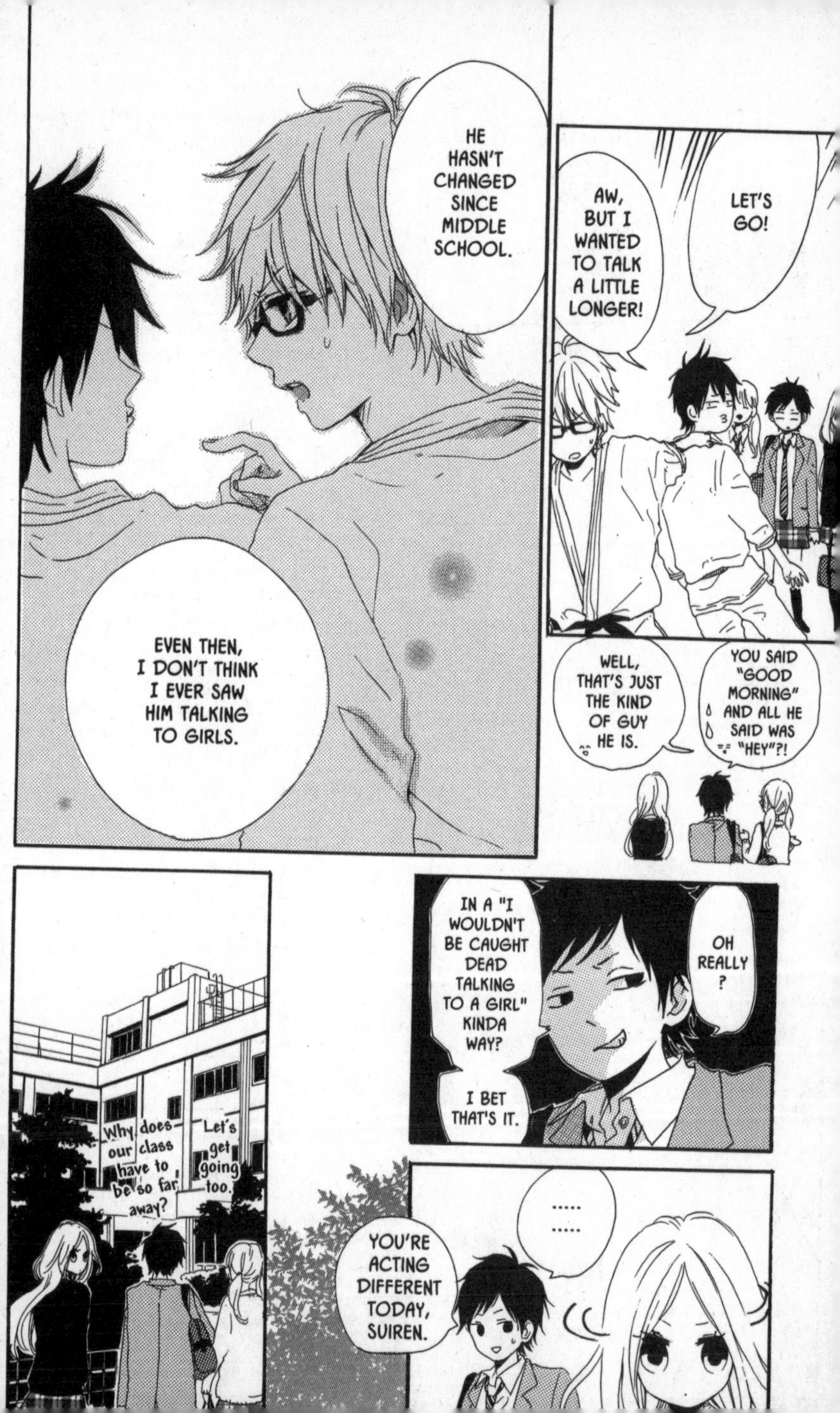
LET'S GO!
AW, BUT I WANTED TO TALK A LITTLE LONGER!
YOU SAID "GOOD MORNING" AND ALL HE SAID WAS "HEY"?!
WELL, THAT'S JUST THE KIND OF GUY HE IS.
HE HASN'T CHANGED SINCE MIDDLE SCHOOL.
EVEN THEN, I DON'T THINK I EVER SAW HIM TALKING TO GIRLS.
OH REALLY?
IN A "I WOULDN'T BE CAUGHT DEAD TALKING TO A GIRL" KINDA WAY?
I BET THAT'S IT.
....
YOU'RE ACTING DIFFERENT TODAY, SUIREN.
Let's get going too.
Why does our class have to be so far away?

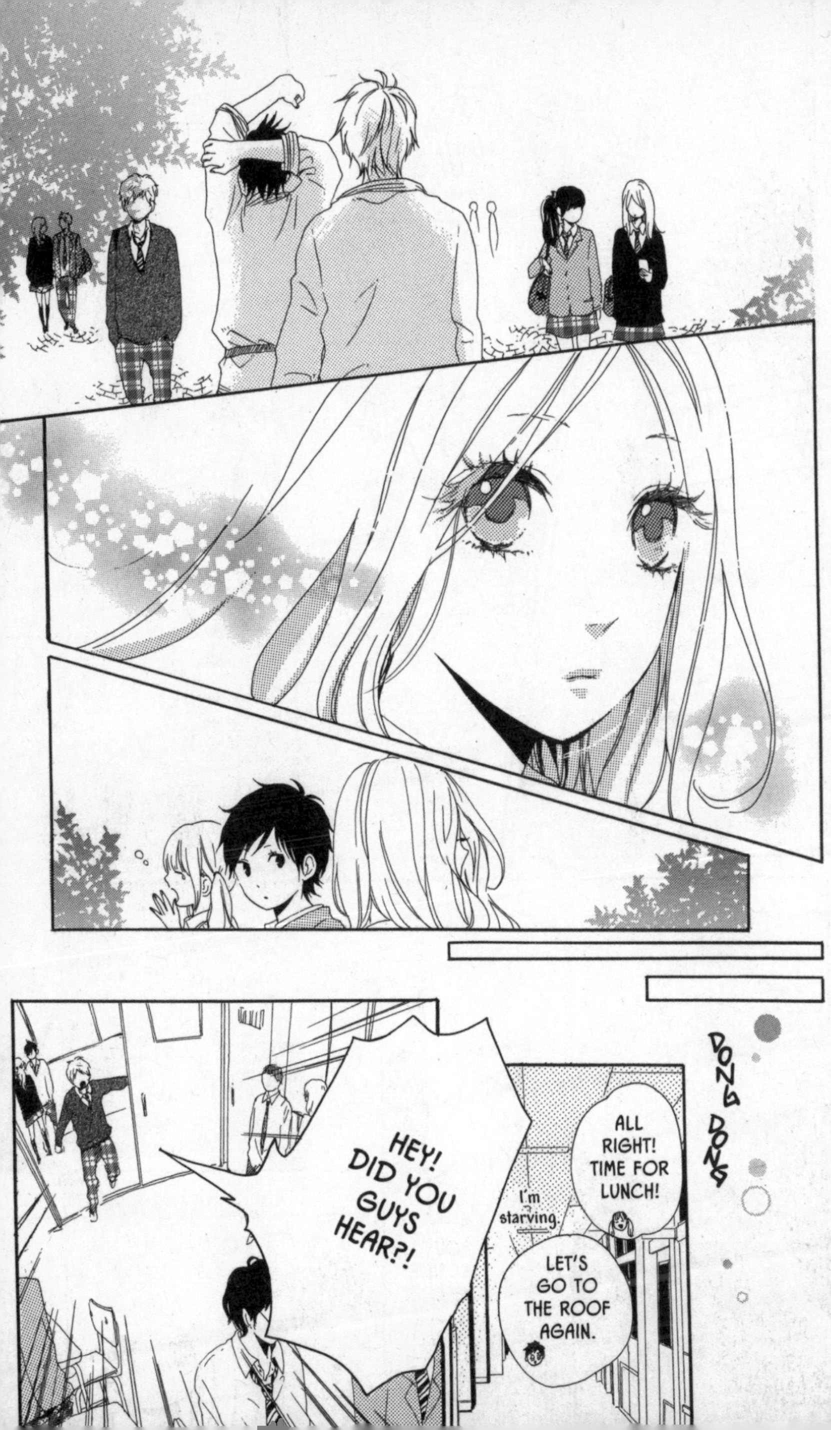
DONG DONG
ALL RIGHT! TIME FOR LUNCH!
I'm starving.
LET'S GO TO THE ROOF AGAIN.
HEY! DID YOU GUYS HEAR?!

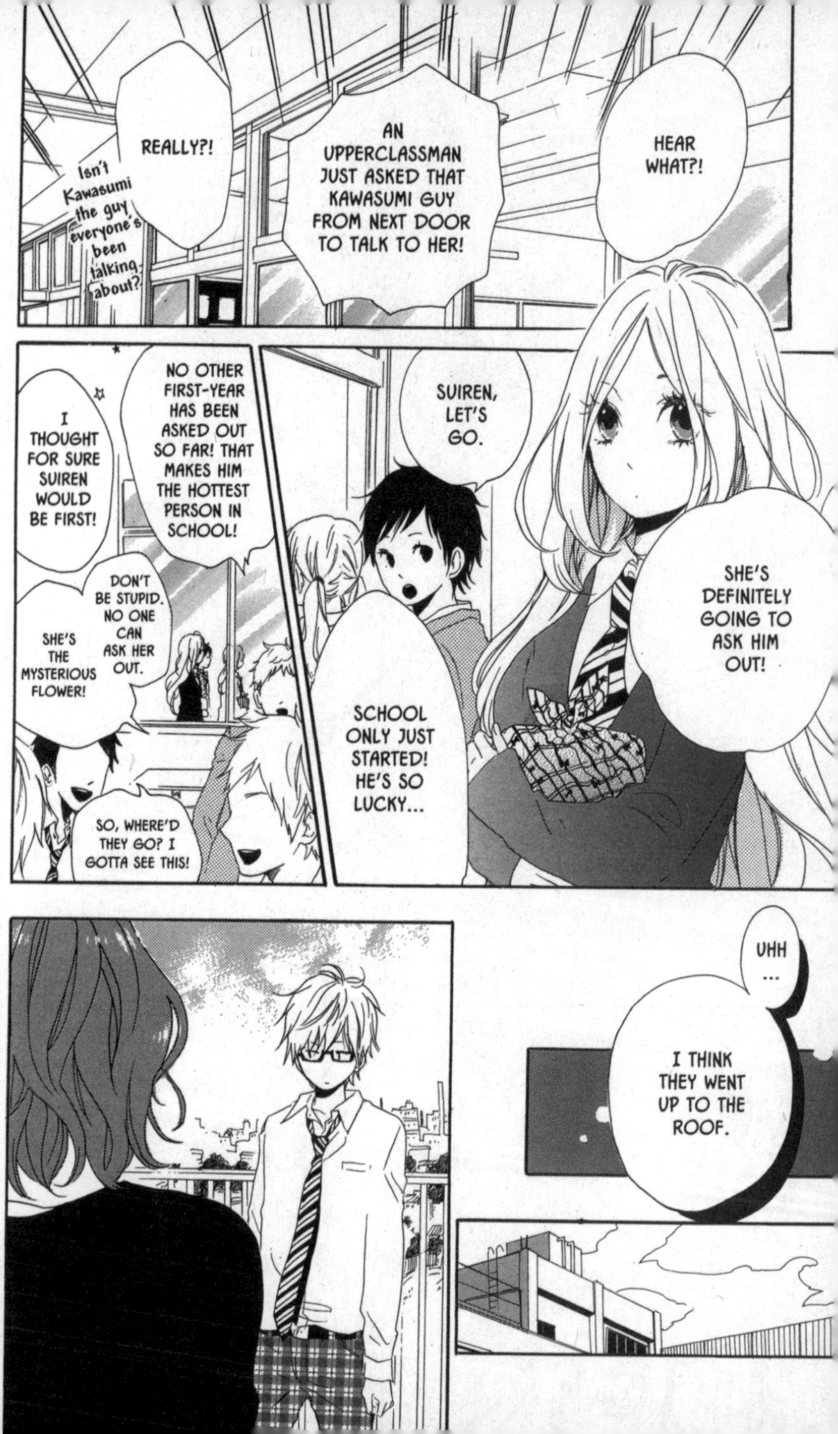
HEAR WHAT?!
AN UPPERCLASSMAN JUST ASKED THAT KAWASUMI GUY FROM NEXT DOOR TO TALK TO HER!
REALLY?!
Isn't Kawasumi the guy everyone's been talking about?
SUIREN, LET'S GO.
SHE'S DEFINITELY GOING TO ASK HIM OUT!
SCHOOL ONLY JUST STARTED! HE'S SO LUCKY...
NO OTHER FIRST-YEAR HAS BEEN ASKED OUT SO FAR! THAT MAKES HIM THE HOTTEST PERSON IN SCHOOL!
I THOUGHT FOR SURE SUIREN WOULD BE FIRST!
DON'T BE STUPID. NO ONE CAN ASK HER OUT.
SHE'S THE MYSTERIOUS FLOWER!
SO, WHERE'D THEY GO? I GOTTA SEE THIS!
UHH...
I THINK THEY WENT UP TO THE ROOF.

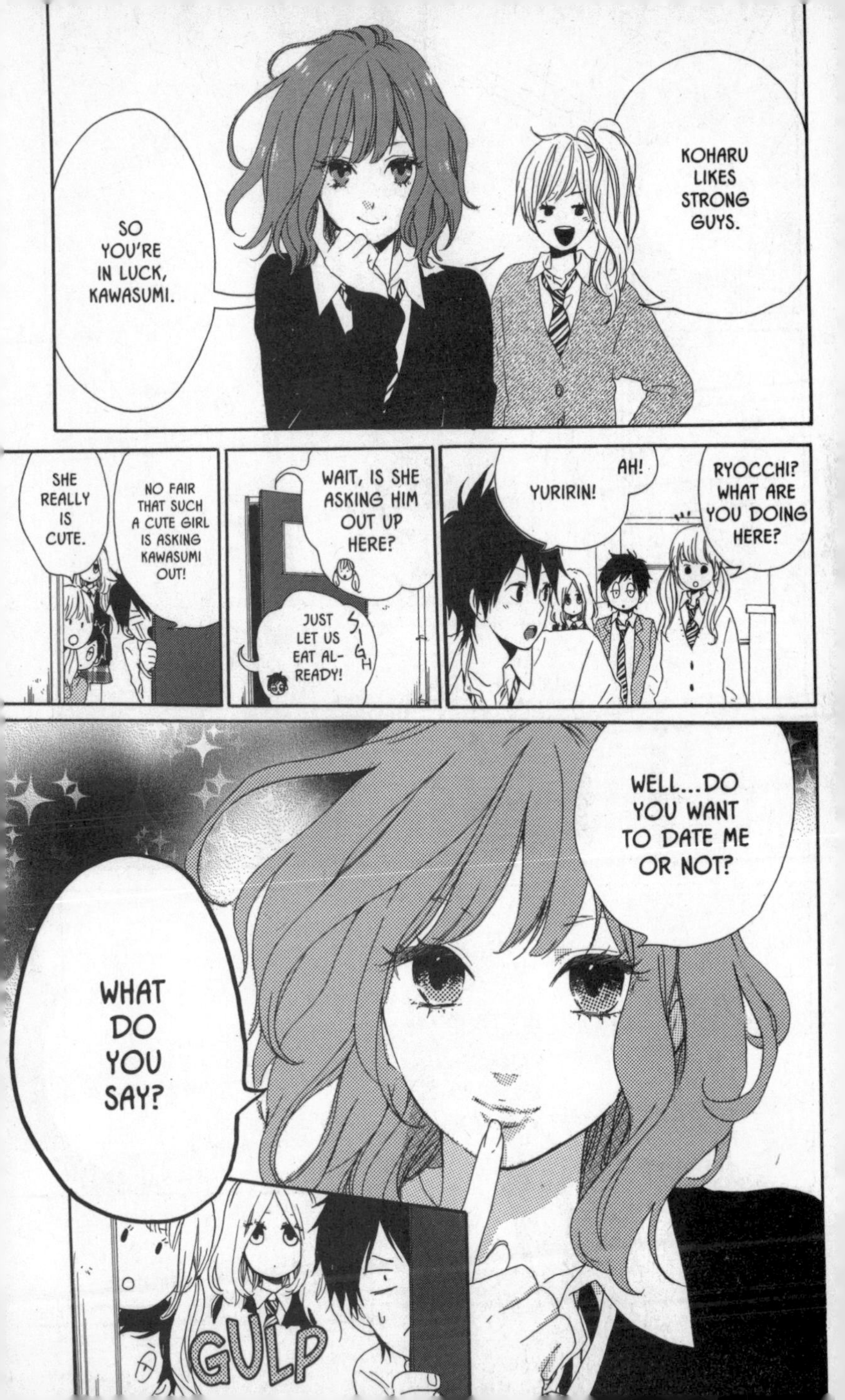
KOHARU LIKES STRONG GUYS.
SO YOU'RE IN LUCK, KAWASUMI.
RYOCCHI? WHAT ARE YOU DOING HERE?
AH!
YURIRIN!
WAIT, IS SHE ASKING HIM OUT UP HERE?
JUST LET US EAT AL-READY!
SIGH
NO FAIR THAT SUCH A CUTE GIRL IS ASKING KAWASUMI OUT!
SHE REALLY IS CUTE.
WELL...DO YOU WANT TO DATE ME OR NOT?
WHAT DO YOU SAY?
GULP

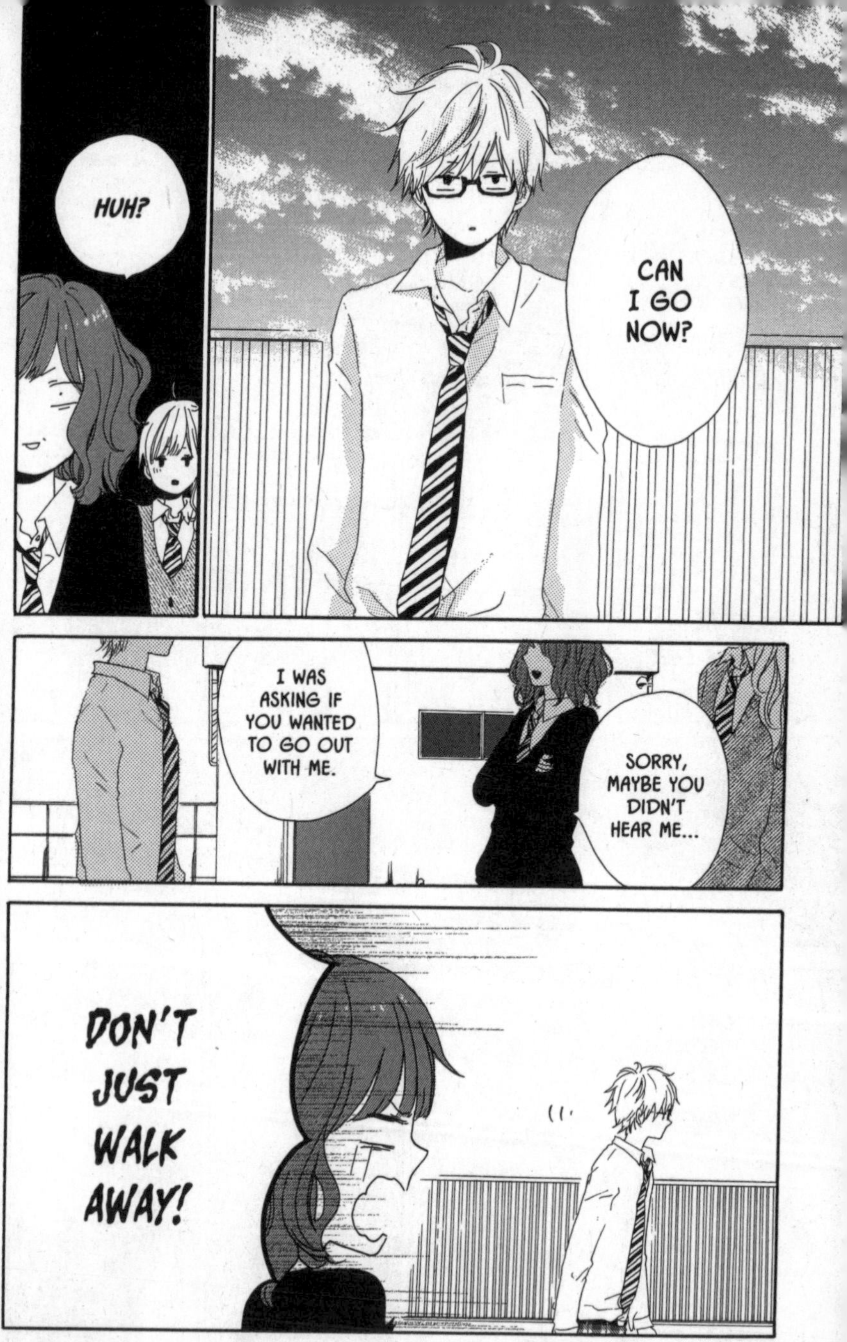
CAN I GO NOW?
HUH?
SORRY, MAYBE YOU DIDN'T HEAR ME...
I WAS ASKING IF YOU WANTED TO GO OUT WITH ME.
DON'T JUST WALK AWAY!

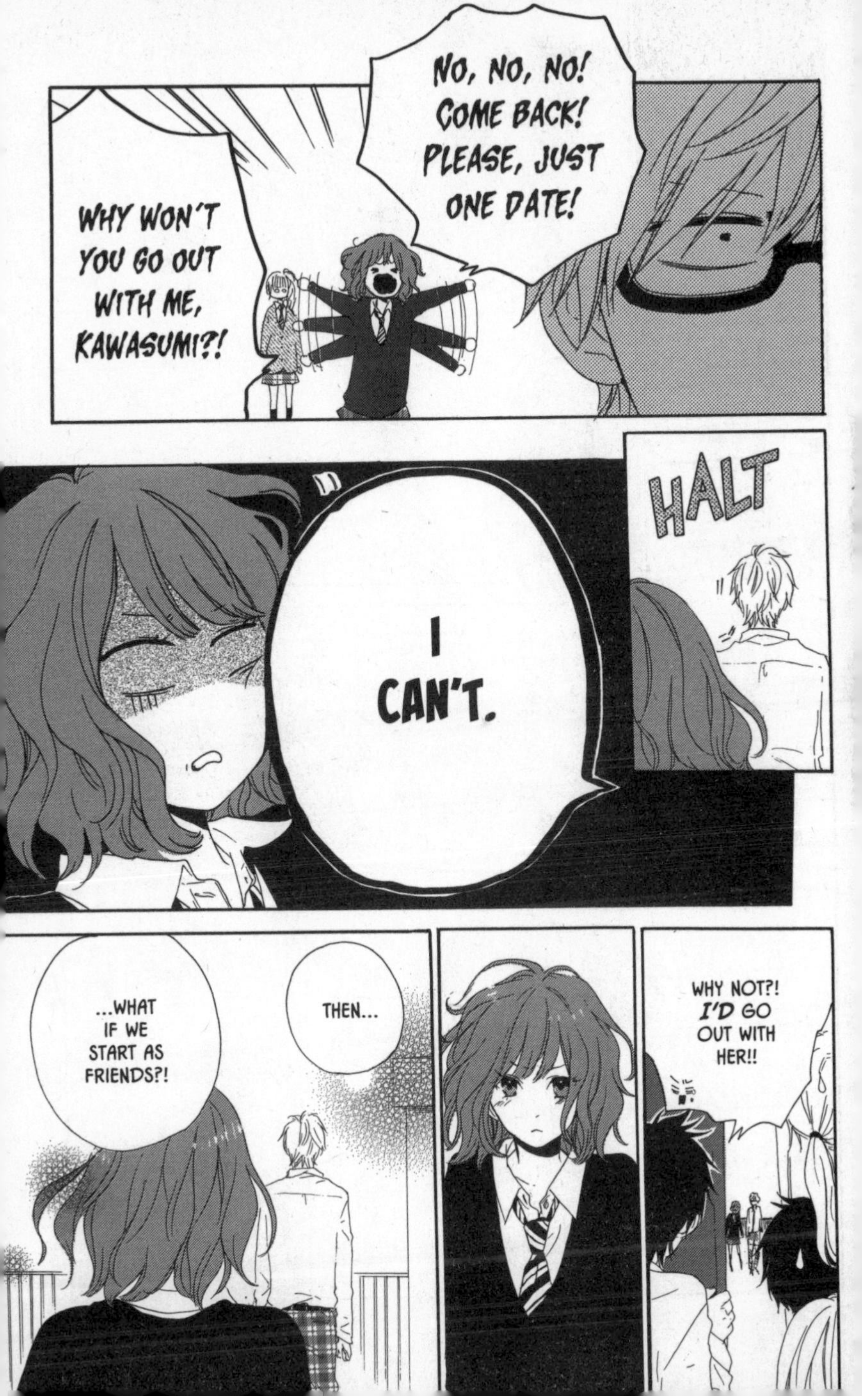
NO, NO, NO! COME BACK! PLEASE, JUST ONE DATE!
WHY WON'T YOU GO OUT WITH ME, KAWASUMI?!
HALT
I CAN'T.
WHY NOT?! I'D GO OUT WITH HER!!
THEN...
...WHAT IF WE START AS FRIENDS?!

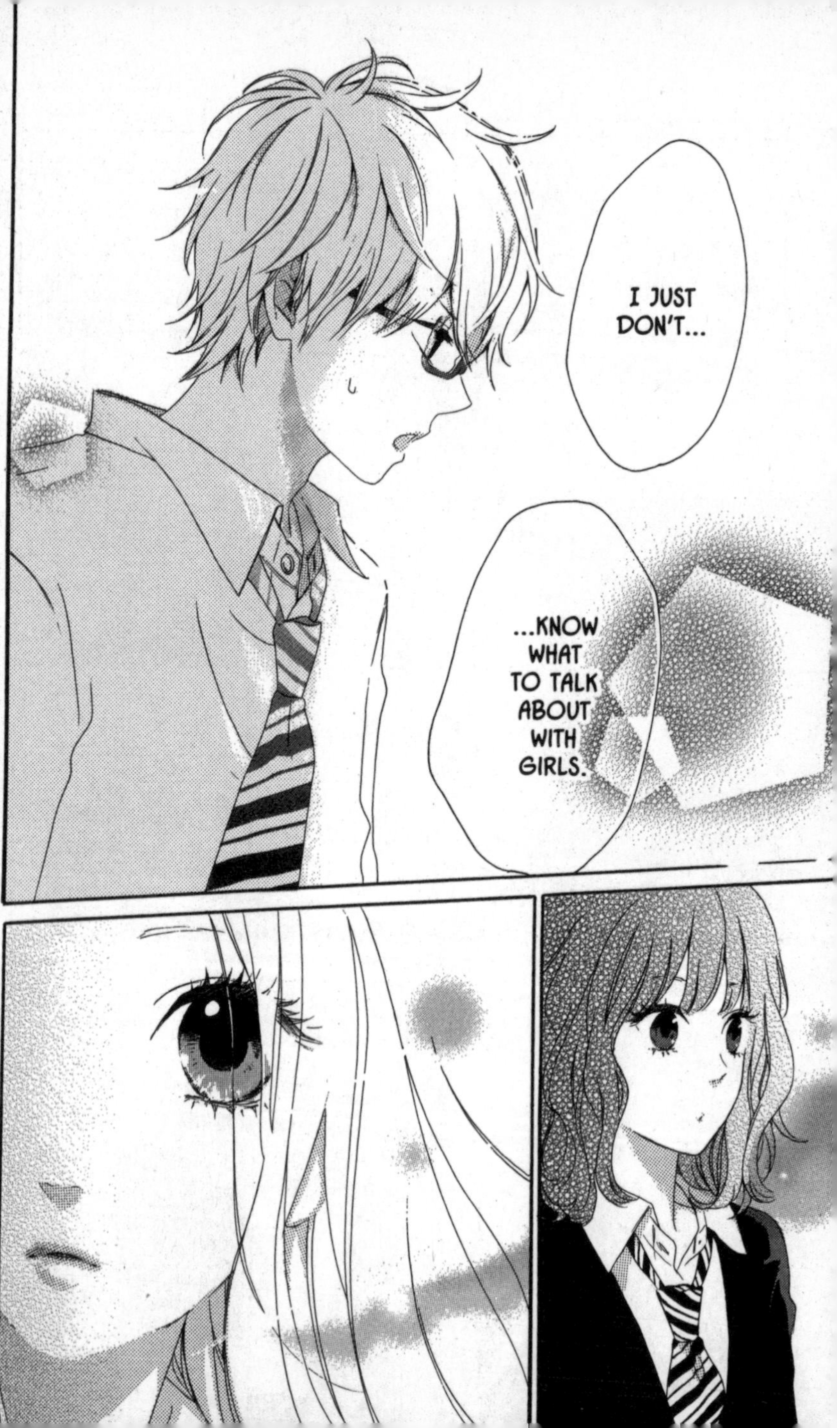
I JUST DON'T...
...KNOW WHAT TO TALK ABOUT WITH GIRLS.

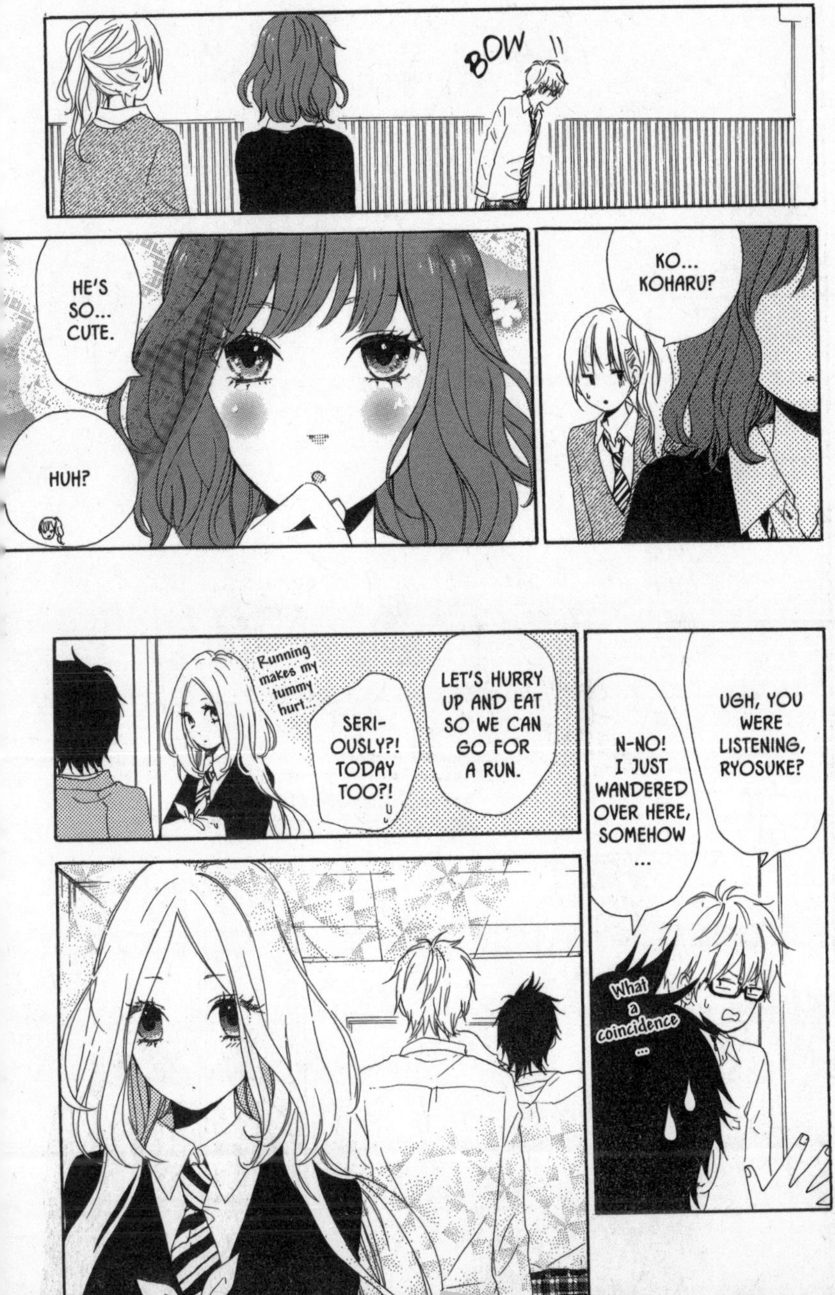
BOW
KO... KOHARU?
HE'S SO... CUTE.
HUH?
UGH, YOU WERE LISTENING, RYOSUKE?
N-NO! I JUST WANDERED OVER HERE, SOMEHOW ...
What a coincidence ...
LET'S HURRY UP AND EAT SO WE CAN GO FOR A RUN.
SERI-OUSLY?! TODAY TOO?!
Running makes my tummy hurt...

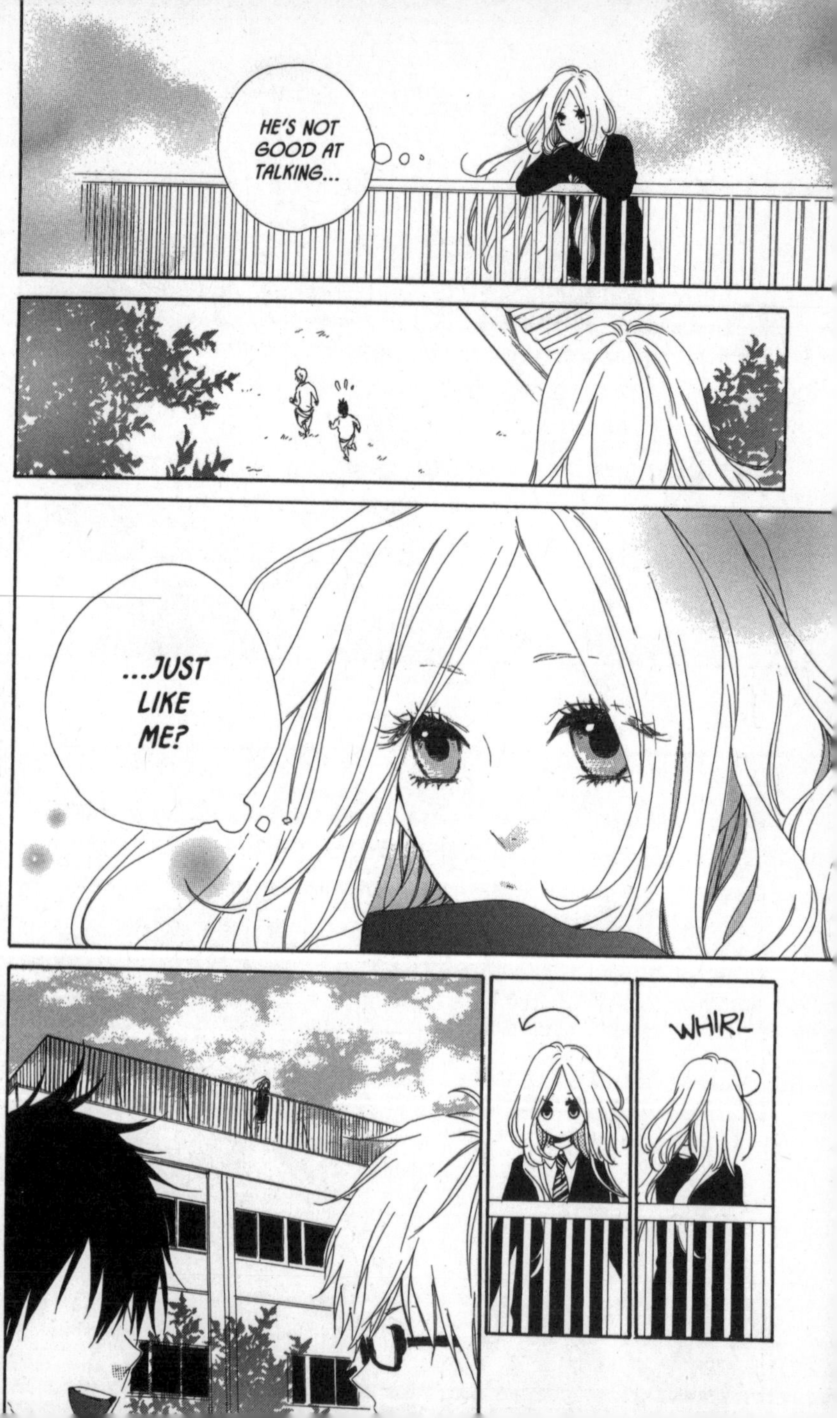
HE'S NOT GOOD AT TALKING...
...JUST LIKE ME?
WHIRL

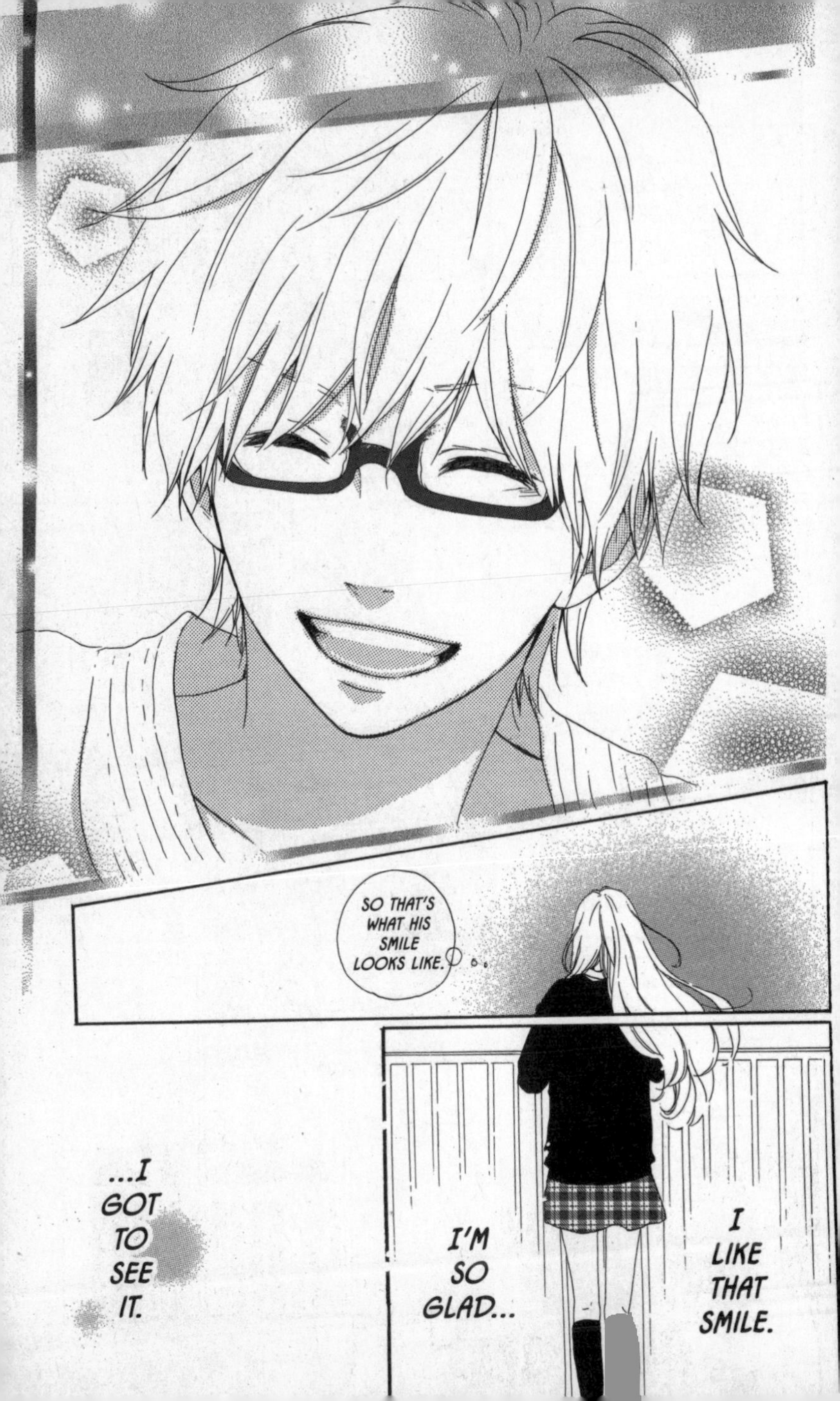
SO THAT'S WHAT HIS SMILE LOOKS LIKE.
I LIKE THAT SMILE.
I'M SO GLAD...
...I GOT TO SEE IT.

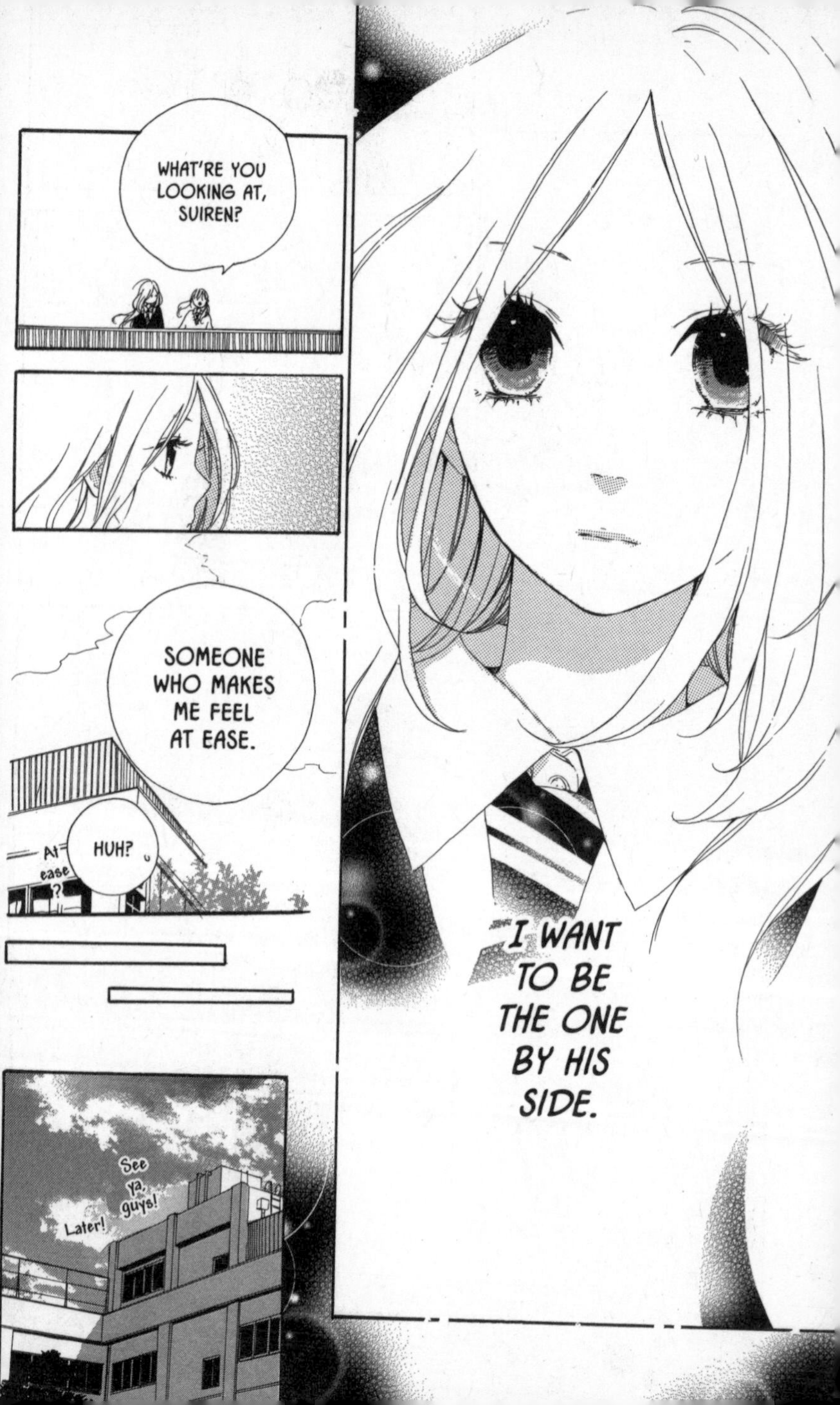
I WANT TO BE THE ONE BY HIS SIDE.
WHAT'RE YOU LOOKING AT, SUIREN?
SOMEONE WHO MAKES ME FEEL AT EASE.
HUH?
At ease?
See ya, guys!
Later!

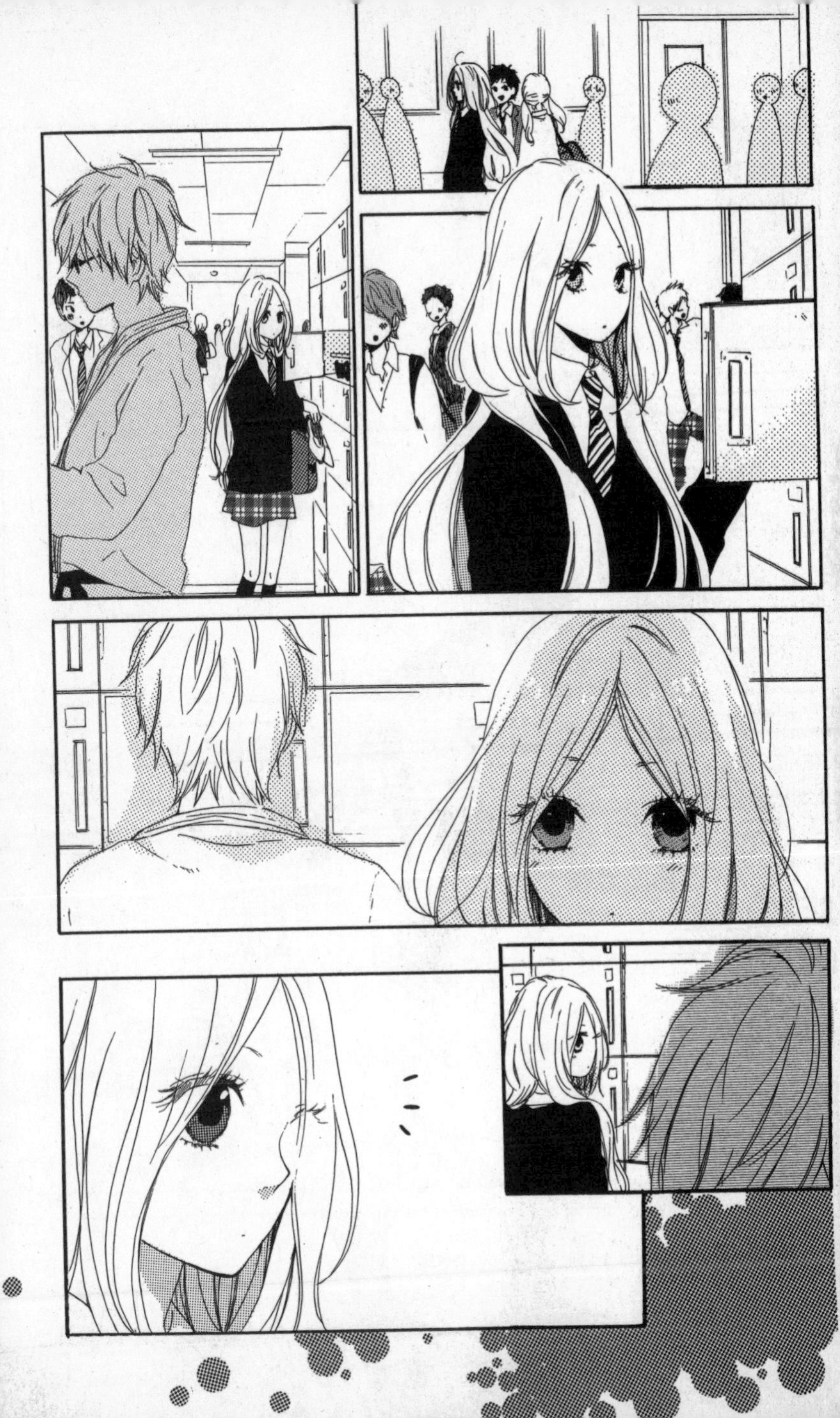

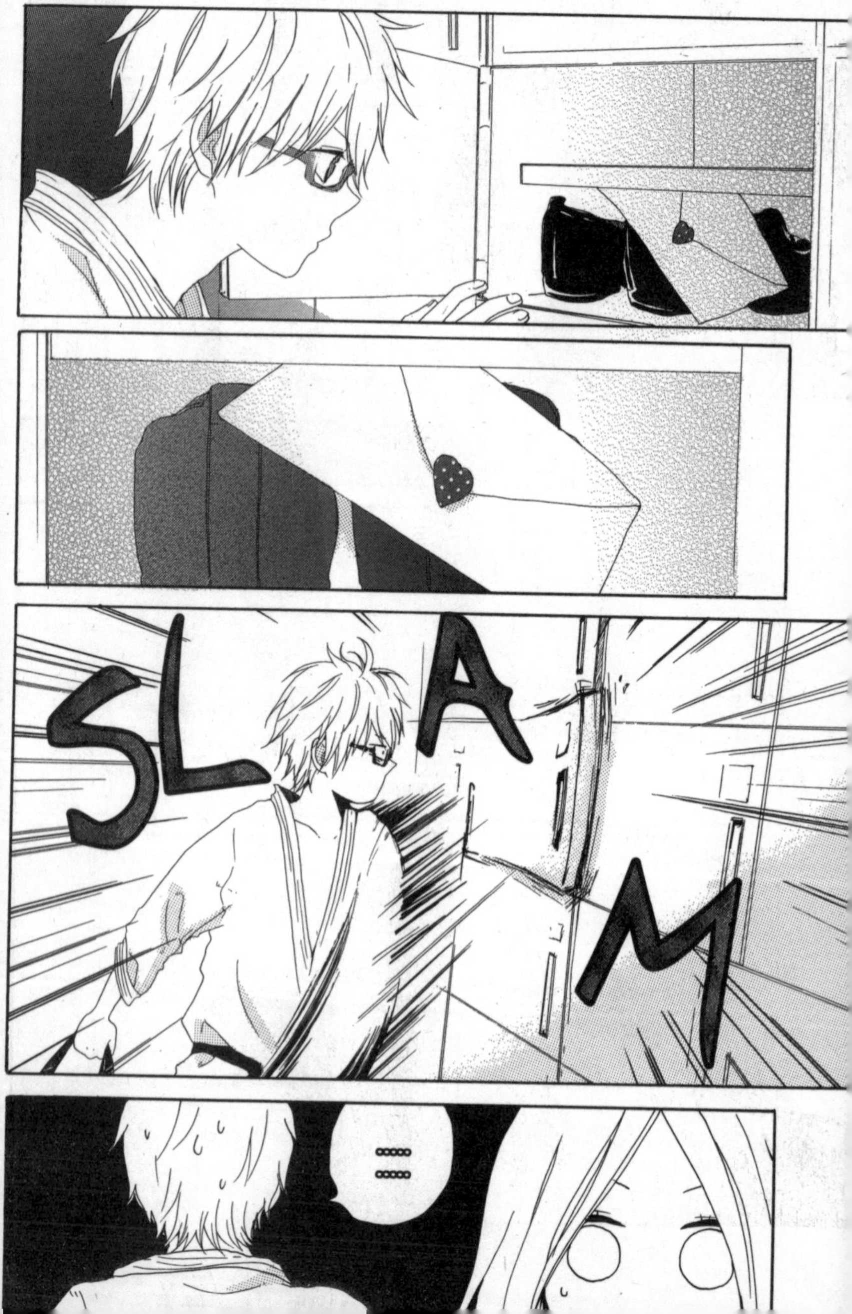
SLAM
......
......

KAWASUUUMI!!

AGH!

WHUMP

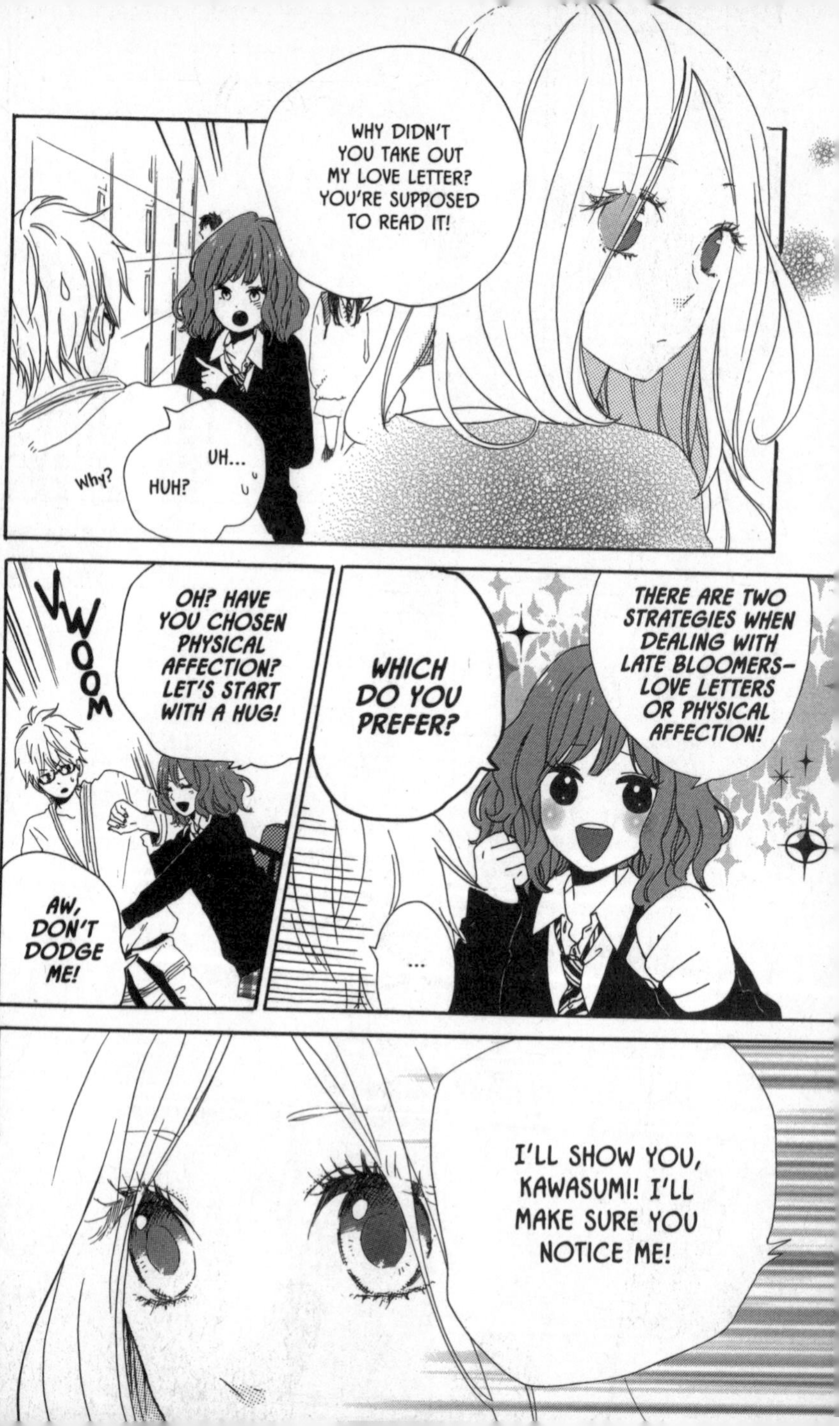
WHY DIDN'T YOU TAKE OUT MY LOVE LETTER? YOU'RE SUPPOSED TO READ IT!
UH...
HUH?
Why?
THERE ARE TWO STRATEGIES WHEN DEALING WITH LATE BLOOMERS-LOVE LETTERS OR PHYSICAL AFFECTION!
WHICH DO YOU PREFER?
...
VWOOM
OH? HAVE YOU CHOSEN PHYSICAL AFFECTION? LET'S START WITH A HUG!
AW, DON'T DODGE ME!
I'LL SHOW YOU, KAWASUMI! I'LL MAKE SURE YOU NOTICE ME!

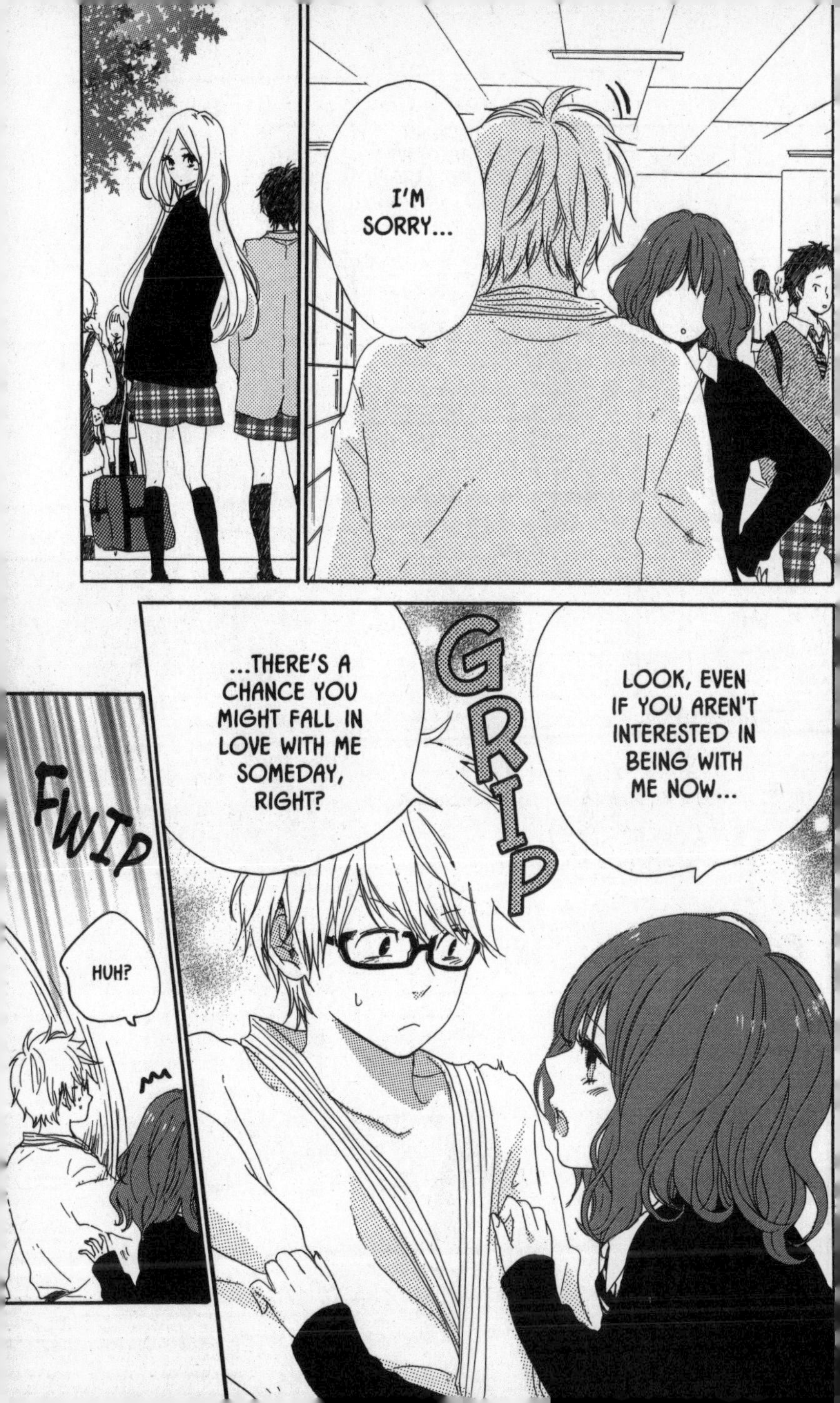
I'M SORRY...
LOOK, EVEN IF YOU AREN'T INTERESTED IN BEING WITH ME NOW...
GRIP
...THERE'S A CHANCE YOU MIGHT FALL IN LOVE WITH ME SOMEDAY, RIGHT?
FWIP
HUH?

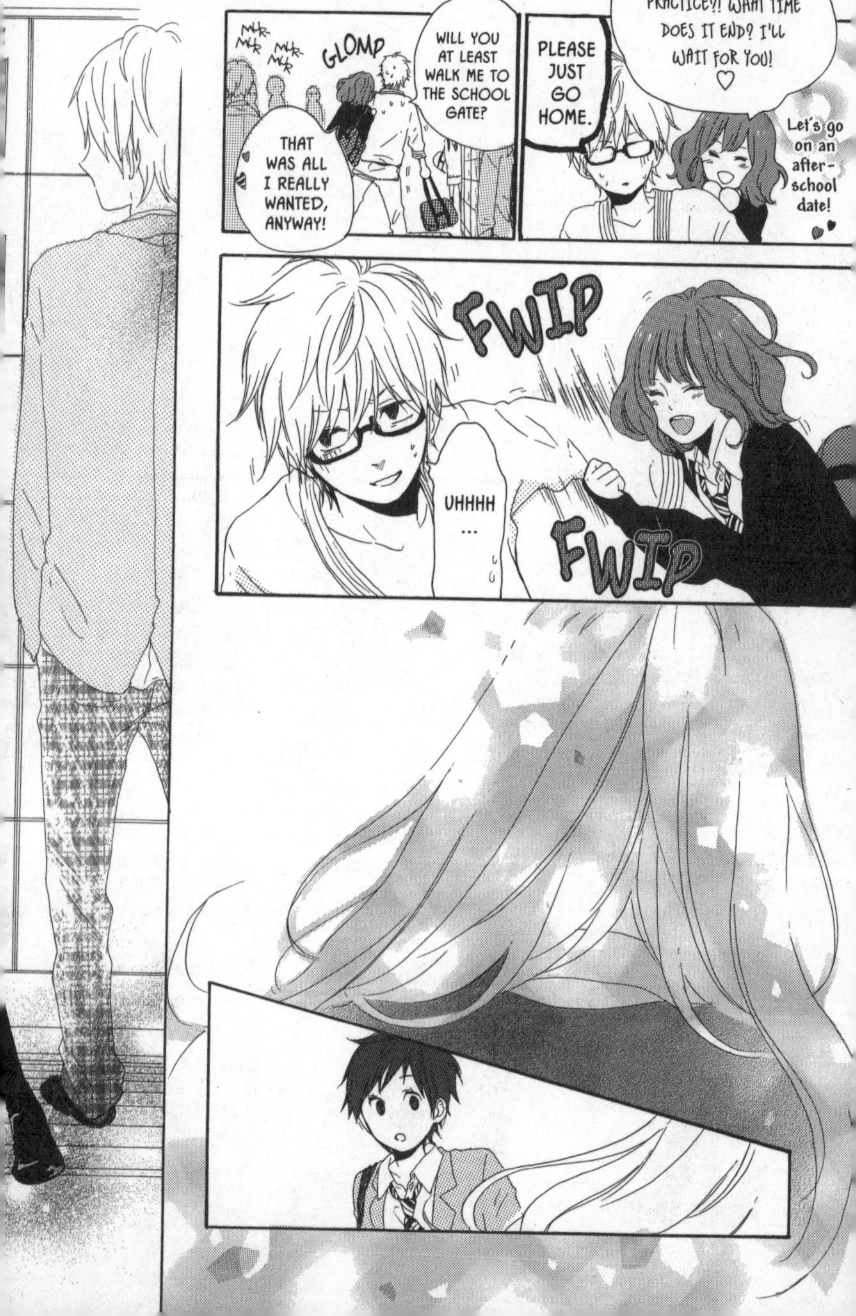
ARE YOU GOING TO PRACTICE?! WHAT TIME DOES IT END? I'LL WAIT FOR YOU! ♡
Let's go on an after-school date!
PLEASE JUST GO HOME.
WILL YOU AT LEAST WALK ME TO THE SCHOOL GATE?
GLOMP
MUR-MUR MUR-MUR
THAT WAS ALL I REALLY WANTED, ANYWAY!
FWIP
UHHHH...
FWIP

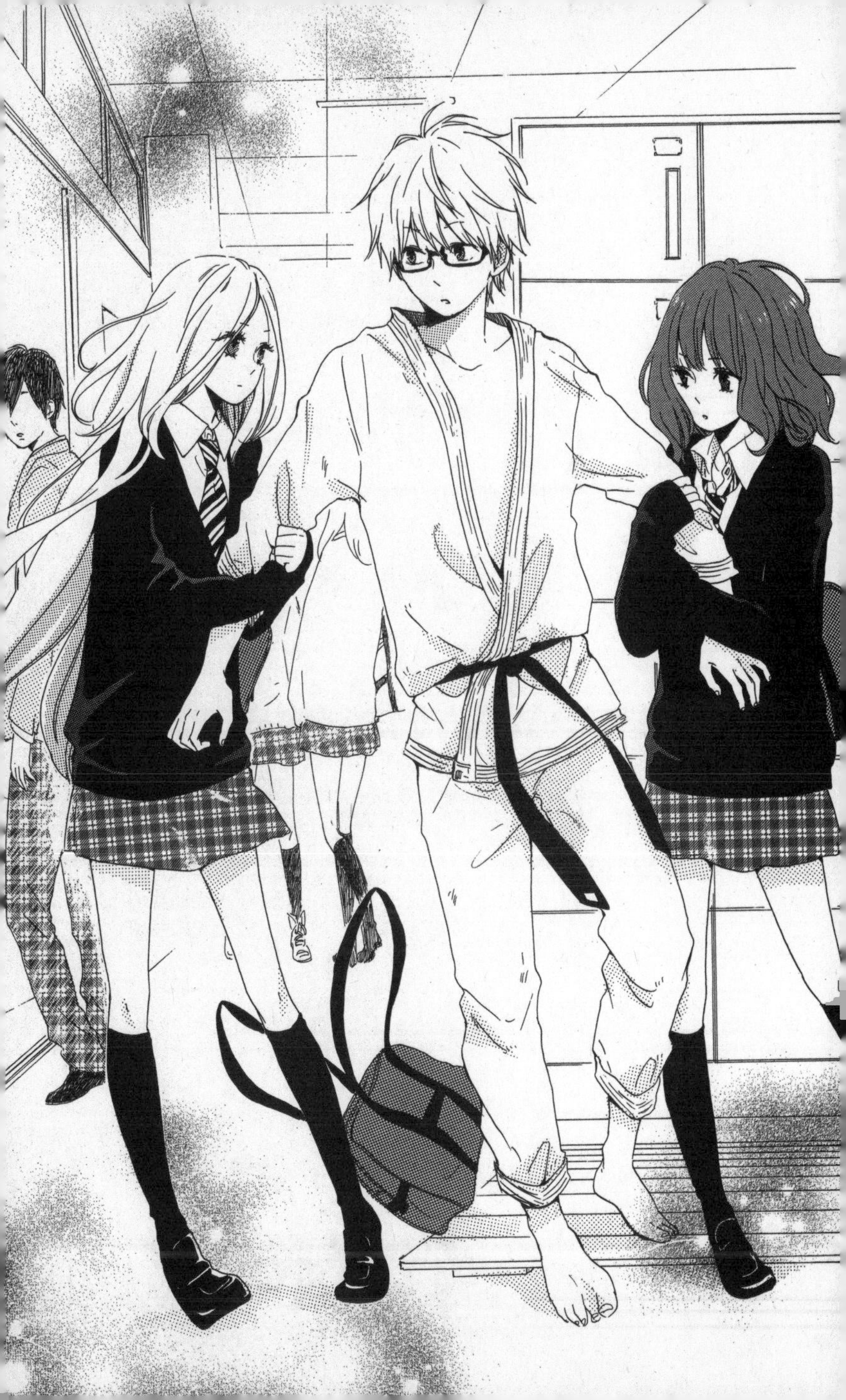

CHAPTER 3

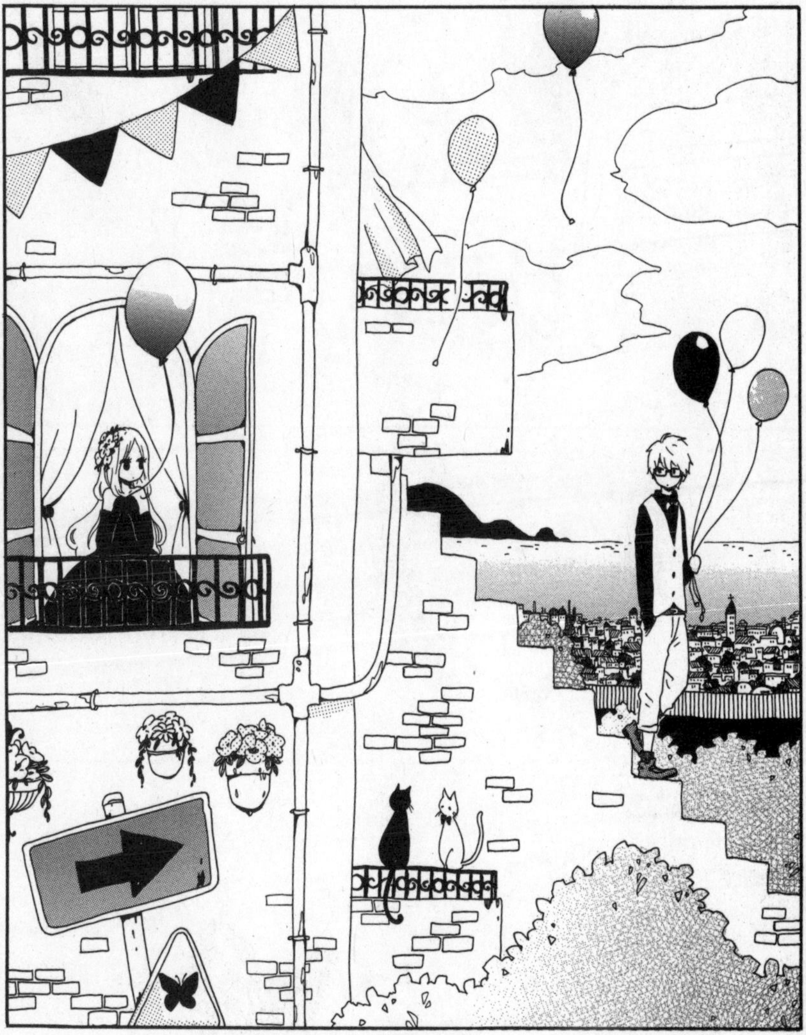

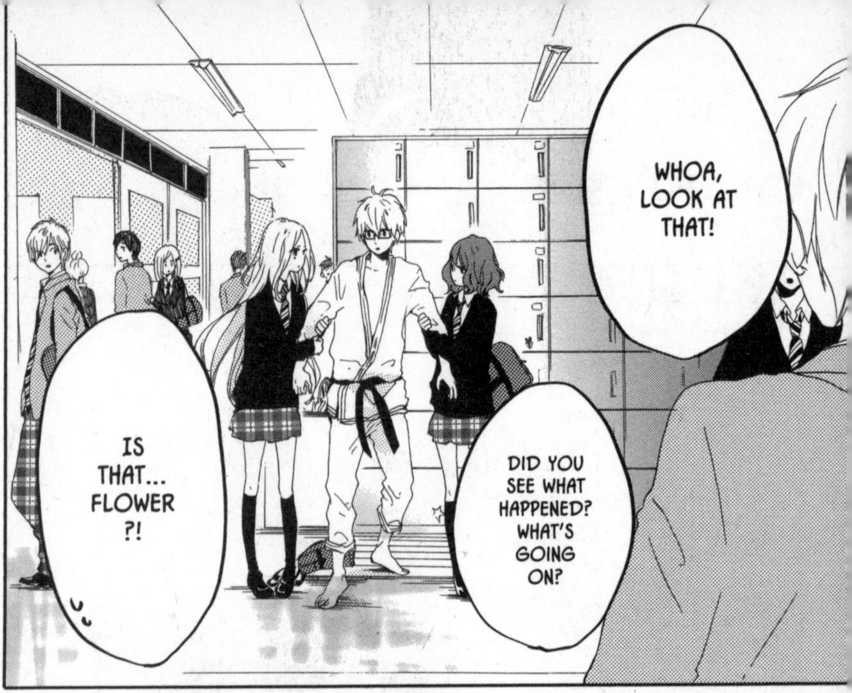
WHOA, LOOK AT THAT!
DID YOU SEE WHAT HAPPENED? WHAT'S GOING ON?
IS THAT... FLOWER ?!

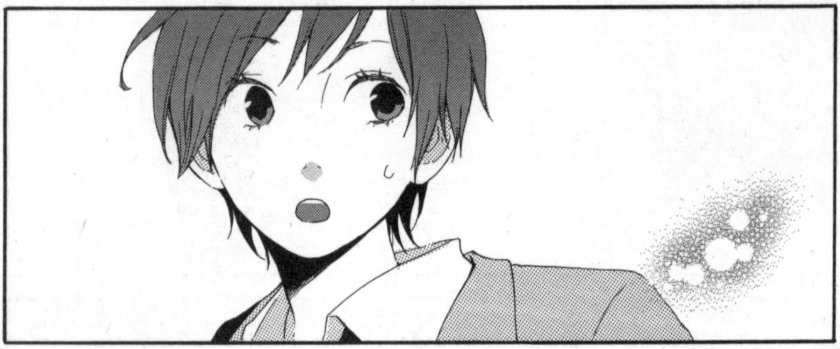

Behind-the-Scenes Introductions

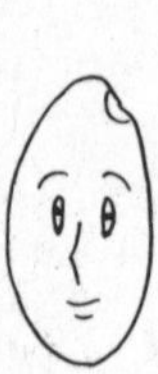

SOBOKU
- MY AVATAR
- A CUTE BUT CREEPY CHARACTER

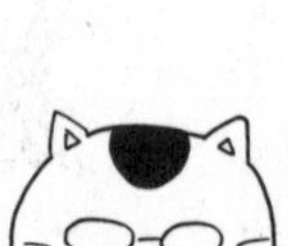

EDITOR NAKACCHI
- AN EDITOR WITH SOME REAL GUTS
- A KIND PERSON

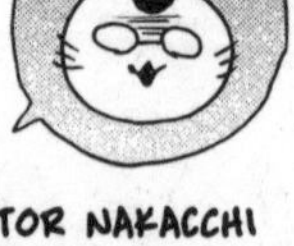

SOMETIMES HE BECOMES ONICCHI THE DEMON...

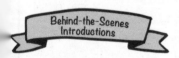

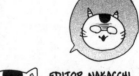

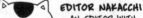

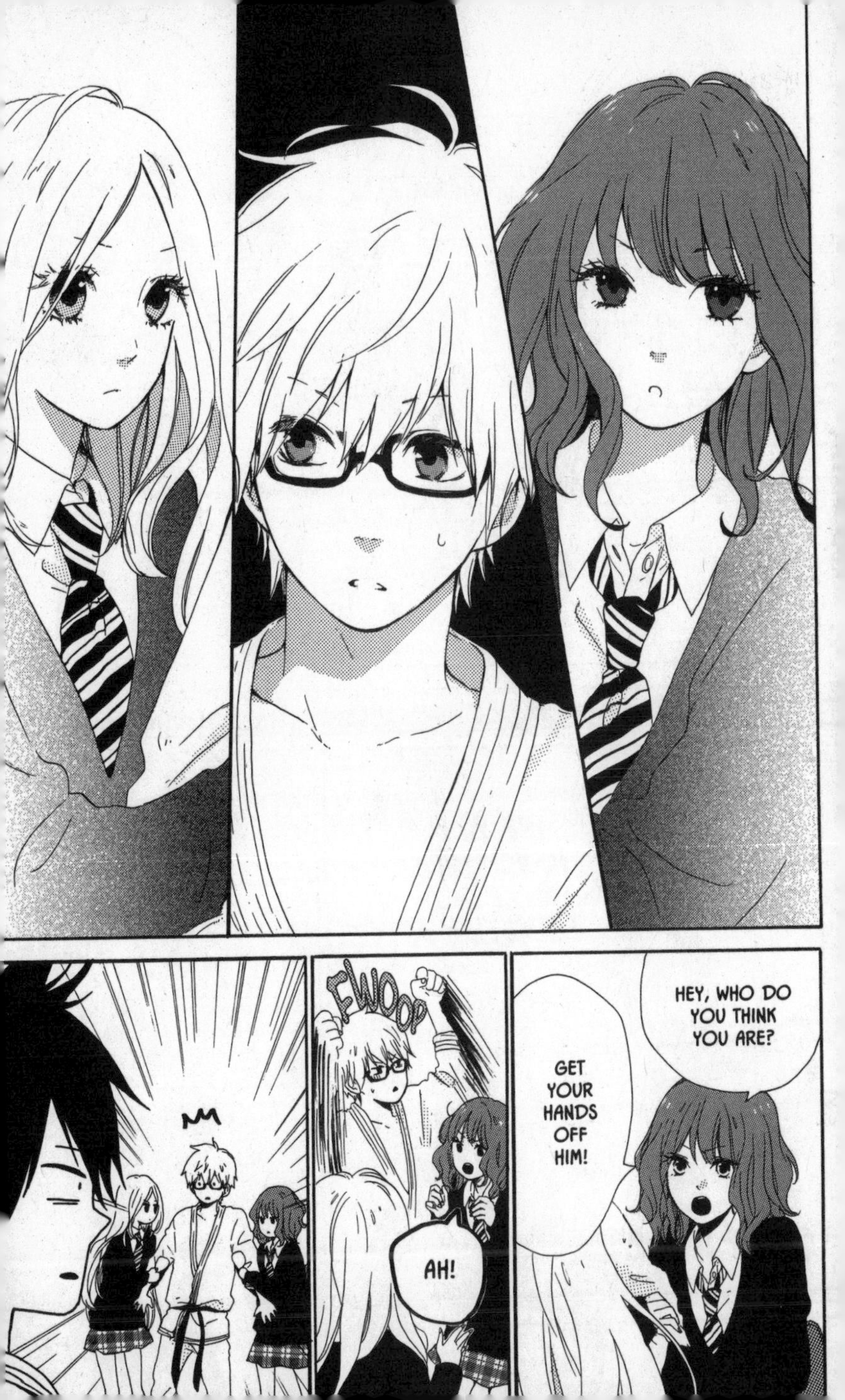
HEY, WHO DO YOU THINK YOU ARE?
GET YOUR HANDS OFF HIM!
FWOOP
AH!

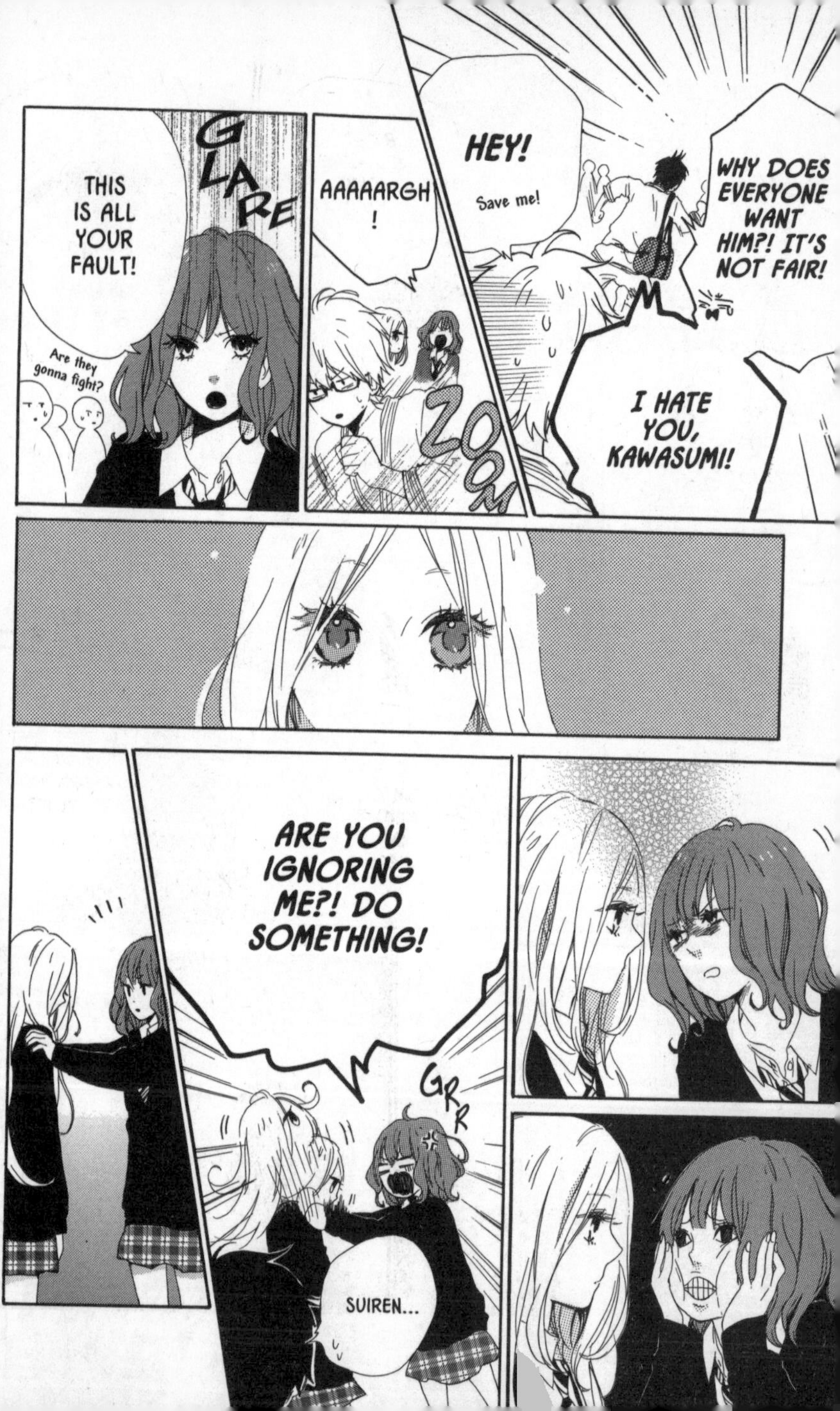
WHY DOES EVERYONE WANT HIM?! IT'S NOT FAIR!
I HATE YOU, KAWASUMI!
HEY!
Save me!
AAAAARGH!
ZOOM
GLARE
THIS IS ALL YOUR FAULT!
Are they gonna fight?
ARE YOU IGNORING ME?! DO SOMETHING!
GRR
SUIREN...

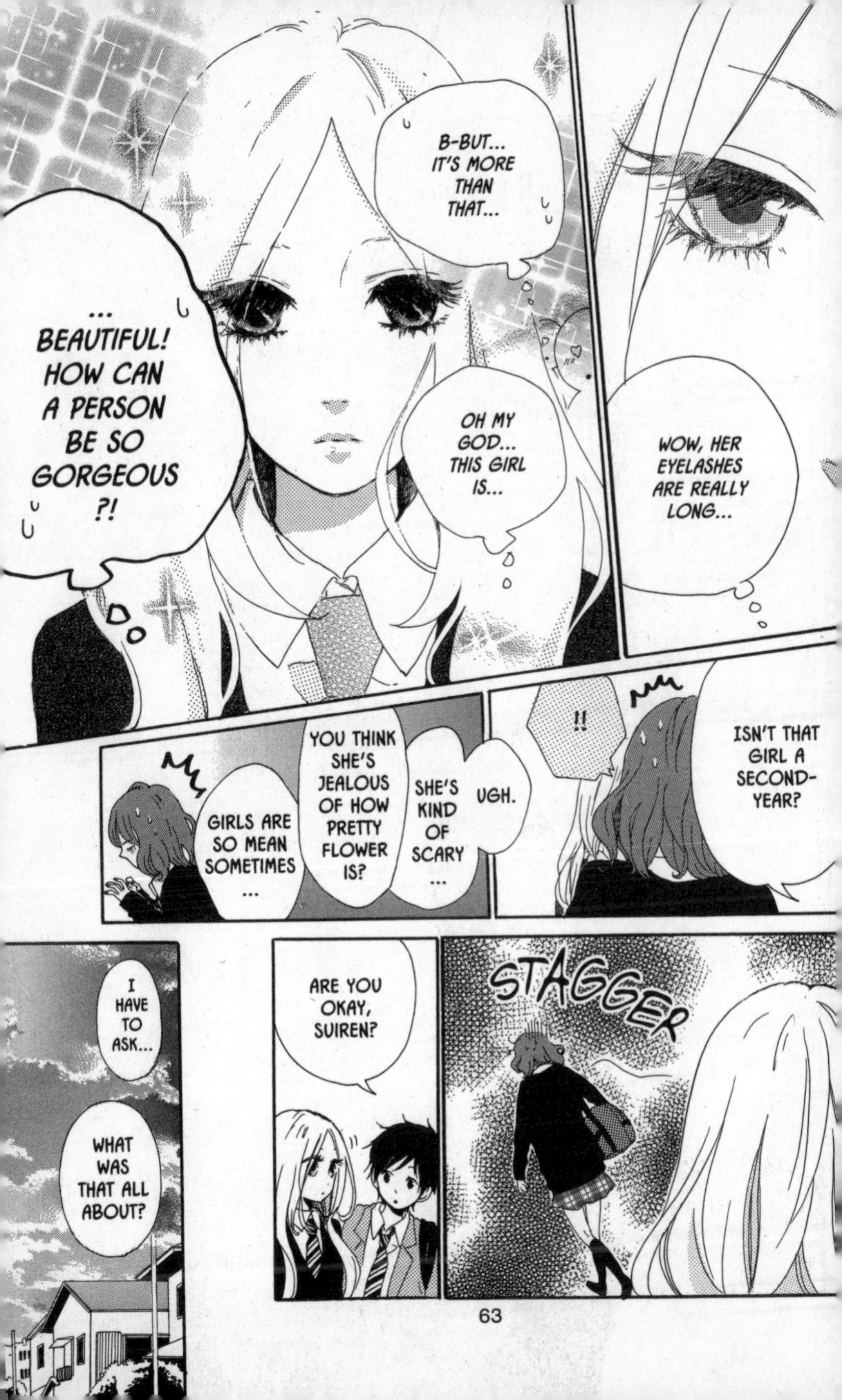
WOW, HER EYELASHES ARE REALLY LONG...
B-BUT... IT'S MORE THAN THAT...
OH MY GOD... THIS GIRL IS...
... BEAUTIFUL! HOW CAN A PERSON BE SO GORGEOUS ?!
ISN'T THAT GIRL A SECOND-YEAR?
!!
UGH.
SHE'S KIND OF SCARY ...
YOU THINK SHE'S JEALOUS OF HOW PRETTY FLOWER IS?
GIRLS ARE SO MEAN SOMETIMES ...
STAGGER
ARE YOU OKAY, SUIREN?
I HAVE TO ASK...
WHAT WAS THAT ALL ABOUT?

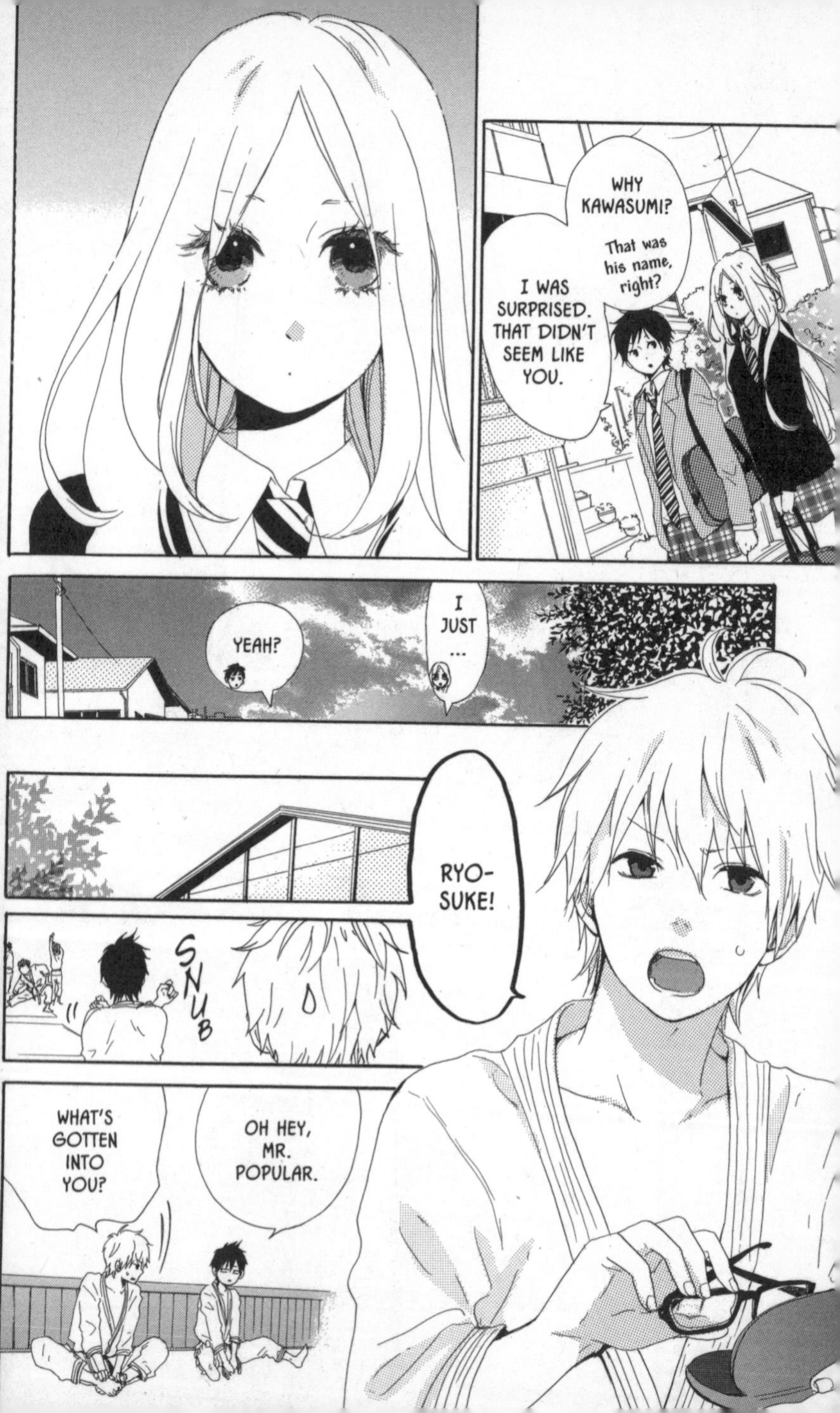
WHY KAWASUMI?
That was his name, right?
I WAS SURPRISED. THAT DIDN'T SEEM LIKE YOU.
I JUST ...
YEAH?
RYO-SUKE!
SNUB
OH HEY, MR. POPULAR.
WHAT'S GOTTEN INTO YOU?

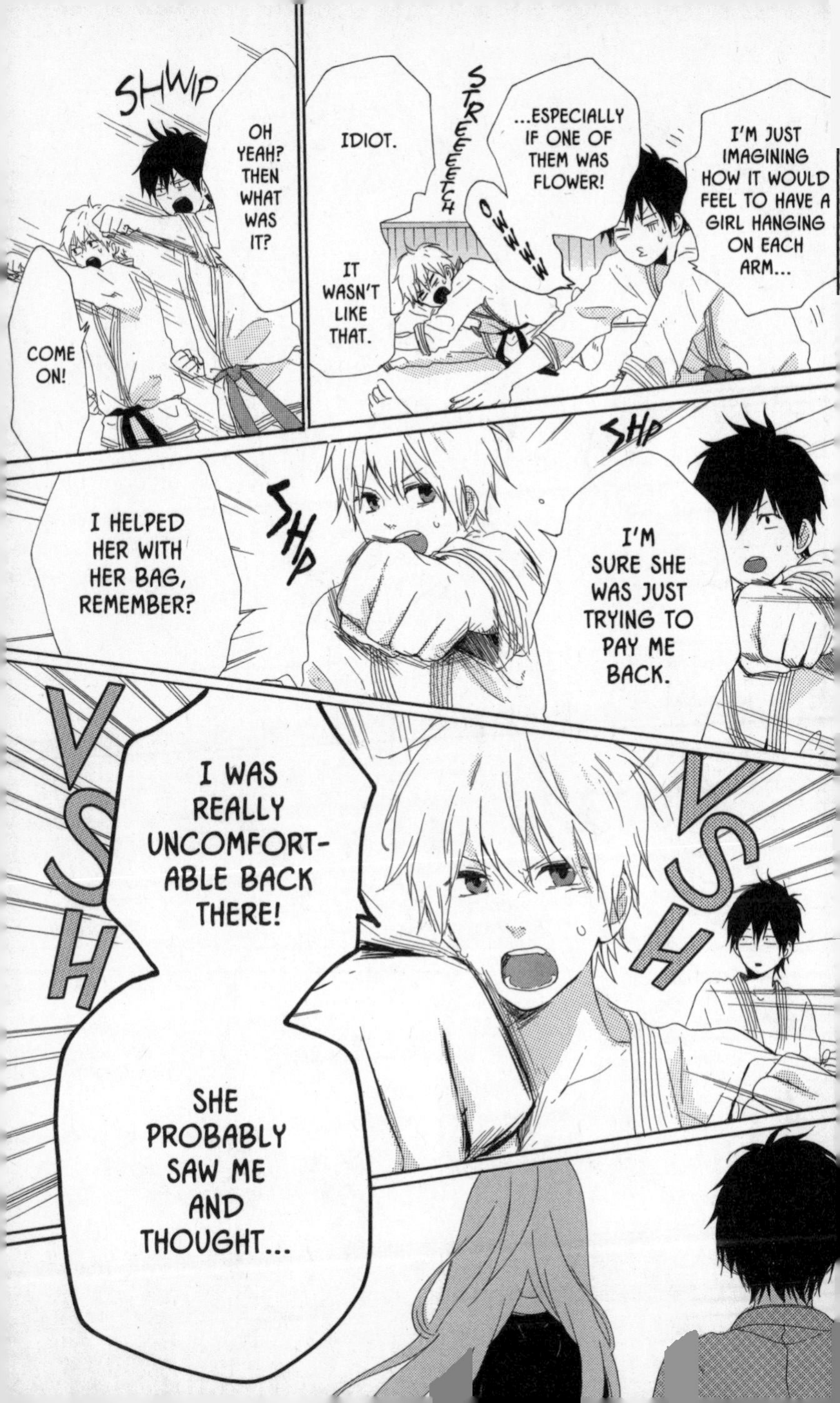
I'M JUST IMAGINING HOW IT WOULD FEEL TO HAVE A GIRL HANGING ON EACH ARM...
...ESPECIALLY IF ONE OF THEM WAS FLOWER!
OWWWW
STREEEEECH
IDIOT.
IT WASN'T LIKE THAT.
SHWIP
OH YEAH? THEN WHAT WAS IT?
COME ON!
SHP
I'M SURE SHE WAS JUST TRYING TO PAY ME BACK.
SHP
I HELPED HER WITH HER BAG, REMEMBER?
VSH
I WAS REALLY UNCOMFORT-ABLE BACK THERE!
VSH
SHE PROBABLY SAW ME AND THOUGHT...

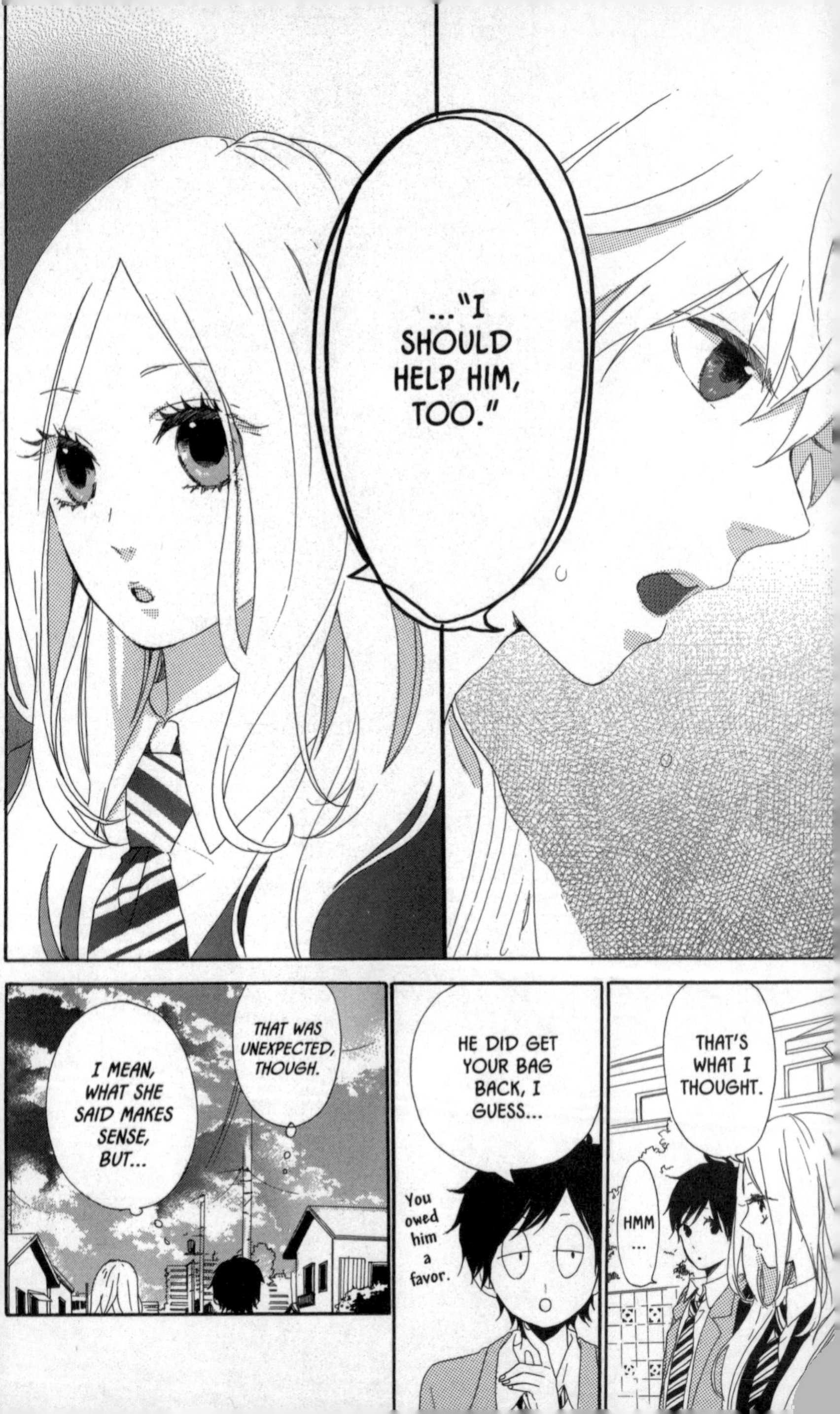

..."I SHOULD HELP HIM, TOO."
THAT'S WHAT I THOUGHT.
HMM...
HE DID GET YOUR BAG BACK, I GUESS...
You owed him a favor.
THAT WAS UNEXPECTED, THOUGH.
I MEAN, WHAT SHE SAID MAKES SENSE, BUT...

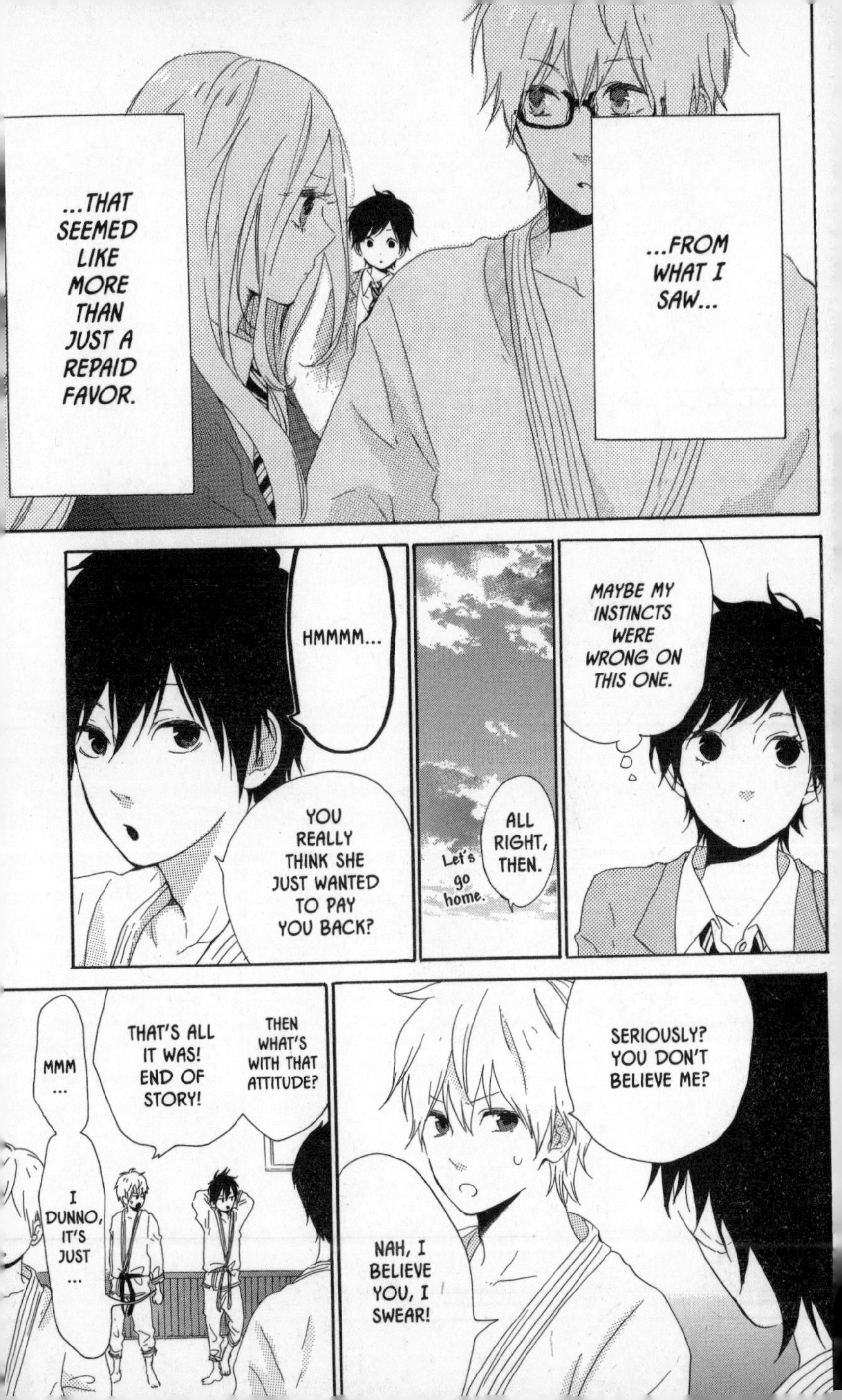
...FROM WHAT I SAW...
...THAT SEEMED LIKE MORE THAN JUST A REPAID FAVOR.
MAYBE MY INSTINCTS WERE WRONG ON THIS ONE.
ALL RIGHT, THEN.
Let's go home.
HMMMM...
YOU REALLY THINK SHE JUST WANTED TO PAY YOU BACK?
SERIOUSLY? YOU DON'T BELIEVE ME?
NAH, I BELIEVE YOU, I SWEAR!
THEN WHAT'S WITH THAT ATTITUDE?
THAT'S ALL IT WAS! END OF STORY!
MMM ...
I DUNNO, IT'S JUST ...

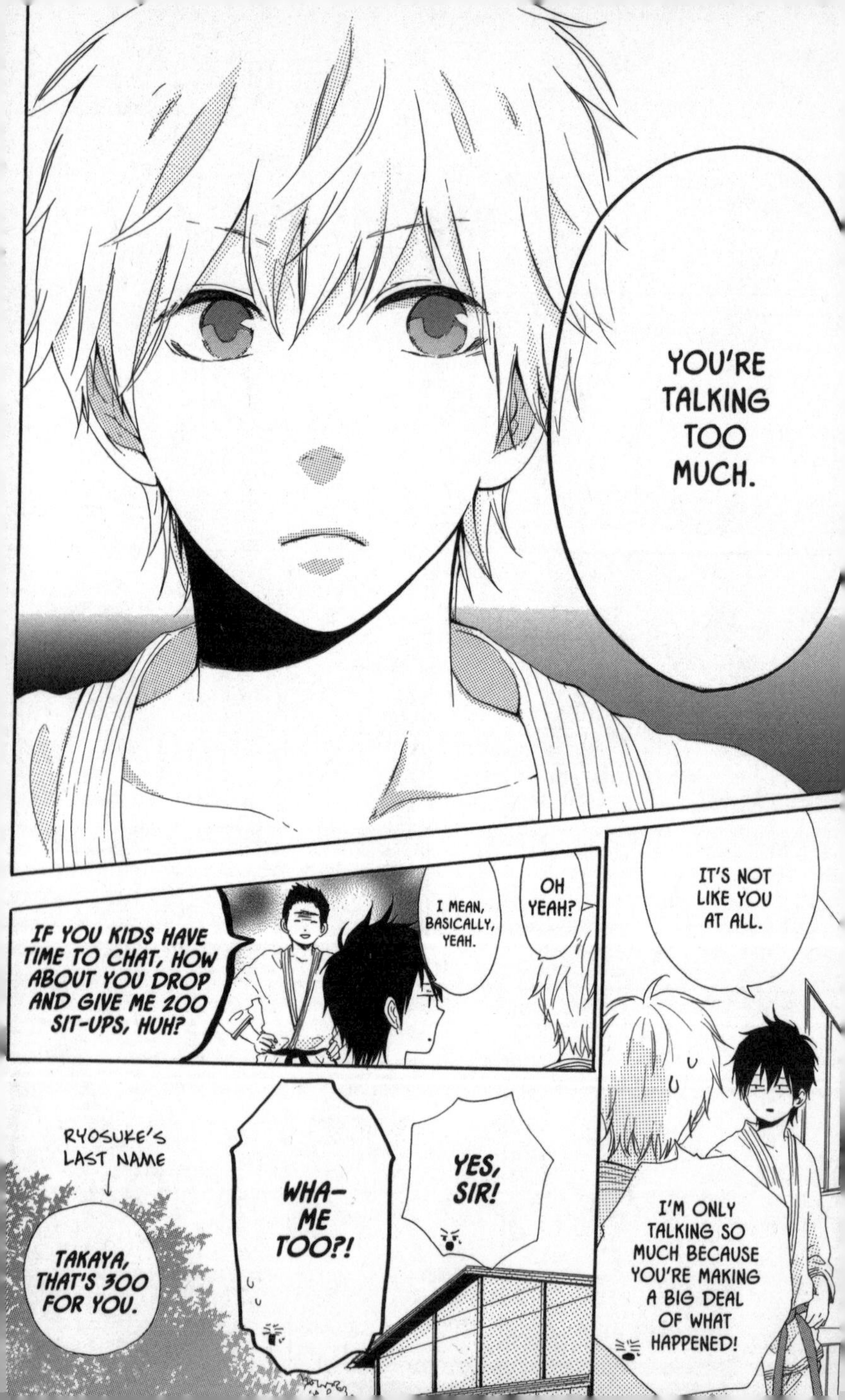
YOU'RE TALKING TOO MUCH.
IT'S NOT LIKE YOU AT ALL.
I'M ONLY TALKING SO MUCH BECAUSE YOU'RE MAKING A BIG DEAL OF WHAT HAPPENED!
OH YEAH?
I MEAN, BASICALLY, YEAH.
IF YOU KIDS HAVE TIME TO CHAT, HOW ABOUT YOU DROP AND GIVE ME 200 SIT-UPS, HUH?
YES, SIR!
WHA- ME TOO?!
RYOSUKE'S LAST NAME
TAKAYA, THAT'S 300 FOR YOU.

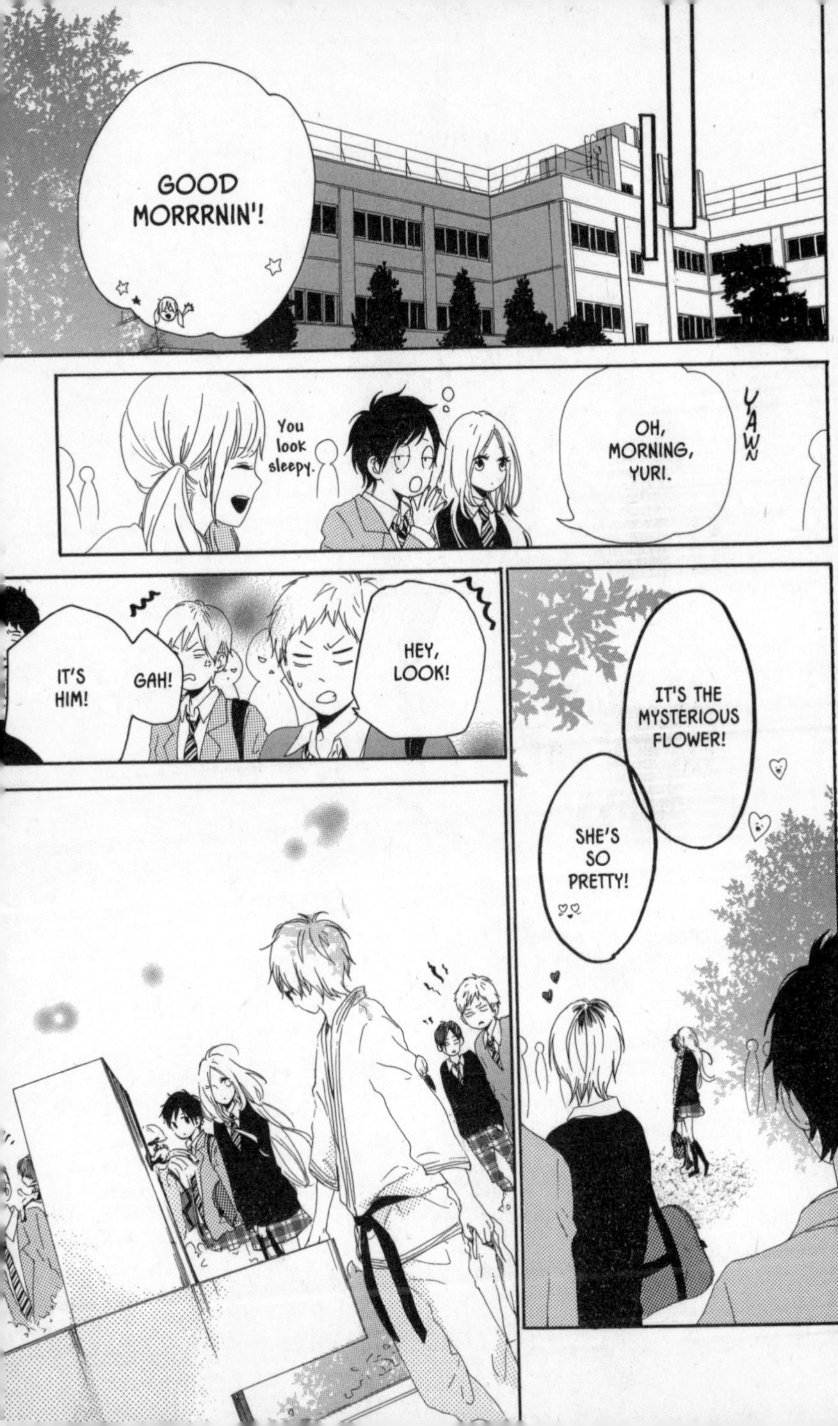
GOOD MORRRNIN'!
OH, MORNING, YURI.
YAWN
You look sleepy.
IT'S THE MYSTERIOUS FLOWER!
SHE'S SO PRETTY!
HEY, LOOK!
GAH!
IT'S HIM!

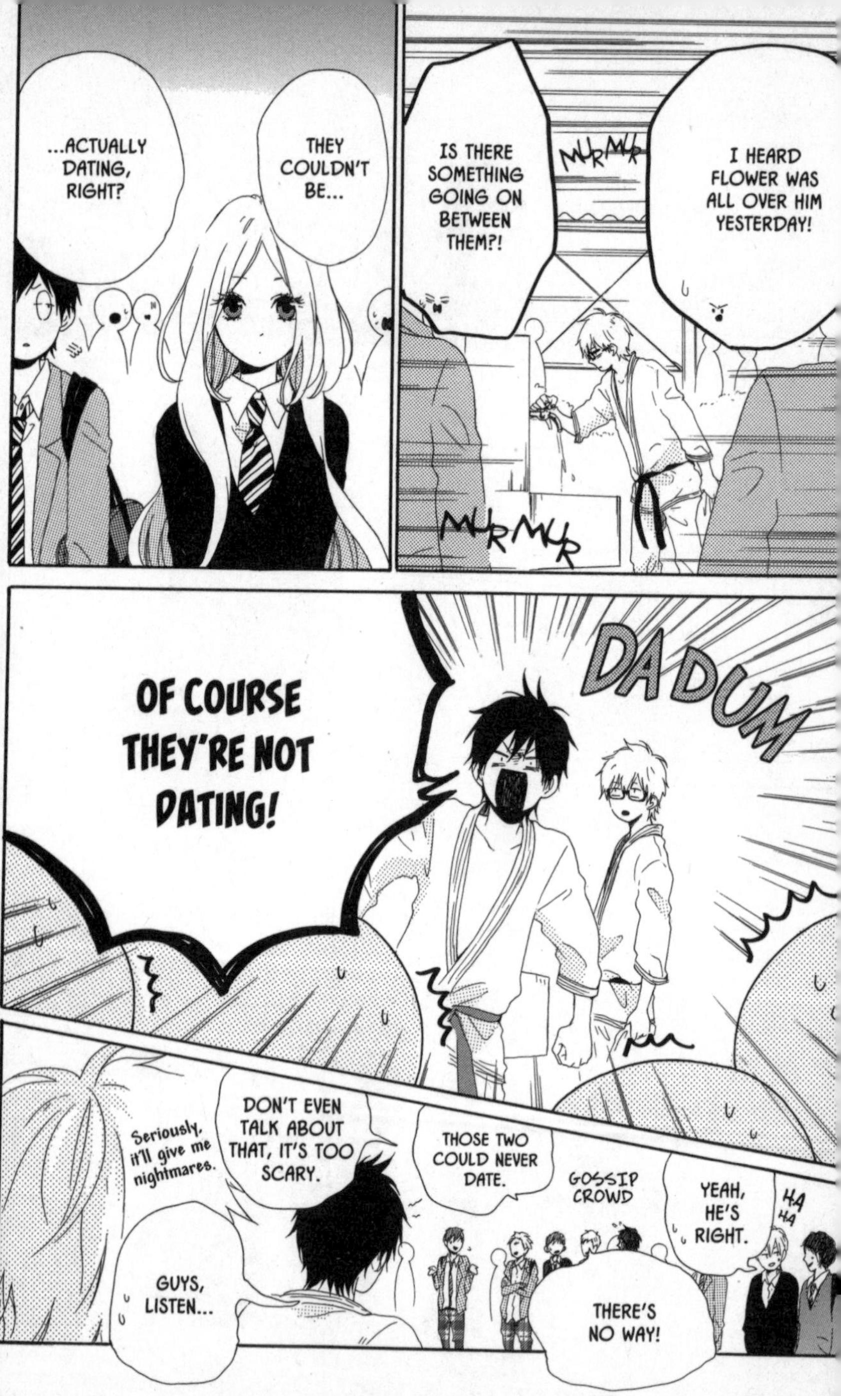
I HEARD FLOWER WAS ALL OVER HIM YESTERDAY!
MURMUR
IS THERE SOMETHING GOING ON BETWEEN THEM?!
MURMUR
THEY COULDN'T BE...
...ACTUALLY DATING, RIGHT?
DADUM
OF COURSE THEY'RE NOT DATING!
HA HA
YEAH, HE'S RIGHT.
THERE'S NO WAY!
GOSSIP CROWD
THOSE TWO COULD NEVER DATE.
DON'T EVEN TALK ABOUT THAT, IT'S TOO SCARY.
Seriously, it'll give me nightmares.
GUYS, LISTEN...

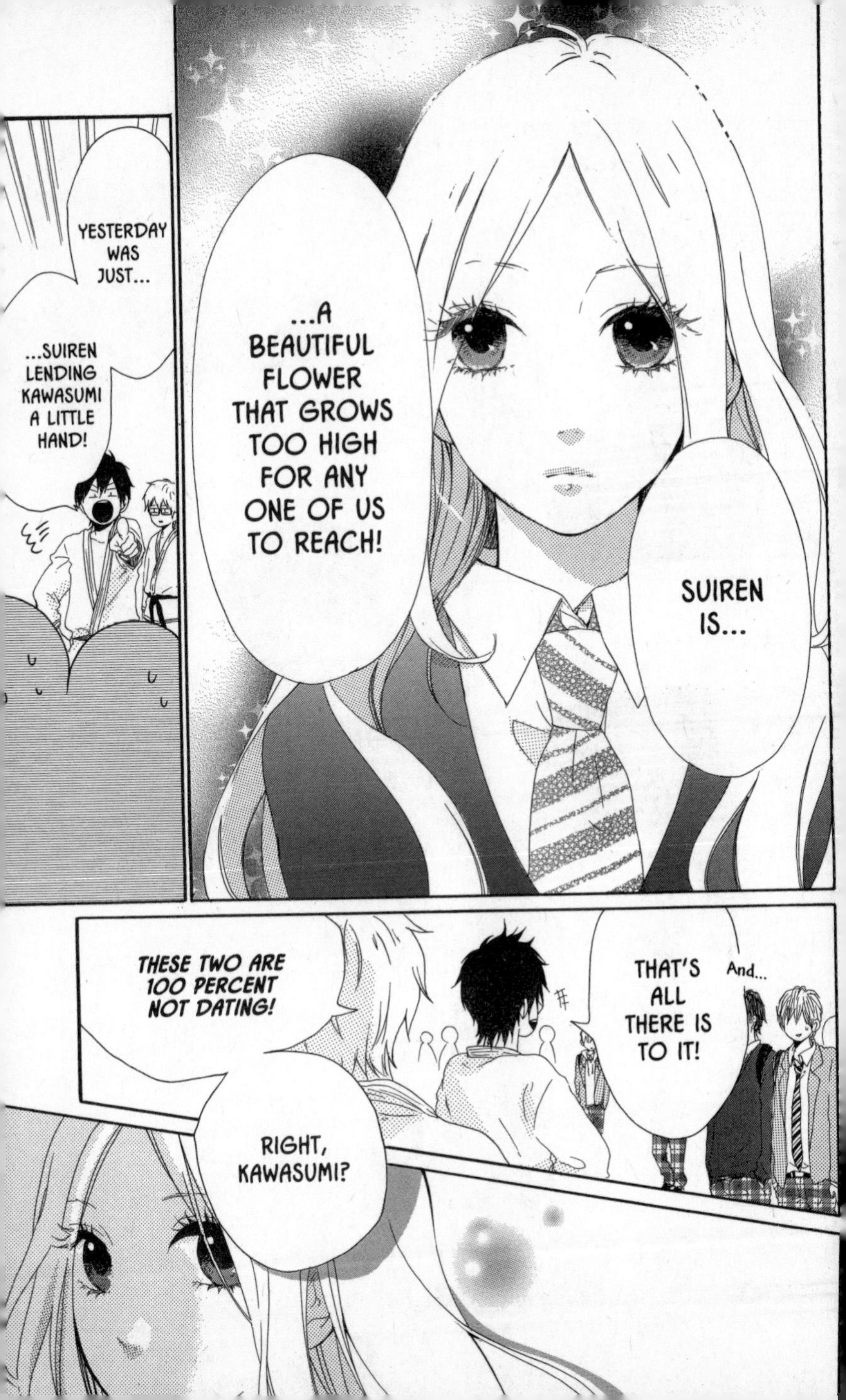
SUIREN IS...
...A BEAUTIFUL FLOWER THAT GROWS TOO HIGH FOR ANY ONE OF US TO REACH!
YESTERDAY WAS JUST...
...SUIREN LENDING KAWASUMI A LITTLE HAND!
THAT'S ALL THERE IS TO IT!
And...
THESE TWO ARE 100 PERCENT NOT DATING!
RIGHT, KAWASUMI?

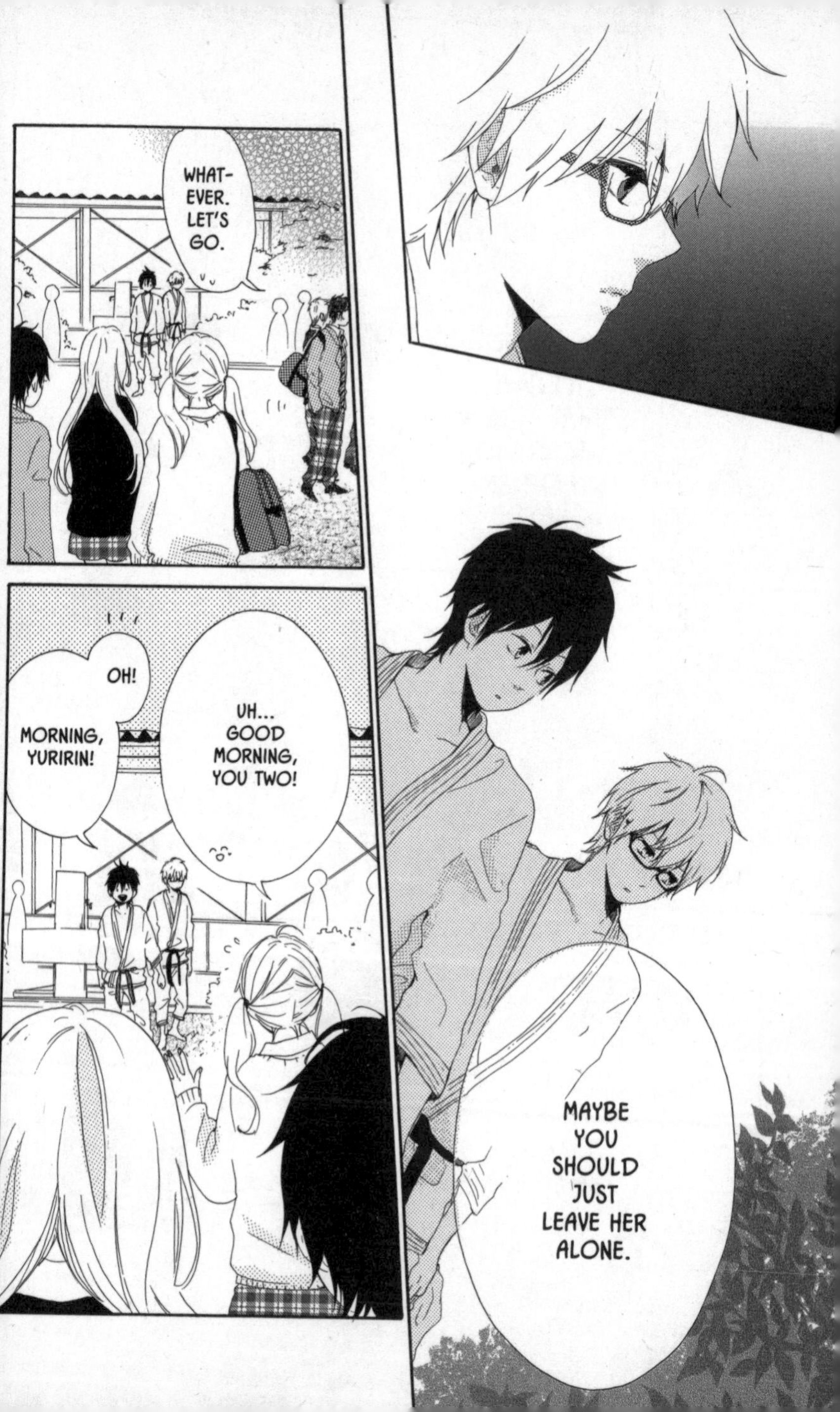
MAYBE YOU SHOULD JUST LEAVE HER ALONE.
WHAT-EVER. LET'S GO.
UH... GOOD MORNING, YOU TWO!
OH!
MORNING, YURIRIN!

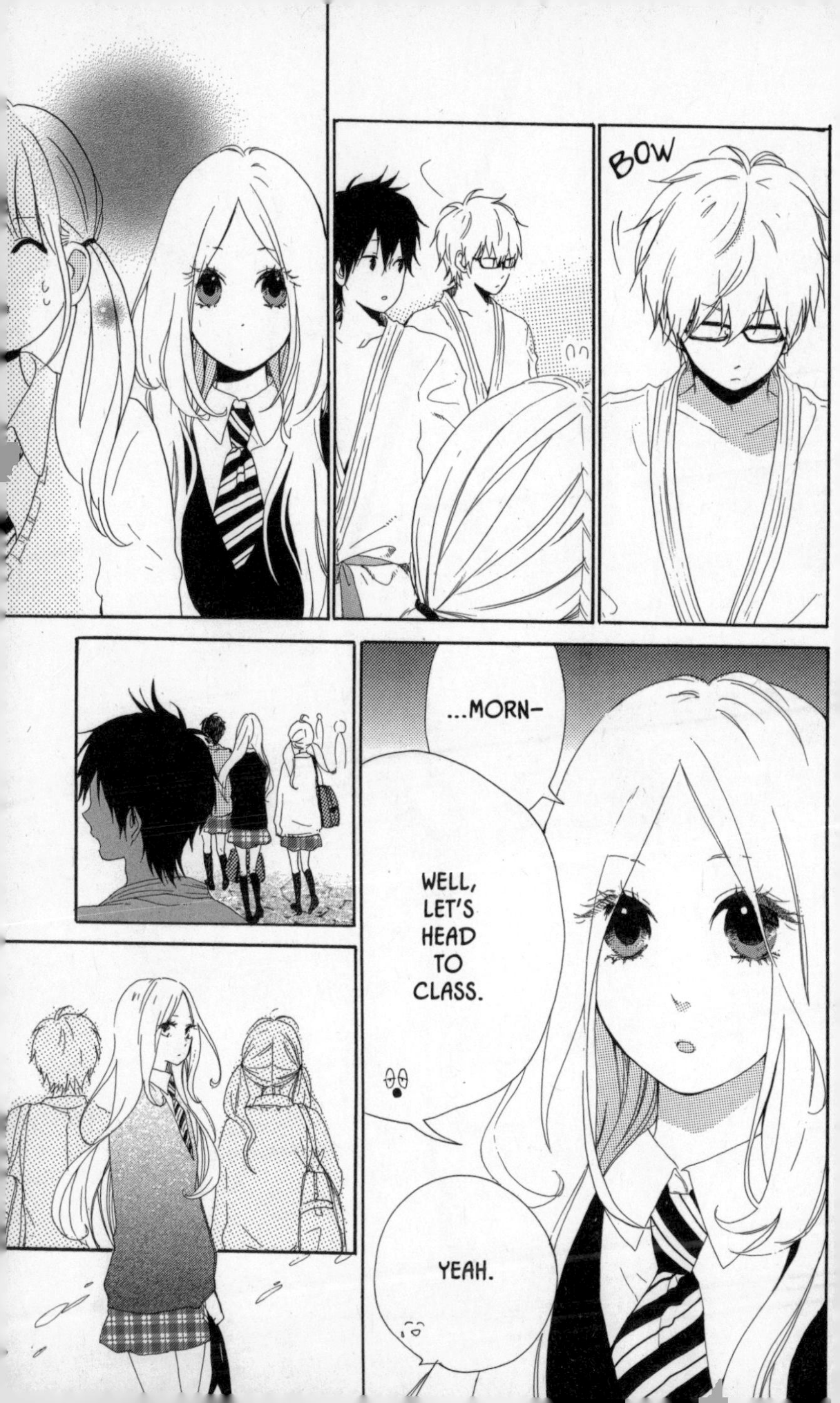
BOW
...MORN-
WELL, LET'S HEAD TO CLASS.
YEAH.

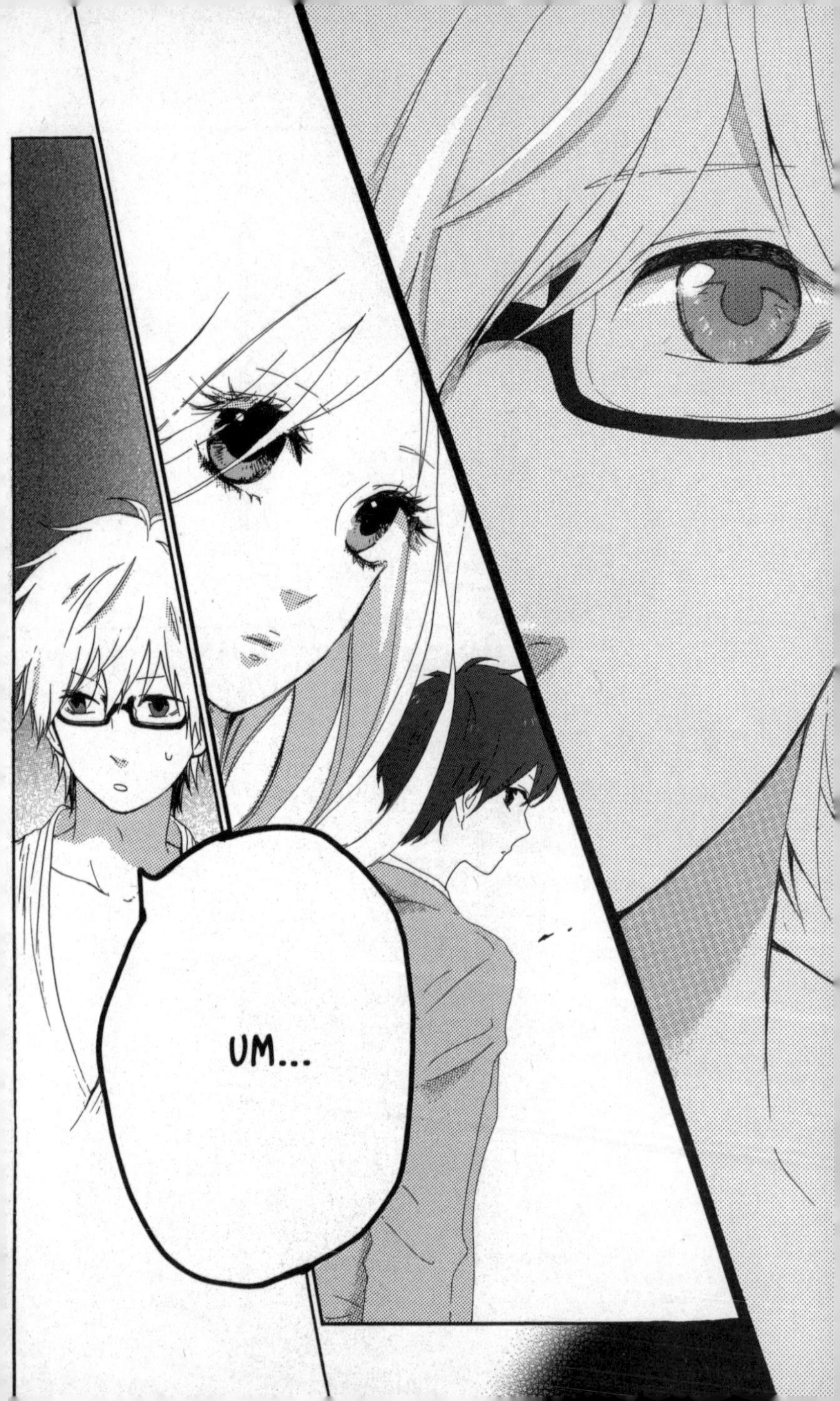
UM...

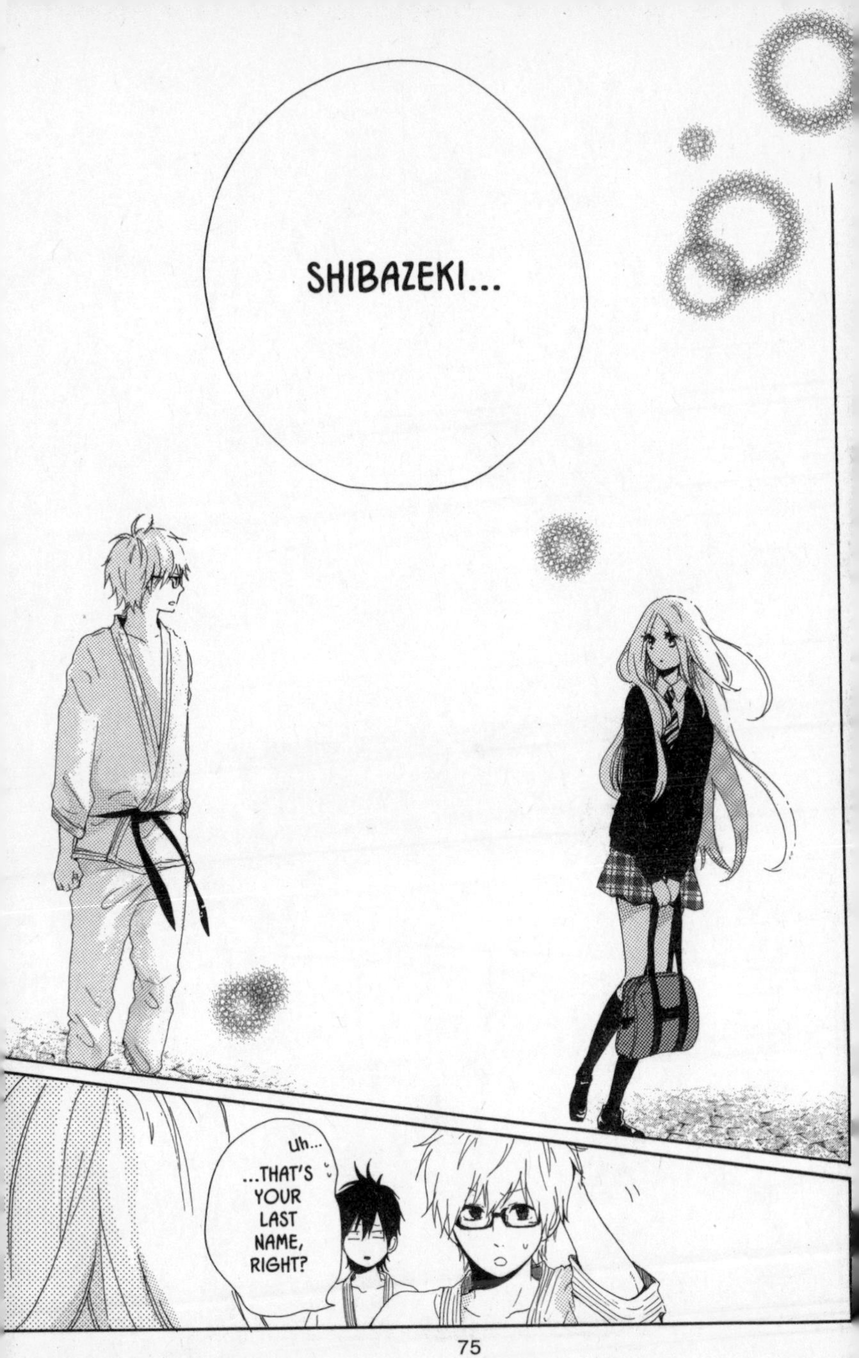
SHIBAZEKI...
Uh...
...THAT'S YOUR LAST NAME, RIGHT?

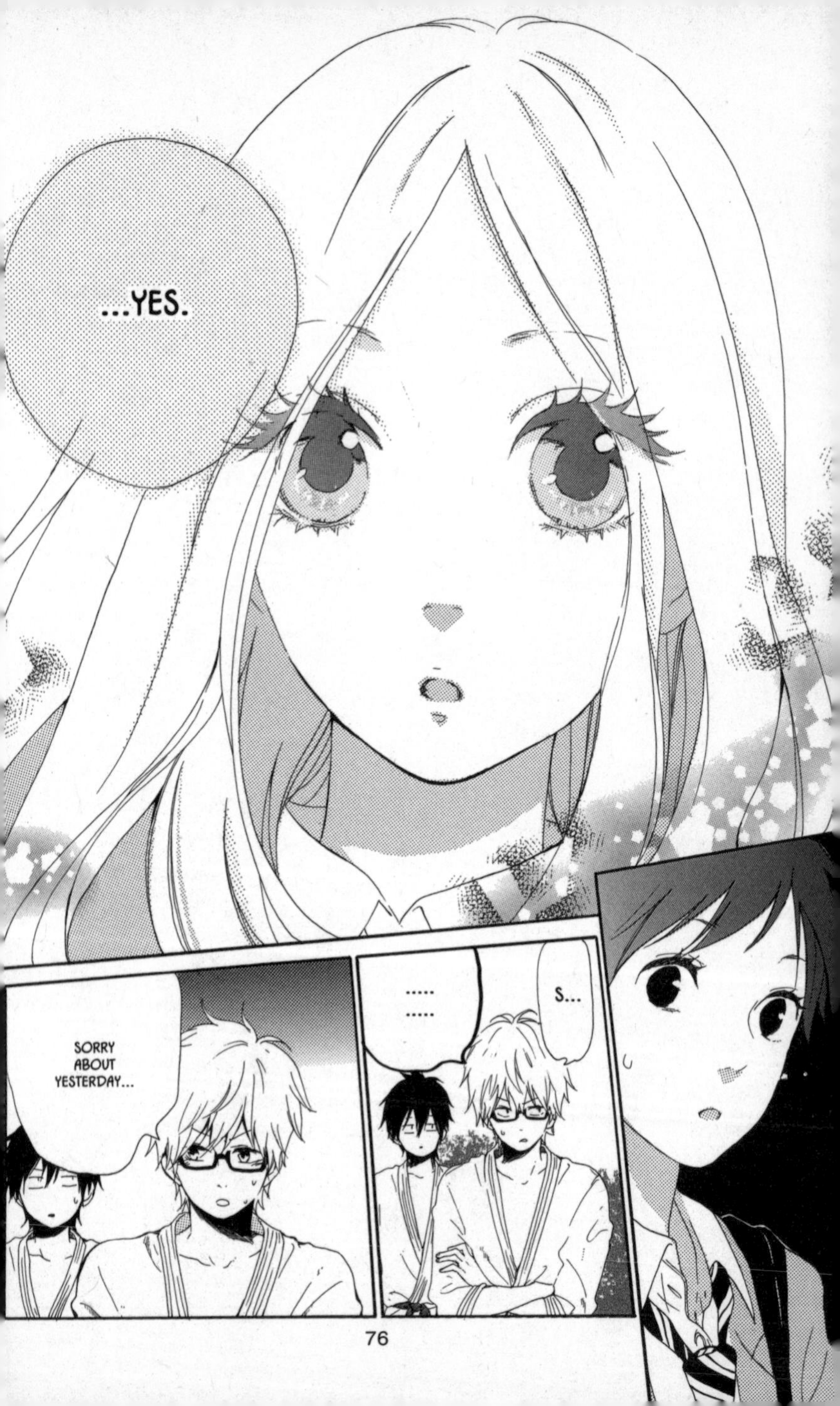
...YES.
S...
.....
.....
SORRY ABOUT YESTERDAY...

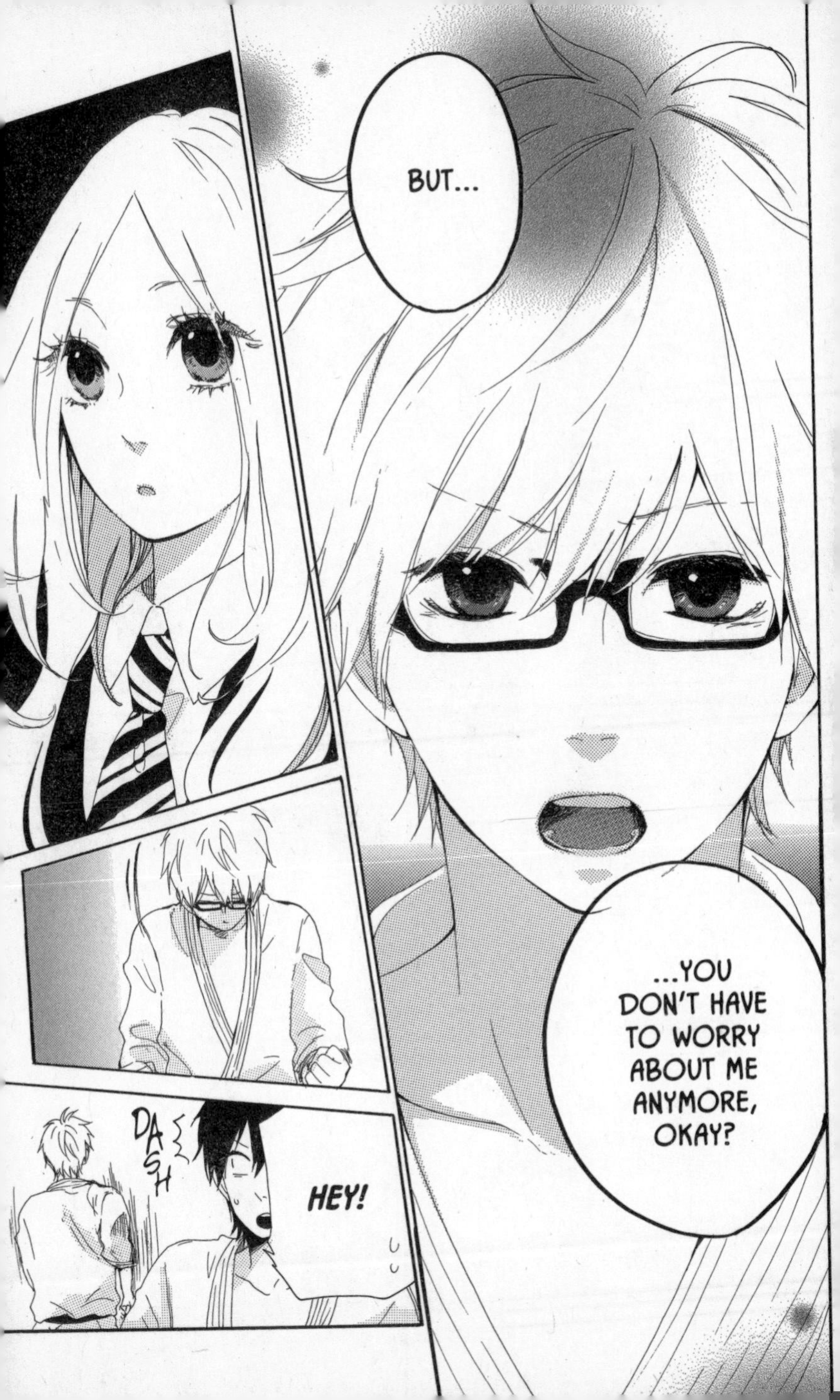
BUT...
...YOU DON'T HAVE TO WORRY ABOUT ME ANYMORE, OKAY?
DASH
HEY!

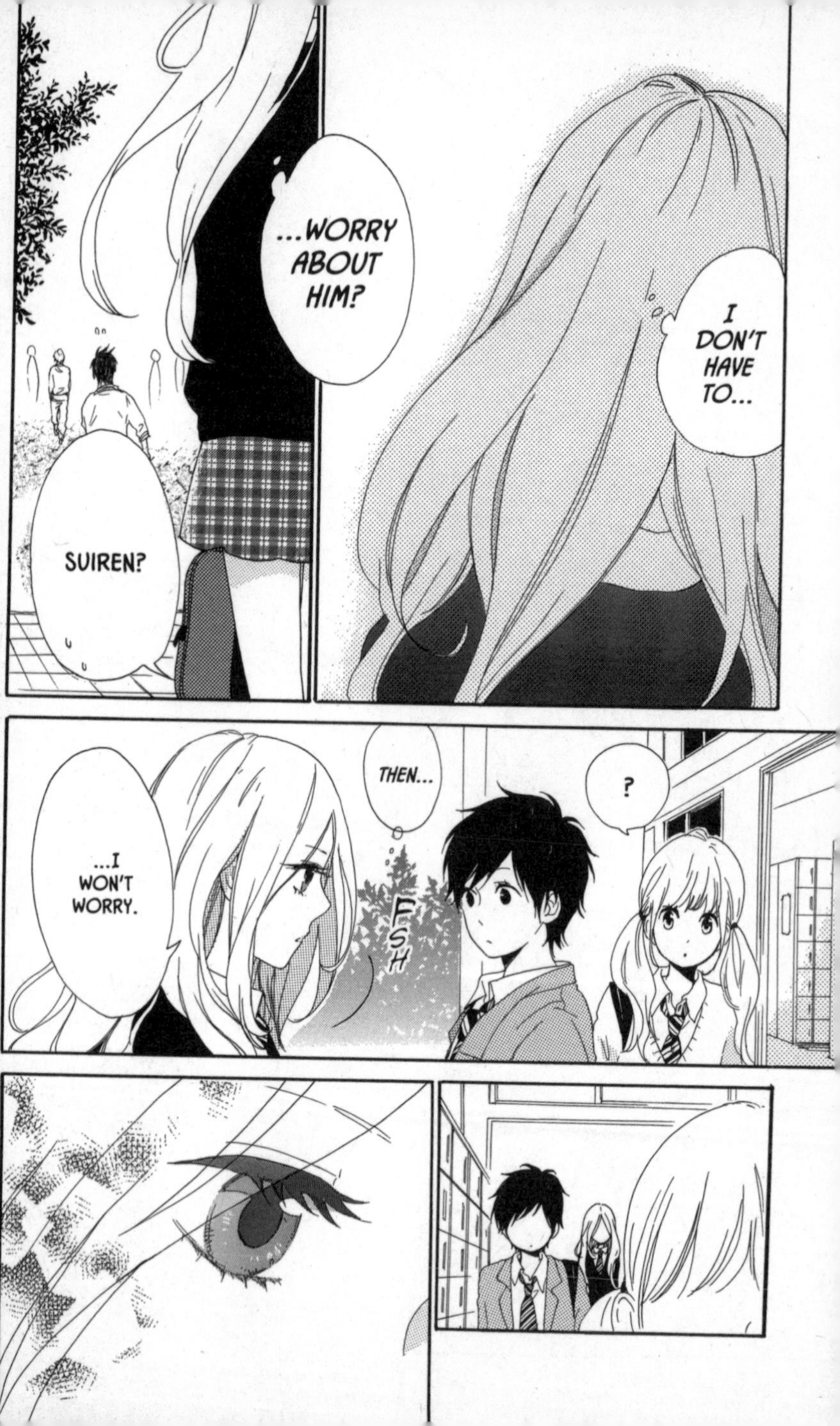
I DON'T HAVE TO...
...WORRY ABOUT HIM?
SUIREN?
?
THEN...
FSH
...I WON'T WORRY.

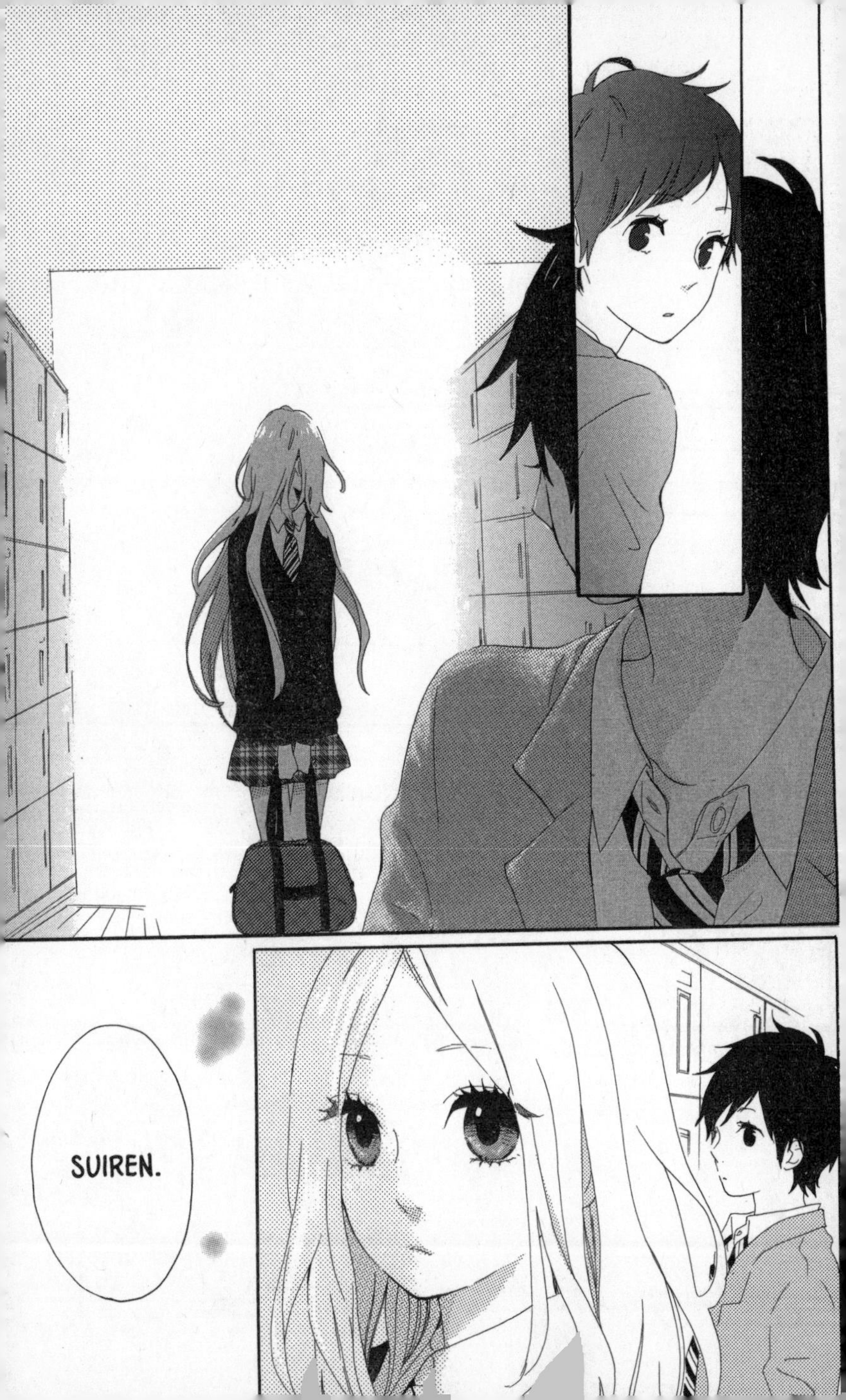
SUIREN.

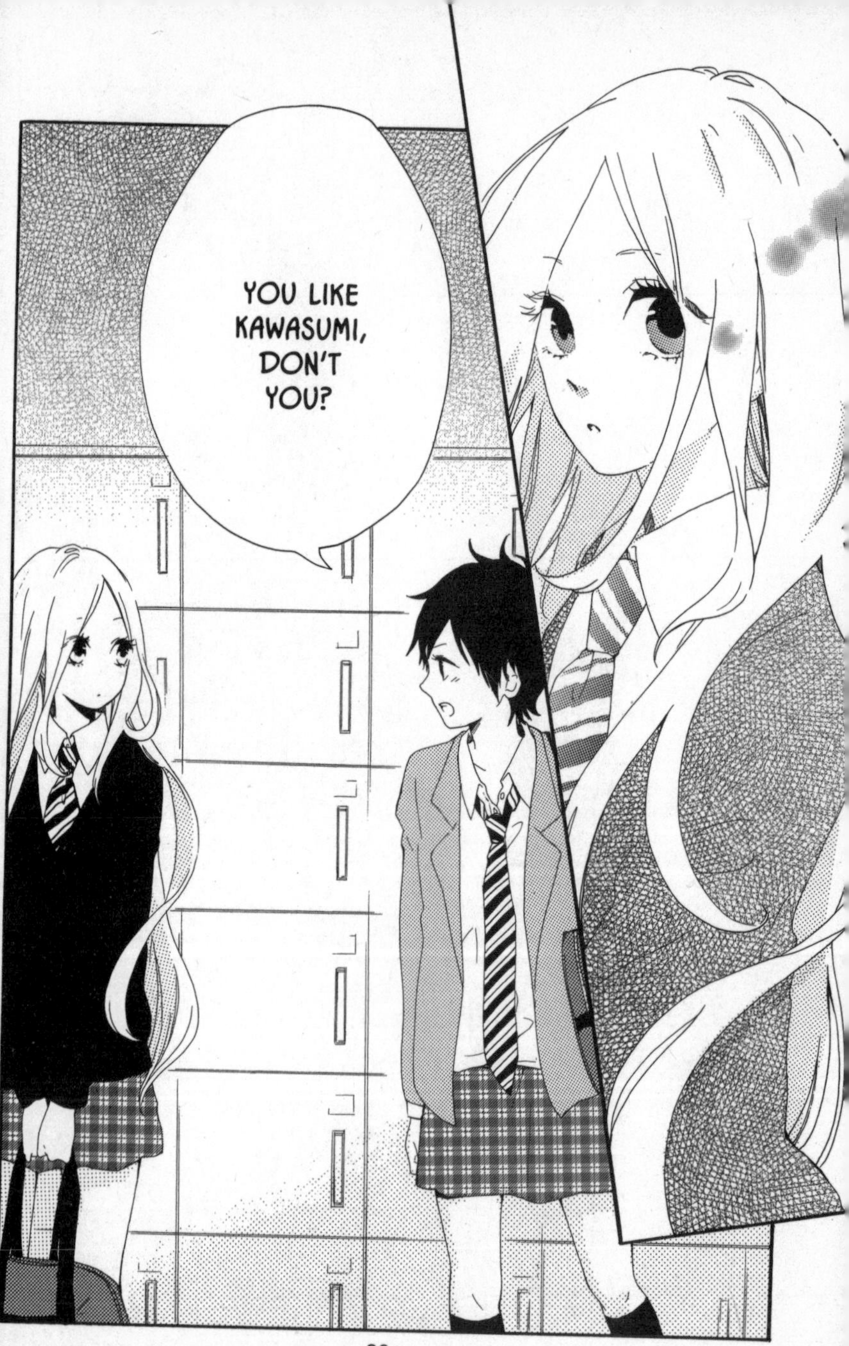
YOU LIKE KAWASUMI, DON'T YOU?

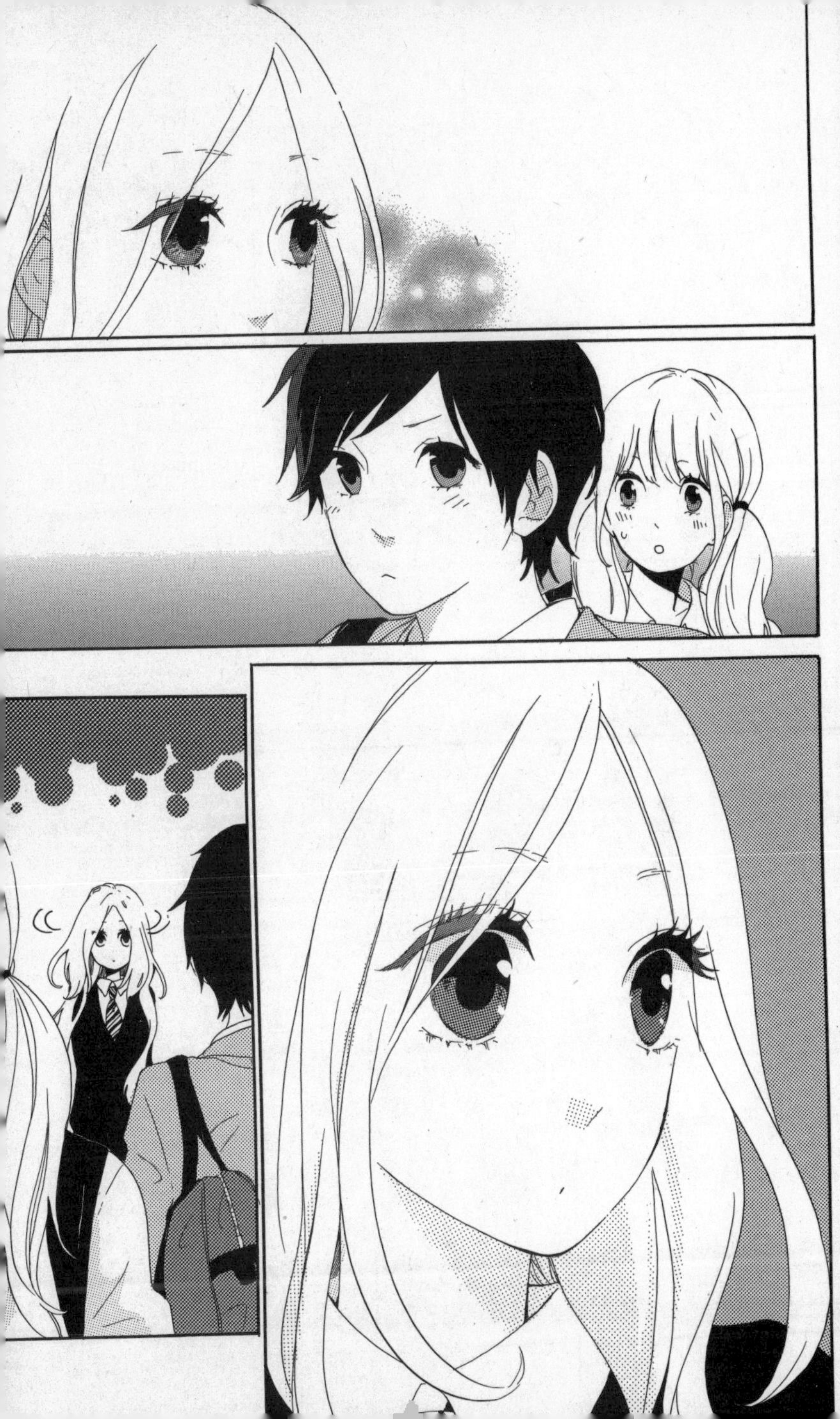

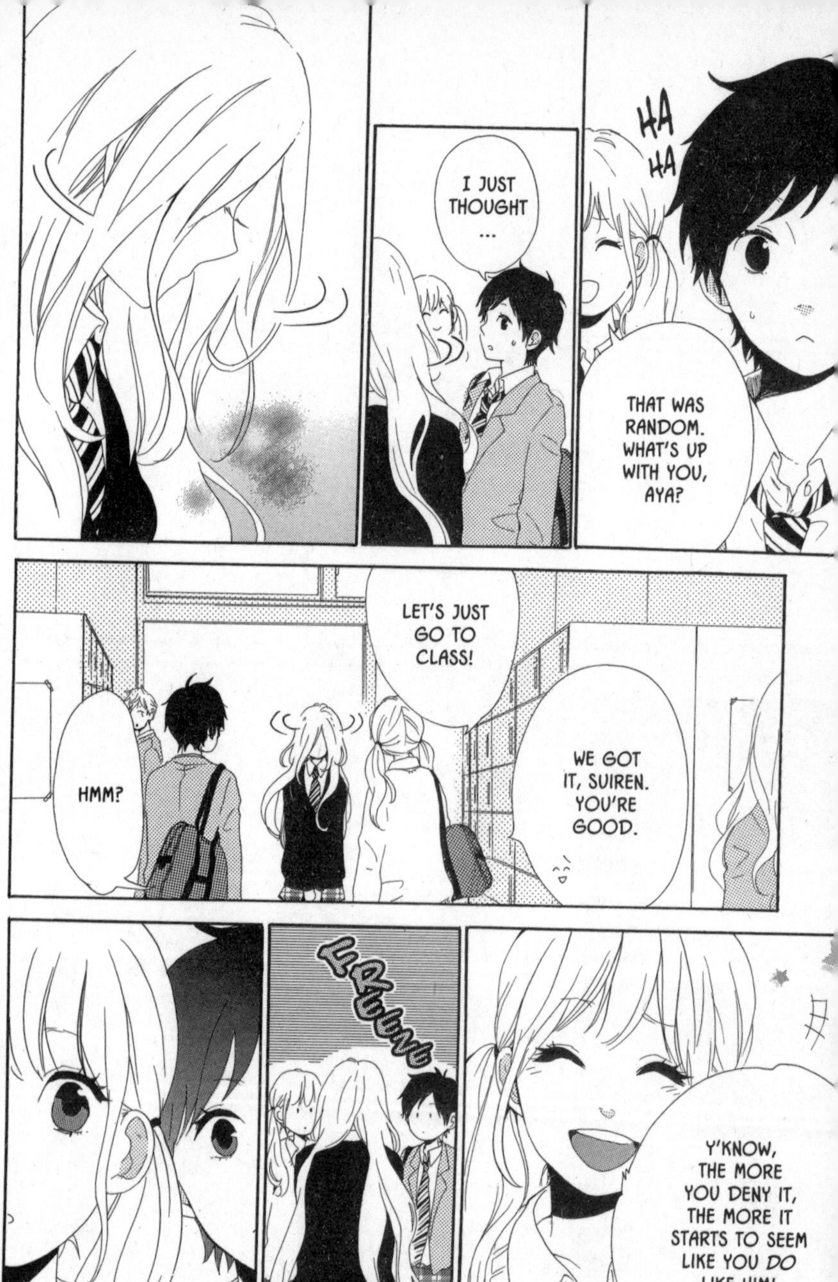
HA HA
THAT WAS RANDOM. WHAT'S UP WITH YOU, AYA?
I JUST THOUGHT ...
LET'S JUST GO TO CLASS!
WE GOT IT, SUIREN. YOU'RE GOOD.
HMM?
Y'KNOW, THE MORE YOU DENY IT, THE MORE IT STARTS TO SEEM LIKE YOU *DO* LIKE HIM!

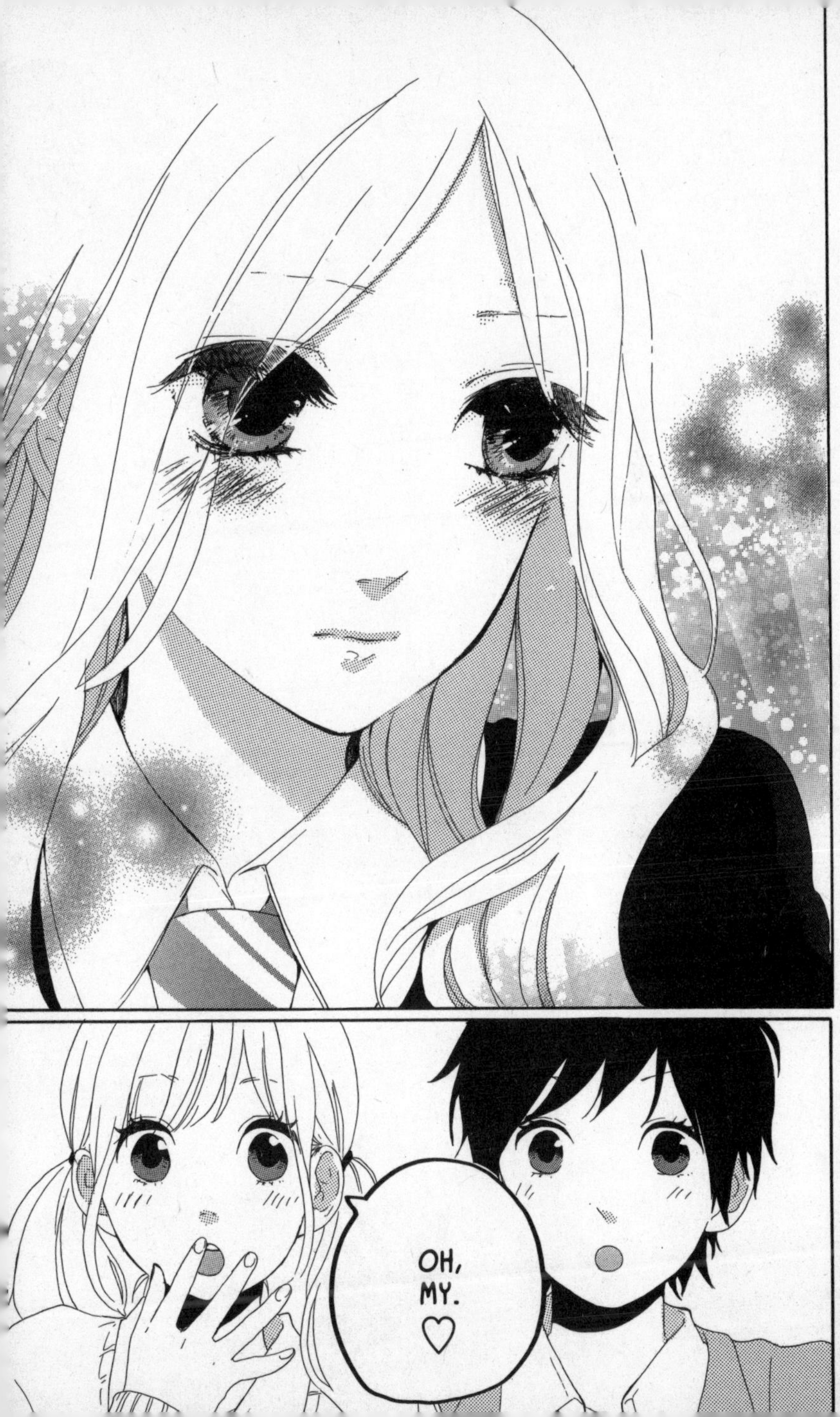
OH, MY. ♡

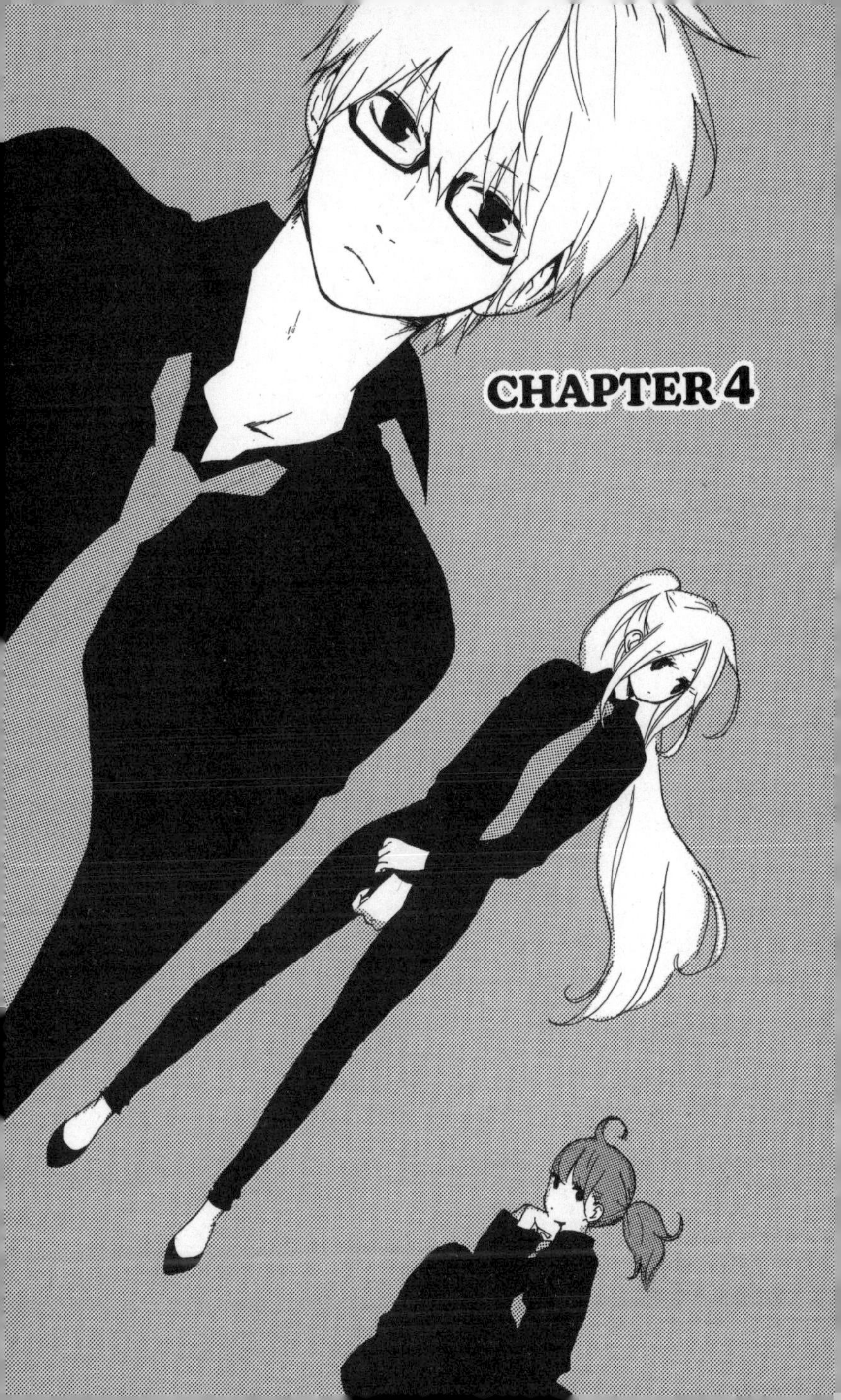
CHAPTER 4

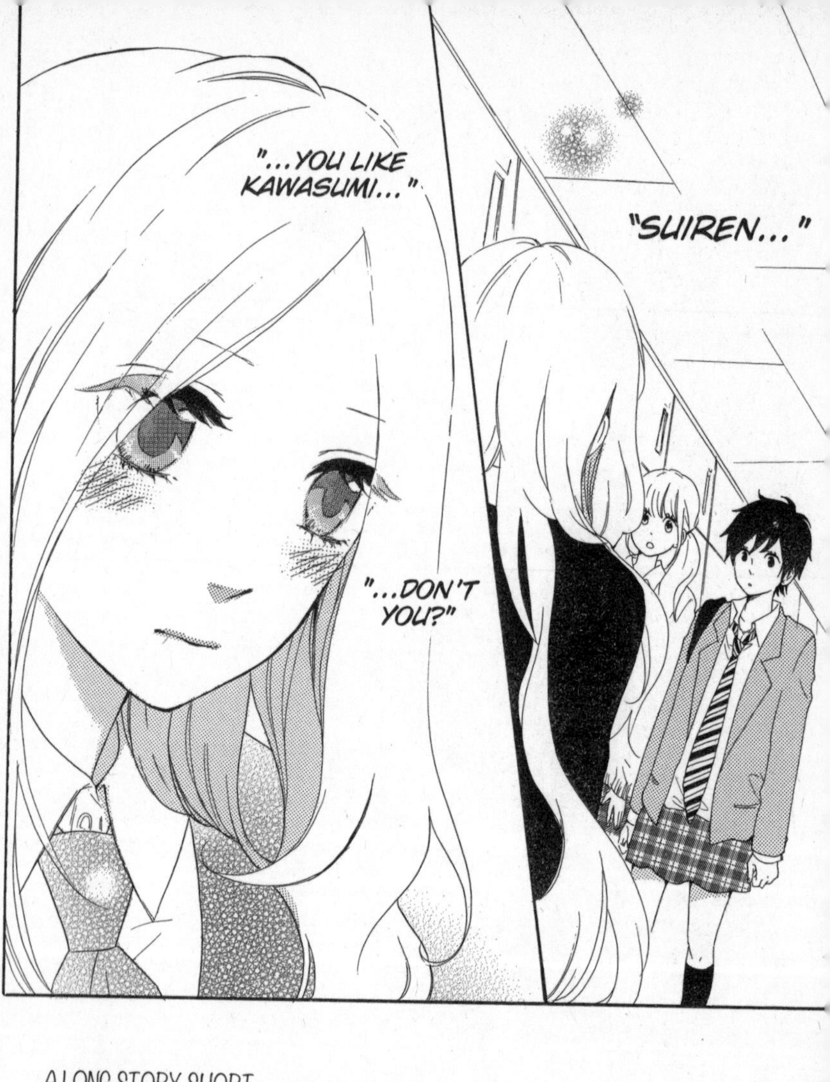
"SUIREN..."
"...YOU LIKE KAWASUMI..."
"...DON'T YOU?"

AROUND 2011, I MADE A "LIKE A BUTTERFLY" ONE-SHOT.

A LONG STORY SHORT...

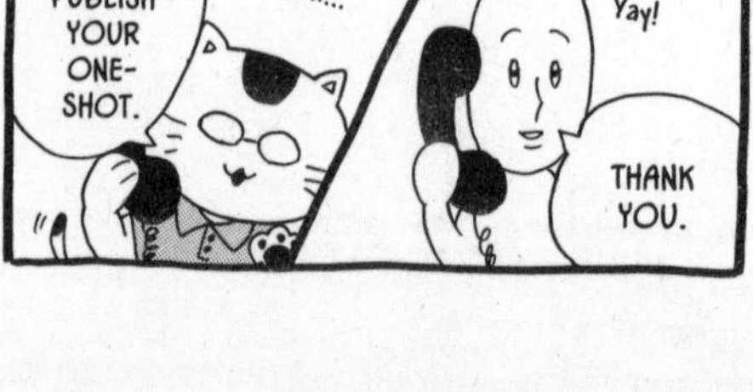
Yay!
THANK YOU.
WE'RE GOING TO PUBLISH YOUR ONE-SHOT.
Mreow...

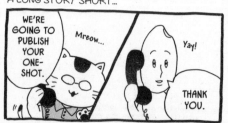

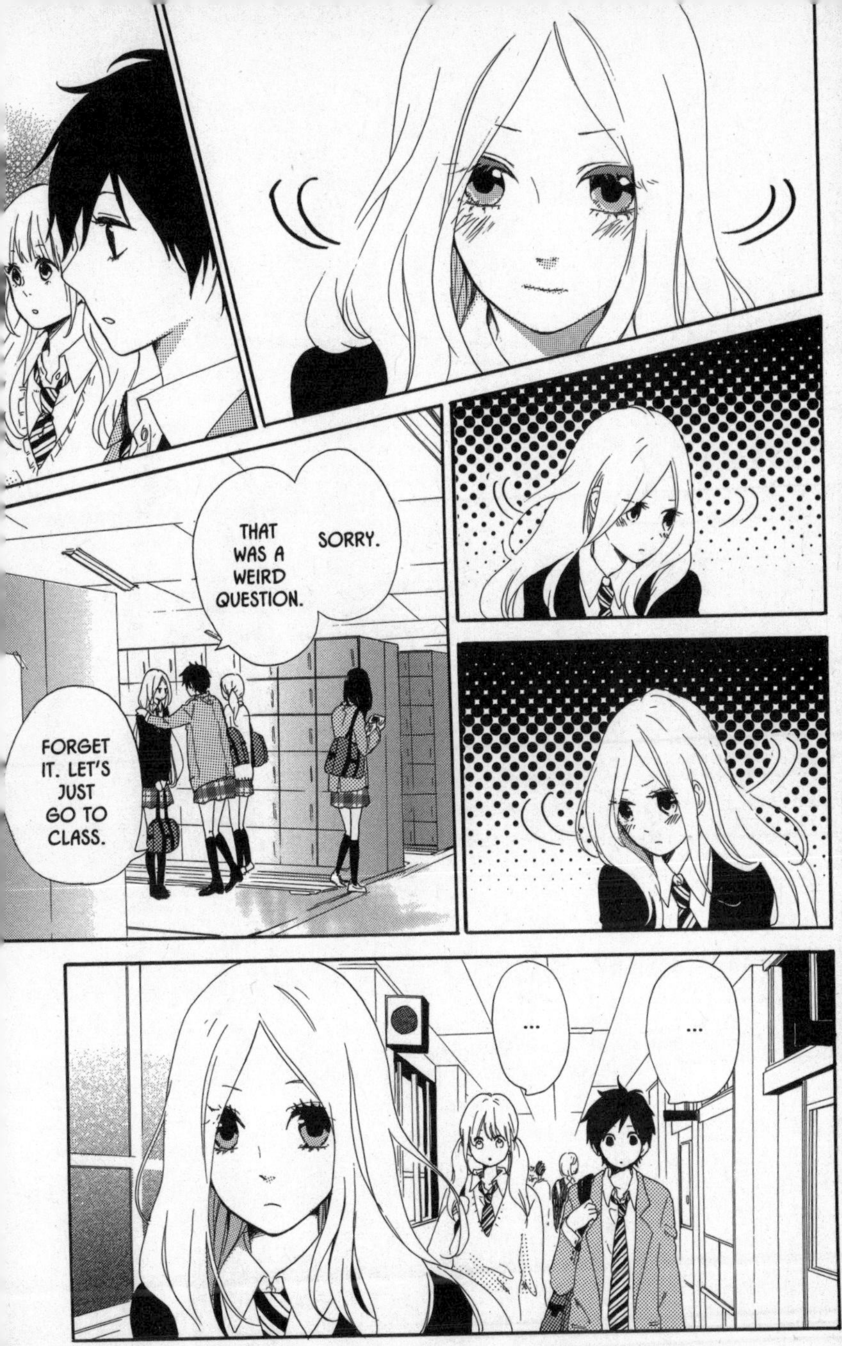
SORRY.
THAT WAS A WEIRD QUESTION.
FORGET IT. LET'S JUST GO TO CLASS.
...
...

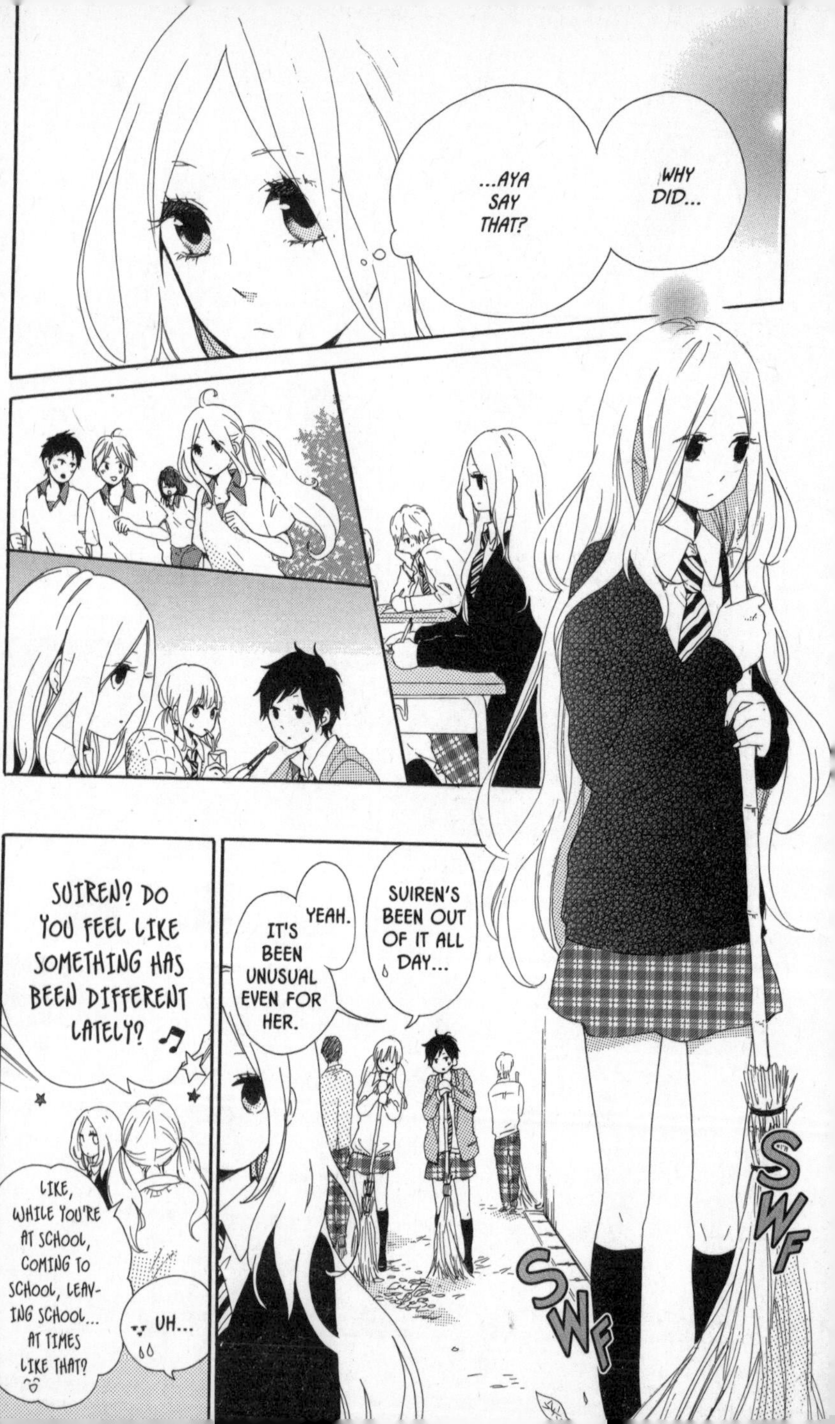
WHY DID...
...AYA SAY THAT?
SUIREN'S BEEN OUT OF IT ALL DAY...
YEAH.
IT'S BEEN UNUSUAL EVEN FOR HER.
SWF
SWF
SUIREN? DO YOU FEEL LIKE SOMETHING HAS BEEN DIFFERENT LATELY? ♪
LIKE, WHILE YOU'RE AT SCHOOL, COMING TO SCHOOL, LEAVING SCHOOL... AT TIMES LIKE THAT?
UH...

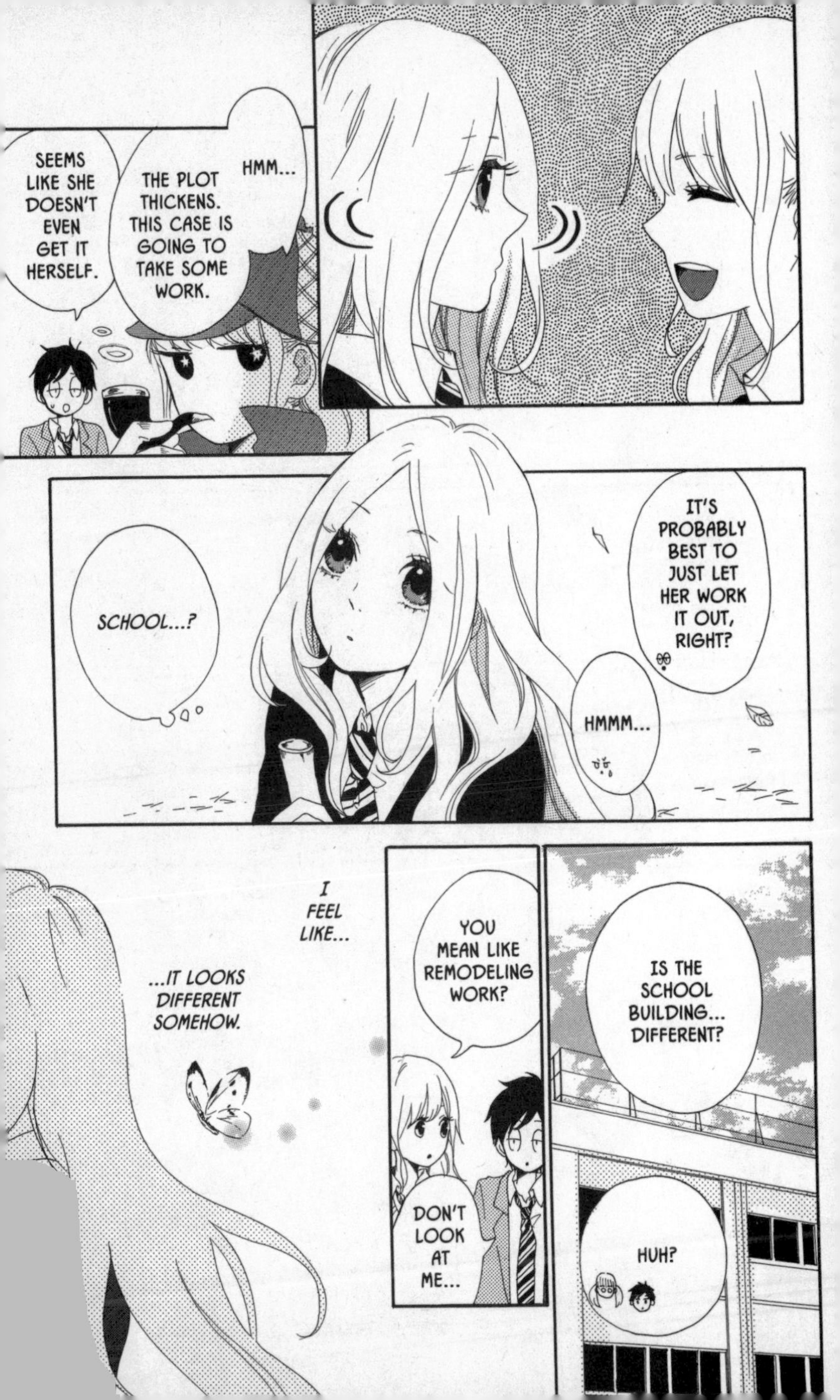
HMM...
THE PLOT THICKENS. THIS CASE IS GOING TO TAKE SOME WORK.
SEEMS LIKE SHE DOESN'T EVEN GET IT HERSELF.
IT'S PROBABLY BEST TO JUST LET HER WORK IT OUT, RIGHT?
HMMM...
SCHOOL...?
IS THE SCHOOL BUILDING... DIFFERENT?
HUH?
YOU MEAN LIKE REMODELING WORK?
DON'T LOOK AT ME...
I FEEL LIKE...
...IT LOOKS DIFFERENT SOMEHOW.

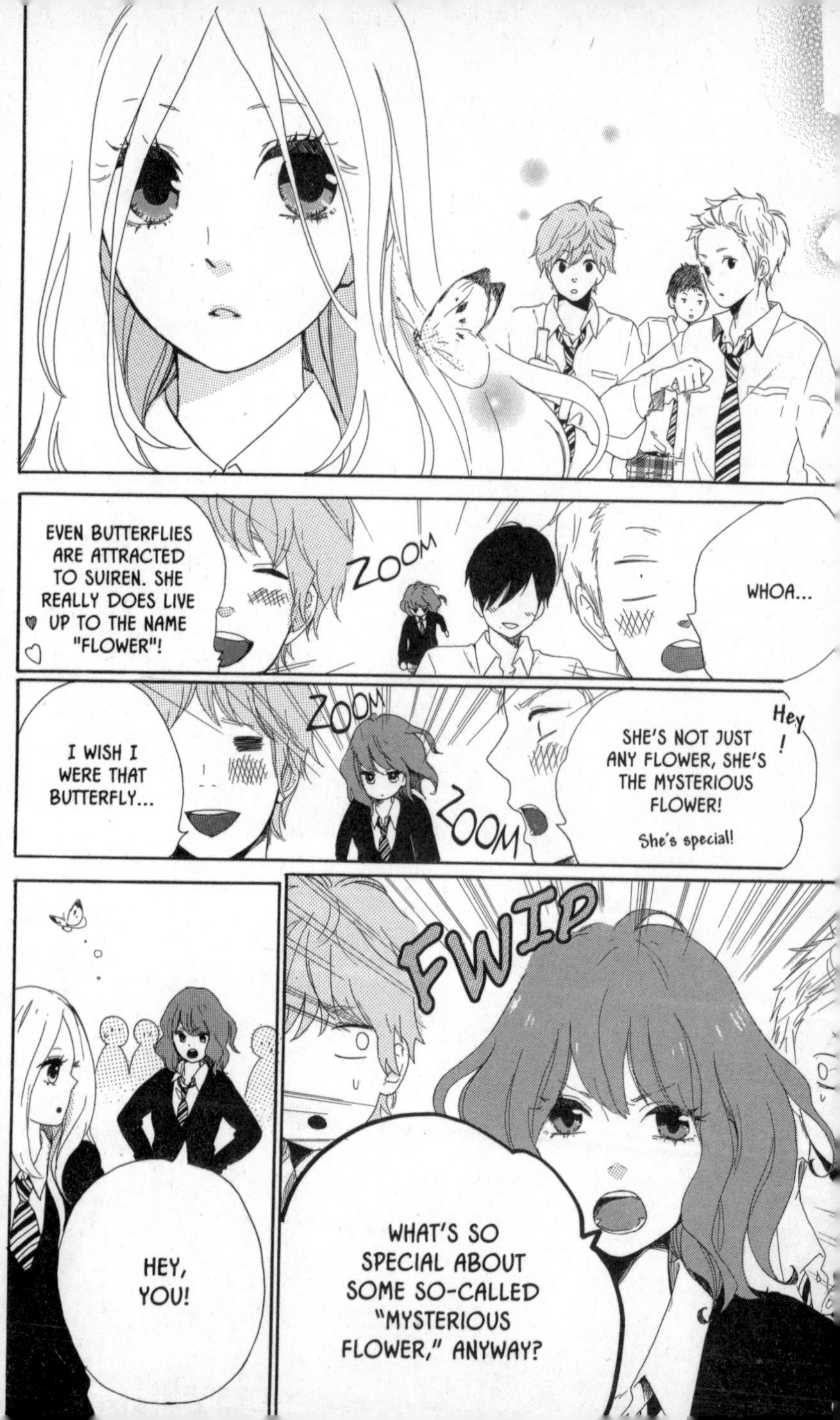
WHOA...
ZOOM
EVEN BUTTERFLIES ARE ATTRACTED TO SUIREN. SHE REALLY DOES LIVE UP TO THE NAME "FLOWER"! ♥ ♡
Hey!
SHE'S NOT JUST ANY FLOWER, SHE'S THE MYSTERIOUS FLOWER!
She's special!
ZOOM
ZOOM
I WISH I WERE THAT BUTTERFLY...
FWIP
WHAT'S SO SPECIAL ABOUT SOME SO-CALLED "MYSTERIOUS FLOWER," ANYWAY?
HEY, YOU!

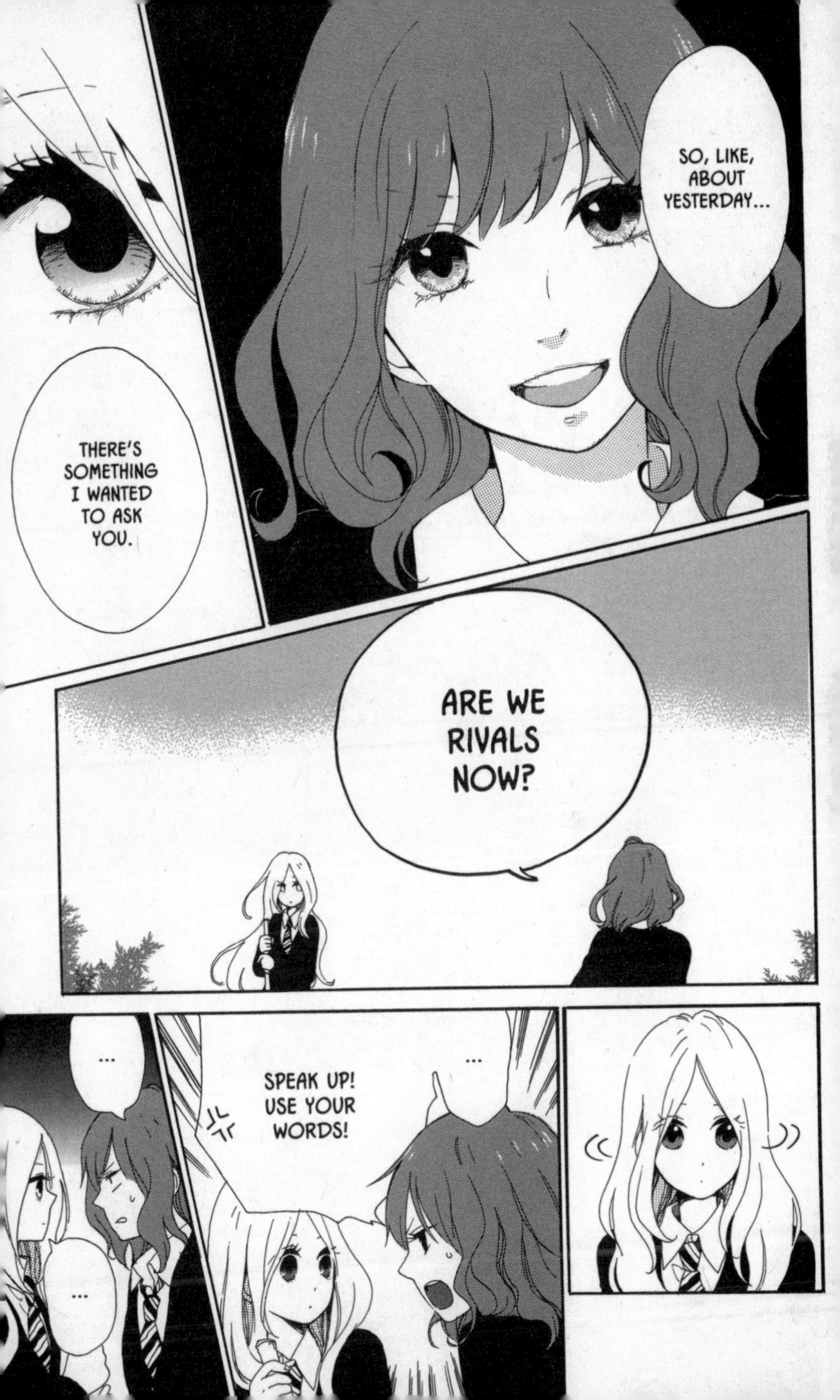
SO, LIKE, ABOUT YESTERDAY...
THERE'S SOMETHING I WANTED TO ASK YOU.
ARE WE RIVALS NOW?
...
SPEAK UP! USE YOUR WORDS!
...
...

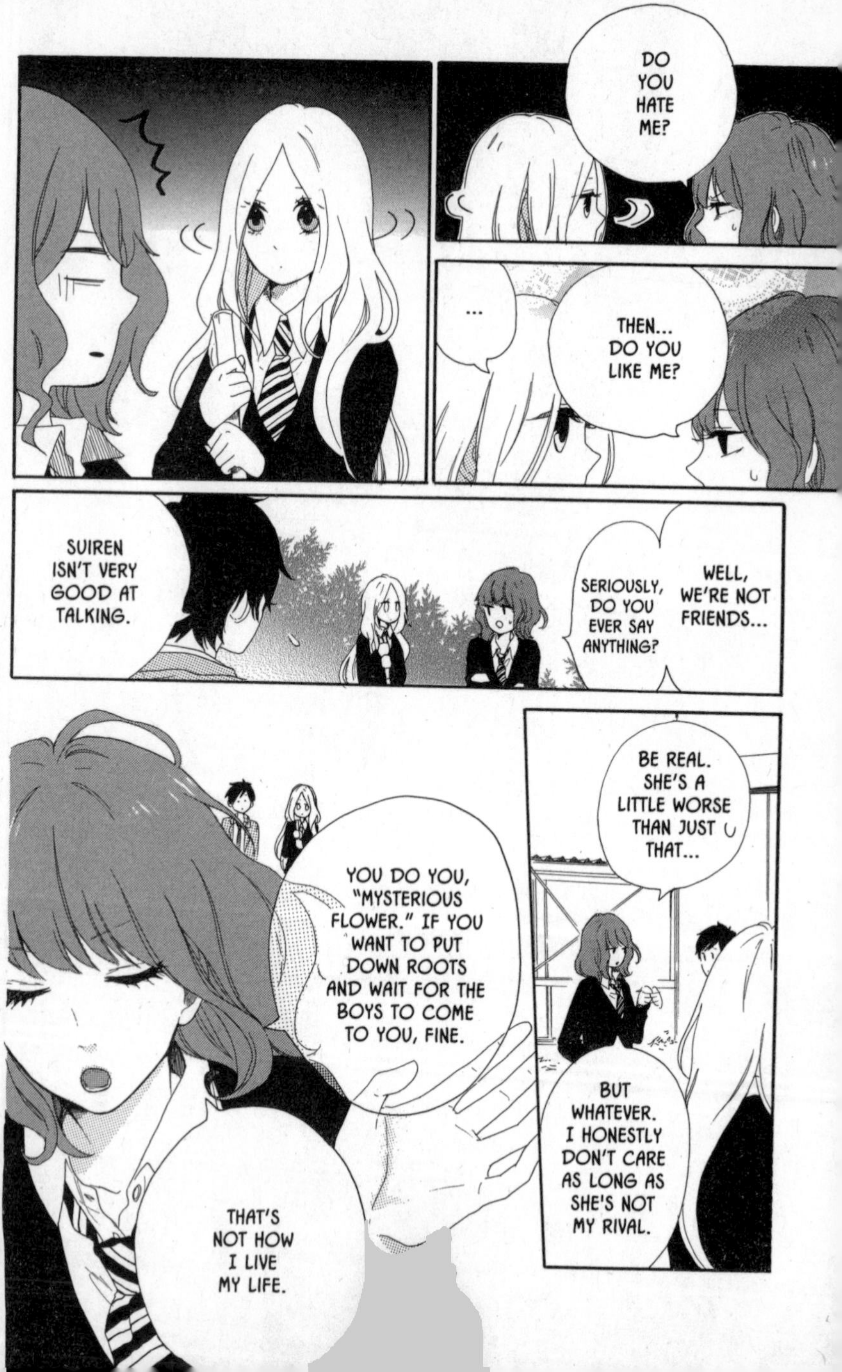
DO YOU HATE ME?
THEN... DO YOU LIKE ME?
...
WELL, WE'RE NOT FRIENDS...
SERIOUSLY, DO YOU EVER SAY ANYTHING?
SUIREN ISN'T VERY GOOD AT TALKING.
BE REAL. SHE'S A LITTLE WORSE THAN JUST THAT...
BUT WHATEVER. I HONESTLY DON'T CARE AS LONG AS SHE'S NOT MY RIVAL.
YOU DO YOU, "MYSTERIOUS FLOWER." IF YOU WANT TO PUT DOWN ROOTS AND WAIT FOR THE BOYS TO COME TO YOU, FINE.
THAT'S NOT HOW I LIVE MY LIFE.

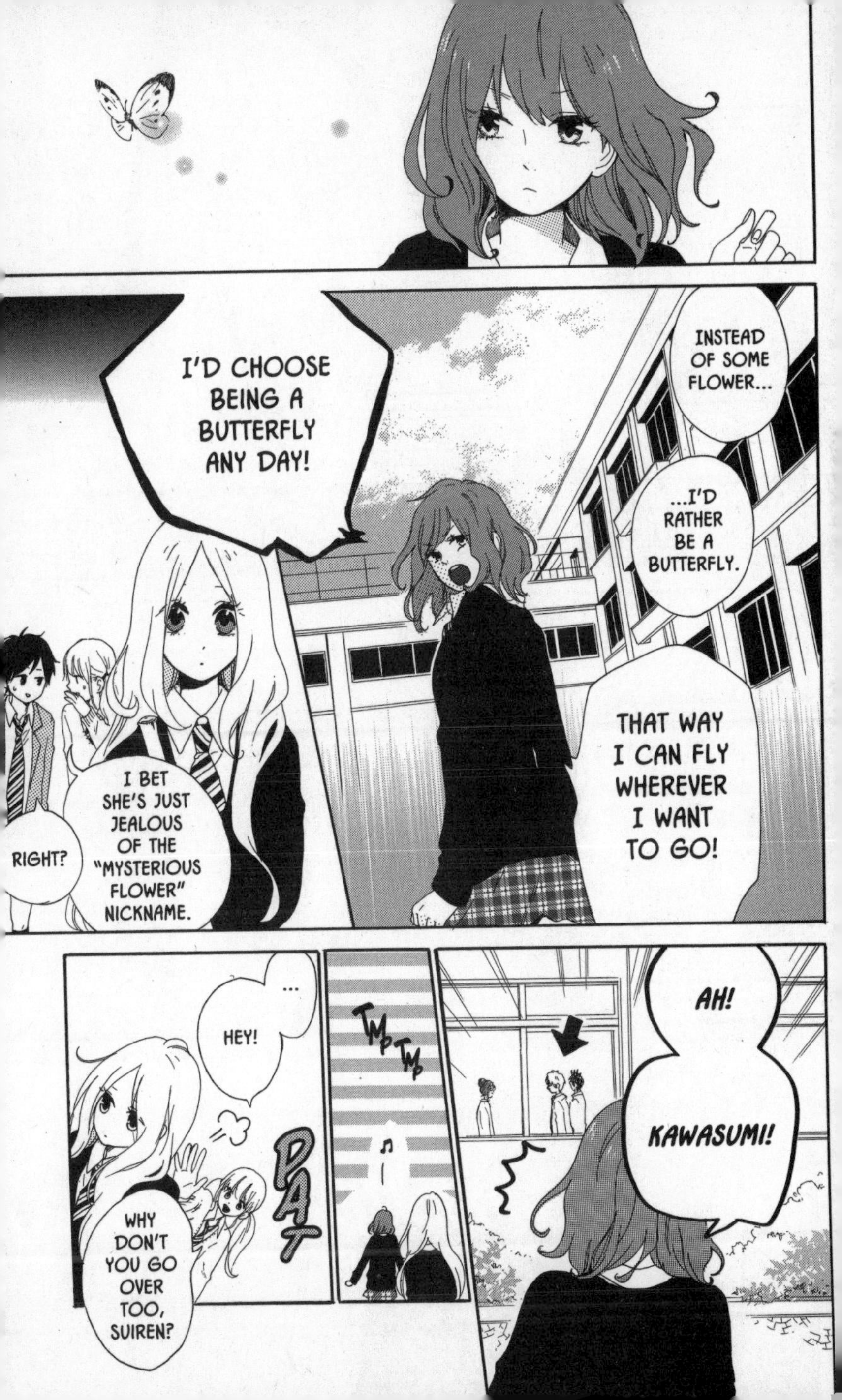
INSTEAD OF SOME FLOWER...
...I'D RATHER BE A BUTTERFLY.
THAT WAY I CAN FLY WHEREVER I WANT TO GO!
I'D CHOOSE BEING A BUTTERFLY ANY DAY!
I BET SHE'S JUST JEALOUS OF THE "MYSTERIOUS FLOWER" NICKNAME.
RIGHT?
AH!
KAWASUMI!
TMP TMP
...
HEY!
PAT
WHY DON'T YOU GO OVER TOO, SUIREN?

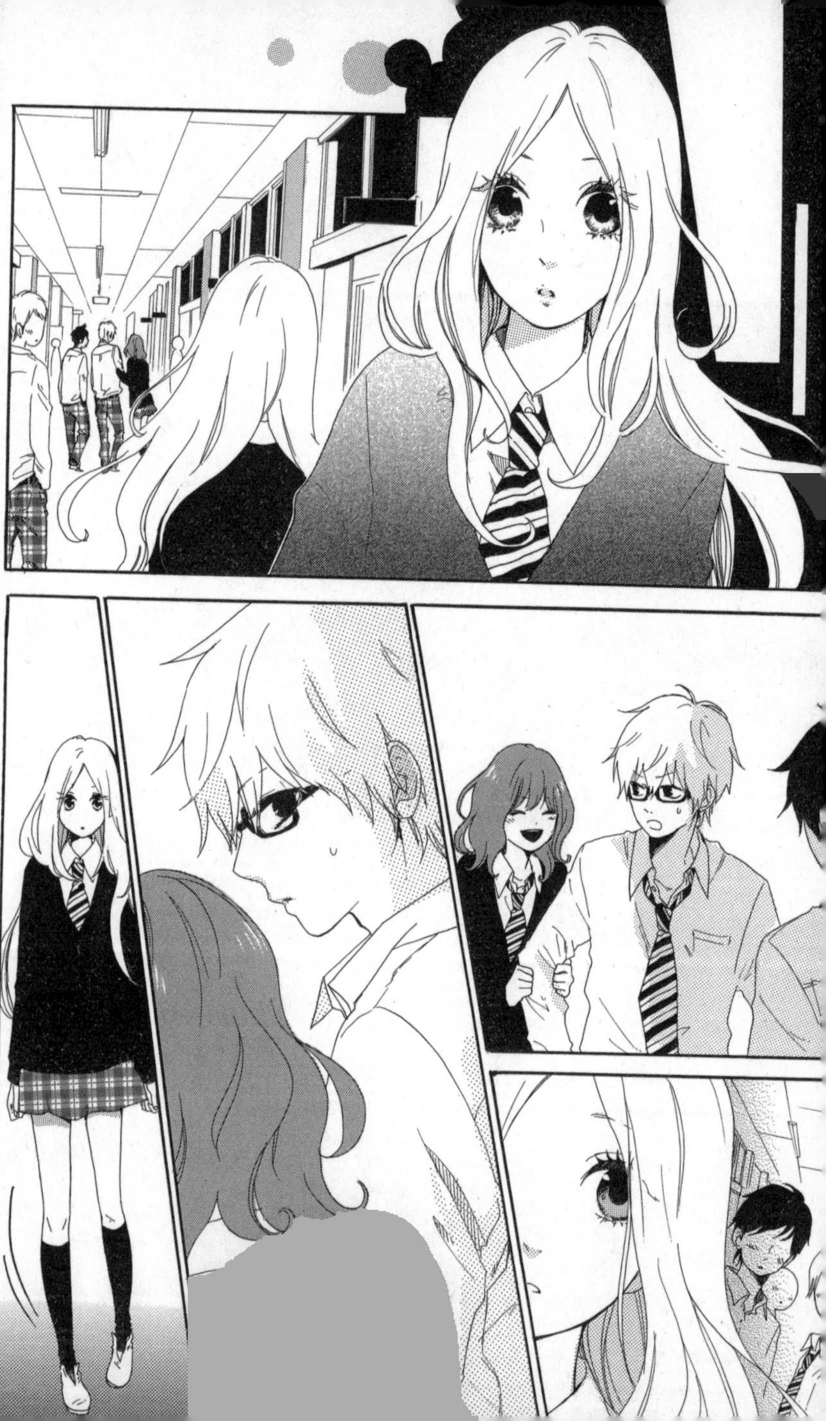

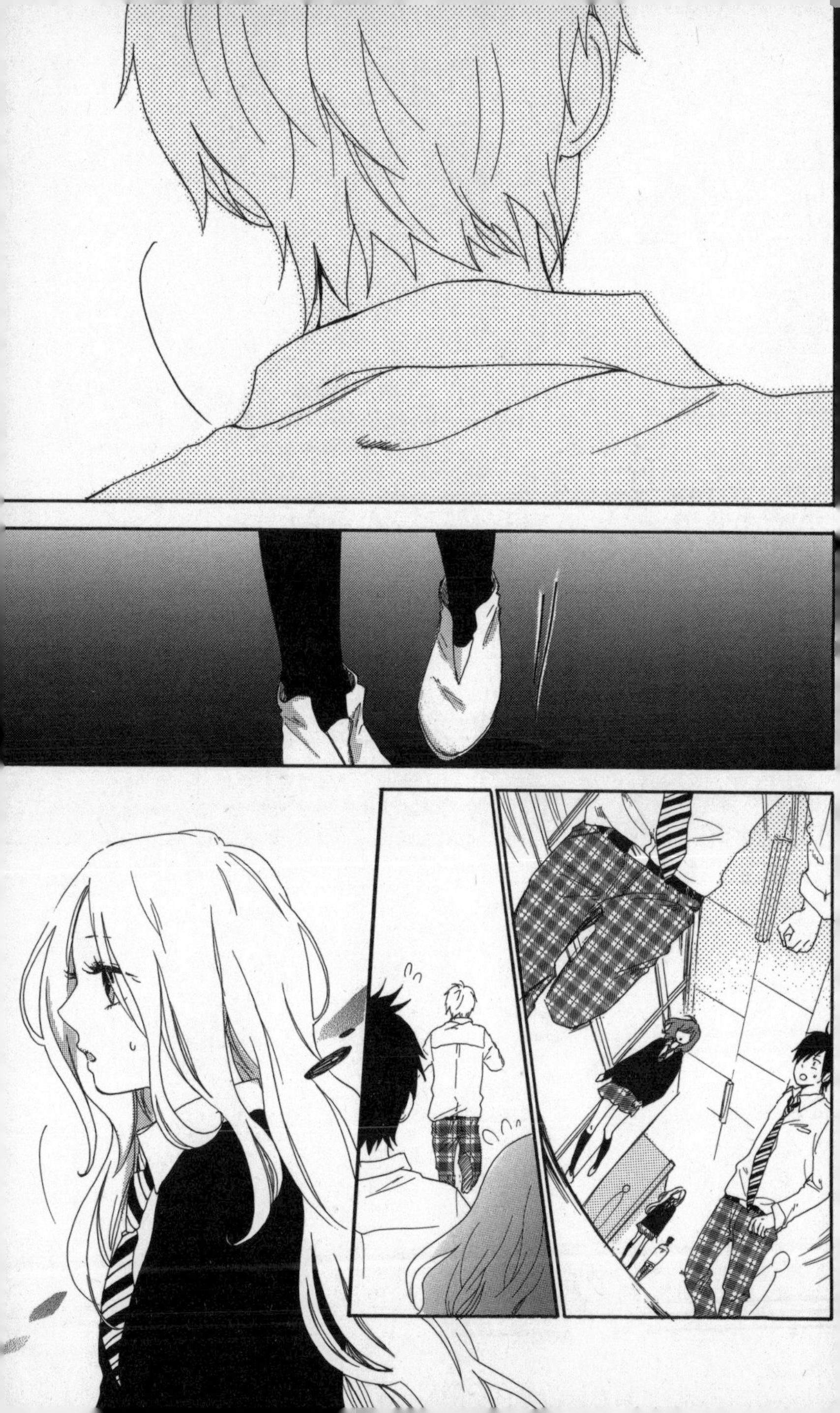

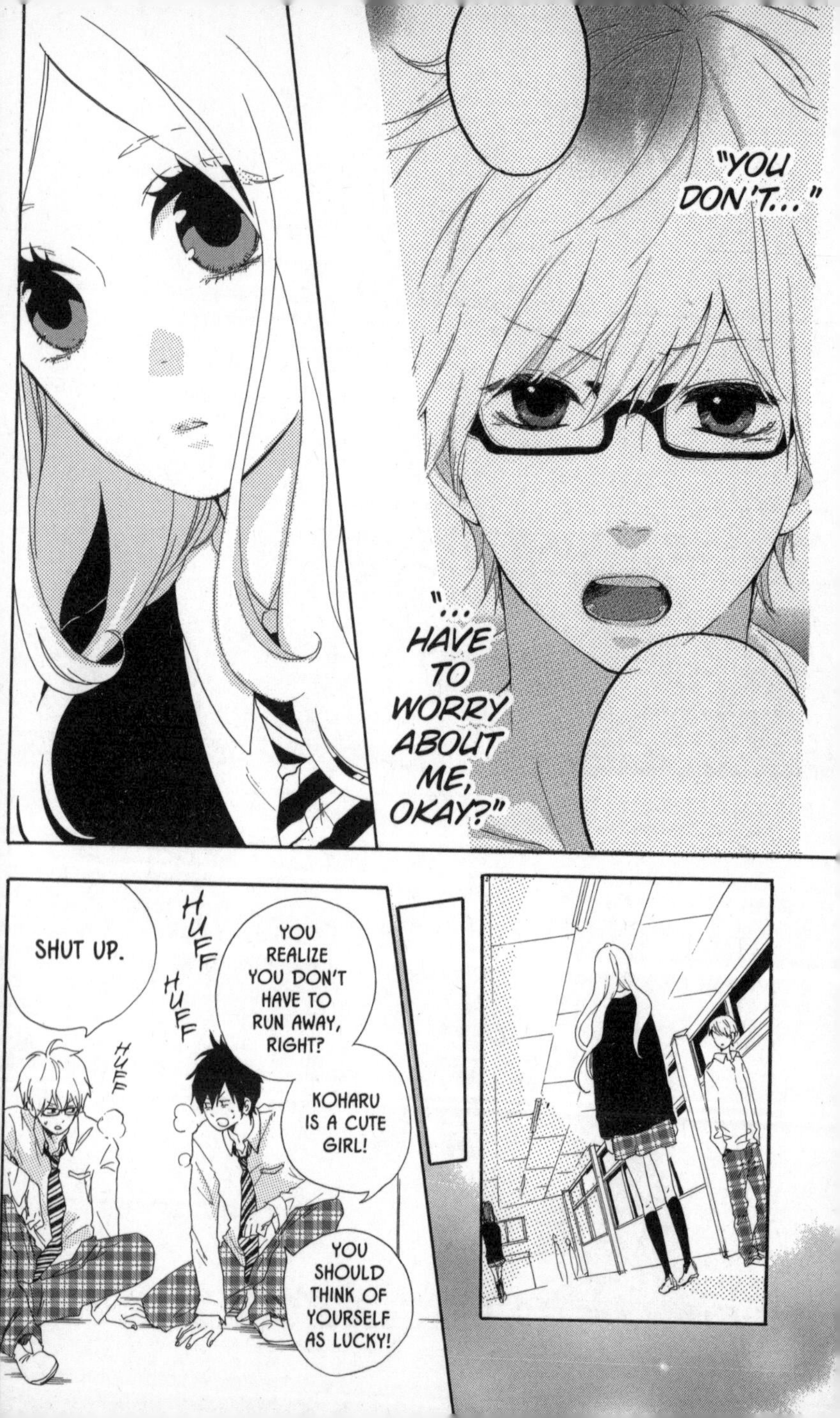
"YOU DON'T..."
"...HAVE TO WORRY ABOUT ME, OKAY?"
HUFF
HUFF
YOU REALIZE YOU DON'T HAVE TO RUN AWAY, RIGHT?
KOHARU IS A CUTE GIRL!
YOU SHOULD THINK OF YOURSELF AS LUCKY!
SHUT UP.
HUFF

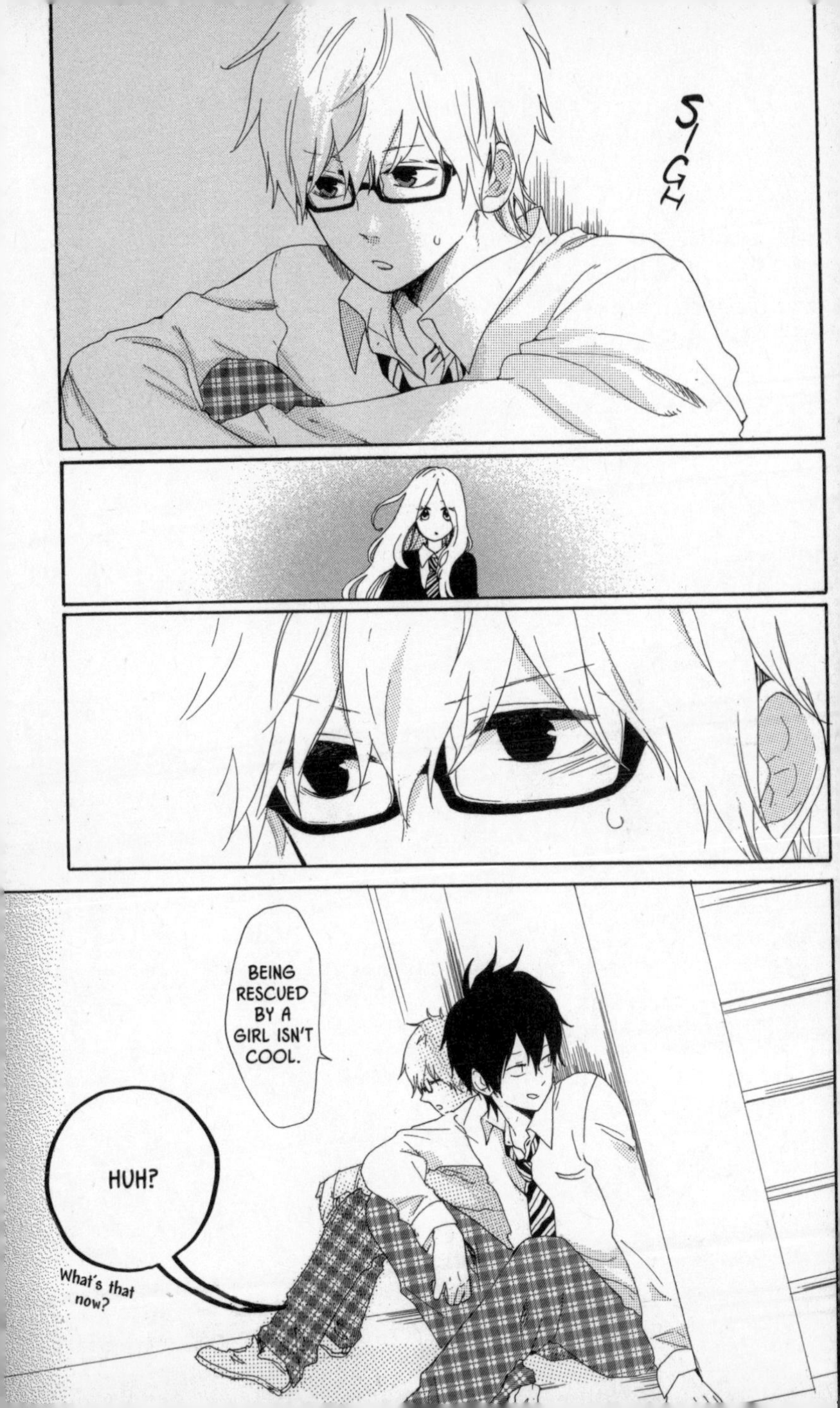
SIGH
BEING RESCUED BY A GIRL ISN'T COOL.
HUH?
What's that now?

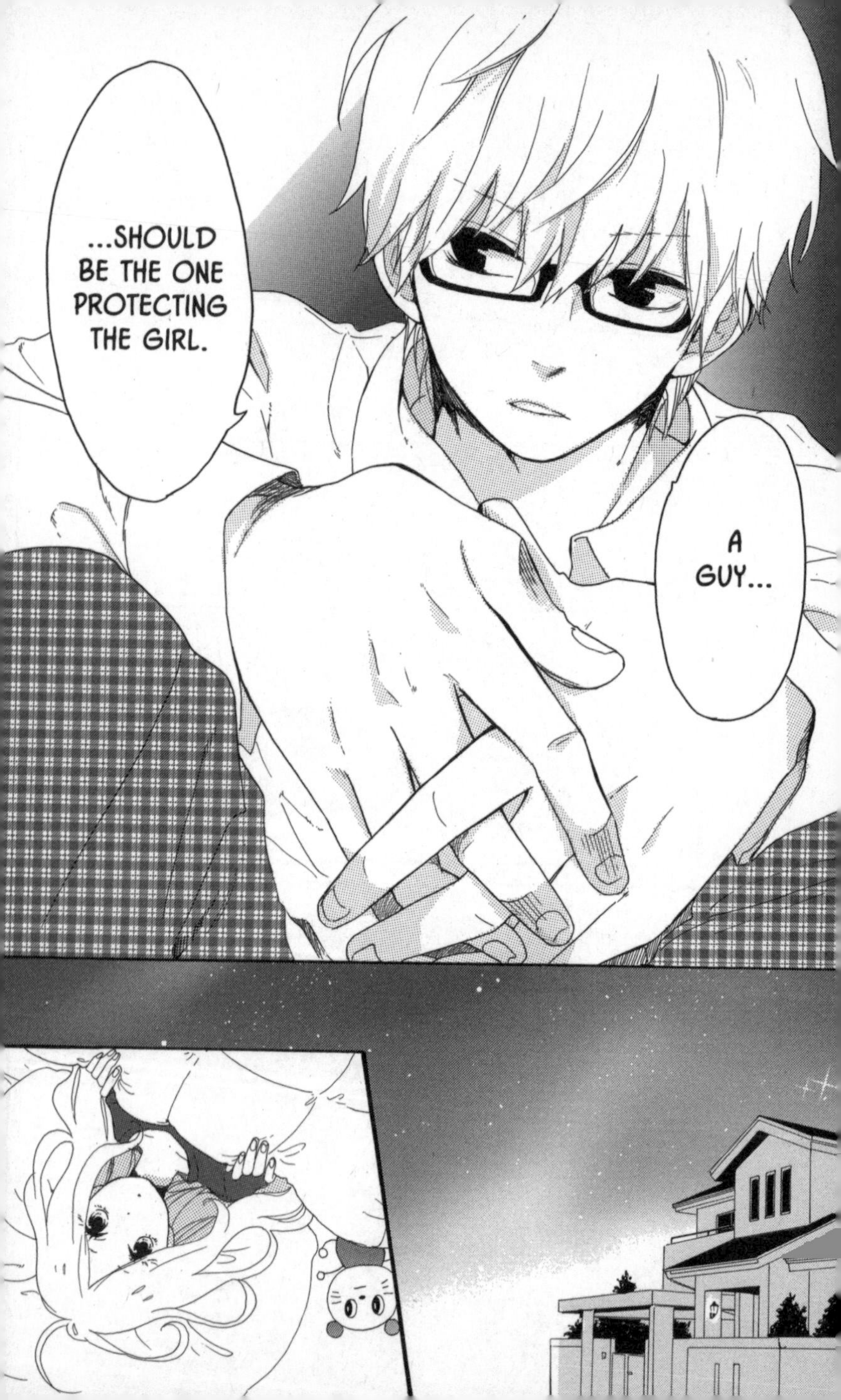
A GUY...
...SHOULD BE THE ONE PROTECTING THE GIRL.

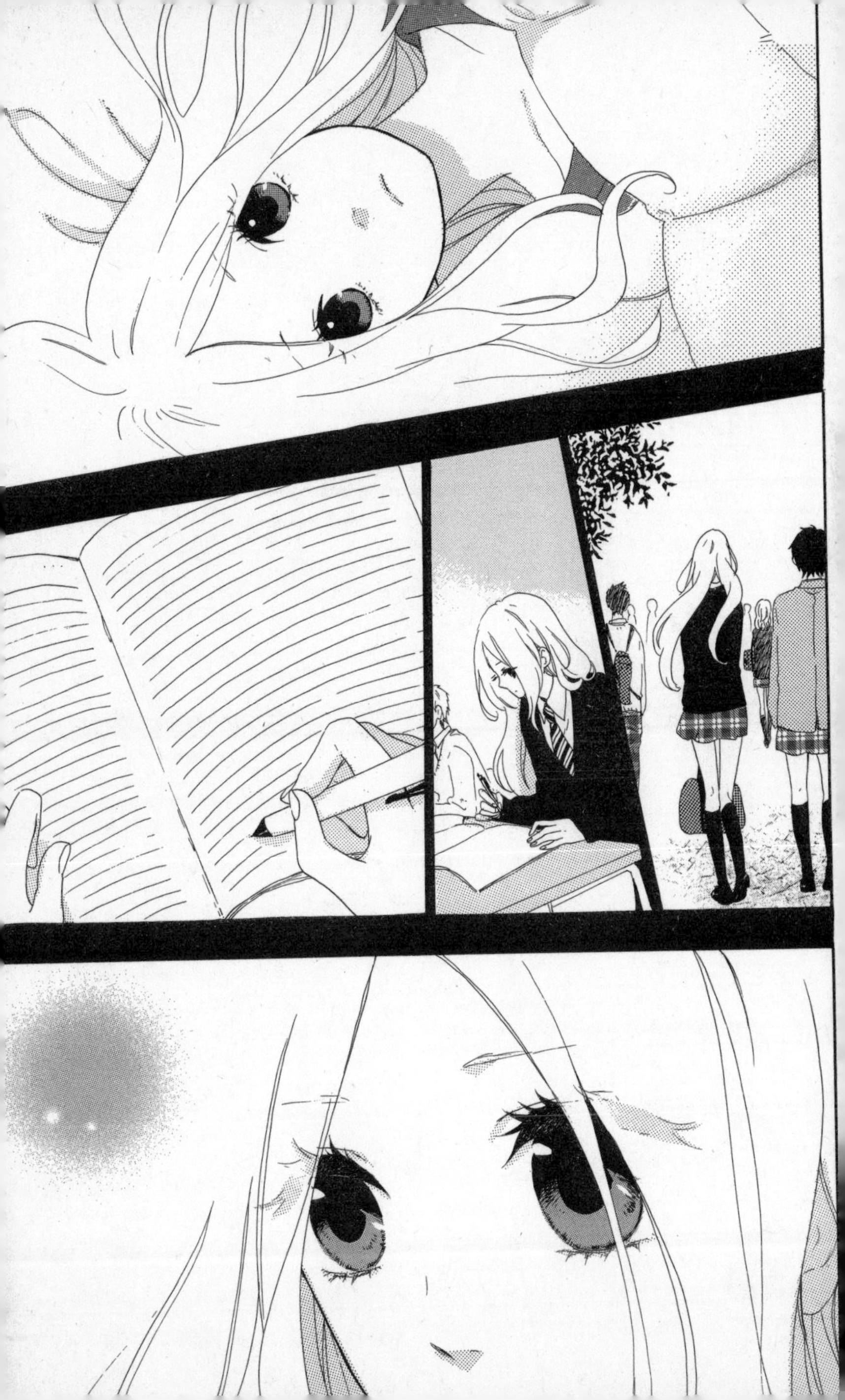

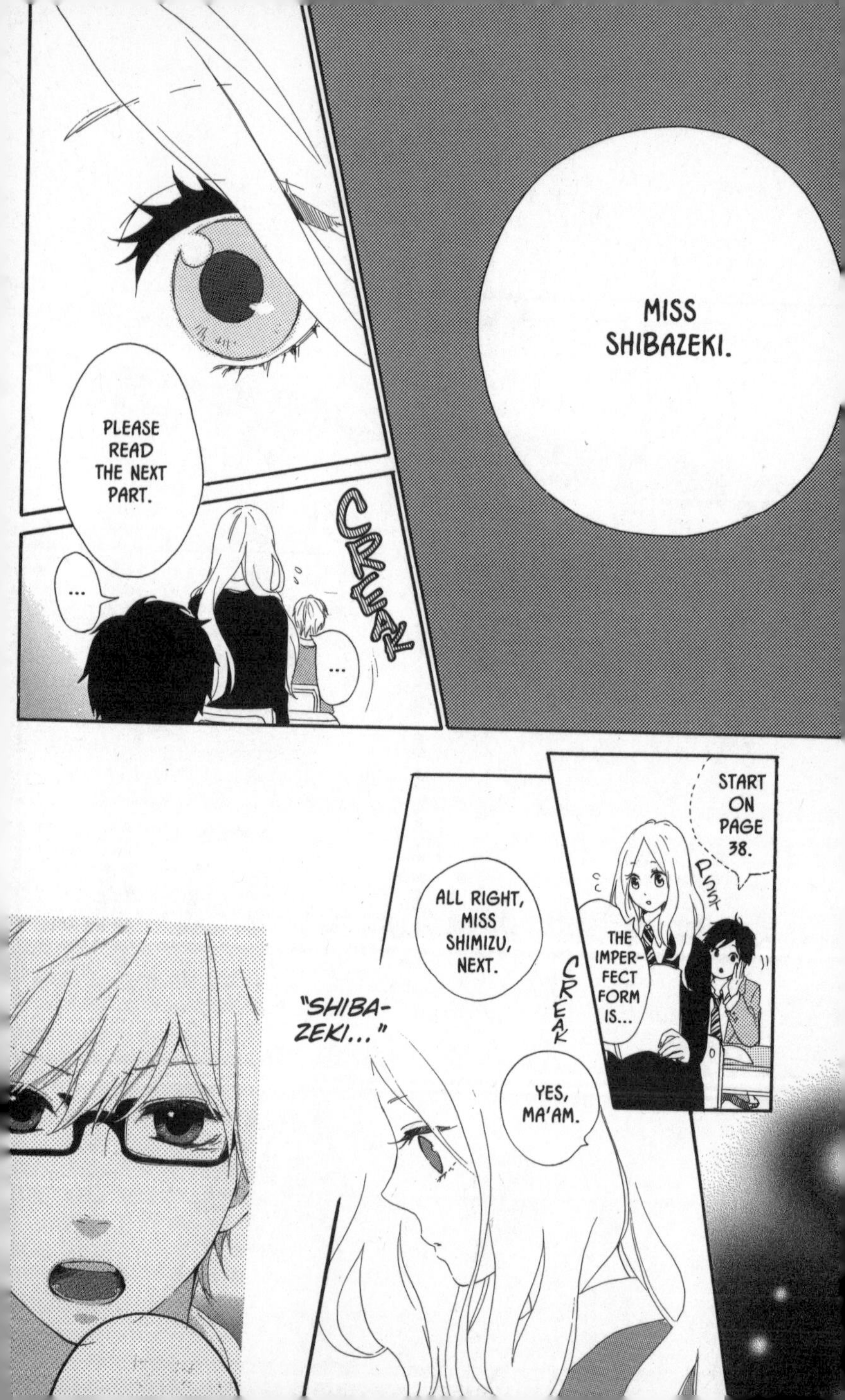
MISS SHIBAZEKI.
PLEASE READ THE NEXT PART.
CREAK
...
...
START ON PAGE 38.
PSST
THE IMPERFECT FORM IS...
ALL RIGHT, MISS SHIMIZU, NEXT.
CREAK
YES, MA'AM.
"SHIBAZEKI..."

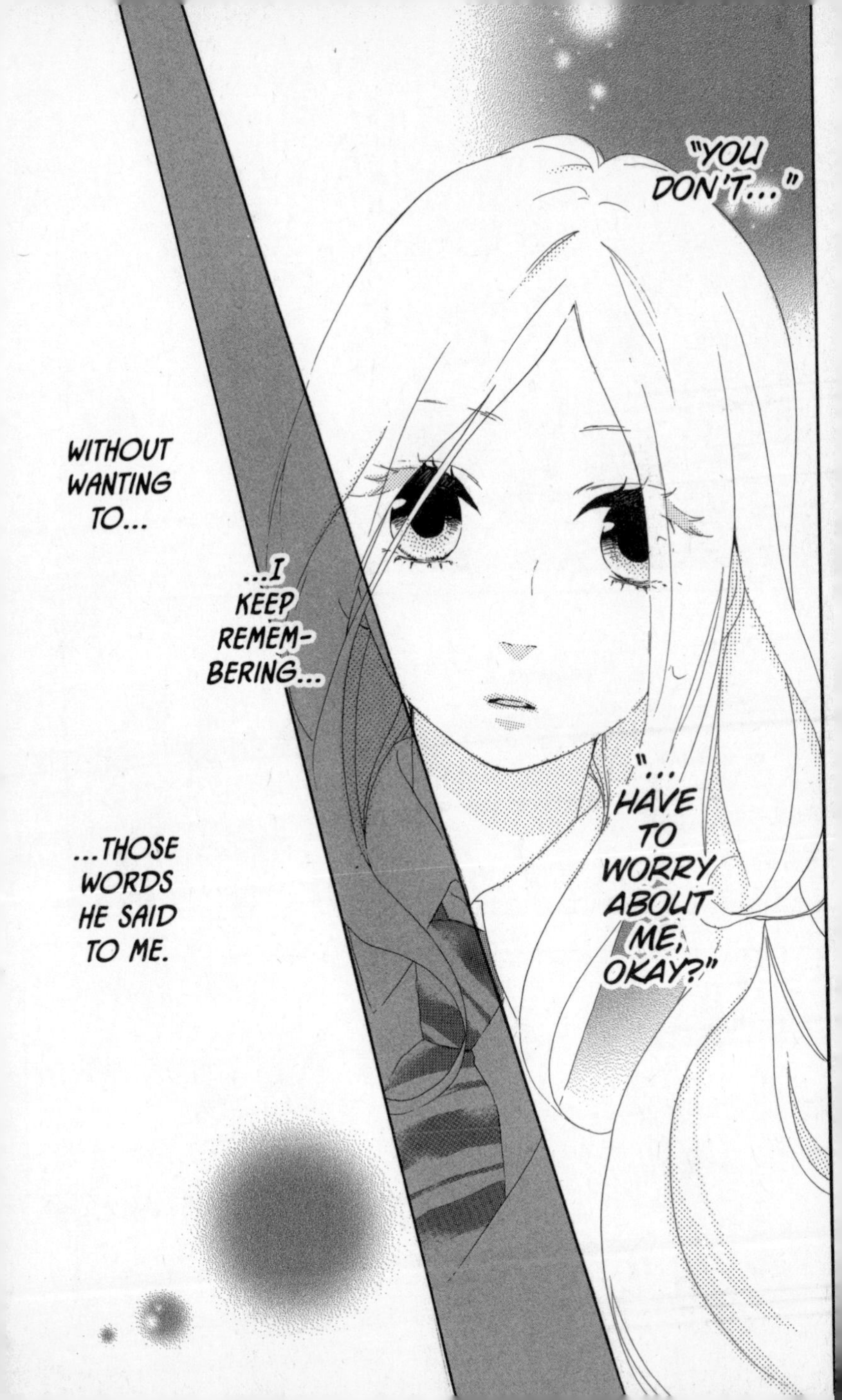
"YOU DON'T..."
"...HAVE TO WORRY ABOUT ME, OKAY?"
WITHOUT WANTING TO...
...I KEEP REMEMBERING...
...THOSE WORDS HE SAID TO ME.

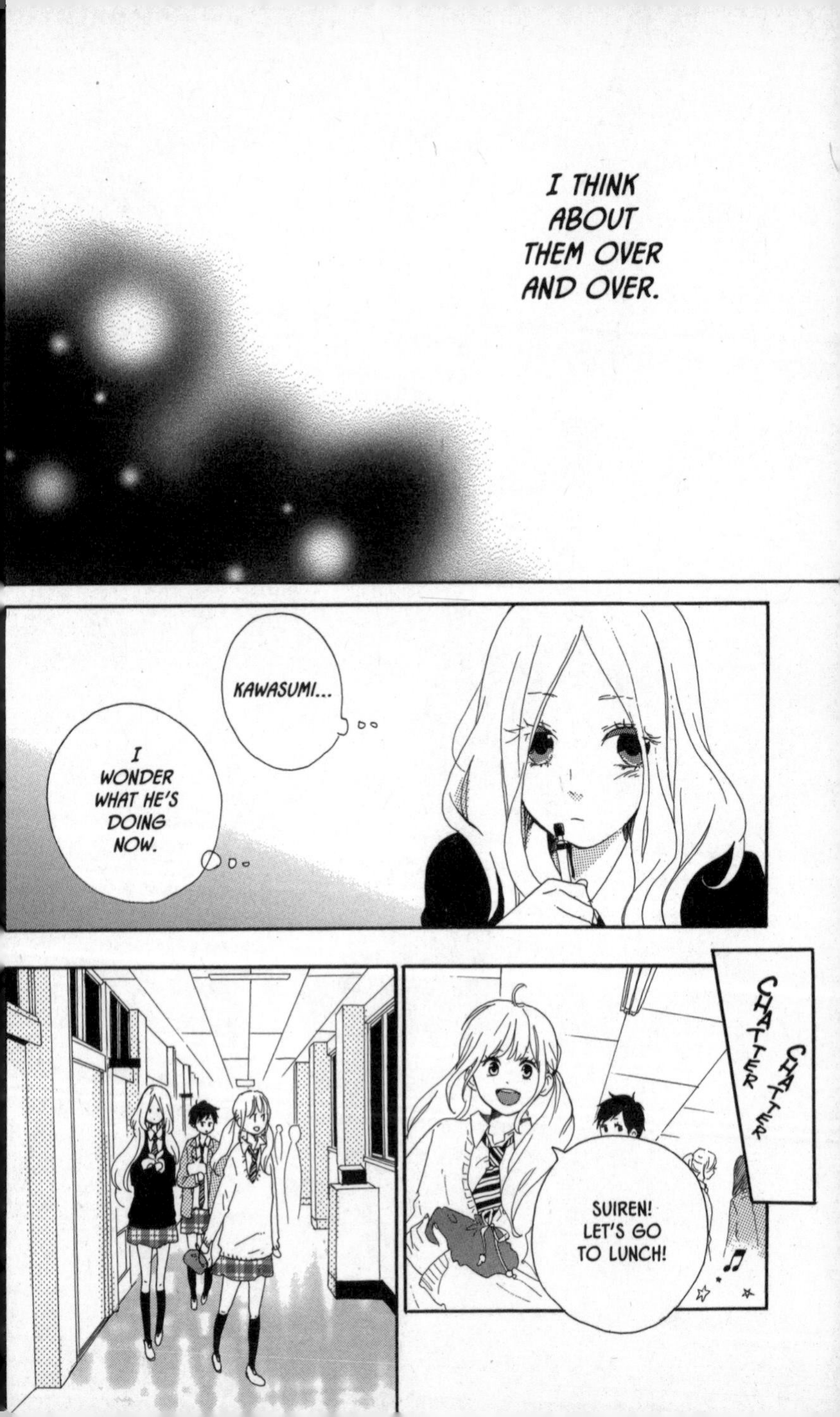
I THINK ABOUT THEM OVER AND OVER.
KAWASUMI...
I WONDER WHAT HE'S DOING NOW.
CHATTER CHATTER
SUIREN! LET'S GO TO LUNCH!

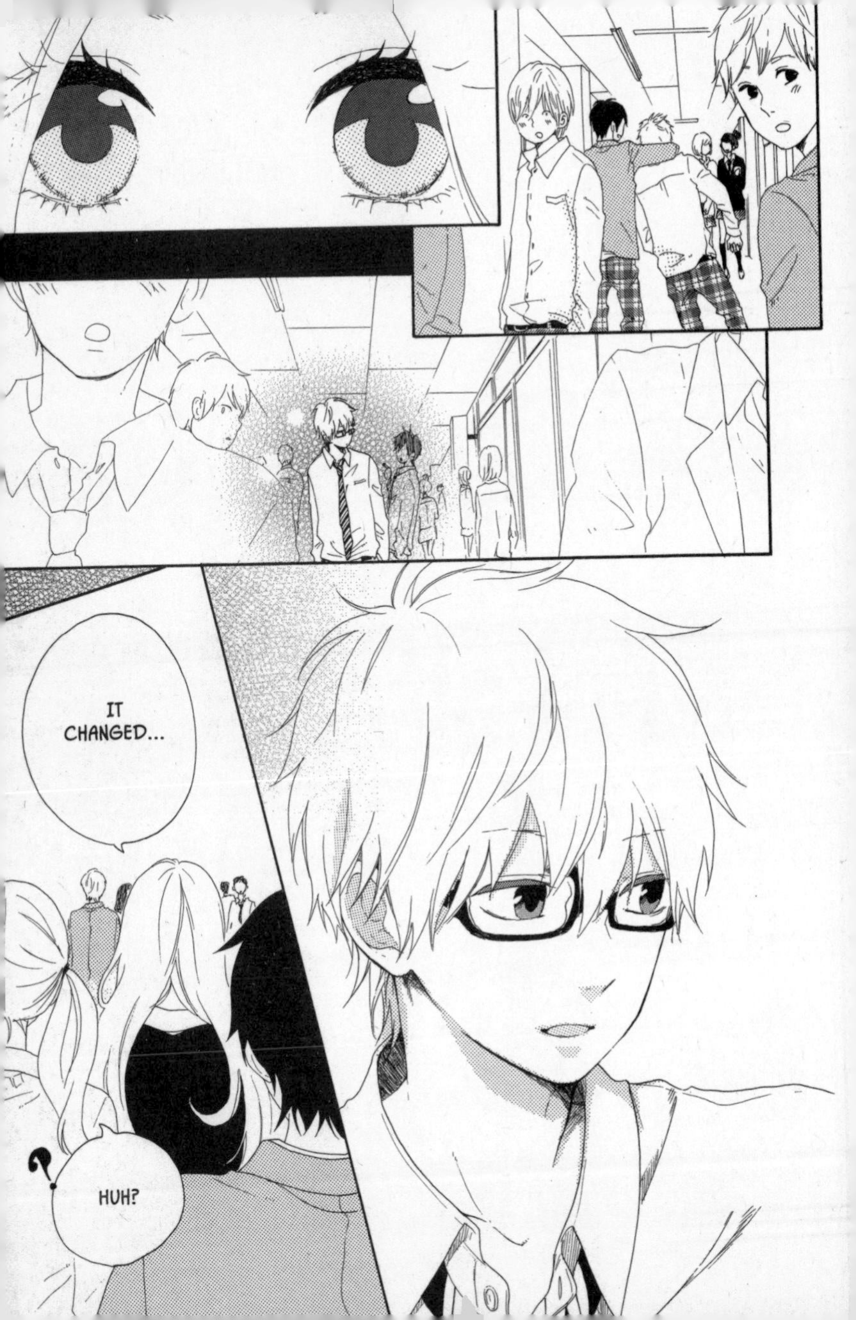
IT CHANGED...
HUH?

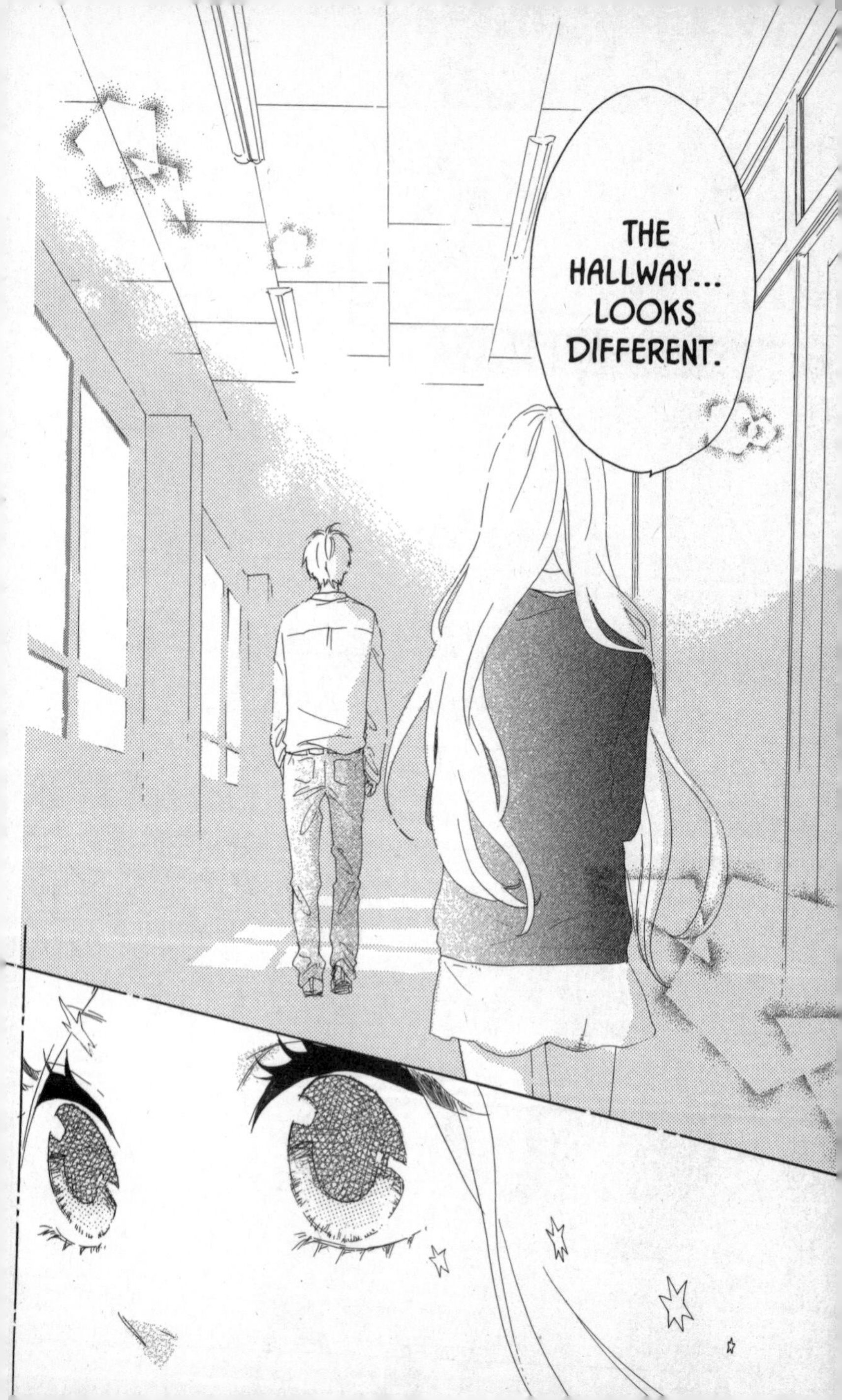
THE HALLWAY... LOOKS DIFFERENT.

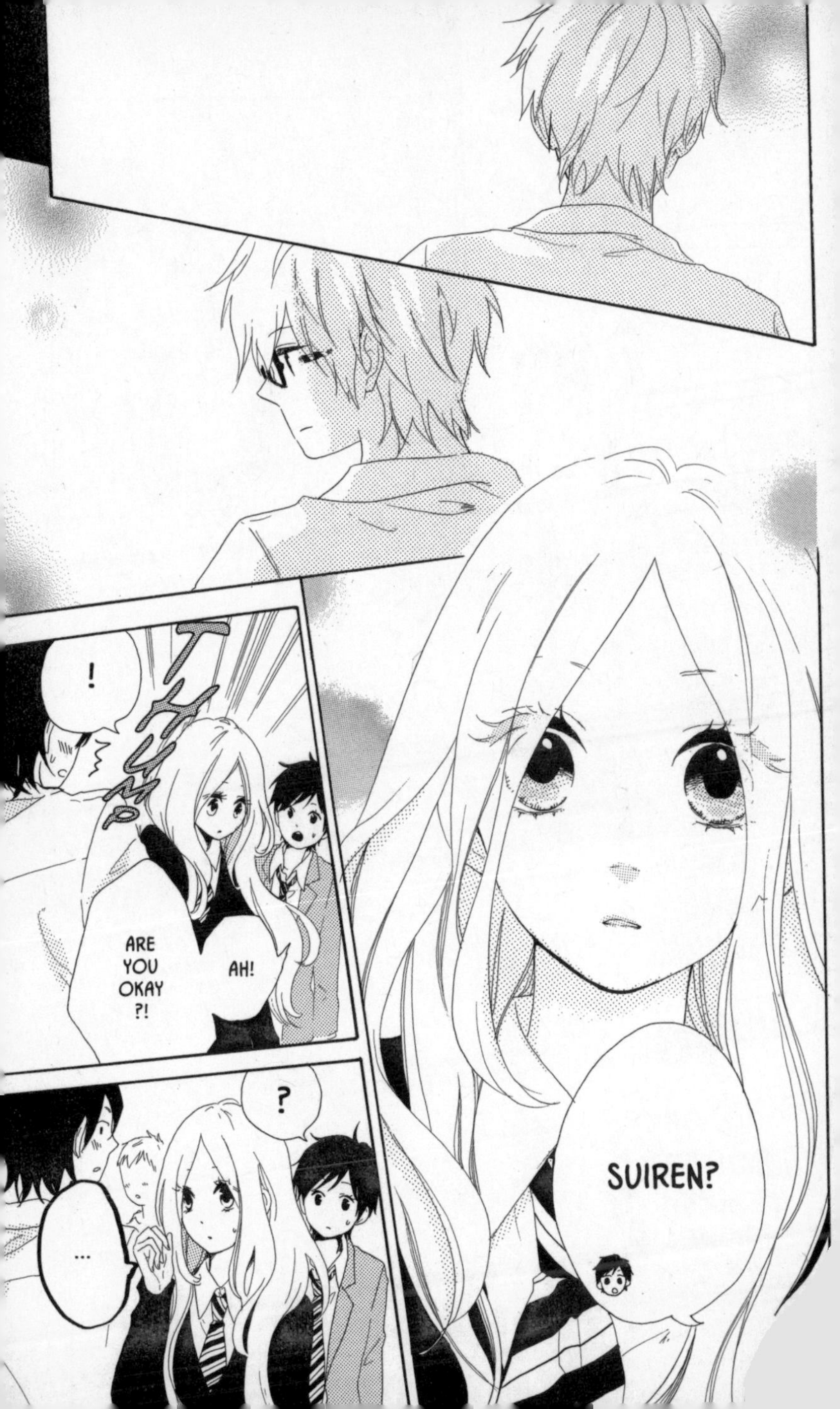
SUIREN?
THUMP
!
AH!
ARE YOU OKAY ?!
?
...

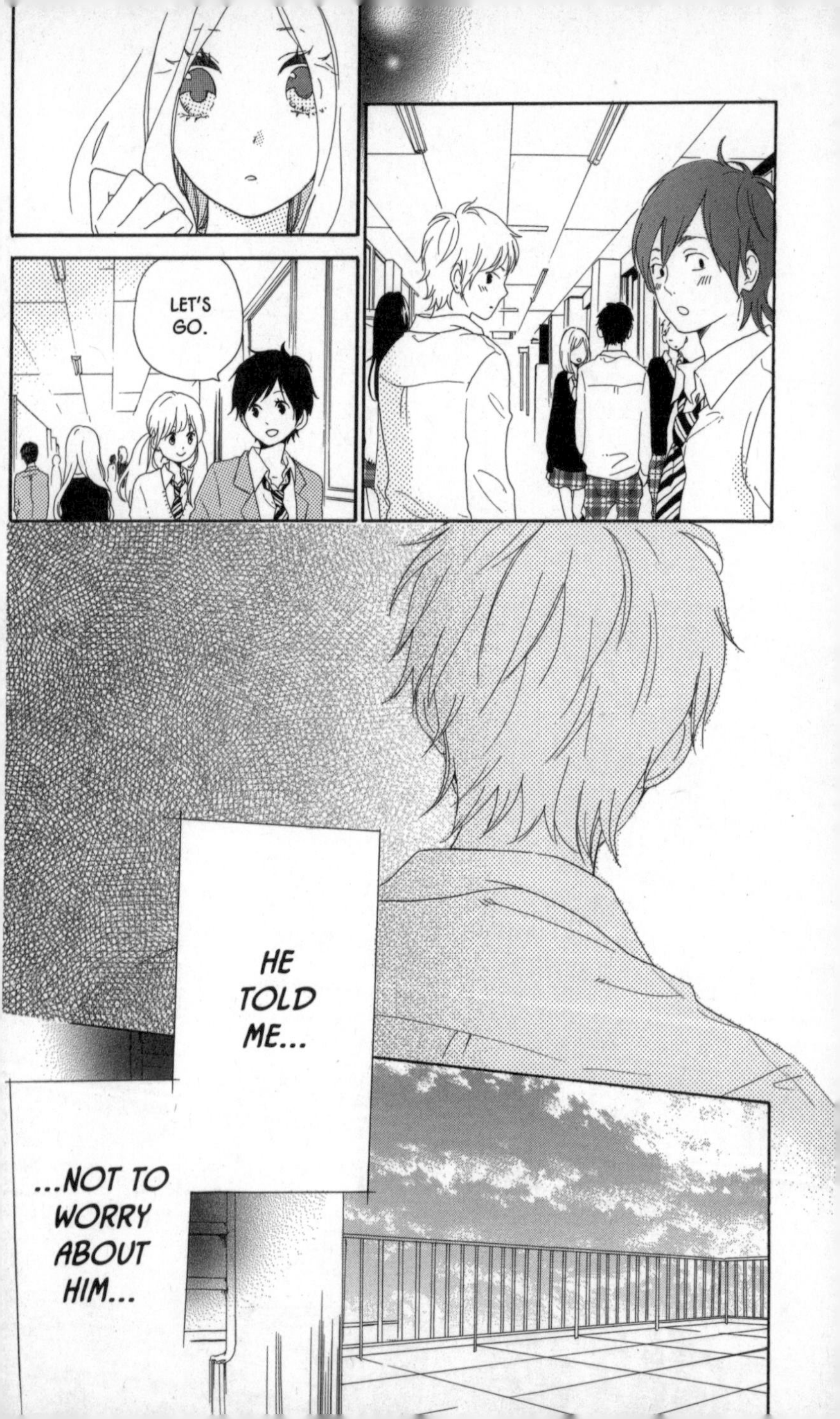
LET'S GO.
HE TOLD ME...
...NOT TO WORRY ABOUT HIM...

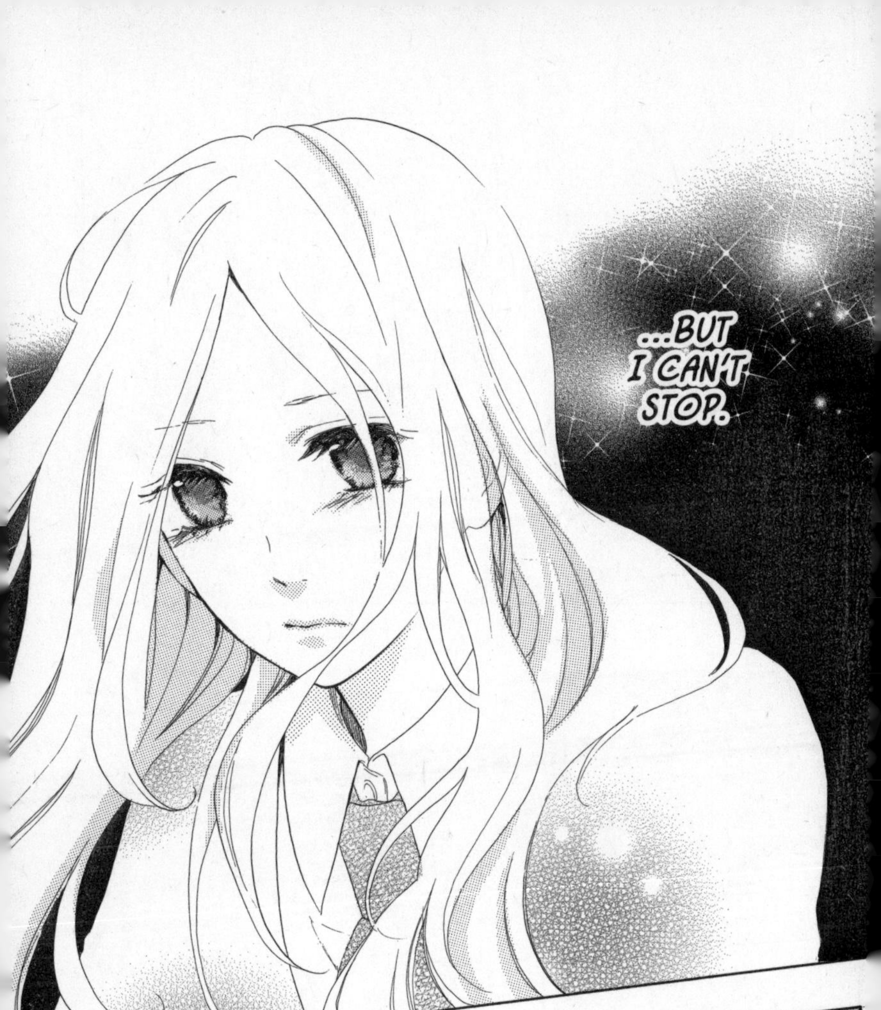
...BUT I CAN'T STOP.
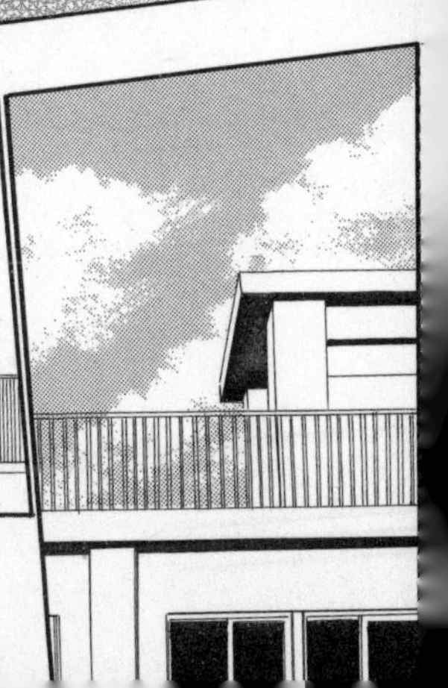
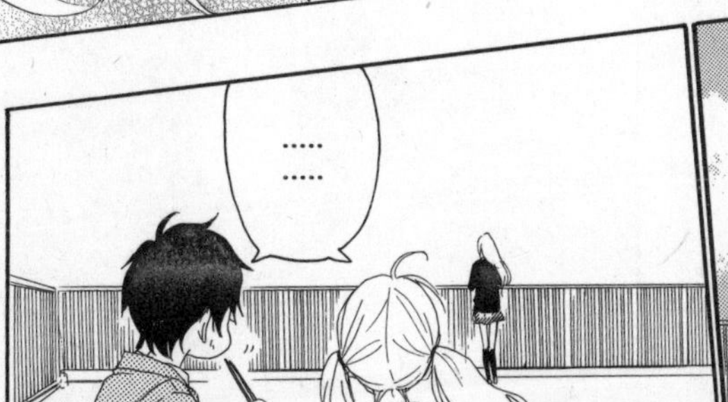
....

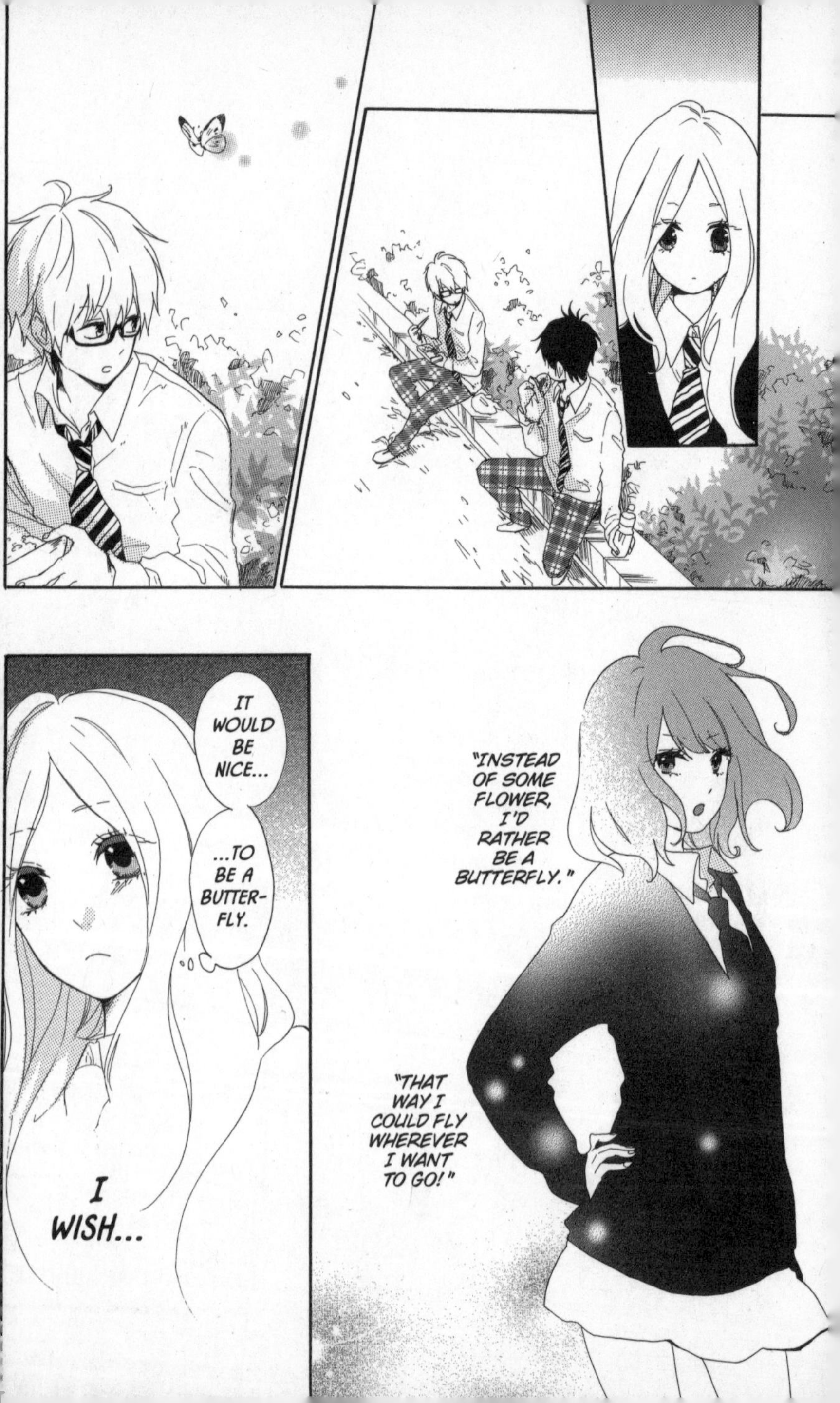
"INSTEAD OF SOME FLOWER, I'D RATHER BE A BUTTERFLY."
"THAT WAY I COULD FLY WHEREVER I WANT TO GO!"
IT WOULD BE NICE...
...TO BE A BUTTER-FLY.
I WISH...

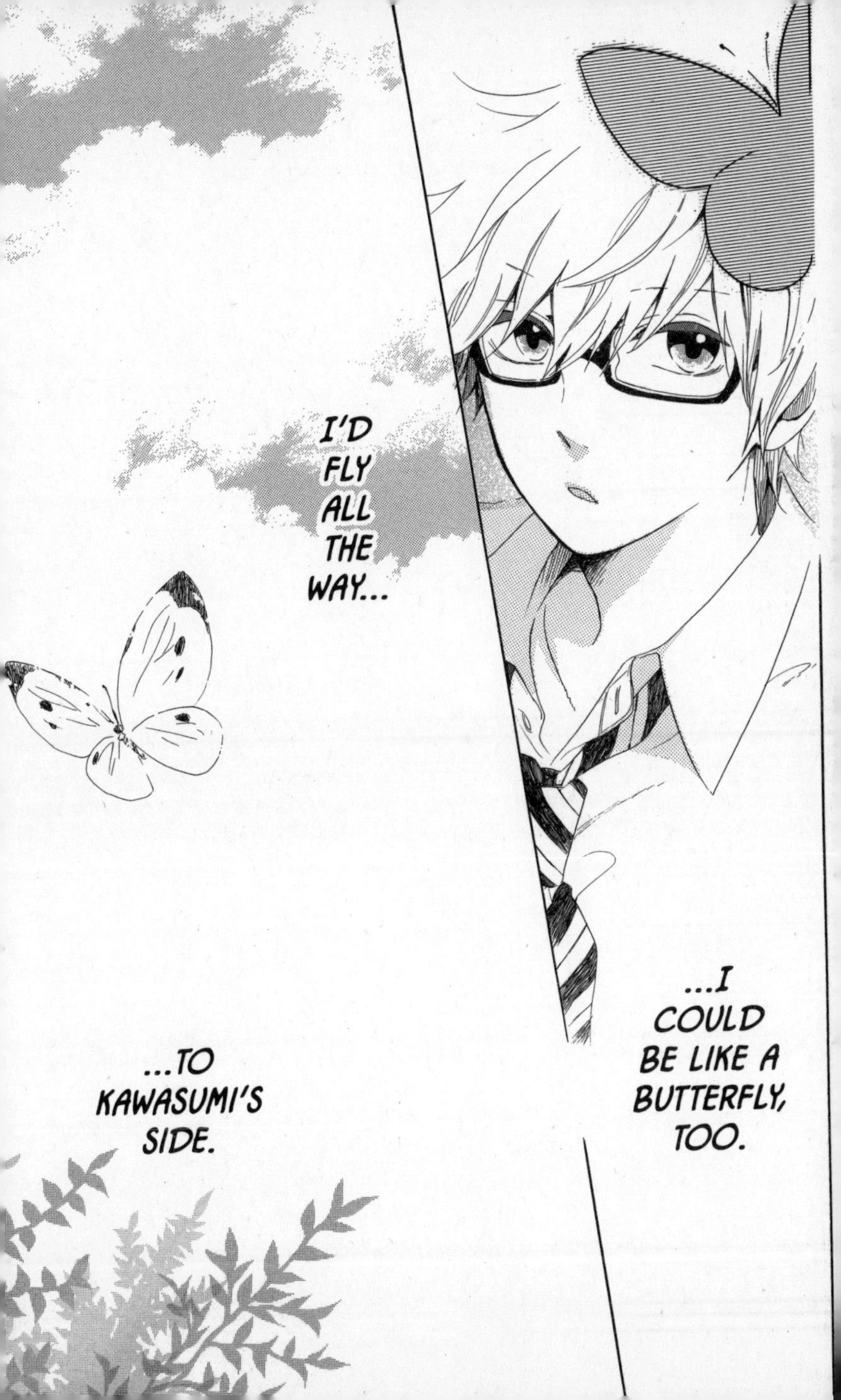
...I COULD BE LIKE A BUTTERFLY, TOO.
I'D FLY ALL THE WAY...
...TO KAWASUMI'S SIDE.

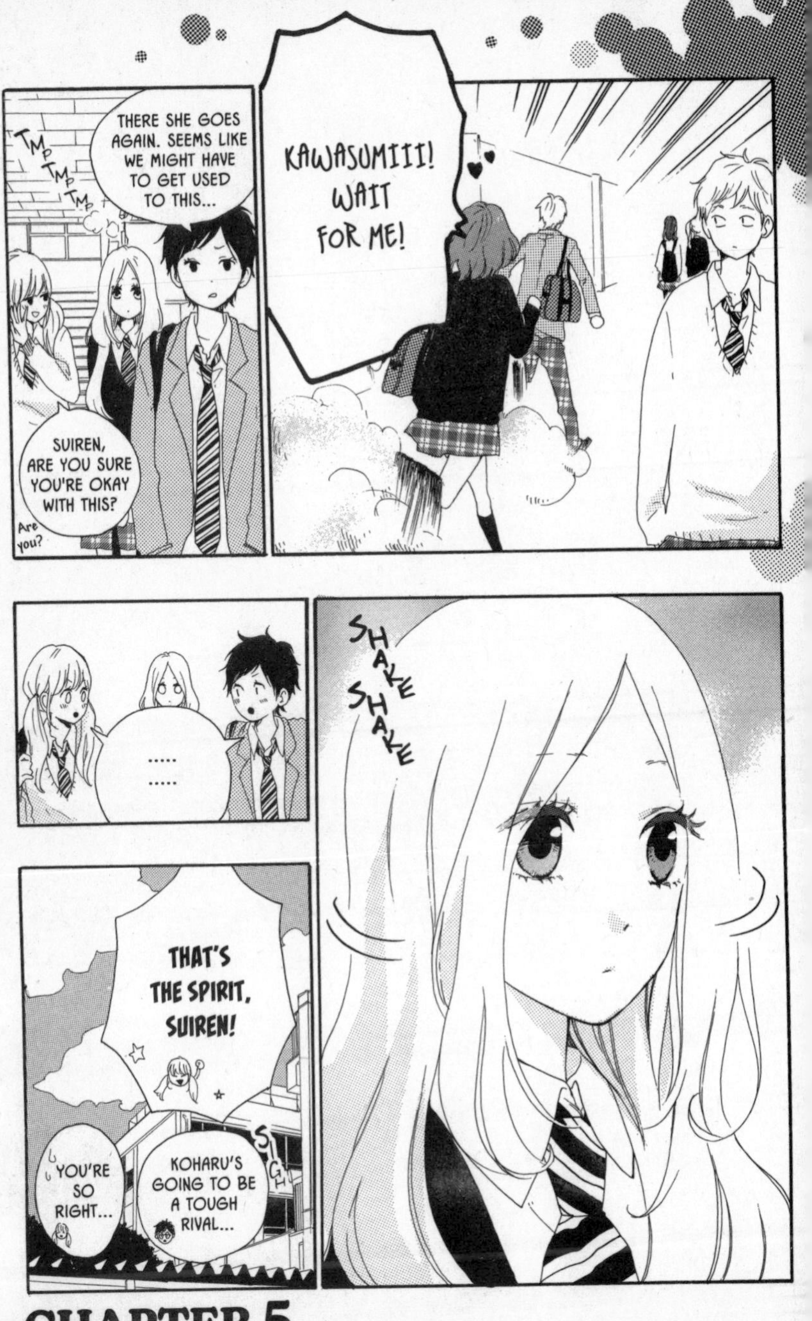
KAWASUMIII! WAIT FOR ME!
TMP TMP TMP
THERE SHE GOES AGAIN. SEEMS LIKE WE MIGHT HAVE TO GET USED TO THIS...
SUIREN, ARE YOU SURE YOU'RE OKAY WITH THIS?
Are you?
SHAKE SHAKE
.....
.....
THAT'S THE SPIRIT, SUIREN!
SIGH
KOHARU'S GOING TO BE A TOUGH RIVAL...
YOU'RE SO RIGHT...

CHAPTER 5

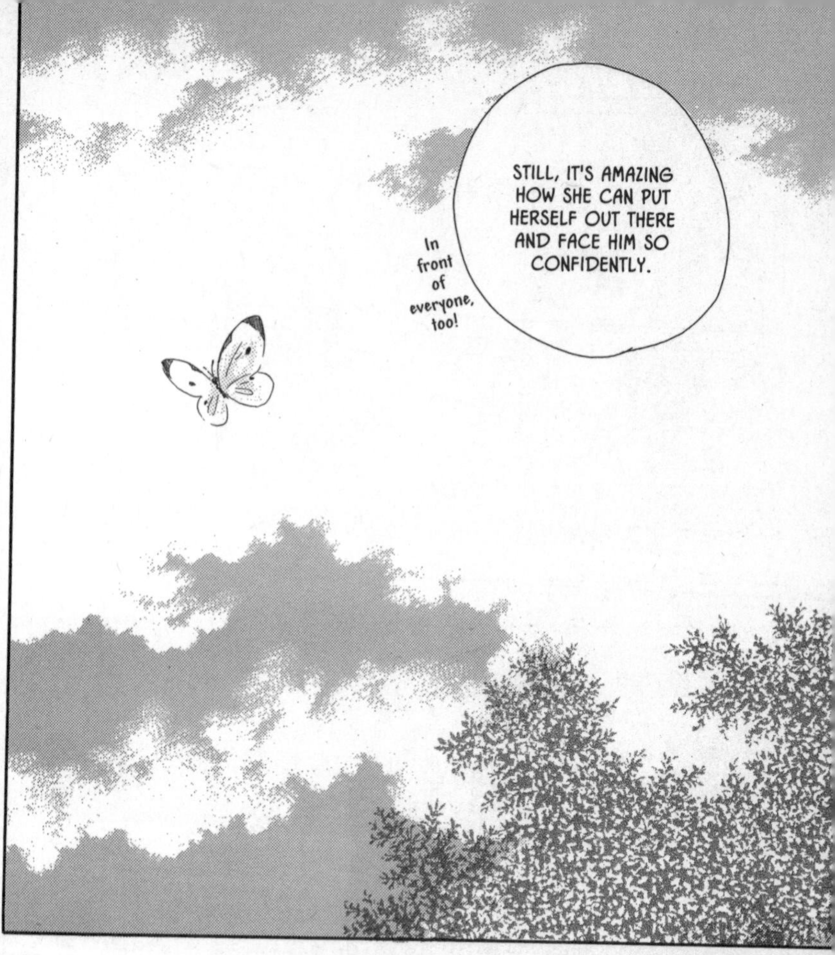
STILL, IT'S AMAZING HOW SHE CAN PUT HERSELF OUT THERE AND FACE HIM SO CONFIDENTLY.
In front of everyone, too!

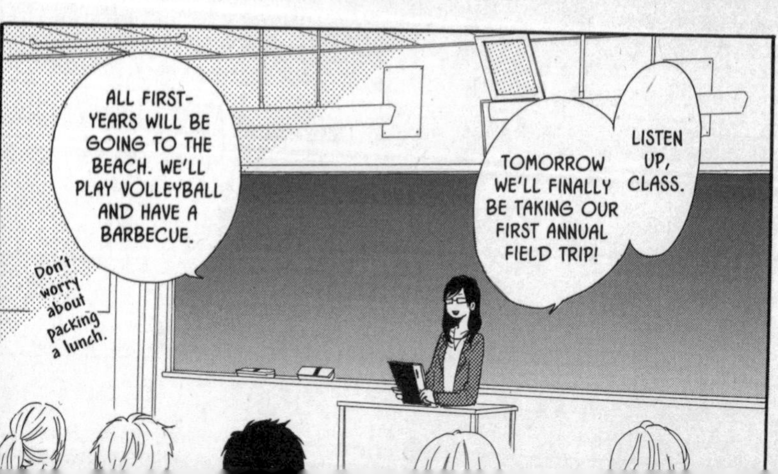
LISTEN UP, CLASS.
TOMORROW WE'LL FINALLY BE TAKING OUR FIRST ANNUAL FIELD TRIP!
ALL FIRST-YEARS WILL BE GOING TO THE BEACH. WE'LL PLAY VOLLEYBALL AND HAVE A BARBECUE.
Don't worry about packing a lunch.

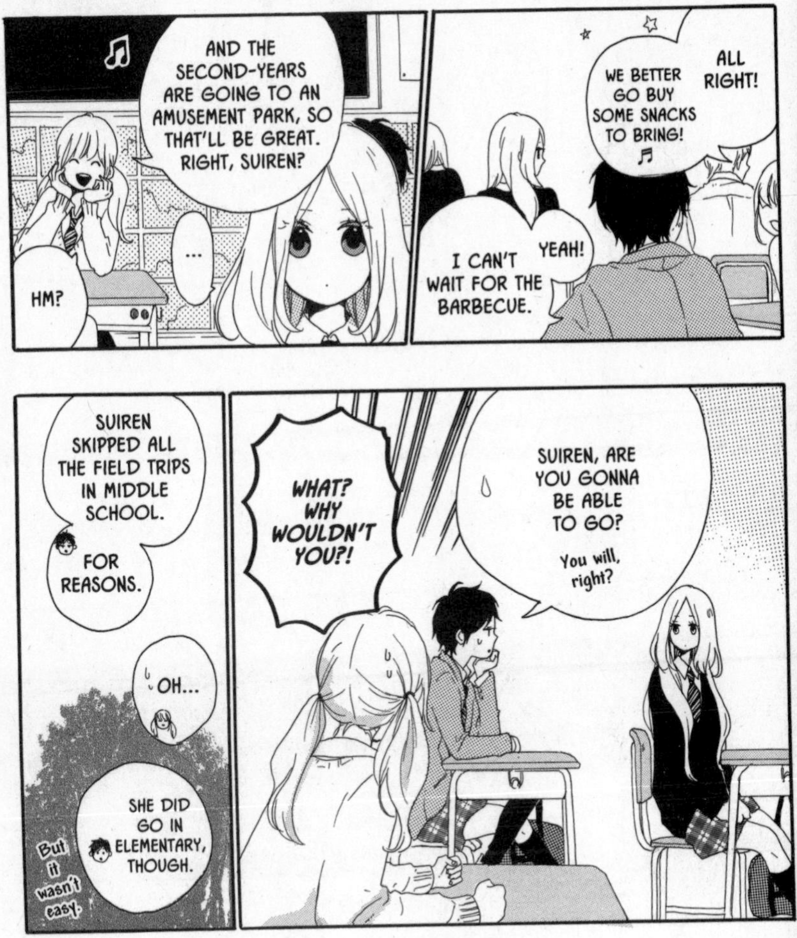
ALL RIGHT!
WE BETTER GO BUY SOME SNACKS TO BRING!
YEAH!
I CAN'T WAIT FOR THE BARBECUE.
AND THE SECOND-YEARS ARE GOING TO AN AMUSEMENT PARK, SO THAT'LL BE GREAT. RIGHT, SUIREN?
...
HM?
SUIREN, ARE YOU GONNA BE ABLE TO GO?
You will, right?
WHAT? WHY WOULDN'T YOU?!
SUIREN SKIPPED ALL THE FIELD TRIPS IN MIDDLE SCHOOL.
FOR REASONS.
OH...
SHE DID GO IN ELEMENTARY, THOUGH.
But it wasn't easy.

ONE DAY...

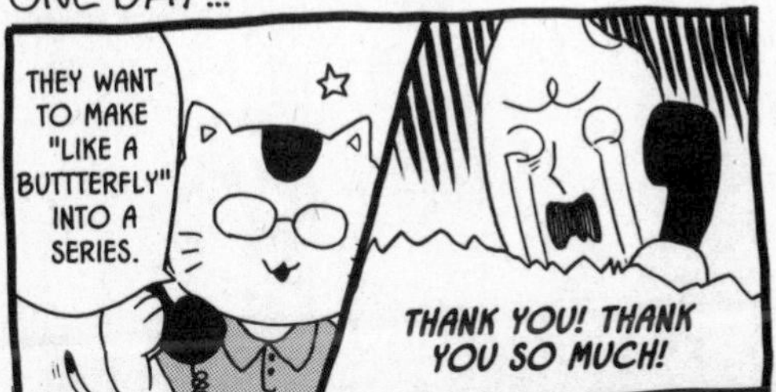
THEY WANT TO MAKE "LIKE A BUTTTERFLY" INTO A SERIES.
THANK YOU! THANK YOU SO MUCH!

OUR NEXT CONVERSATION WAS KIND OF LIKE THIS.

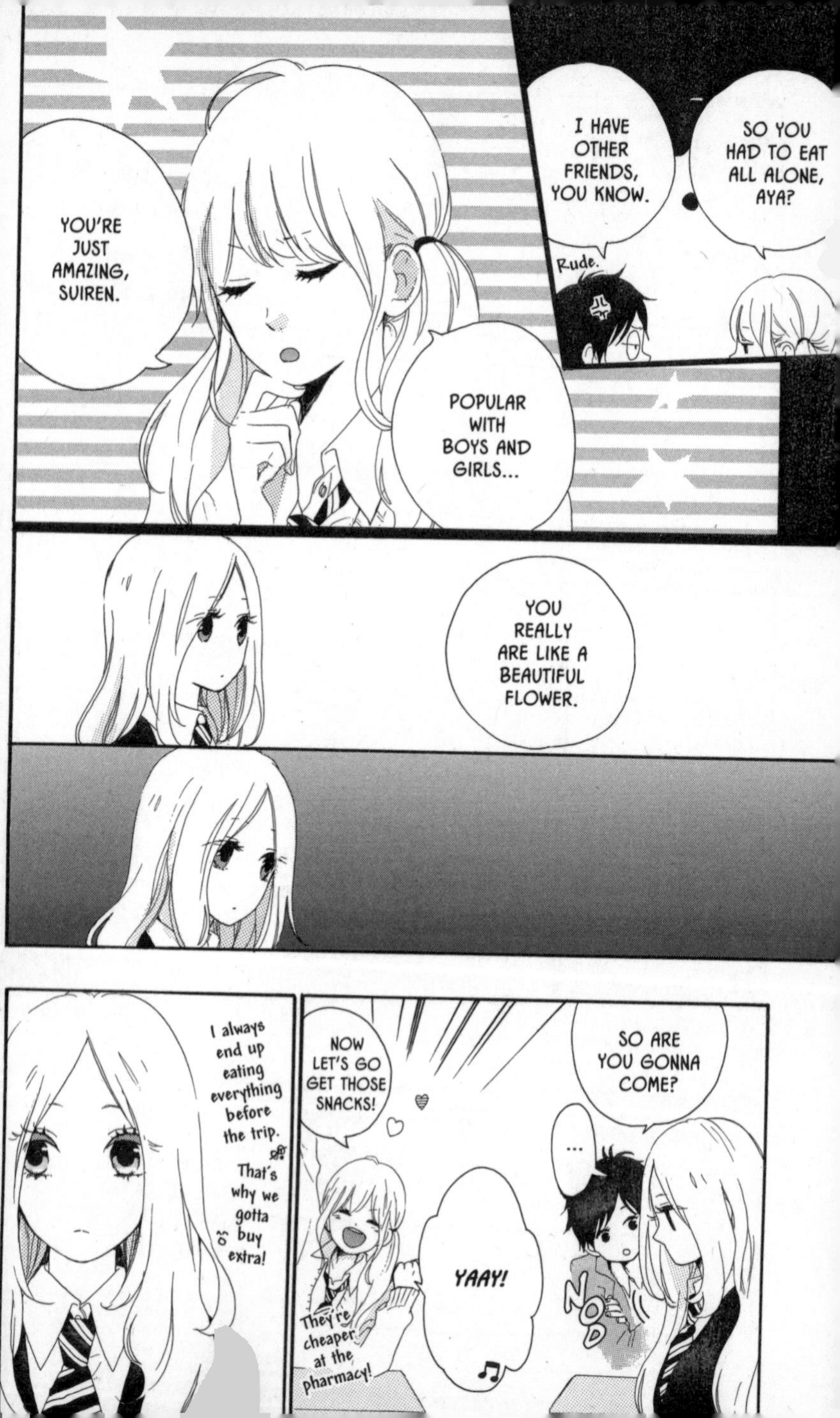
SO YOU HAD TO EAT ALL ALONE, AYA?
I HAVE OTHER FRIENDS, YOU KNOW.
Rude.
POPULAR WITH BOYS AND GIRLS...
YOU'RE JUST AMAZING, SUIREN.
YOU REALLY ARE LIKE A BEAUTIFUL FLOWER.
SO ARE YOU GONNA COME?
...
NOD
NOW LET'S GO GET THOSE SNACKS!
YAAY!
They're cheaper at the pharmacy!
I always end up eating everything before the trip.
That's why we gotta buy extra!

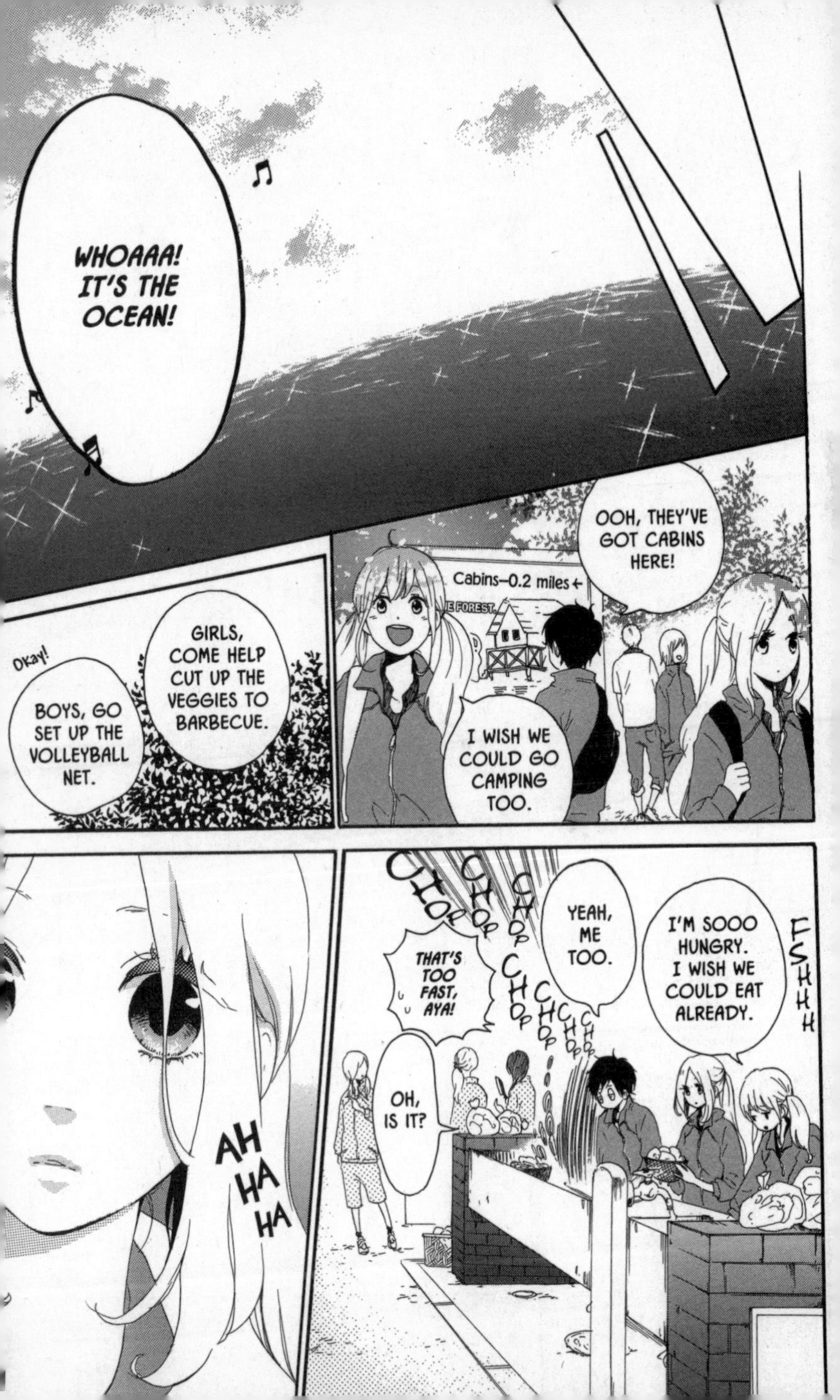
WHOAAA! IT'S THE OCEAN!
OOH, THEY'VE GOT CABINS HERE!
Cabins—0.2 miles ←
I WISH WE COULD GO CAMPING TOO.
GIRLS, COME HELP CUT UP THE VEGGIES TO BARBECUE.
BOYS, GO SET UP THE VOLLEYBALL NET.
Okay!
FSHHH
I'M SOOO HUNGRY. I WISH WE COULD EAT ALREADY.
YEAH, ME TOO.
CHOP CHOP CHOP CHOP CHOP CHOP CHOP
THAT'S TOO FAST, AYA!
OH, IS IT?
AH HA HA

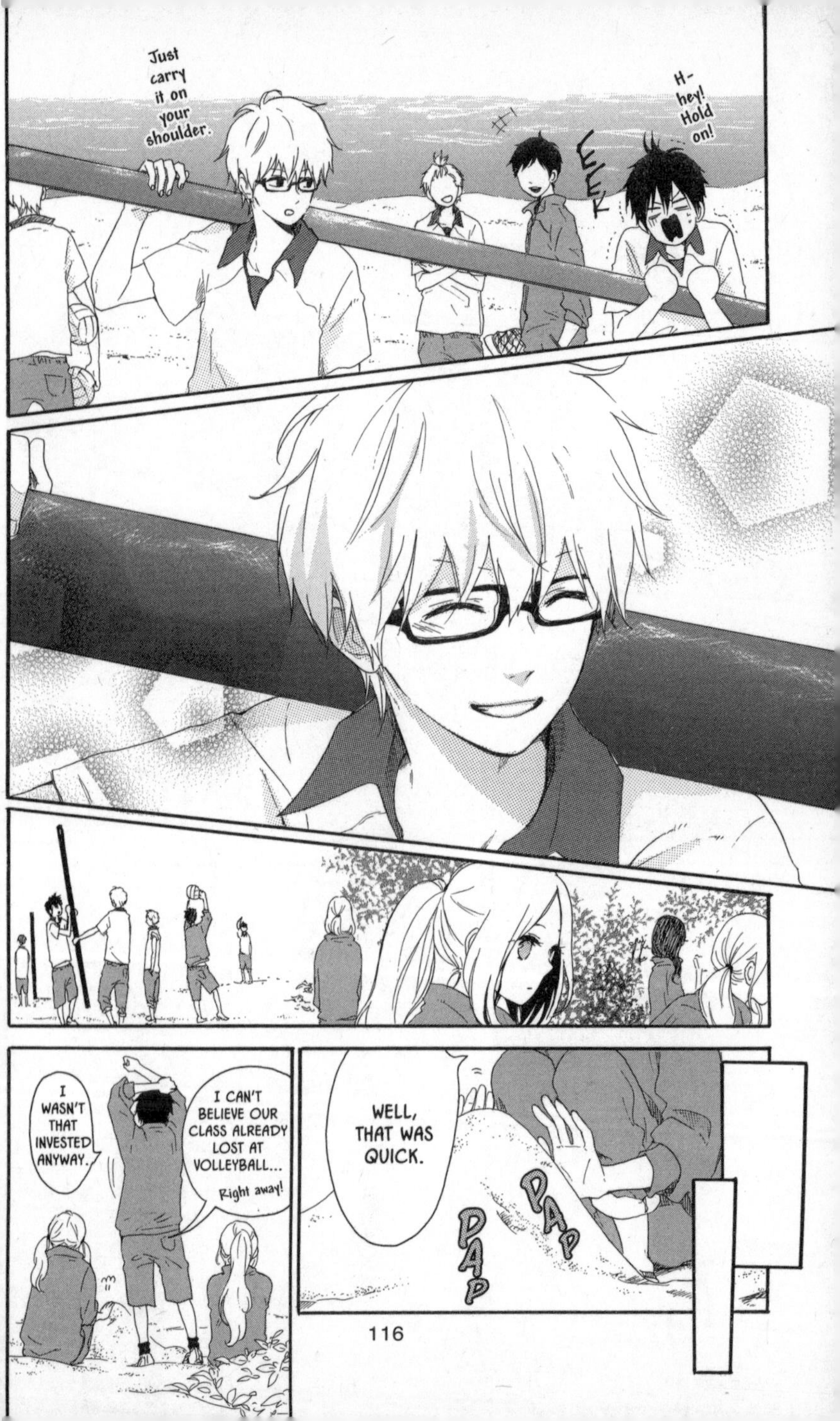
H-hey! Hold on!
EEK
Just carry it on your shoulder.
WELL, THAT WAS QUICK.
DAP DAP
I CAN'T BELIEVE OUR CLASS ALREADY LOST AT VOLLEYBALL...
Right away!
I WASN'T THAT INVESTED ANYWAY.

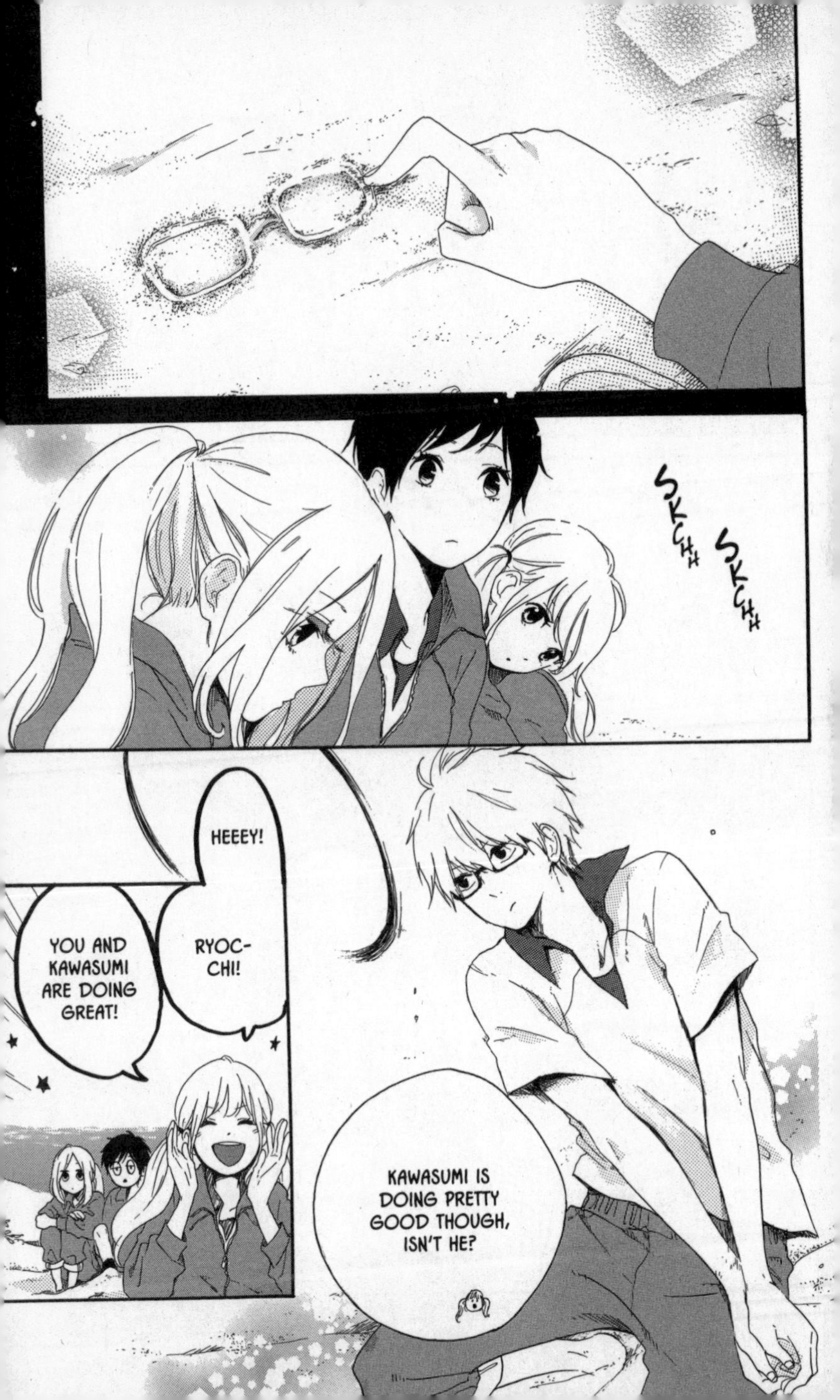
SKCHH
SKCHH
HEEEY!
RYOC-CHI!
YOU AND KAWASUMI ARE DOING GREAT!
KAWASUMI IS DOING PRETTY GOOD THOUGH, ISN'T HE?

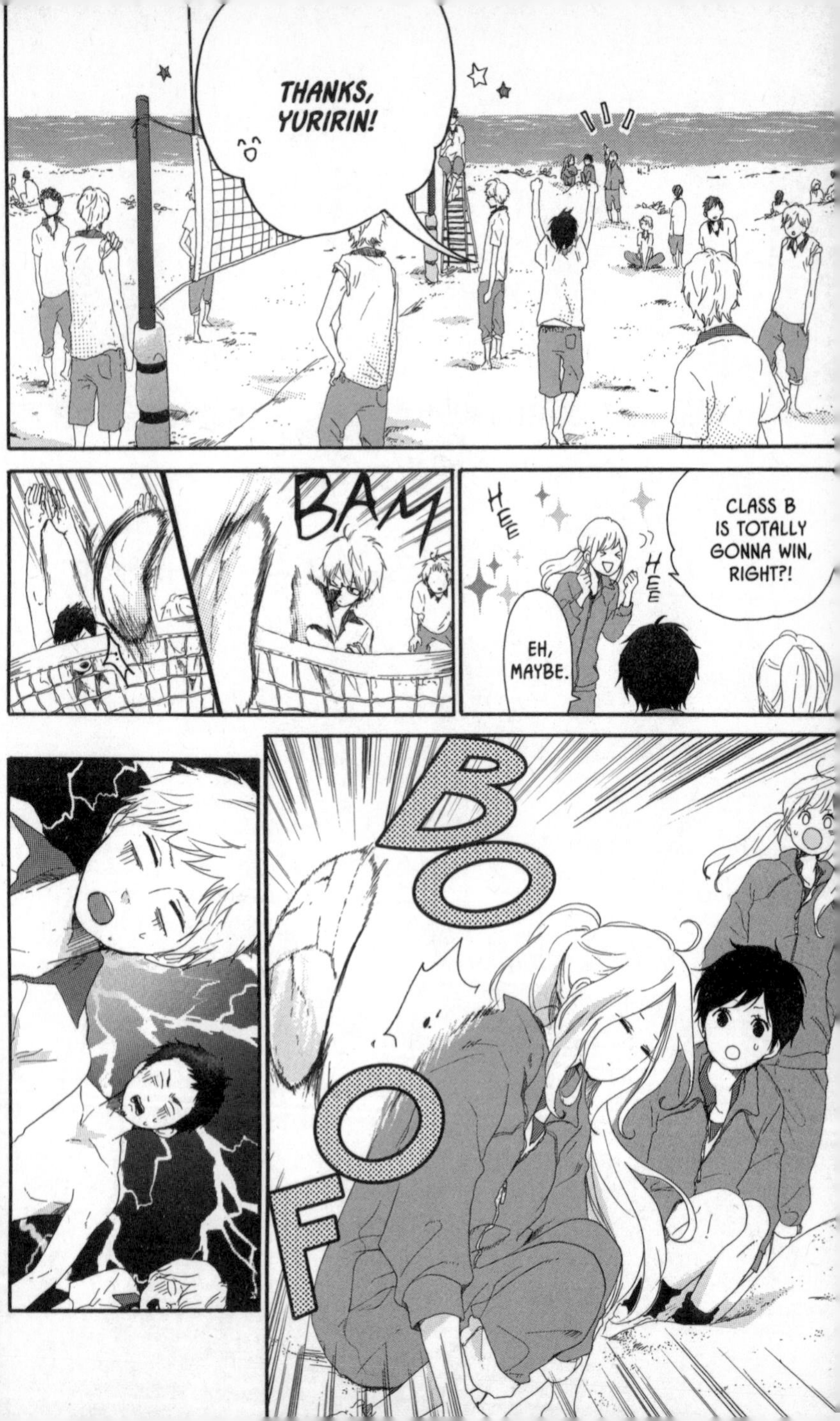
THANKS, YURIRIN!
HEE HEE
CLASS B IS TOTALLY GONNA WIN, RIGHT?!
EH, MAYBE.
BAM
BOOF

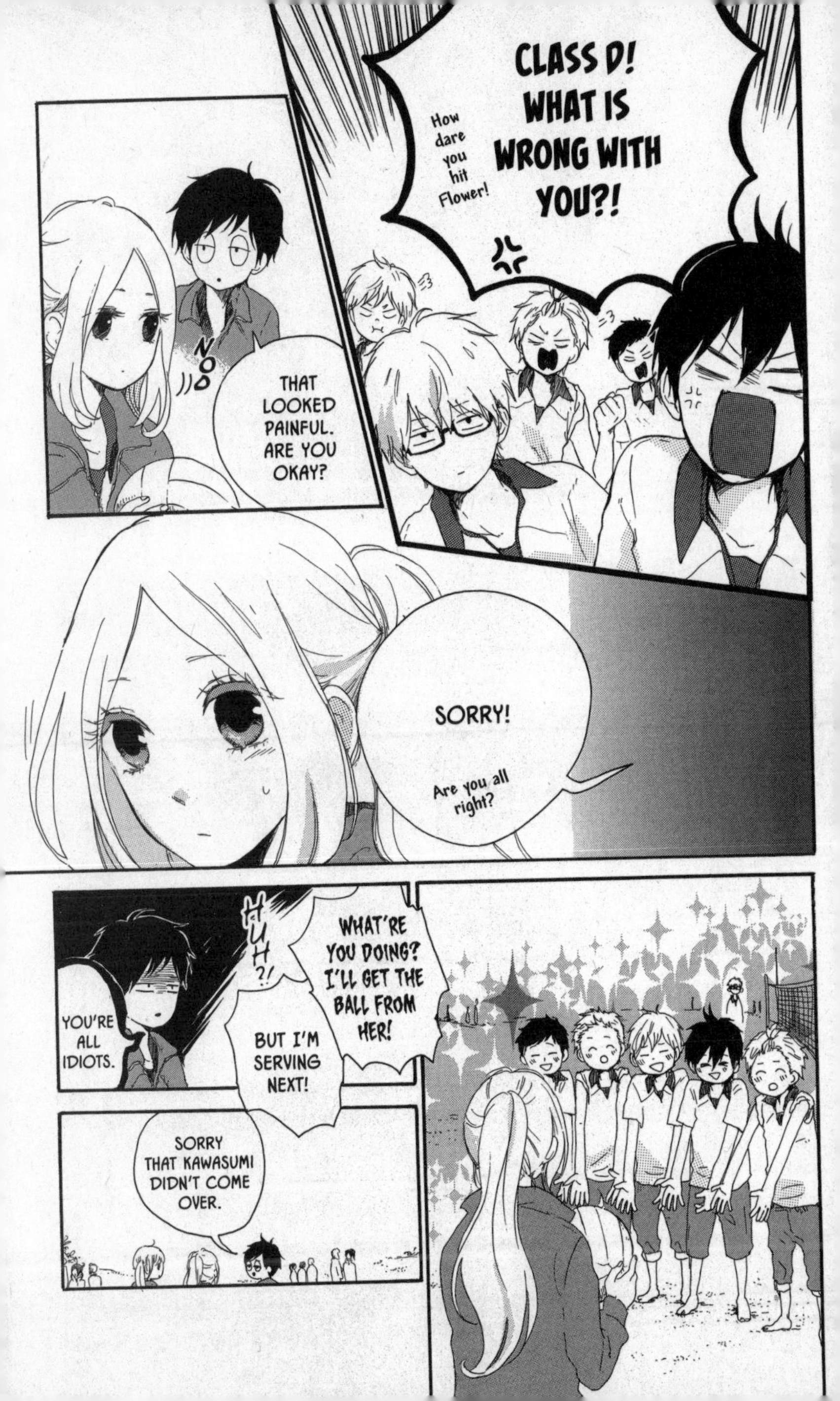
CLASS D! WHAT IS WRONG WITH YOU?!
How dare you hit Flower!
NOD
THAT LOOKED PAINFUL. ARE YOU OKAY?
SORRY!
Are you all right?
HUH?!
WHAT'RE YOU DOING? I'LL GET THE BALL FROM HER!
BUT I'M SERVING NEXT!
YOU'RE ALL IDIOTS.
SORRY THAT KAWASUMI DIDN'T COME OVER.

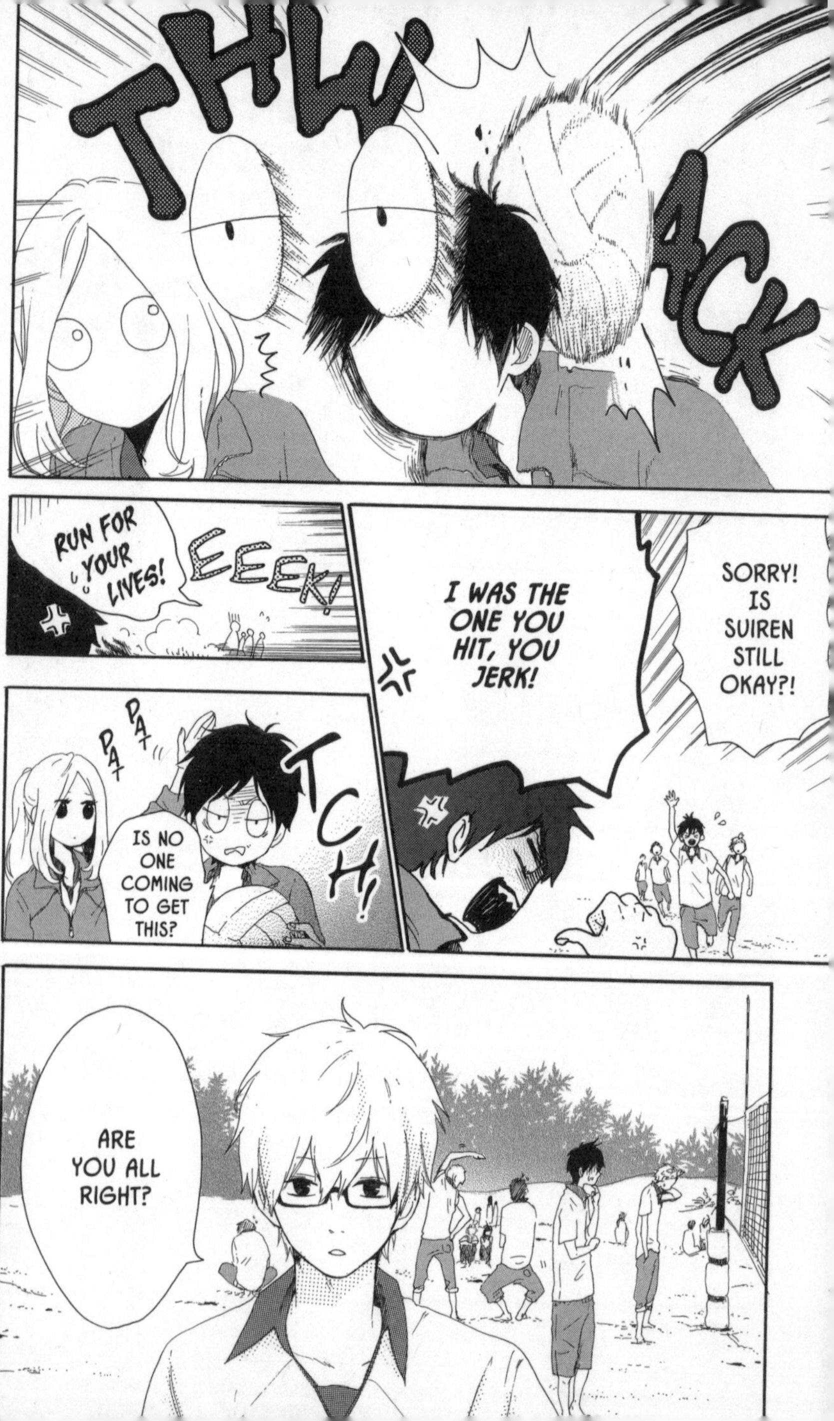
THWACK
SORRY! IS SUIREN STILL OKAY?!
I WAS THE ONE YOU HIT, YOU JERK!
RUN FOR YOUR LIVES!
EEEK!
PAT PAT
TCH!
IS NO ONE COMING TO GET THIS?
ARE YOU ALL RIGHT?

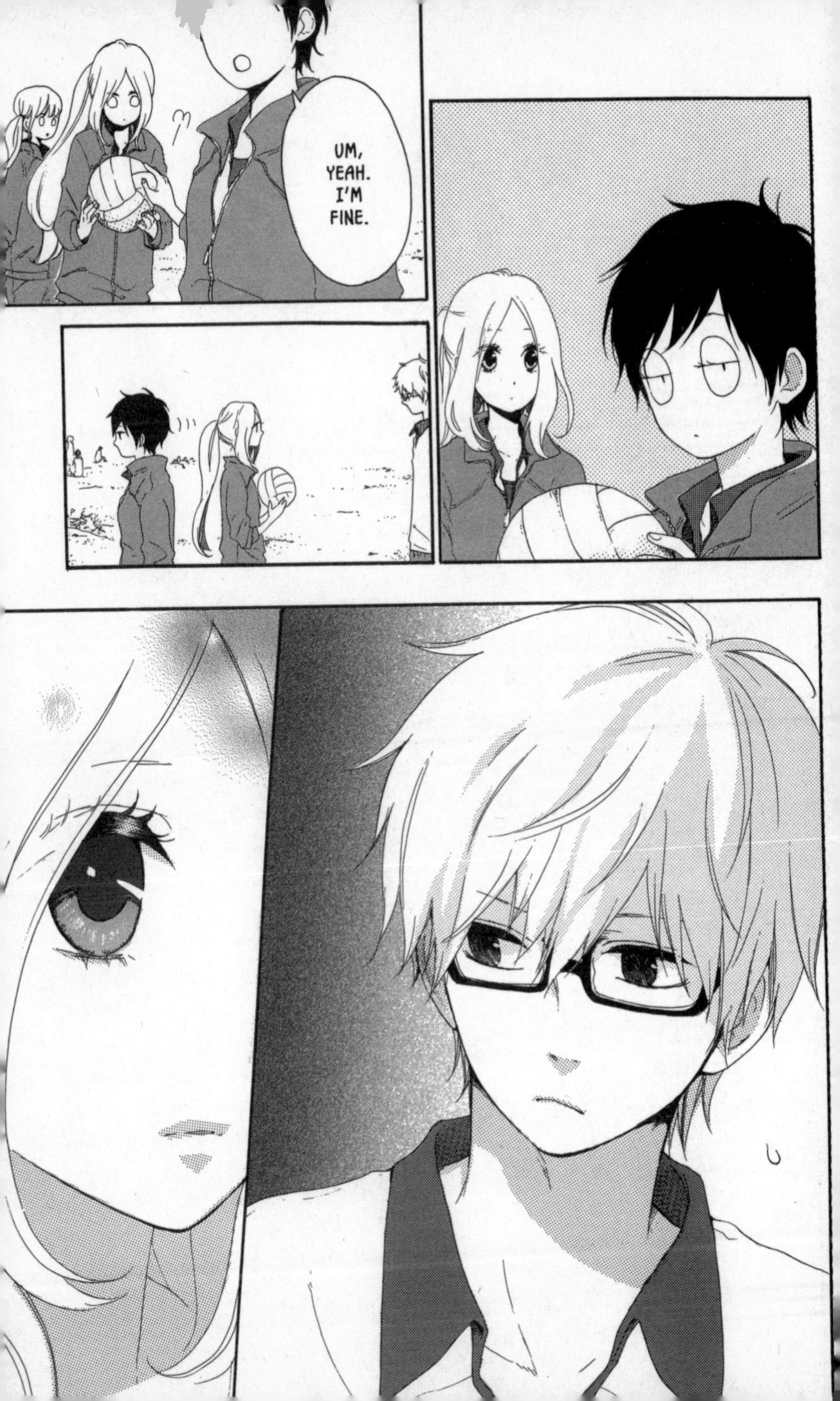
UM, YEAH. I'M FINE.

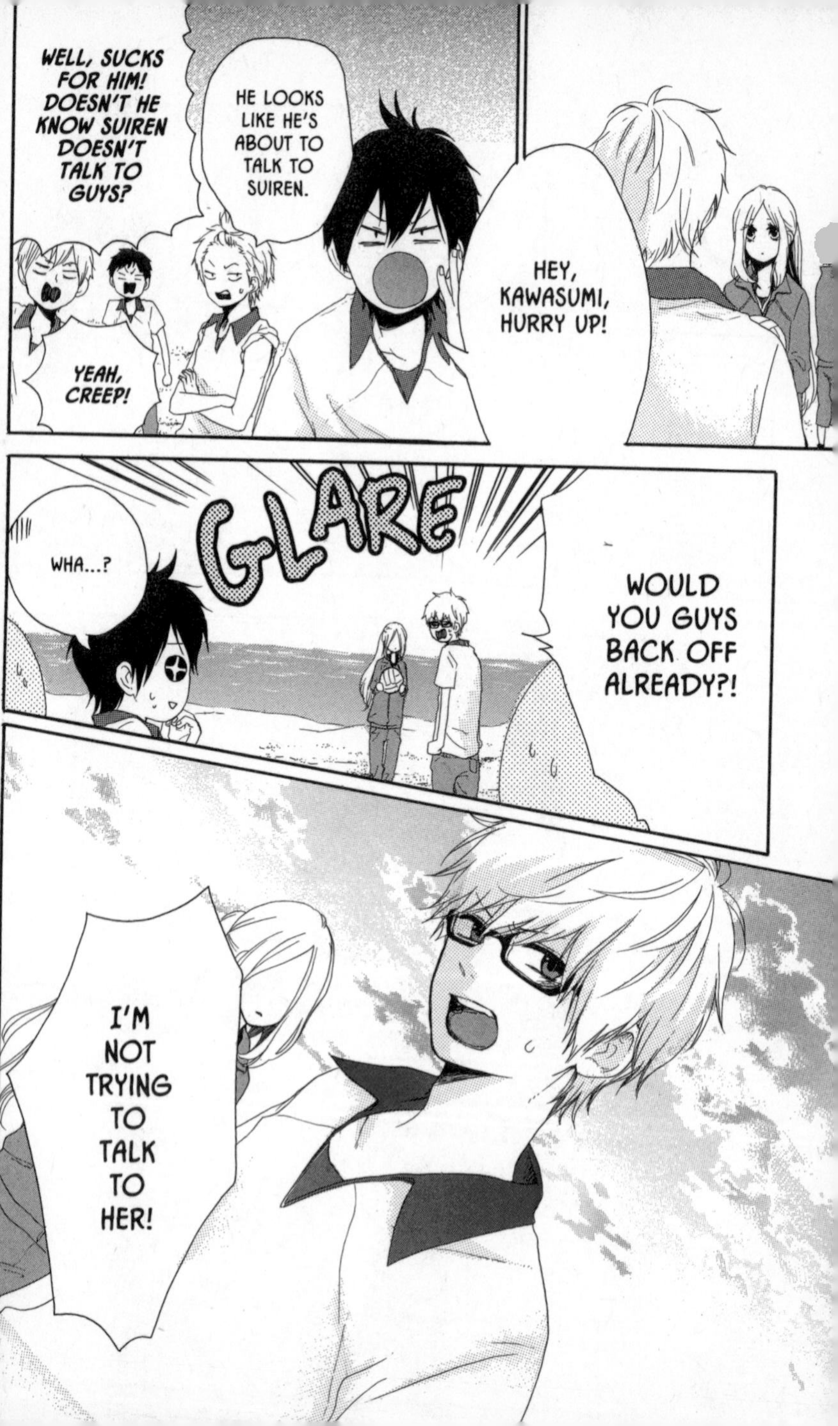
HEY, KAWASUMI, HURRY UP!
HE LOOKS LIKE HE'S ABOUT TO TALK TO SUIREN.
WELL, SUCKS FOR HIM! DOESN'T HE KNOW SUIREN DOESN'T TALK TO GUYS?
YEAH, CREEP!
WOULD YOU GUYS BACK OFF ALREADY?!
GLARE
WHA...?
I'M NOT TRYING TO TALK TO HER!

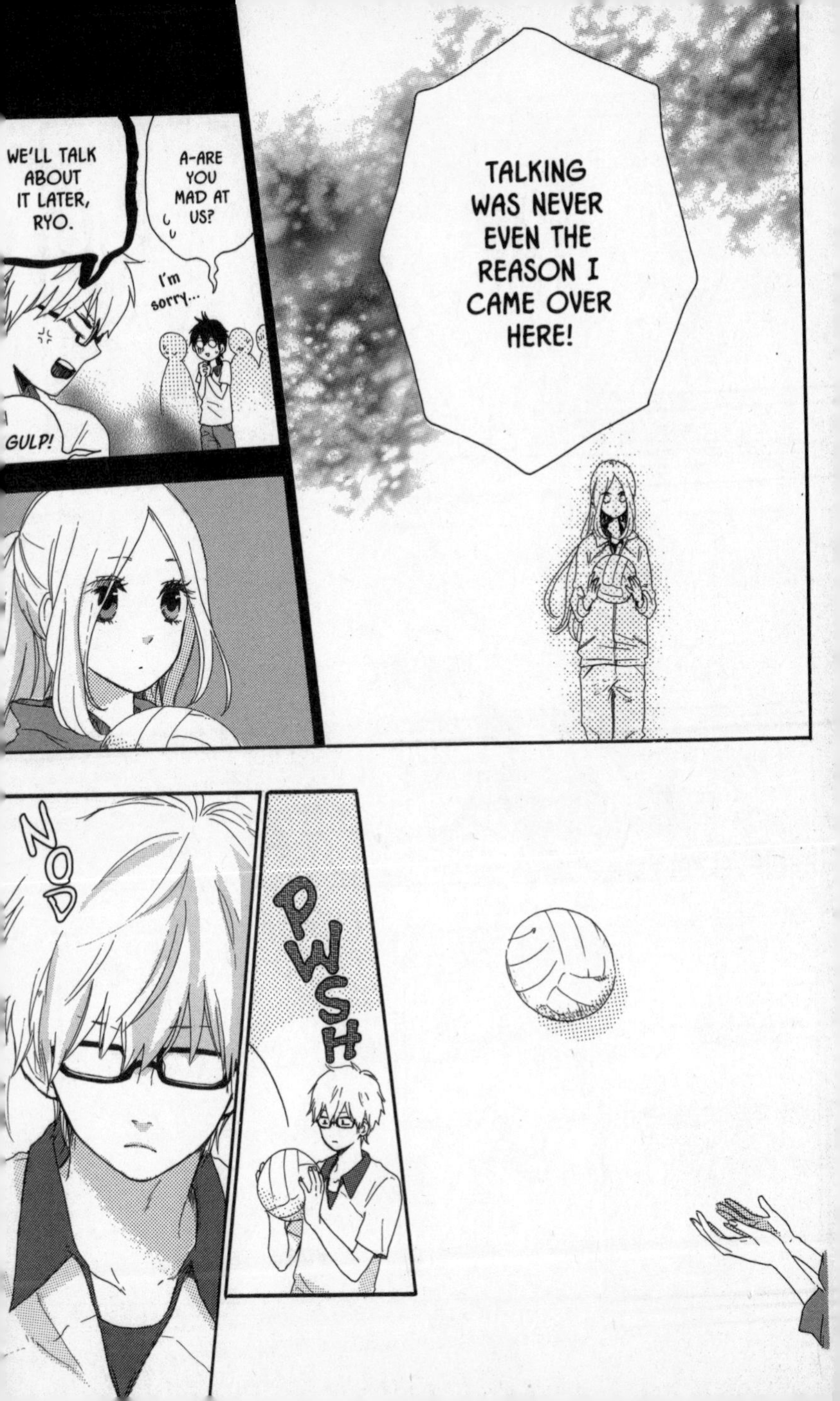
TALKING WAS NEVER EVEN THE REASON I CAME OVER HERE!
A-ARE YOU MAD AT US?
WE'LL TALK ABOUT IT LATER, RYO.
I'm sorry...
GULP!
PWSH
NOD

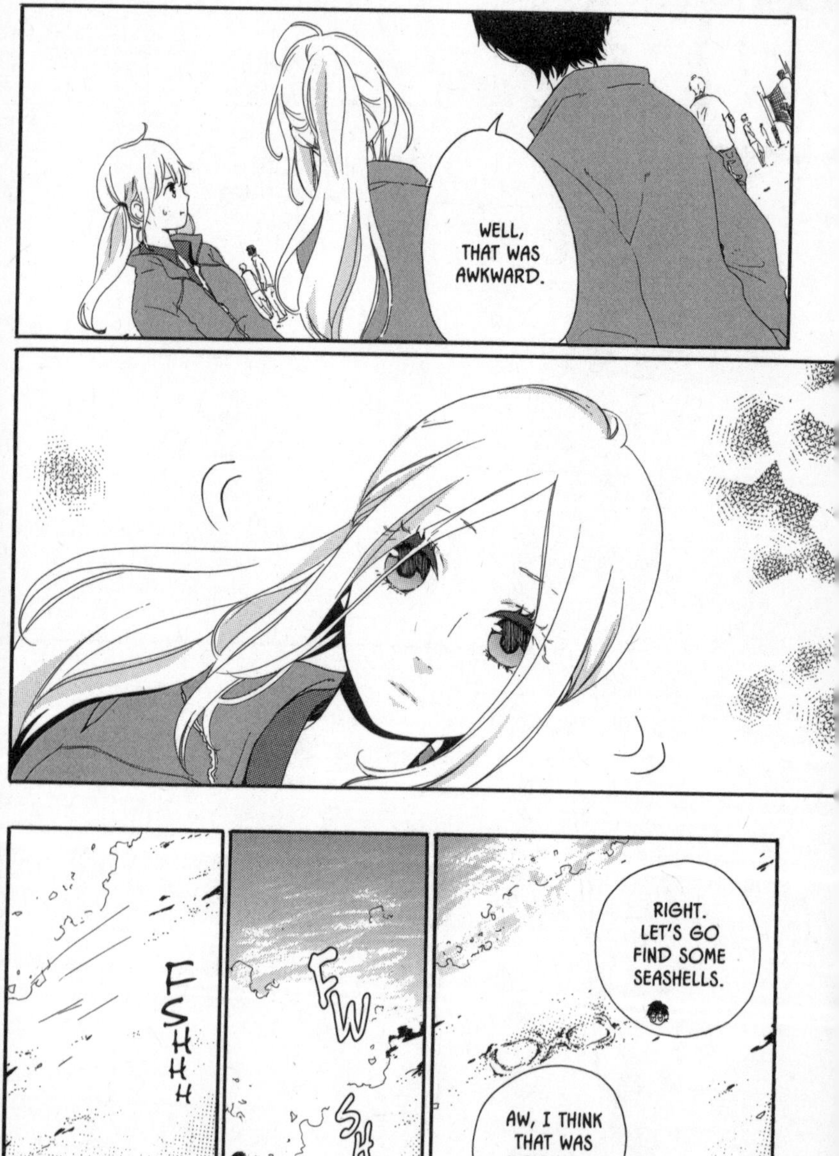
WELL, THAT WAS AWKWARD.
RIGHT. LET'S GO FIND SOME SEASHELLS.
AW, I THINK THAT WAS ROMANTIC!
FWSH
FSHHH

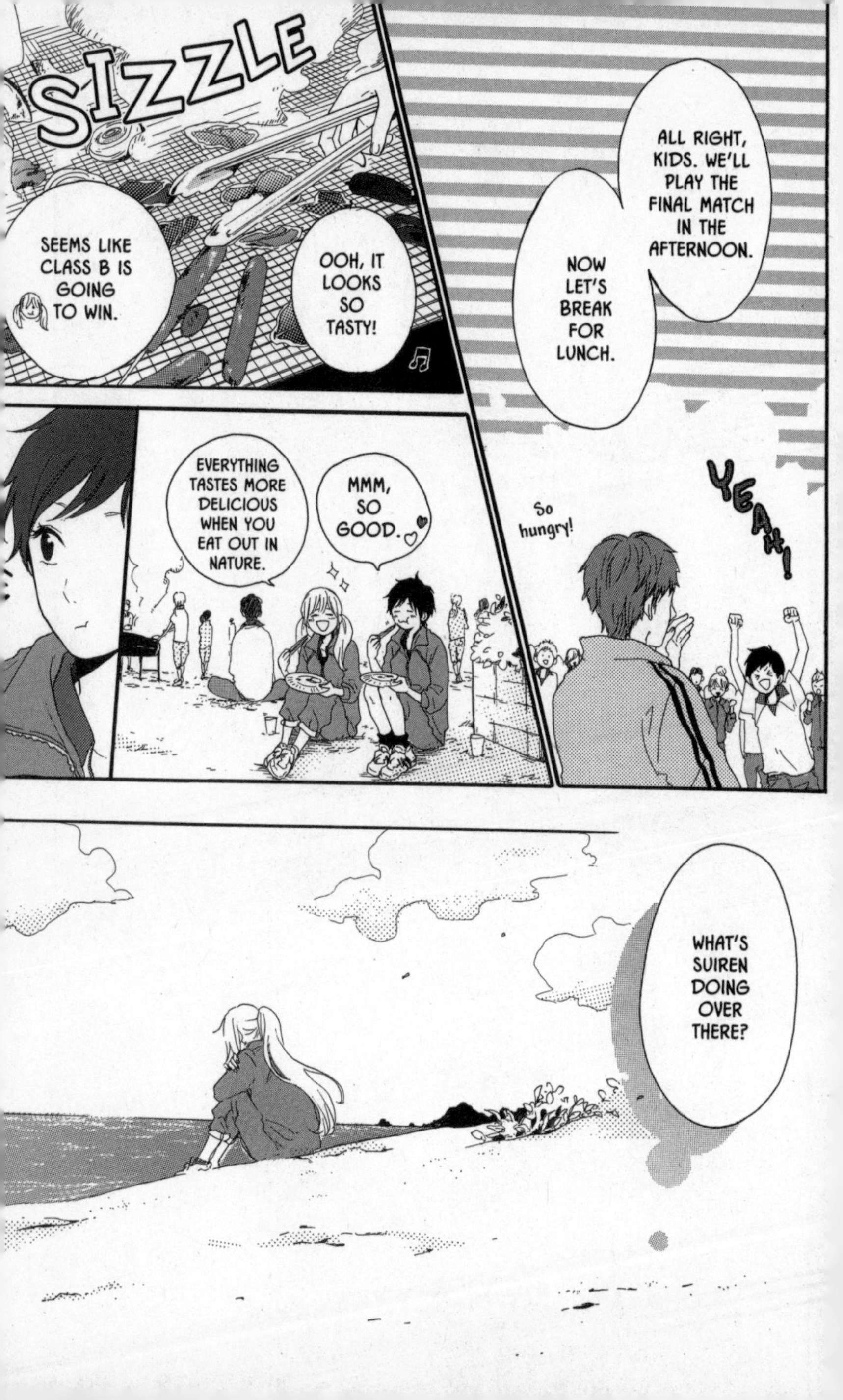
ALL RIGHT, KIDS. WE'LL PLAY THE FINAL MATCH IN THE AFTERNOON.
NOW LET'S BREAK FOR LUNCH.
YEAH!
So hungry!
SIZZLE
OOH, IT LOOKS SO TASTY!
SEEMS LIKE CLASS B IS GOING TO WIN.
MMM, SO GOOD.
EVERYTHING TASTES MORE DELICIOUS WHEN YOU EAT OUT IN NATURE.
WHAT'S SUIREN DOING OVER THERE?

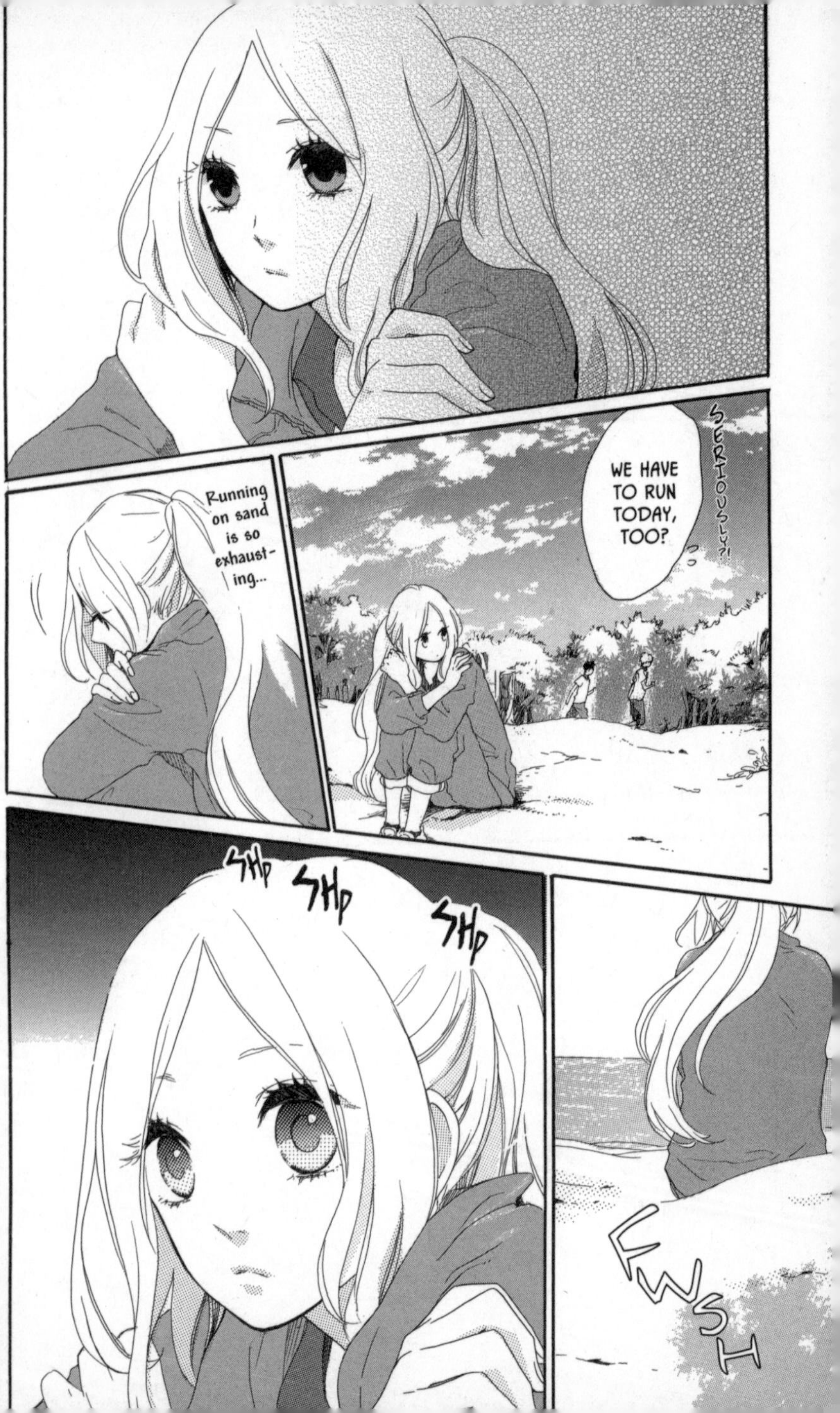
SERIOUSLY?!
WE HAVE TO RUN TODAY, TOO?
Running on sand is so exhaust-ing...
FWSH
SHP
SHP
SHP

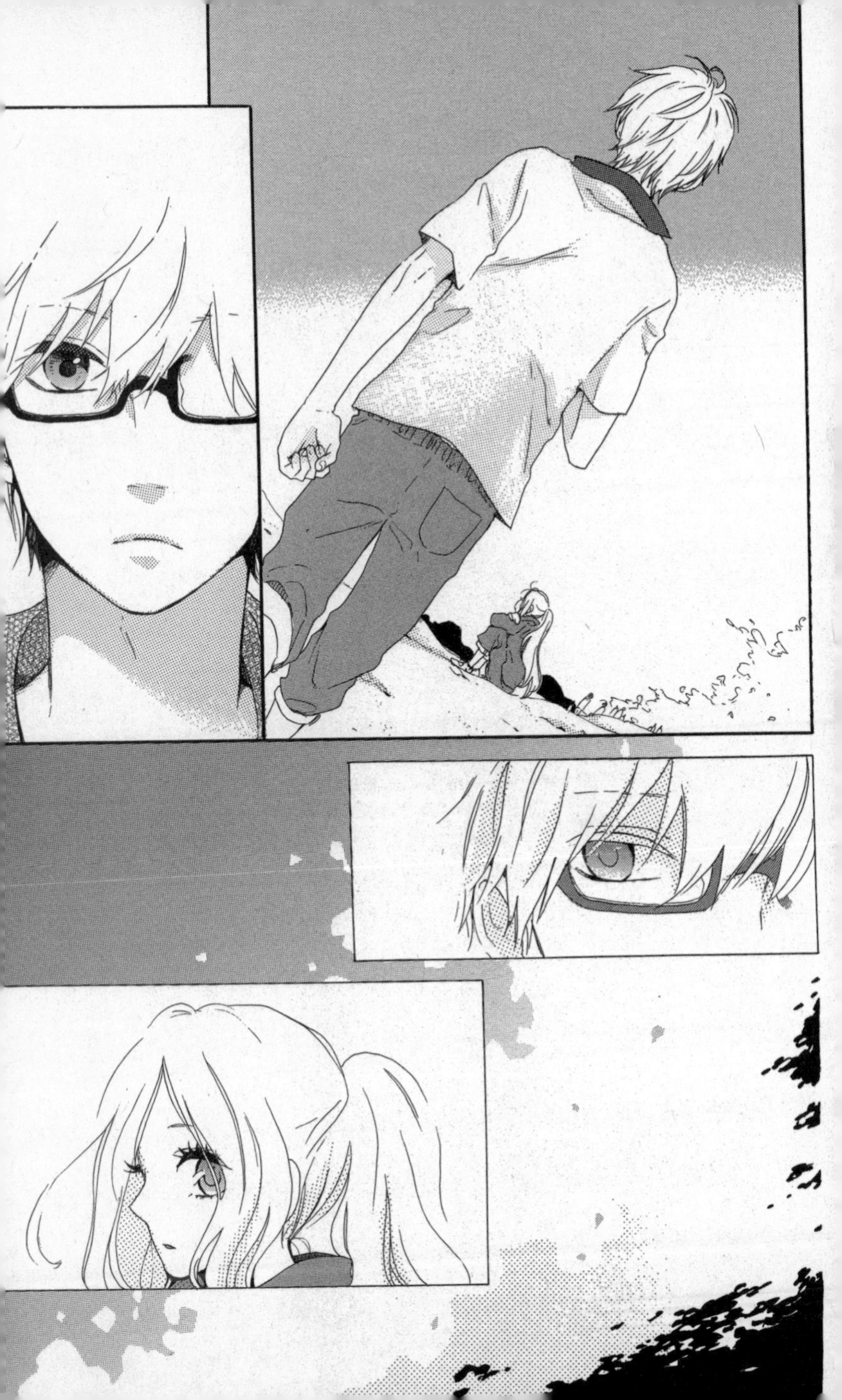

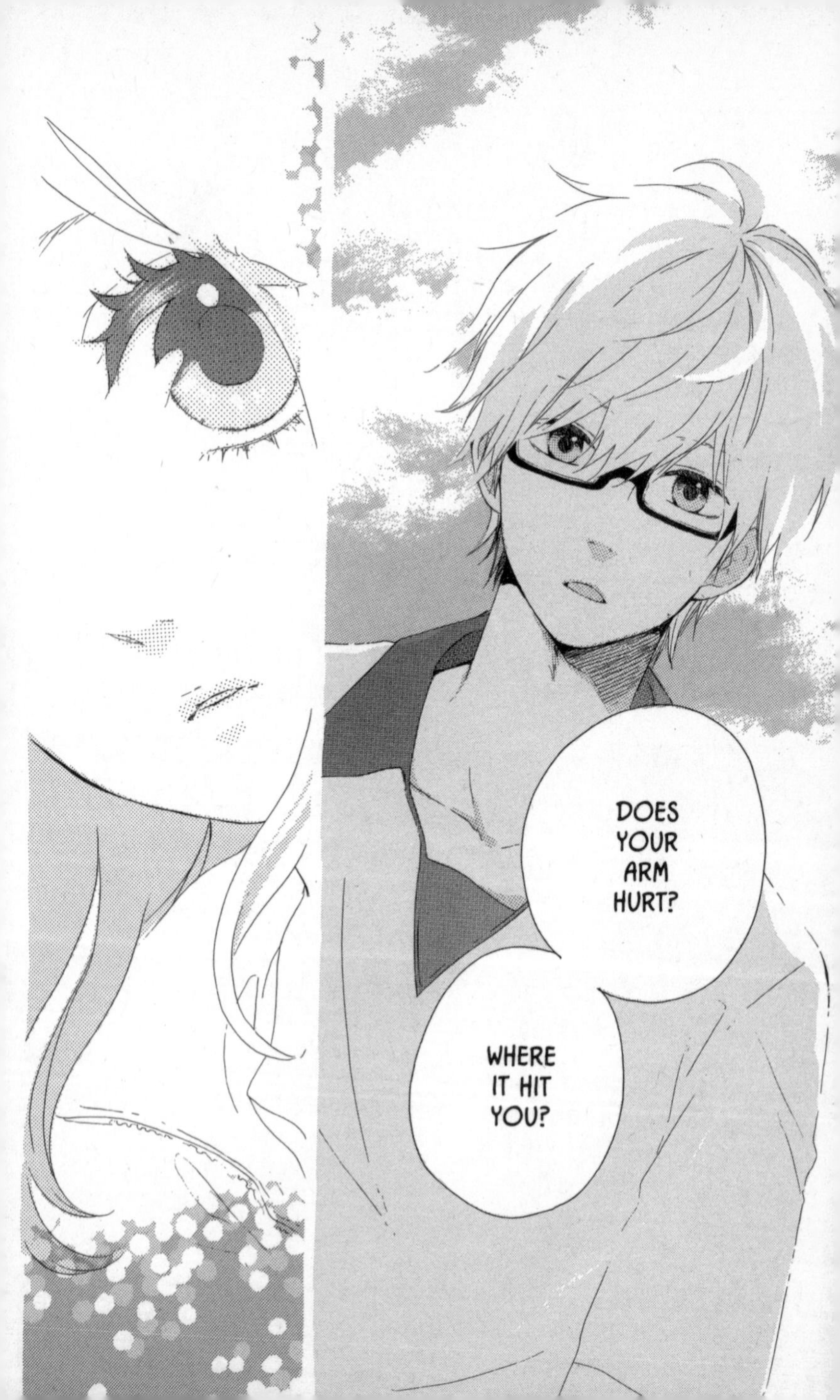
DOES YOUR ARM HURT?
WHERE IT HIT YOU?

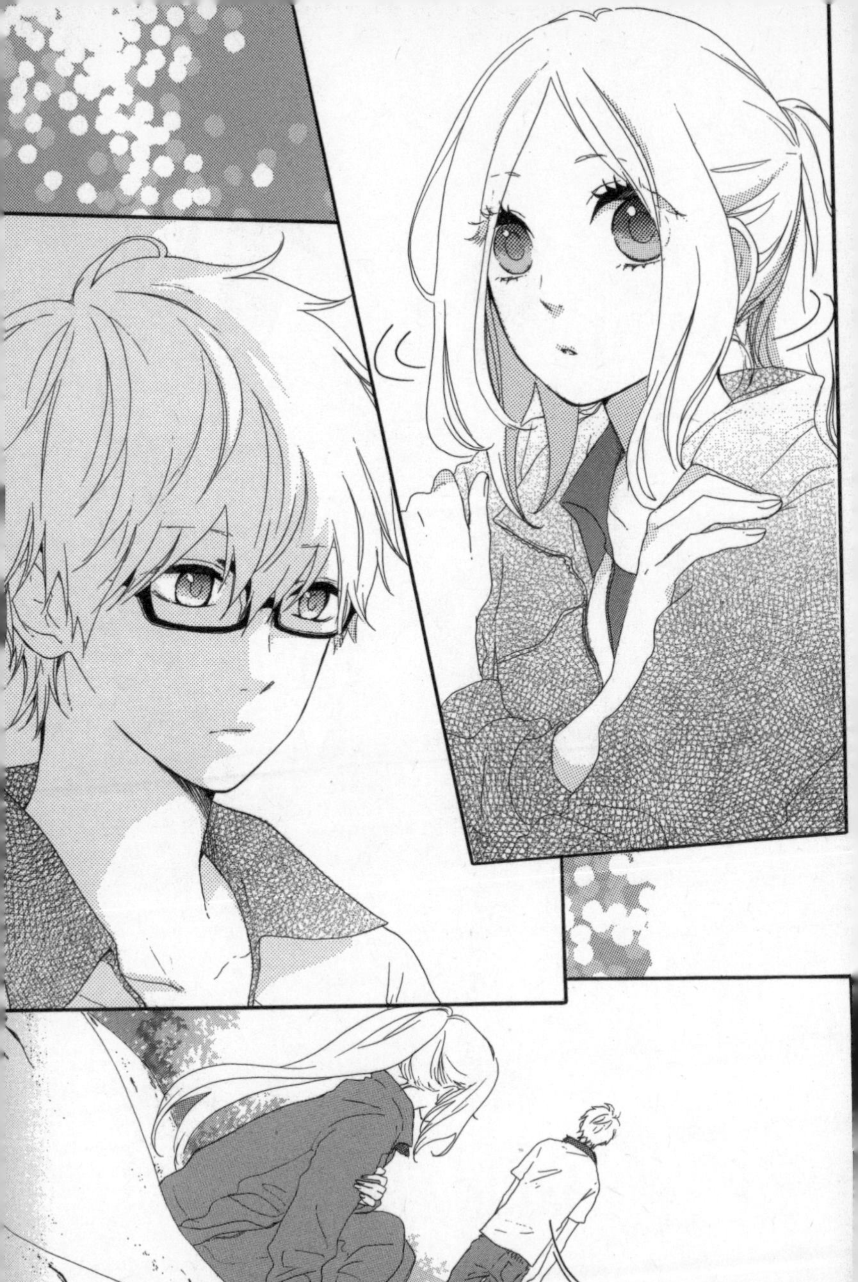

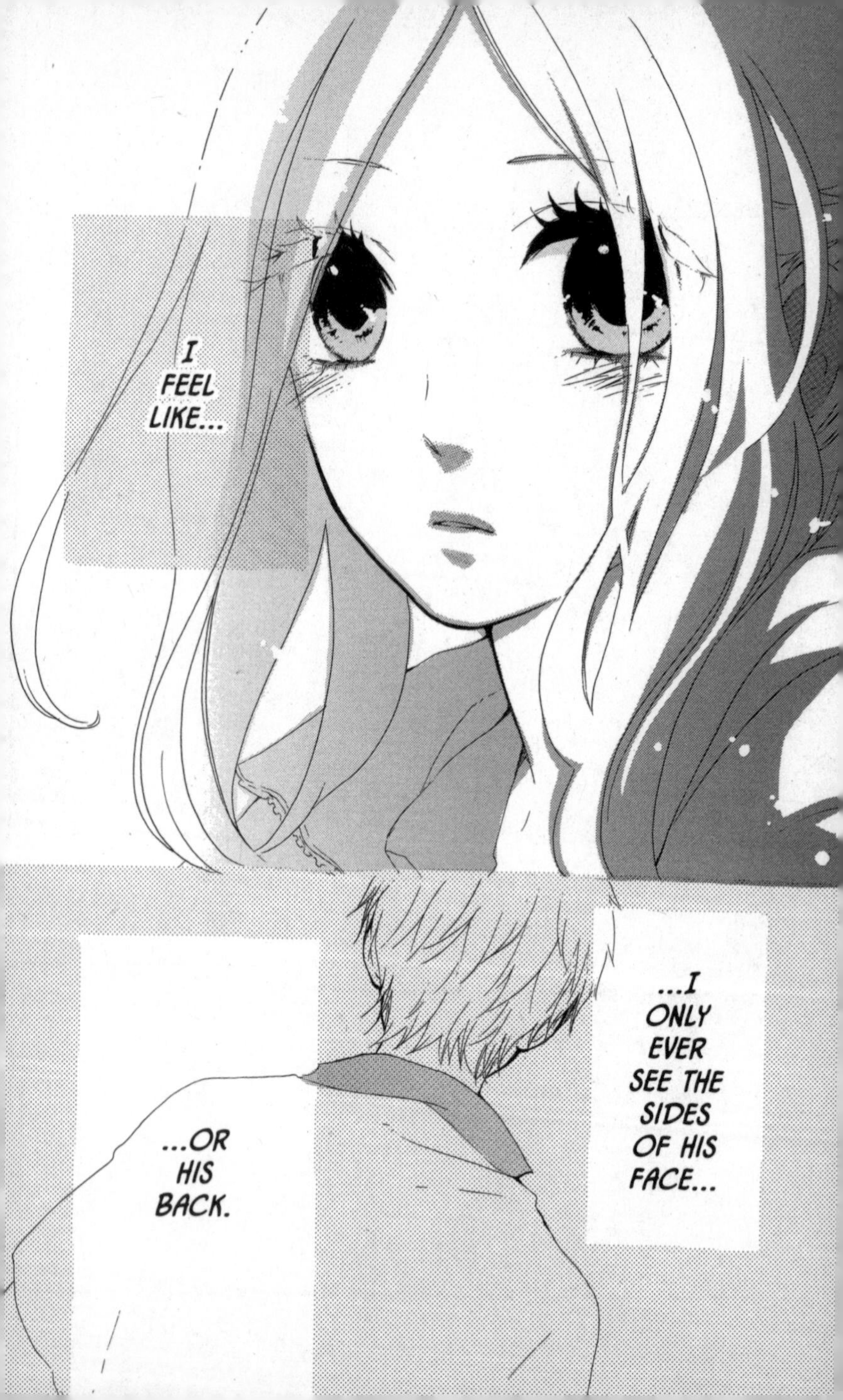
I FEEL LIKE...
...I ONLY EVER SEE THE SIDES OF HIS FACE...
...OR HIS BACK.

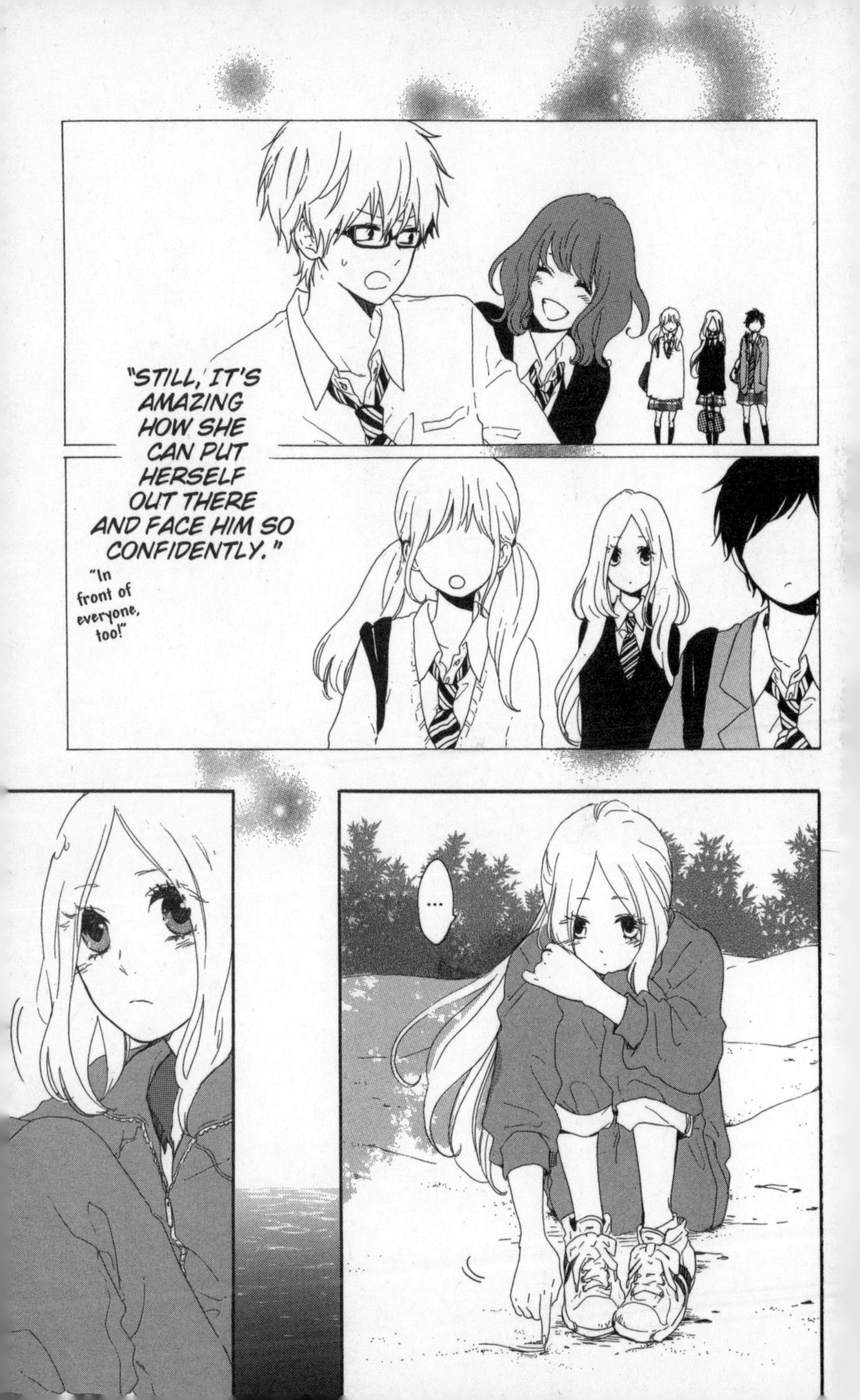
"STILL, IT'S AMAZING HOW SHE CAN PUT HERSELF OUT THERE AND FACE HIM SO CONFIDENTLY."
"In front of everyone, too!"
...

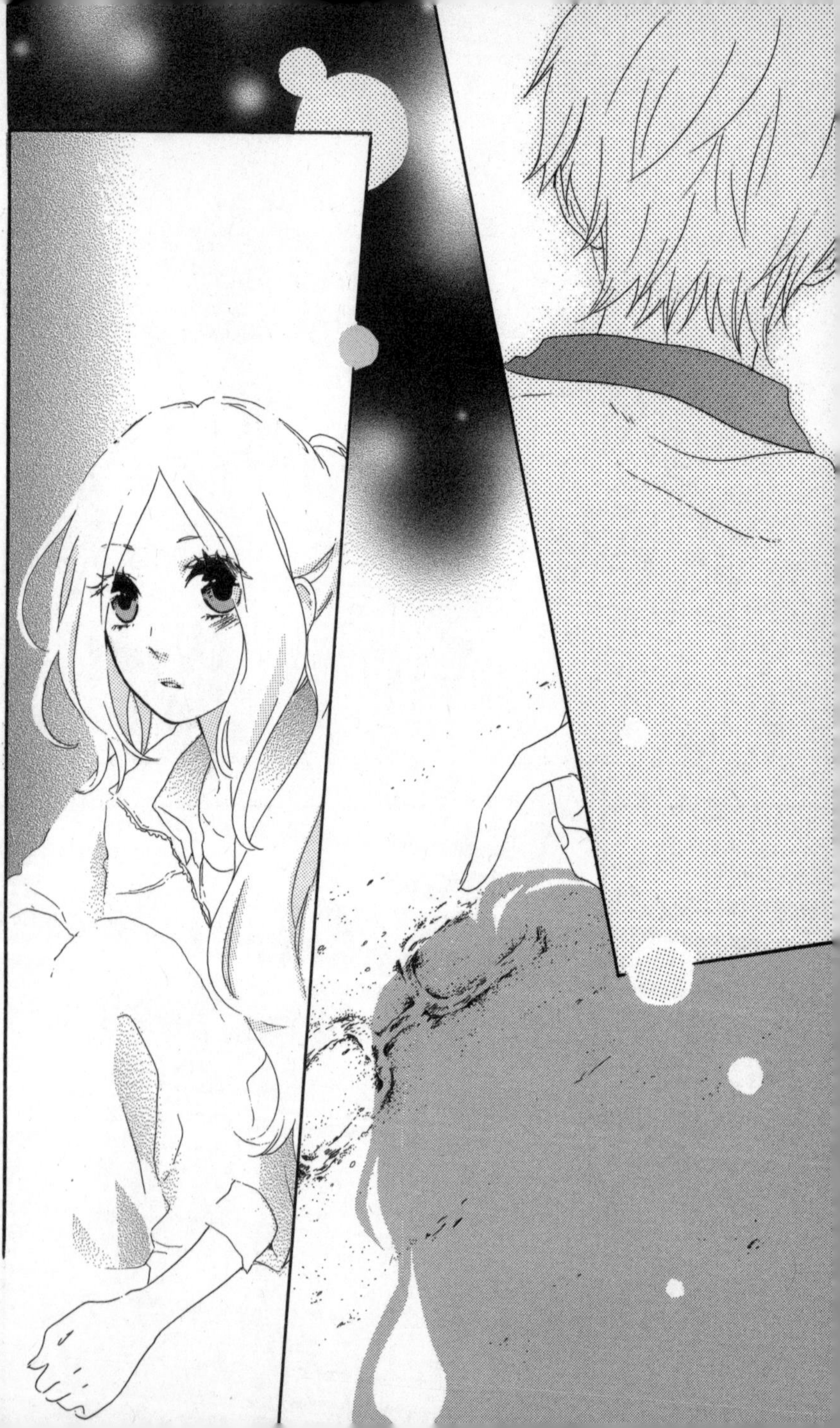

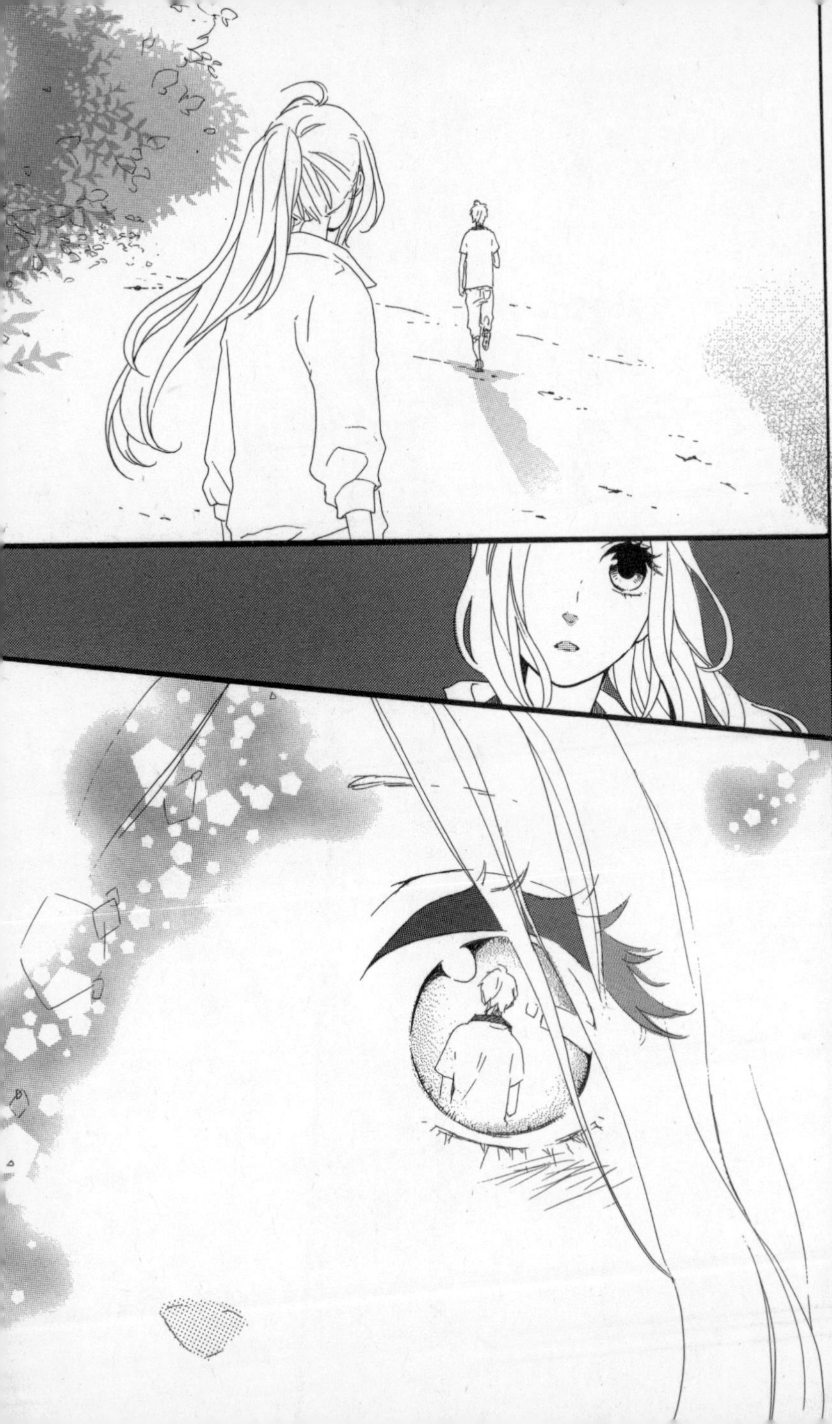

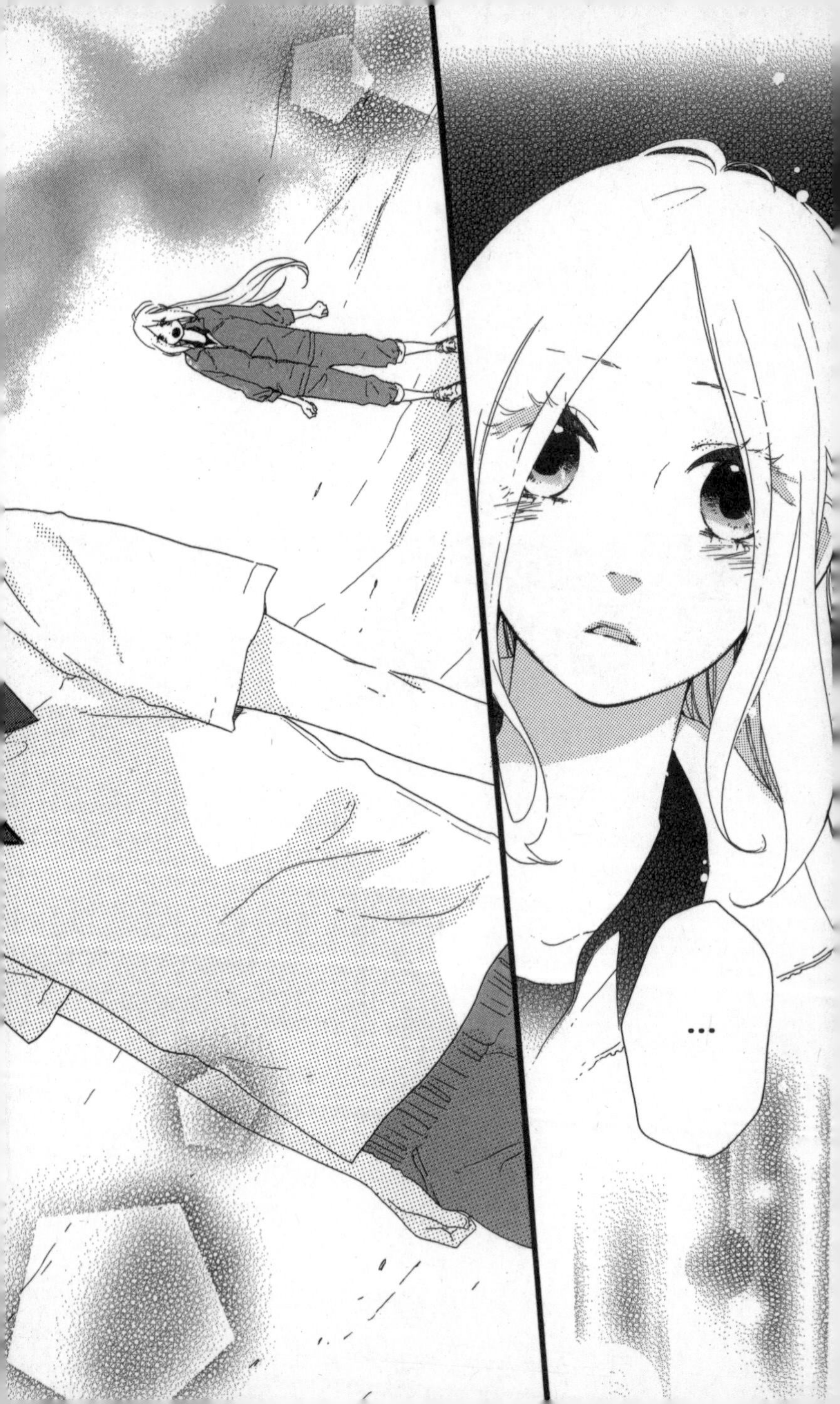
...

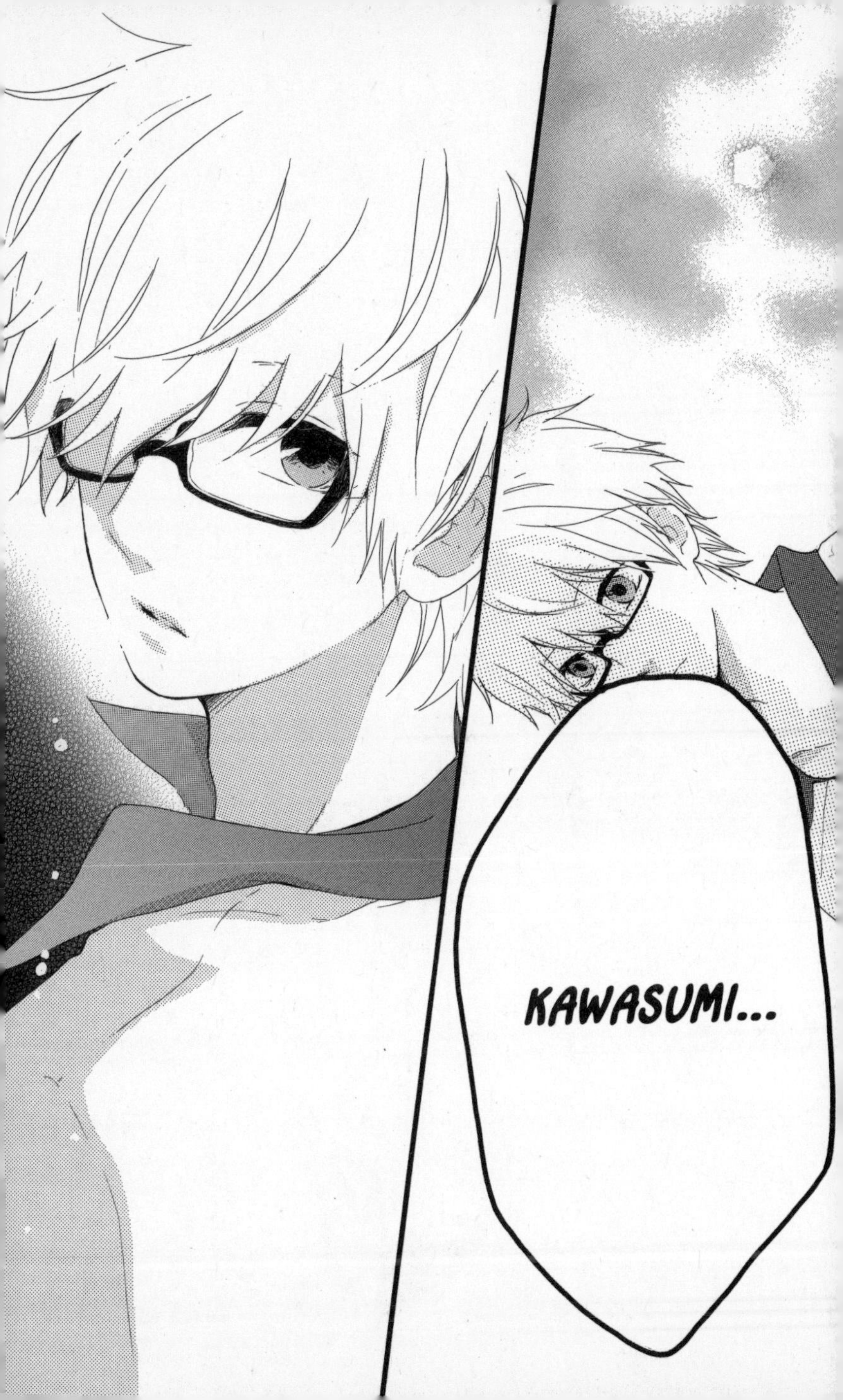
KAWASUMI...

CHAPTER 6

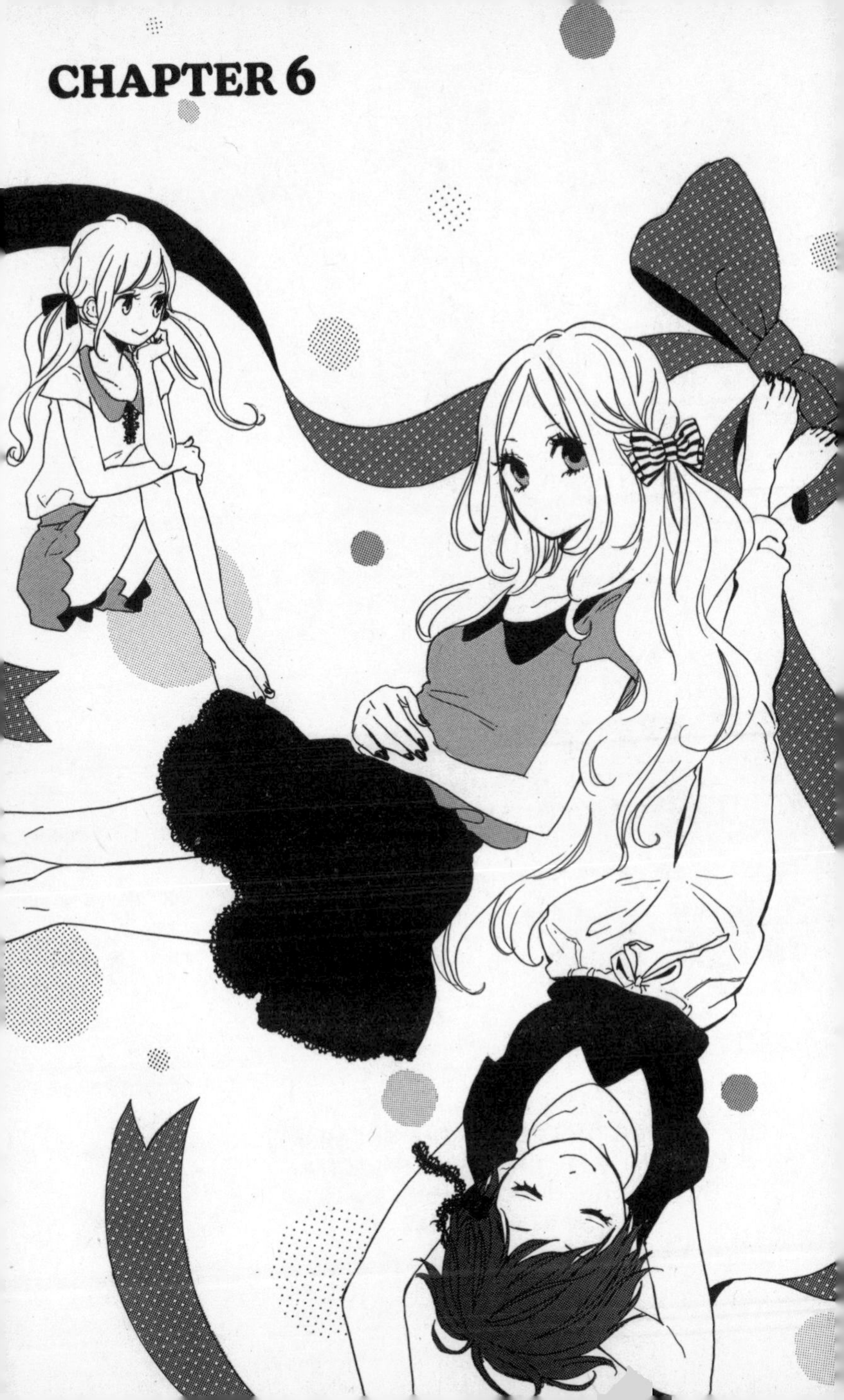

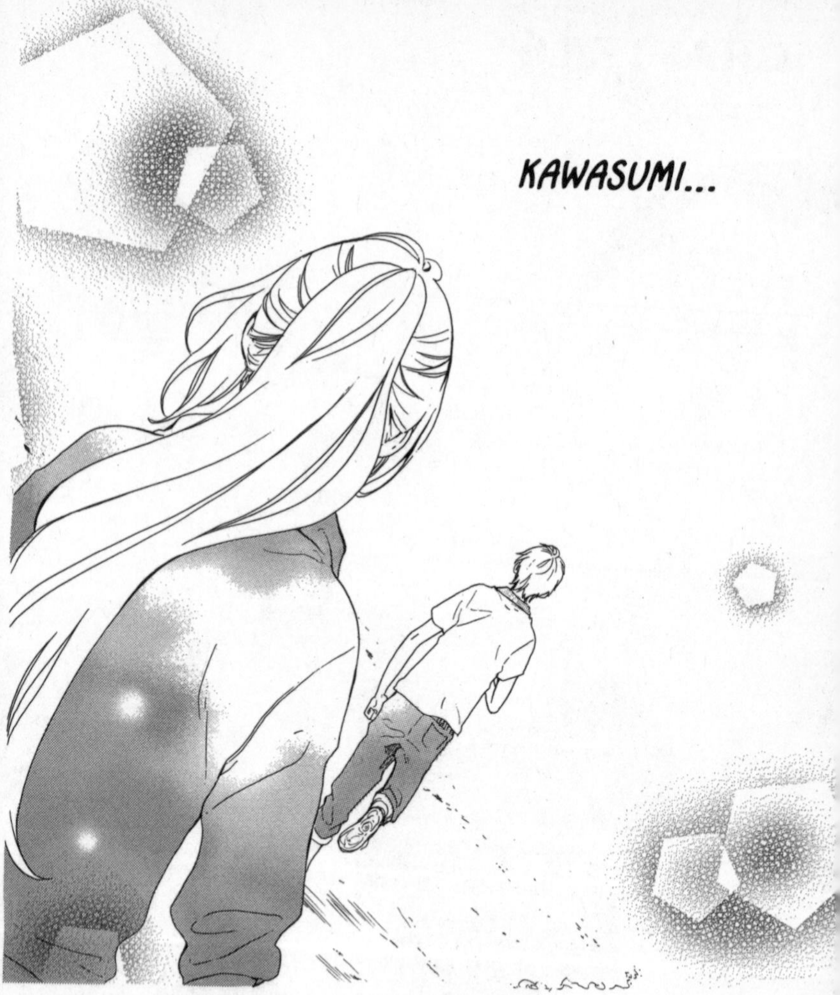
KAWASUMI...

I WAS SO HAPPY WHEN I GOT MY FIRST COLOR INSERT. IN THE ONE-SHOT, KAWASUMI WAS THE MAIN CHARACTER, BUT IN THIS VERSION, SUIREN IS THE MAIN CHARACTER.

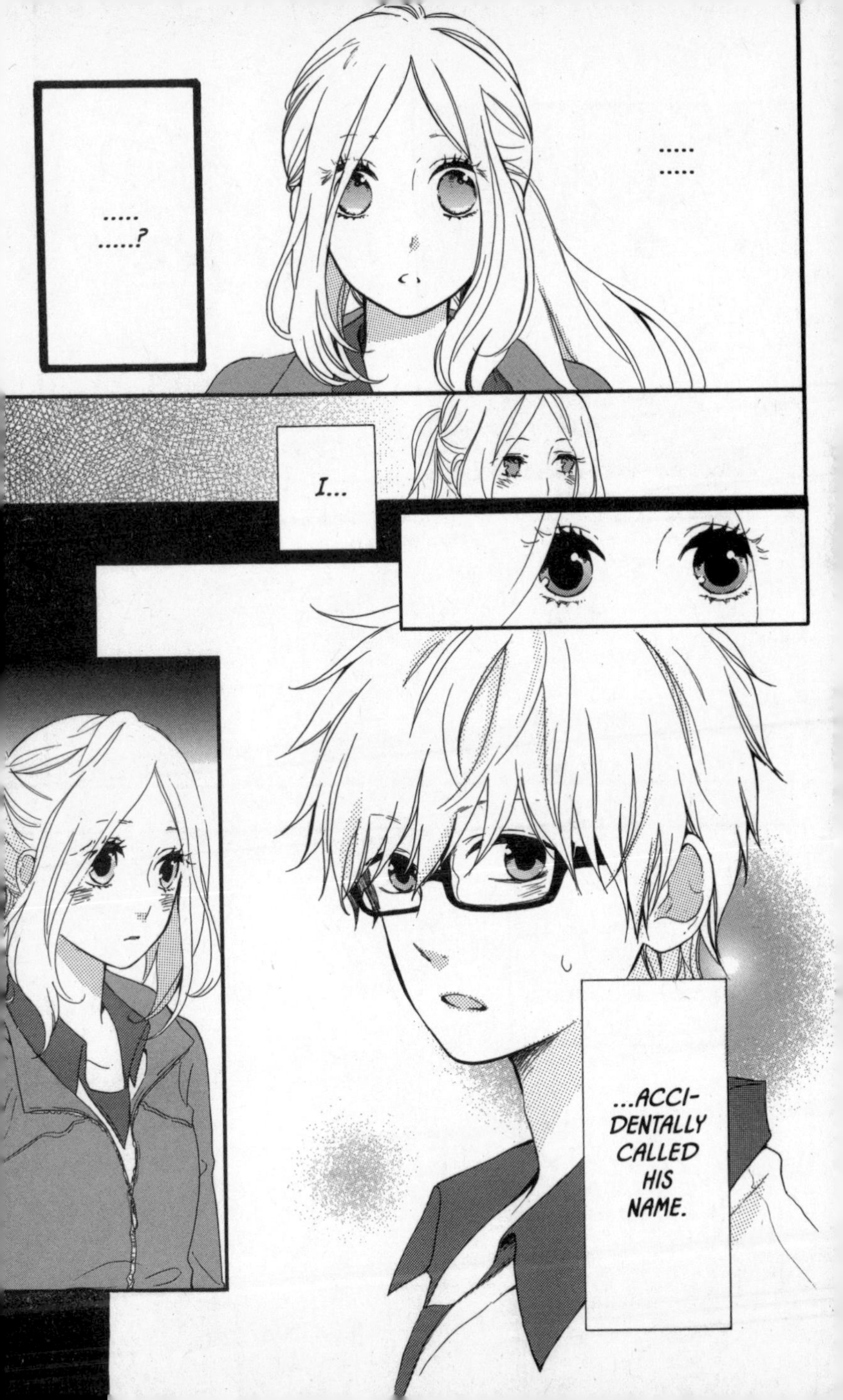
.....
.....
.....
.....?
I...
...ACCI-
DENTALLY
CALLED
HIS
NAME.

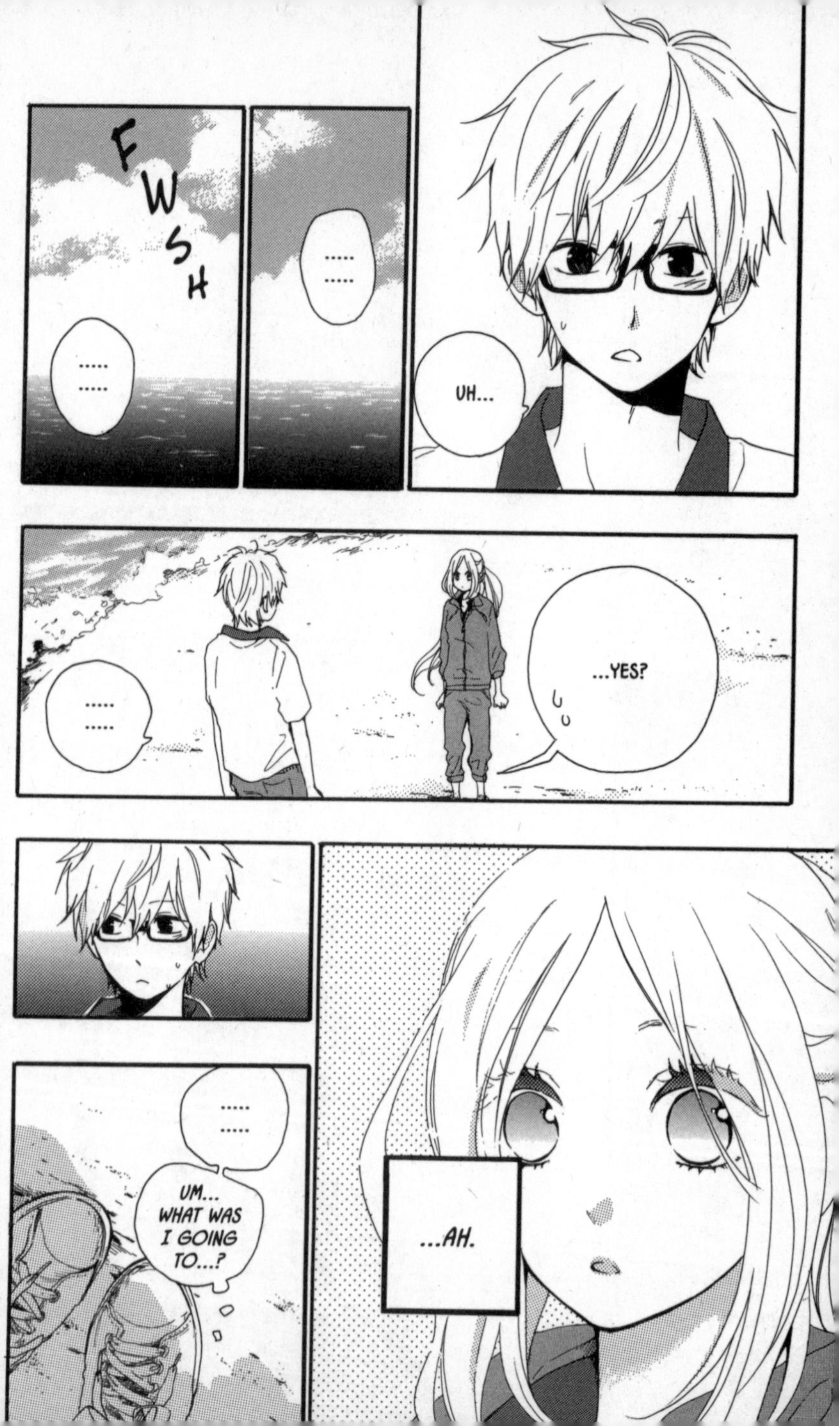
UH...
......
......
FWSH
......
......
...YES?
......
......
...AH.
......
......
UM... WHAT WAS I GOING TO...?

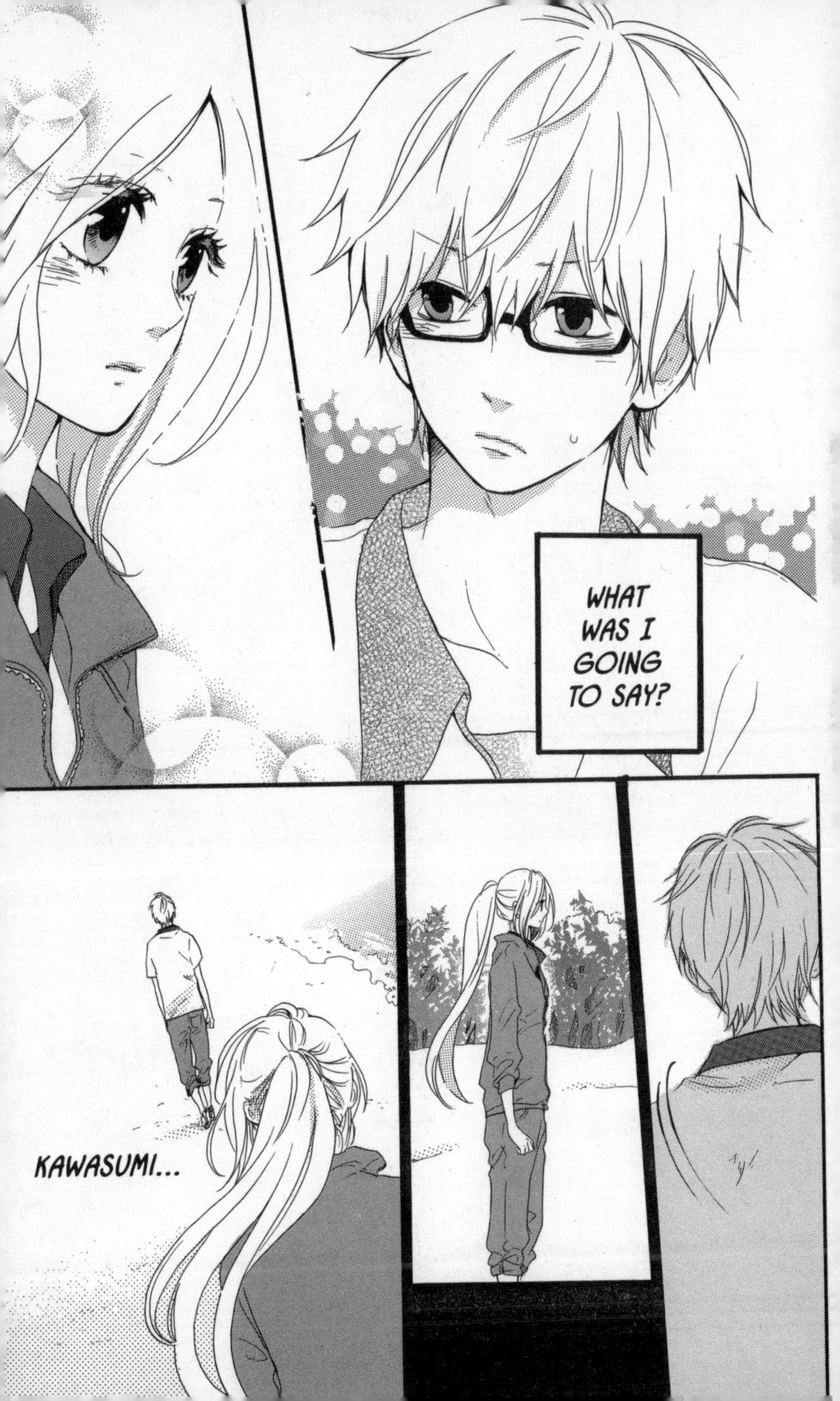
WHAT WAS I GOING TO SAY?
KAWASUMI...

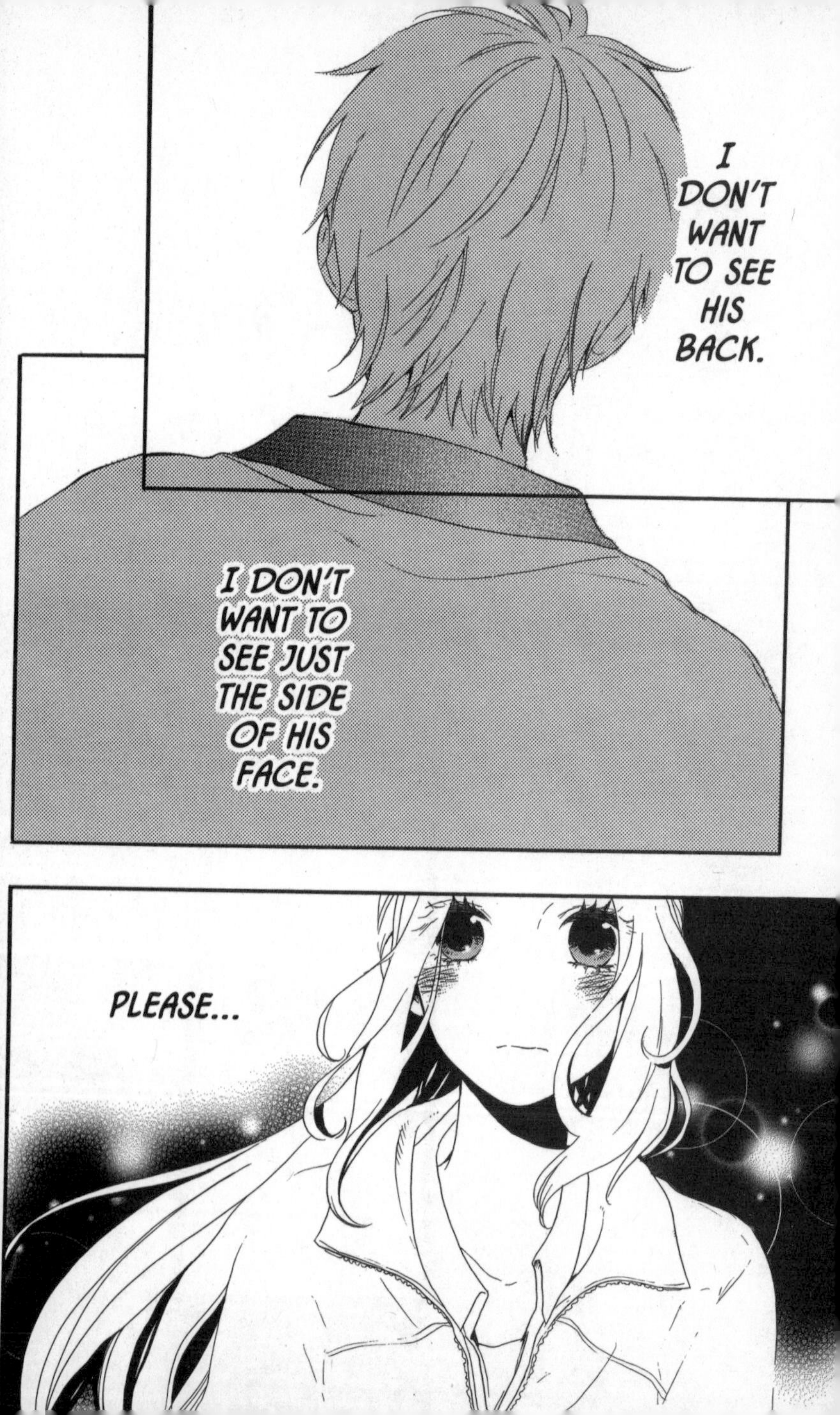
I DON'T WANT TO SEE HIS BACK.
I DON'T WANT TO SEE JUST THE SIDE OF HIS FACE.
PLEASE...

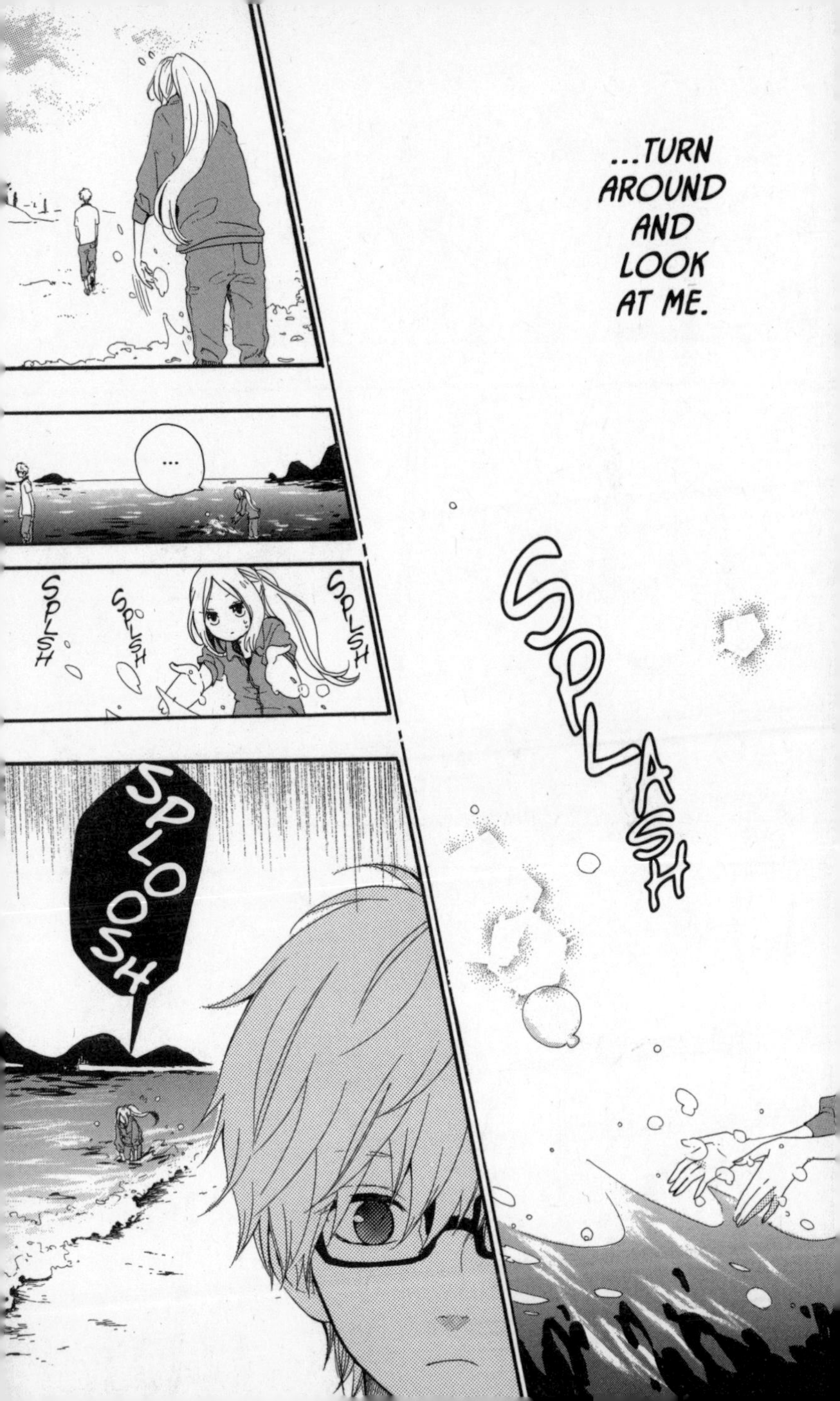
...TURN AROUND AND LOOK AT ME.
SPLASH
...
SPLSH
SPLSH
SPLSH
SPLOOSH

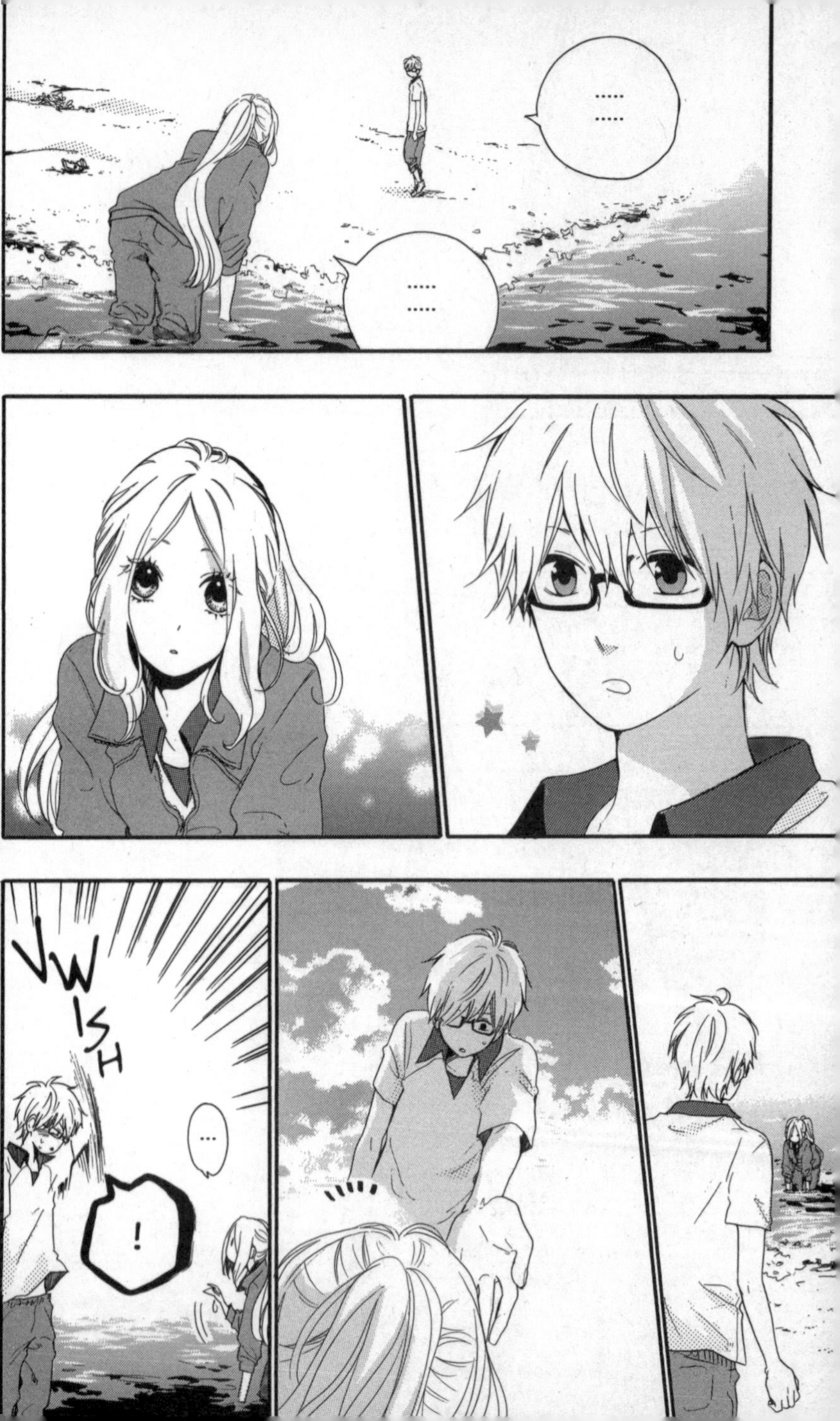
....
....
SWISH
...
!

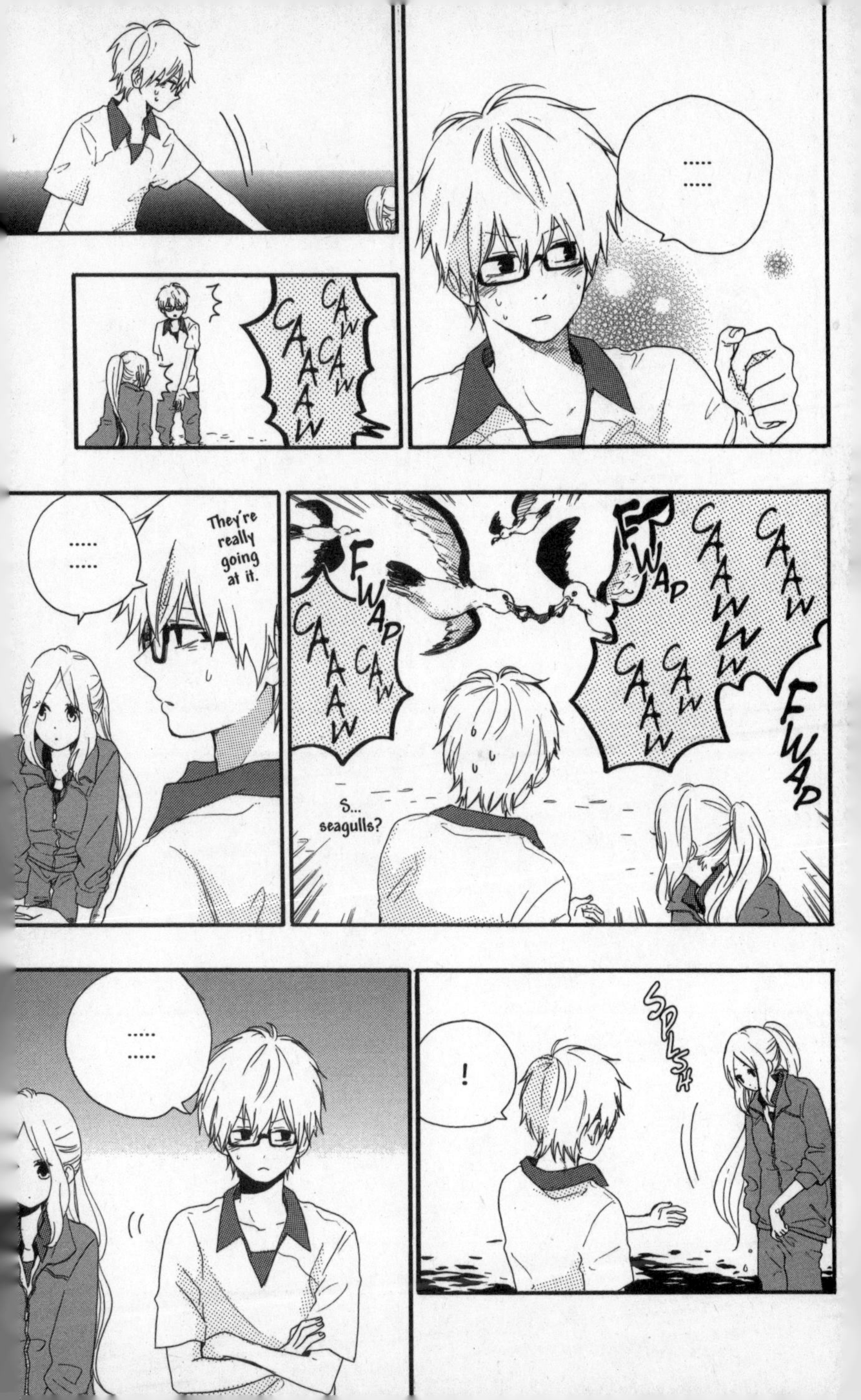

......
......
CAW CAW
CAAAAW
FTWAP
CAAAWWW
CAAAW
CAW
CAAAW
FWAP
FWAP
CAW
CAAAAW
S... seagulls?
They're really going at it.
......
......
SPLSH
!
......
......

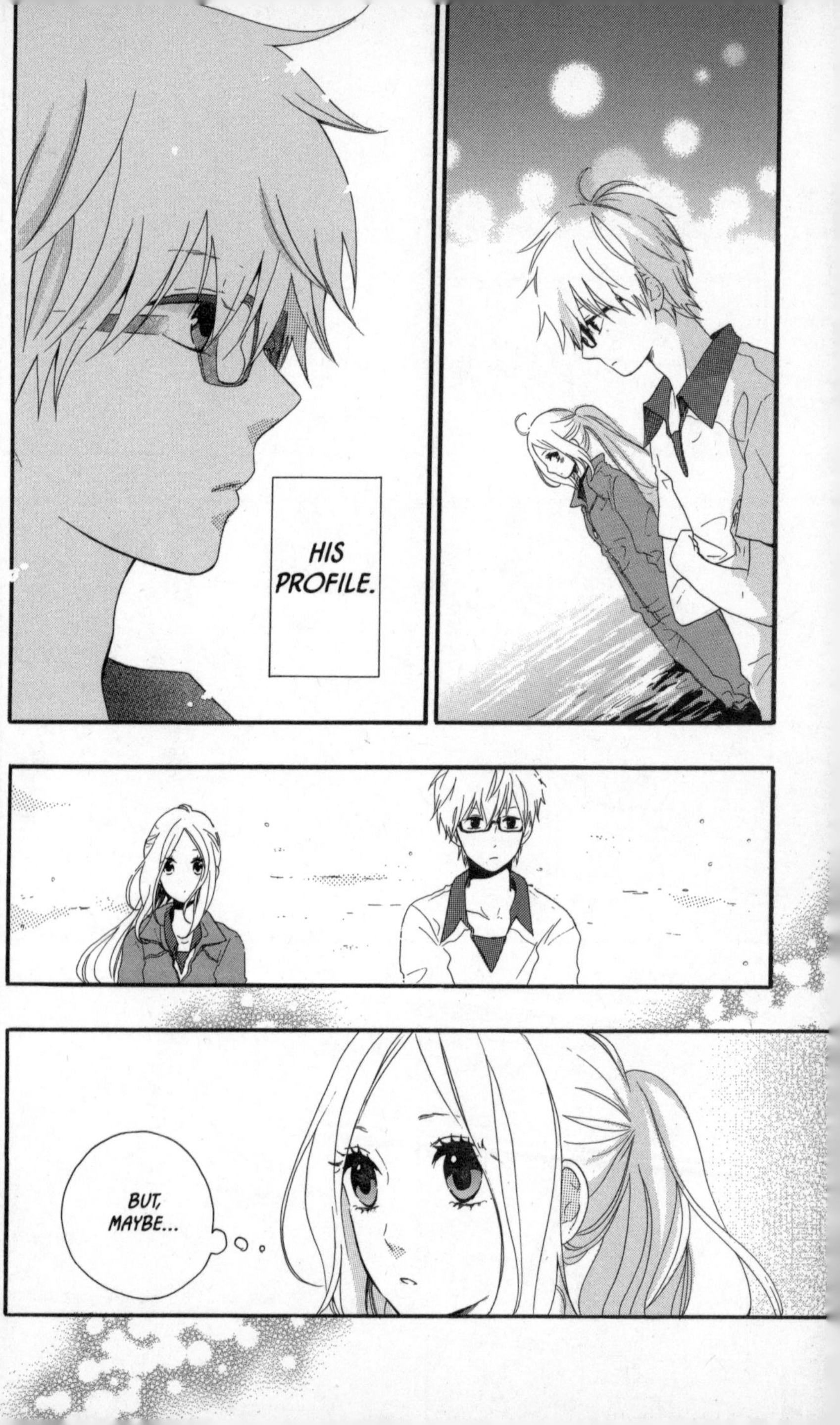
HIS PROFILE.
BUT, MAYBE...

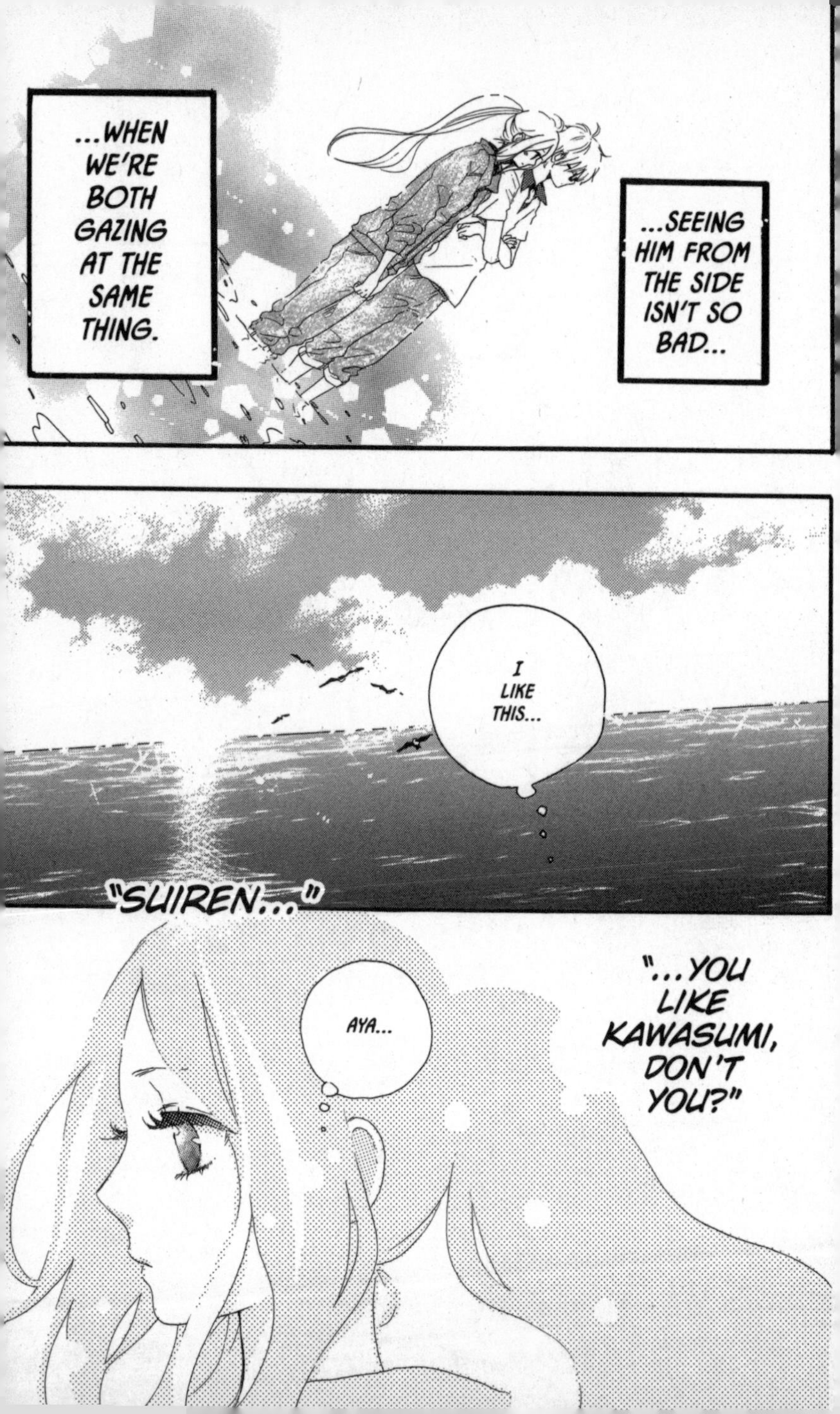
...SEEING HIM FROM THE SIDE ISN'T SO BAD...
...WHEN WE'RE BOTH GAZING AT THE SAME THING.
I LIKE THIS...
"SUIREN..."
"...YOU LIKE KAWASUMI, DON'T YOU?"
AYA...

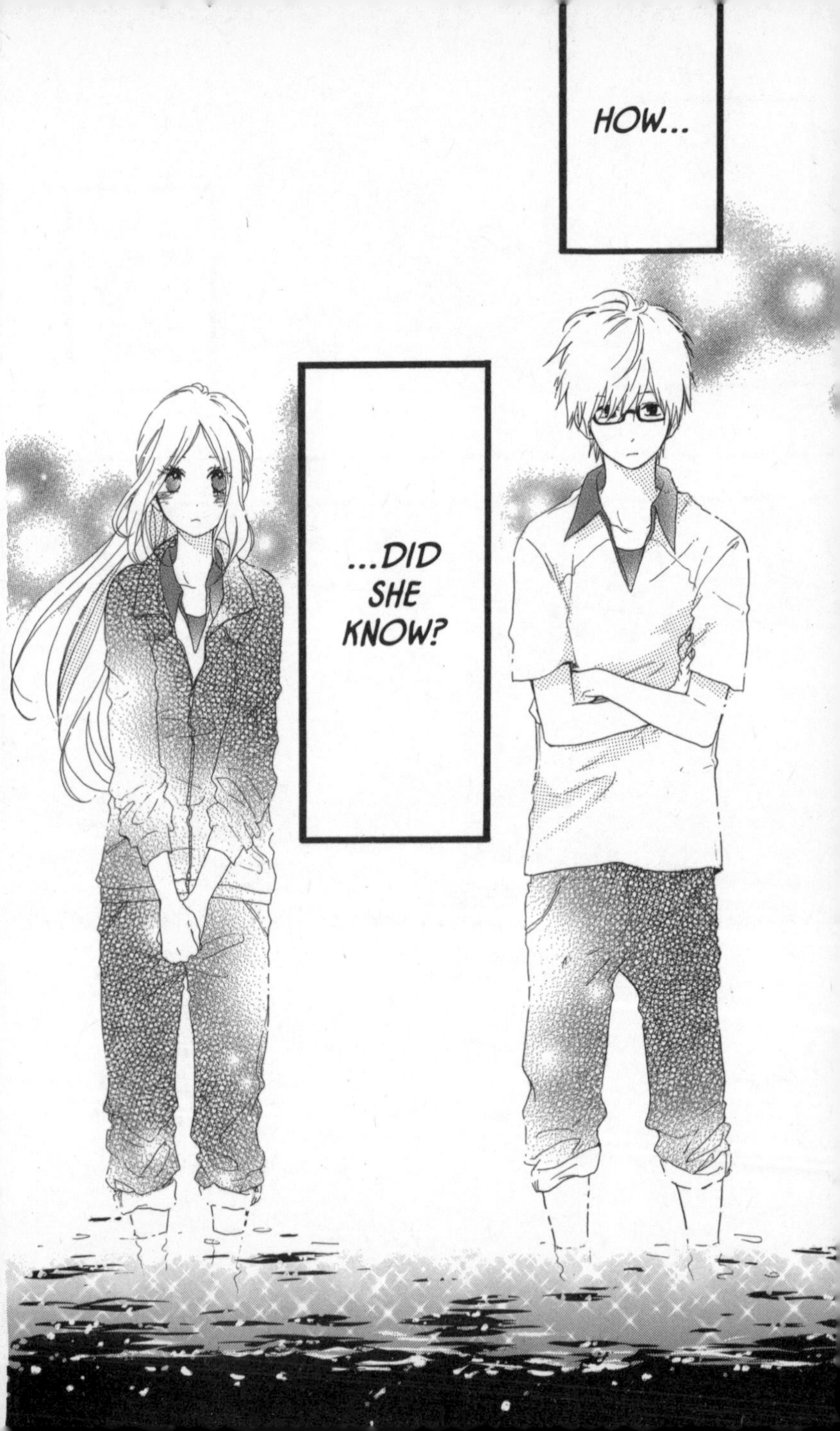
HOW...
...DID SHE KNOW?

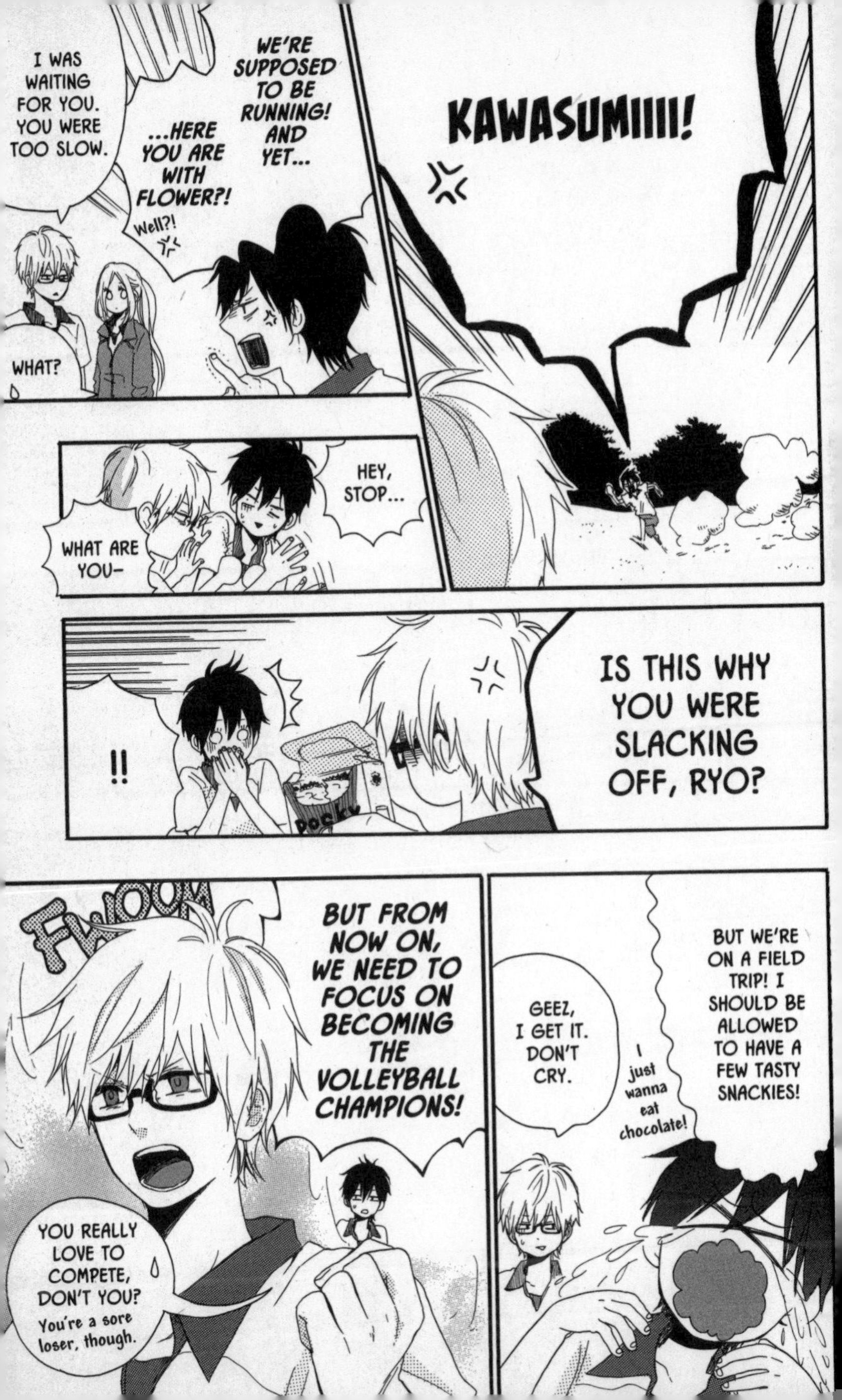
KAWASUMIIIII!
WE'RE SUPPOSED TO BE RUNNING! AND YET...
...HERE YOU ARE WITH FLOWER?!
I WAS WAITING FOR YOU. YOU WERE TOO SLOW.
Well?!
WHAT?
HEY, STOP...
WHAT ARE YOU–
IS THIS WHY YOU WERE SLACKING OFF, RYO?
!!
BUT WE'RE ON A FIELD TRIP! I SHOULD BE ALLOWED TO HAVE A FEW TASTY SNACKIES!
I just wanna eat chocolate!
GEEZ, I GET IT. DON'T CRY.
FWOOM
BUT FROM NOW ON, WE NEED TO FOCUS ON BECOMING THE VOLLEYBALL CHAMPIONS!
YOU REALLY LOVE TO COMPETE, DON'T YOU?
You're a sore loser, though.

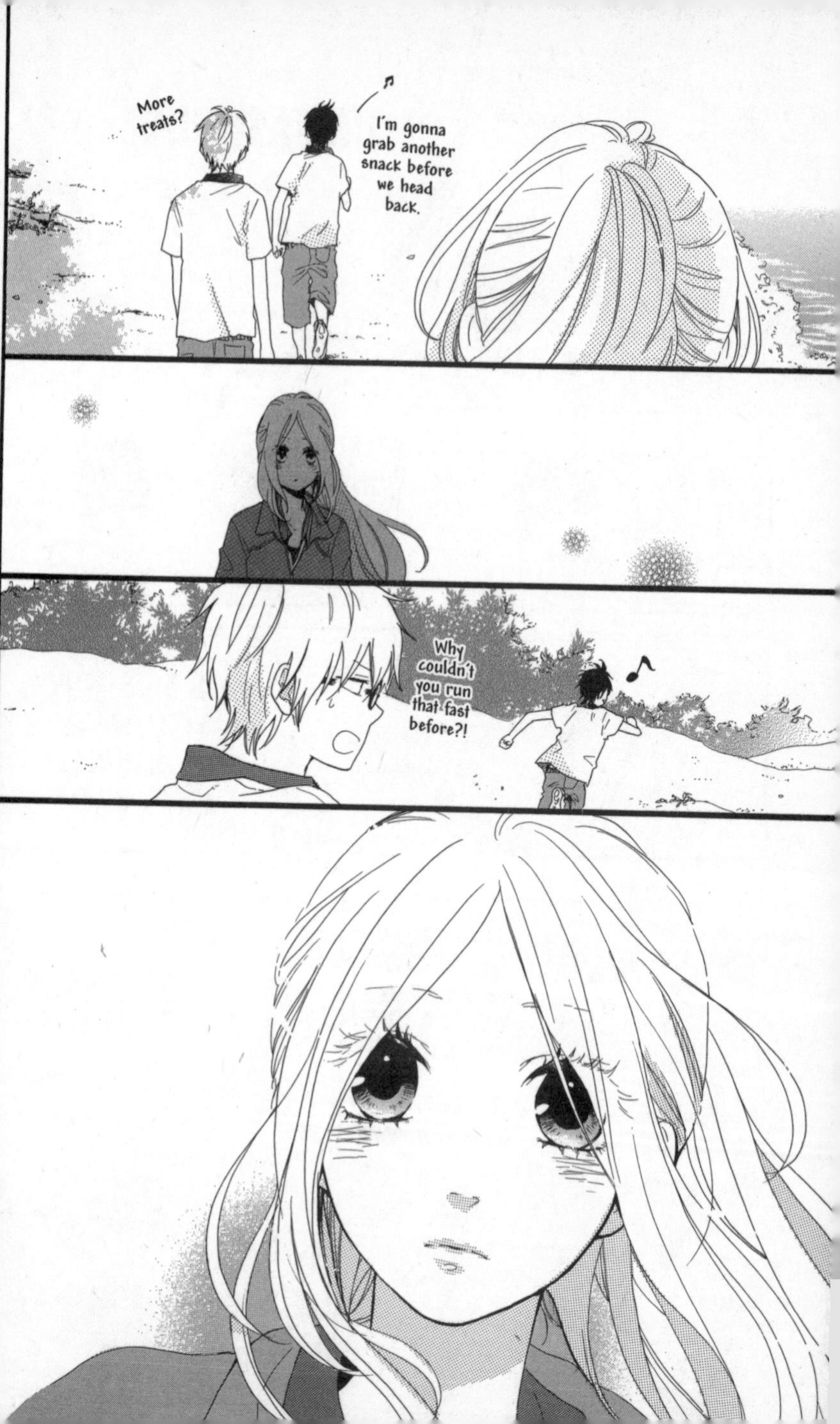
♪
I'm gonna grab another snack before we head back.
More treats?
Why couldn't you run that fast before?!
♪

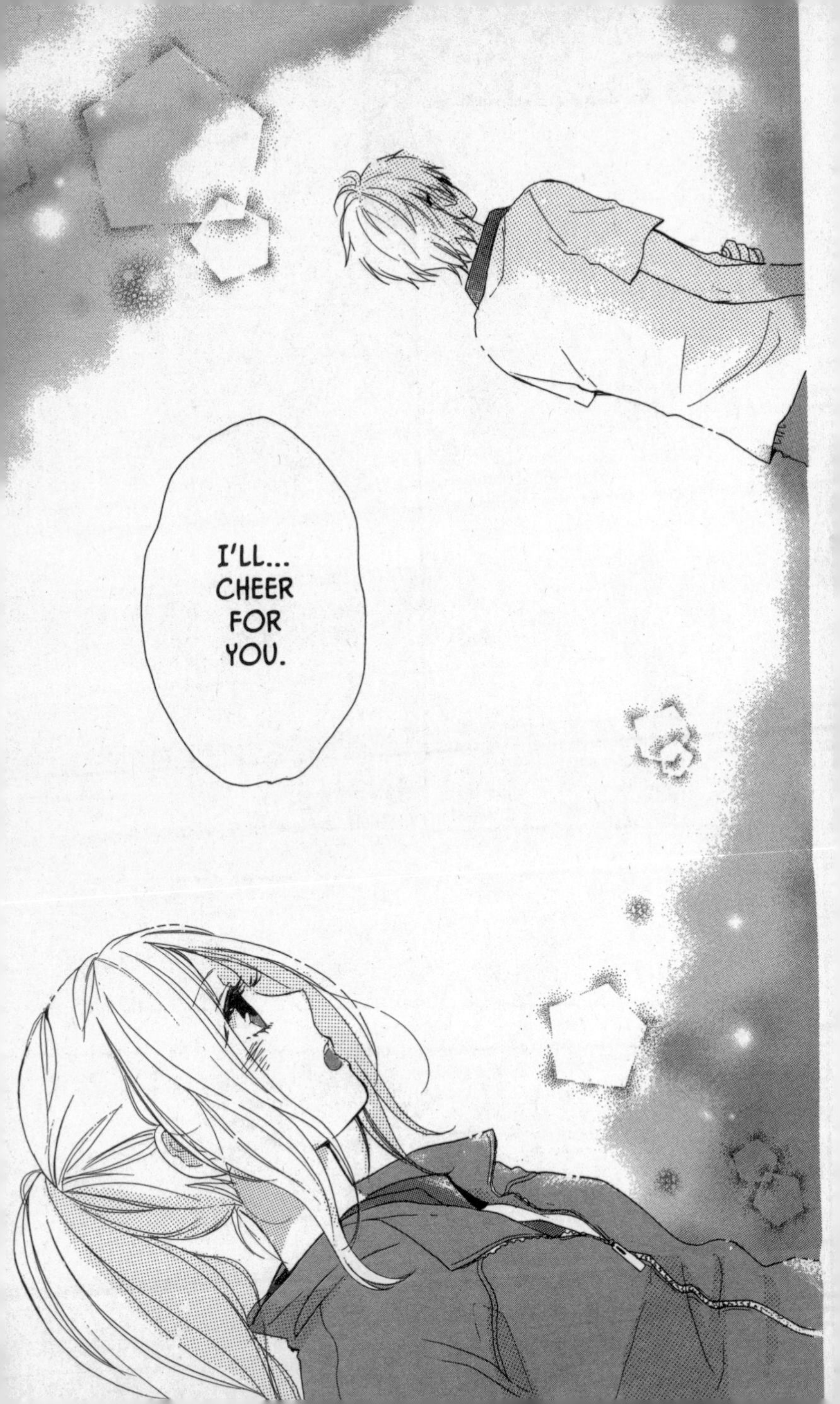
I'LL... CHEER FOR YOU.

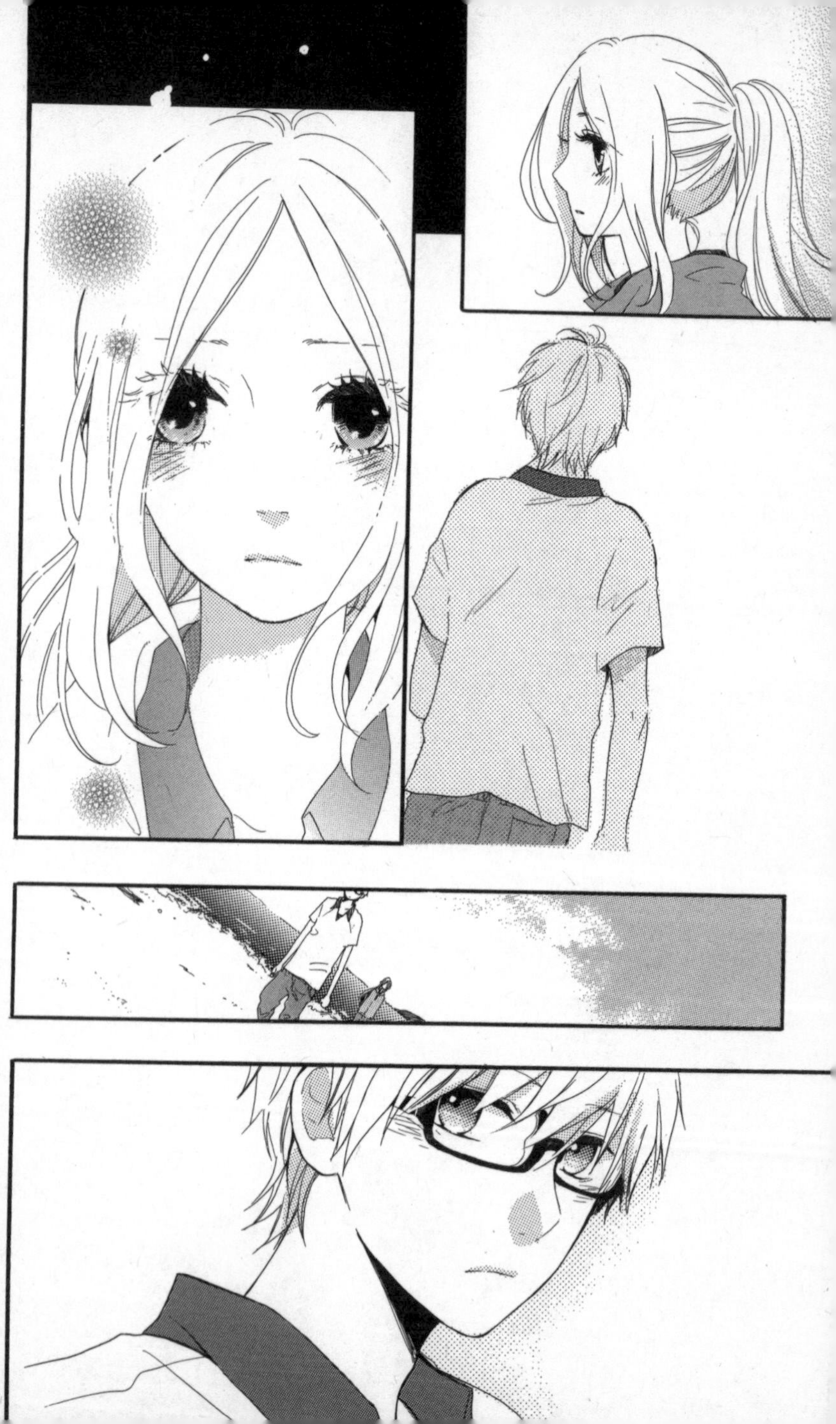

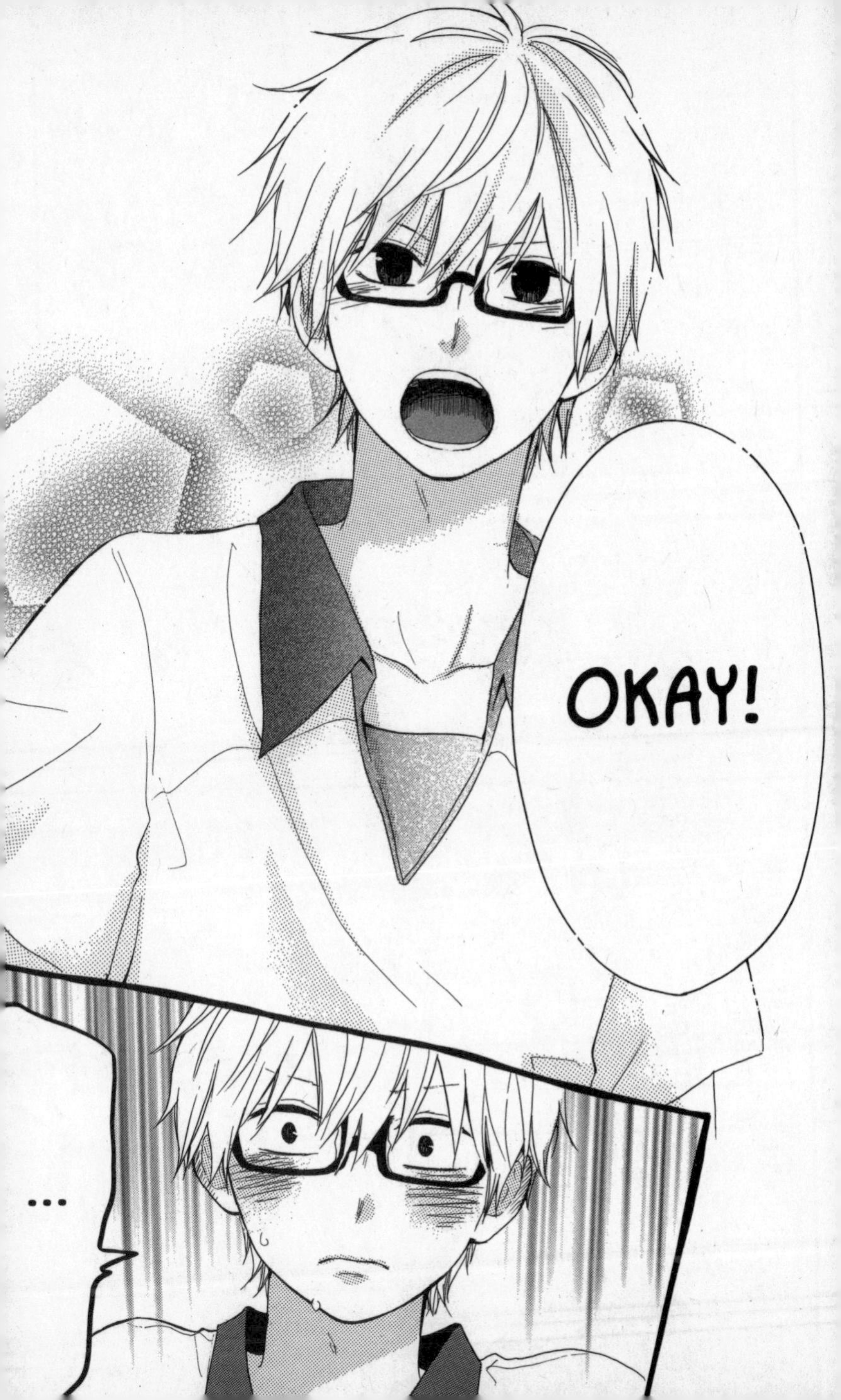
OKAY!
...

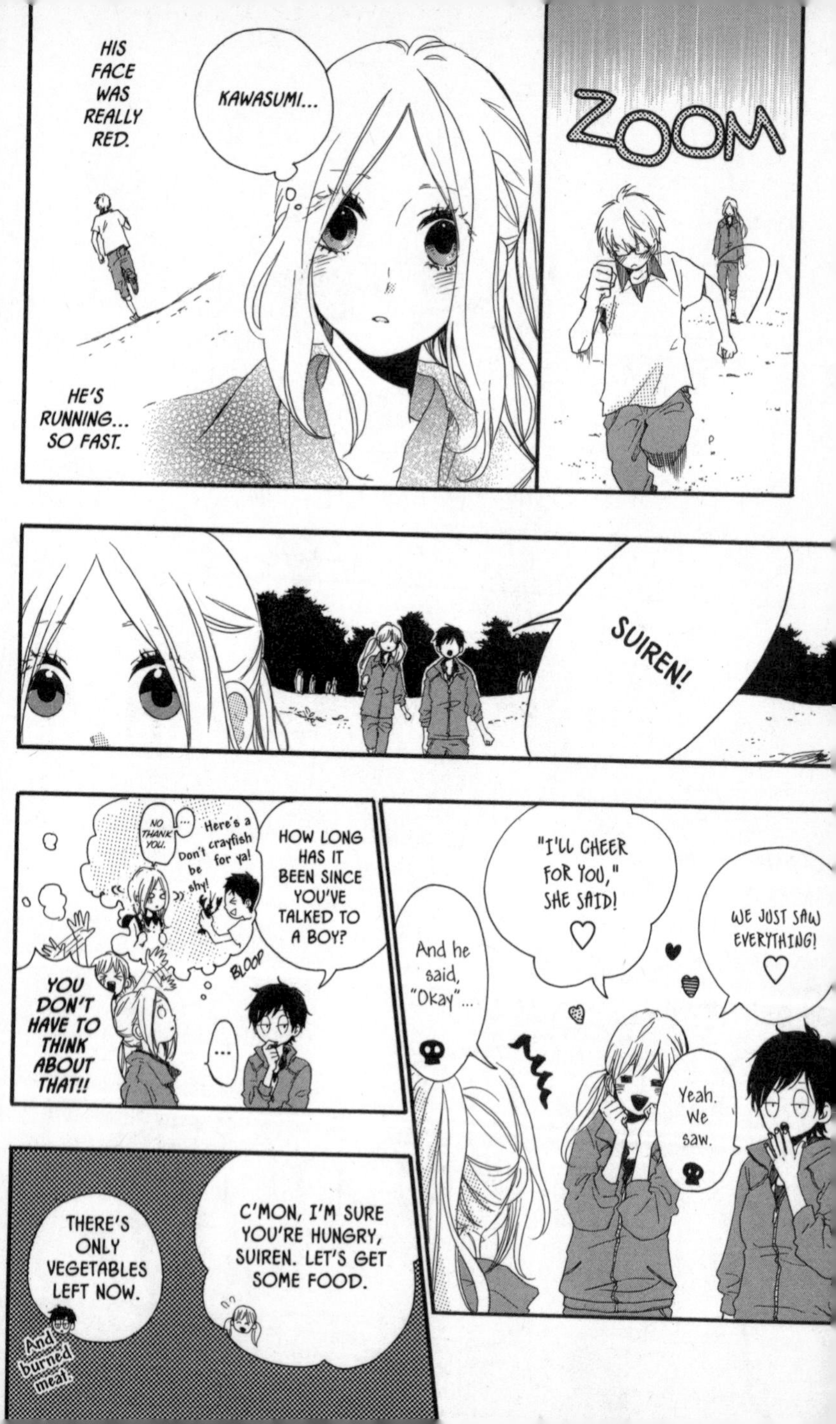
ZOOM
KAWASUMI...
HIS FACE WAS REALLY RED.
HE'S RUNNING... SO FAST.
SUIREN!
WE JUST SAW EVERYTHING!
"I'LL CHEER FOR YOU," SHE SAID!
And he said, "Okay"...
Yeah. We saw.
HOW LONG HAS IT BEEN SINCE YOU'VE TALKED TO A BOY?
Here's a crayfish for ya!
...
NO THANK YOU.
Don't be shy!
BLOOP
YOU DON'T HAVE TO THINK ABOUT THAT!!
...
C'MON, I'M SURE YOU'RE HUNGRY, SUIREN. LET'S GET SOME FOOD.
THERE'S ONLY VEGETABLES LEFT NOW.
And burned meat.

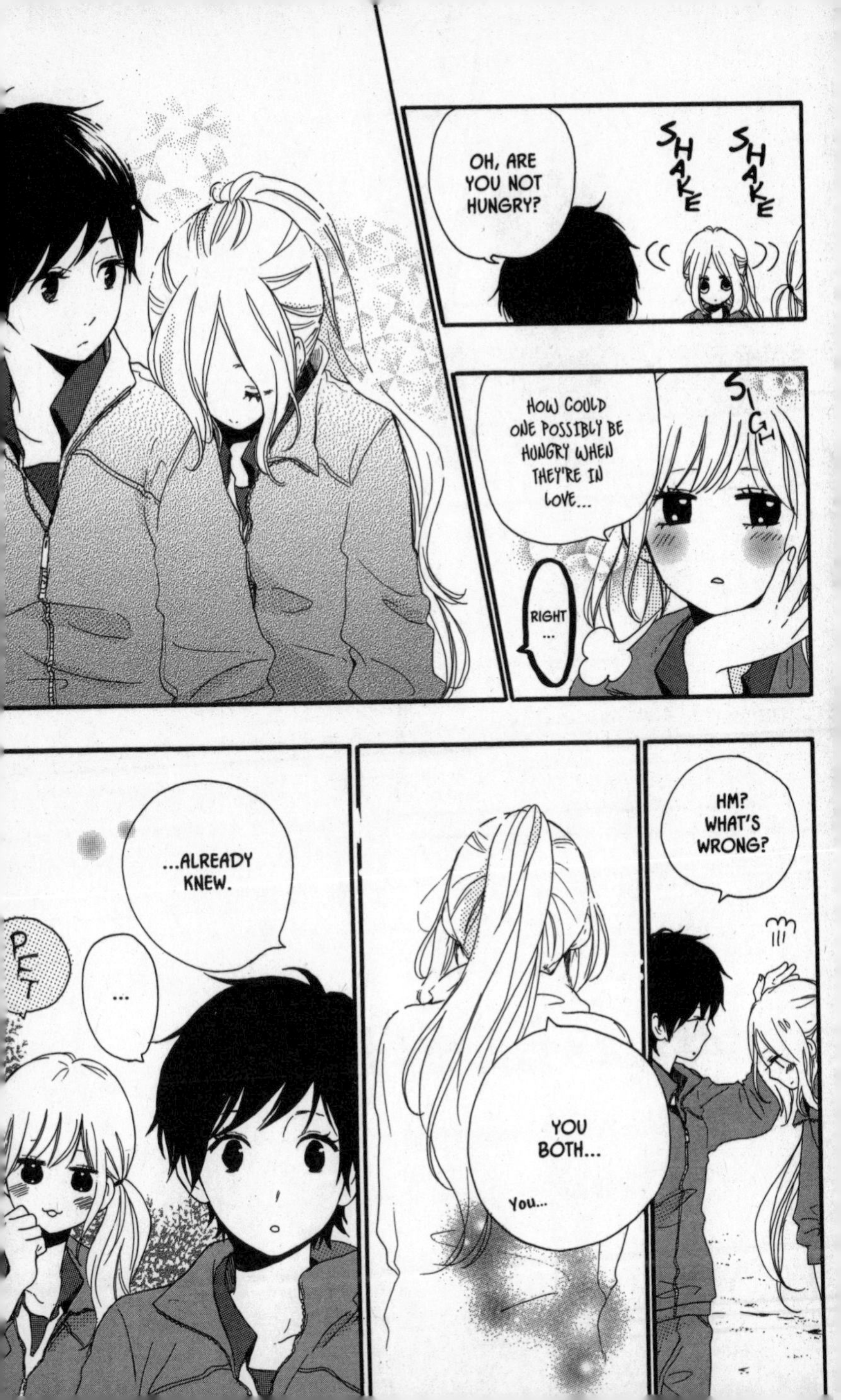
OH, ARE YOU NOT HUNGRY?
SHAKE SHAKE
SIGH
HOW COULD ONE POSSIBLY BE HUNGRY WHEN THEY'RE IN LOVE...
RIGHT...
HM? WHAT'S WRONG?
YOU BOTH...
You...
...ALREADY KNEW.
...
PET

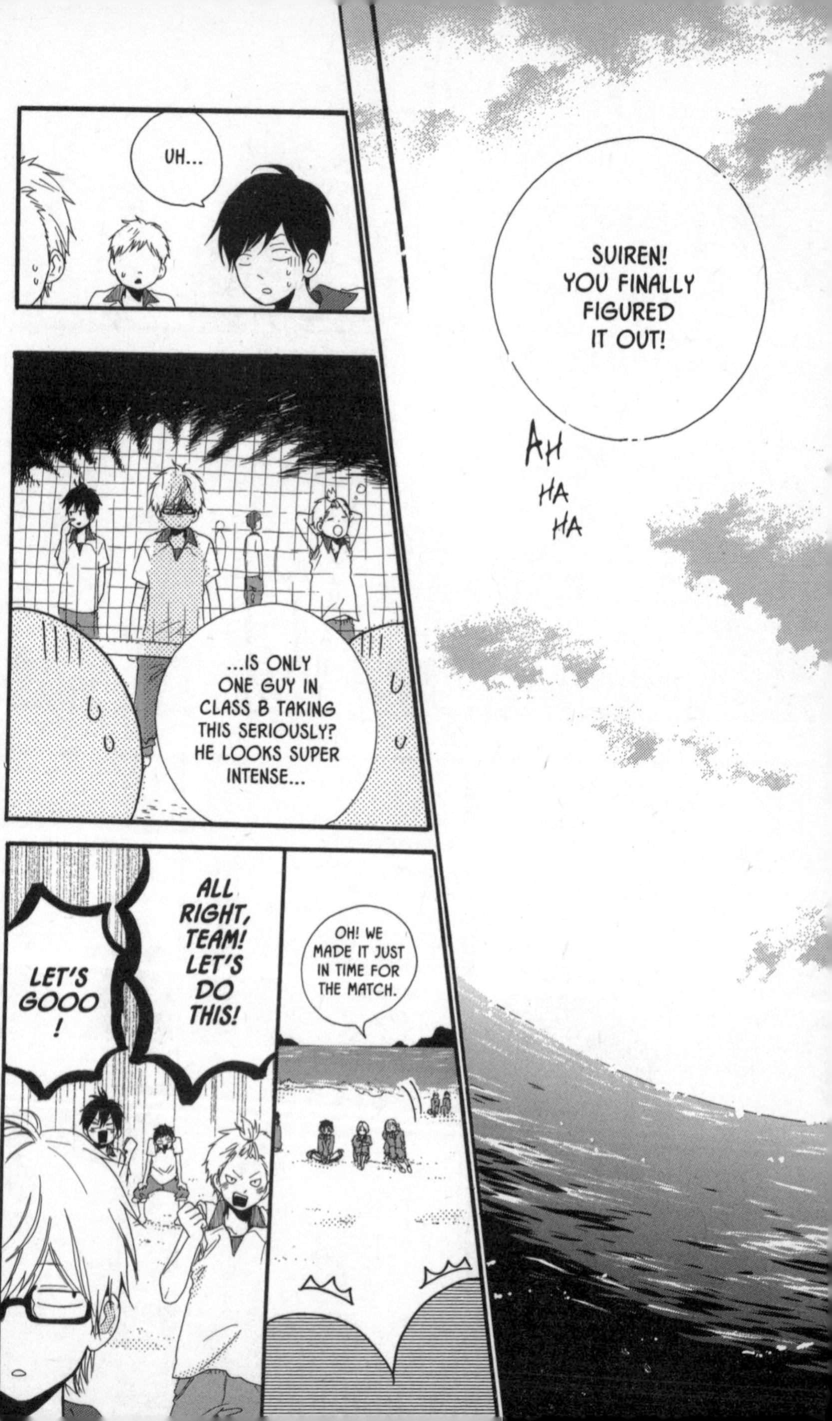
SUIREN! YOU FINALLY FIGURED IT OUT!
AH HA HA
UH...
...IS ONLY ONE GUY IN CLASS B TAKING THIS SERIOUSLY? HE LOOKS SUPER INTENSE...
OH! WE MADE IT JUST IN TIME FOR THE MATCH.
ALL RIGHT, TEAM! LET'S DO THIS!
LET'S GOOO!

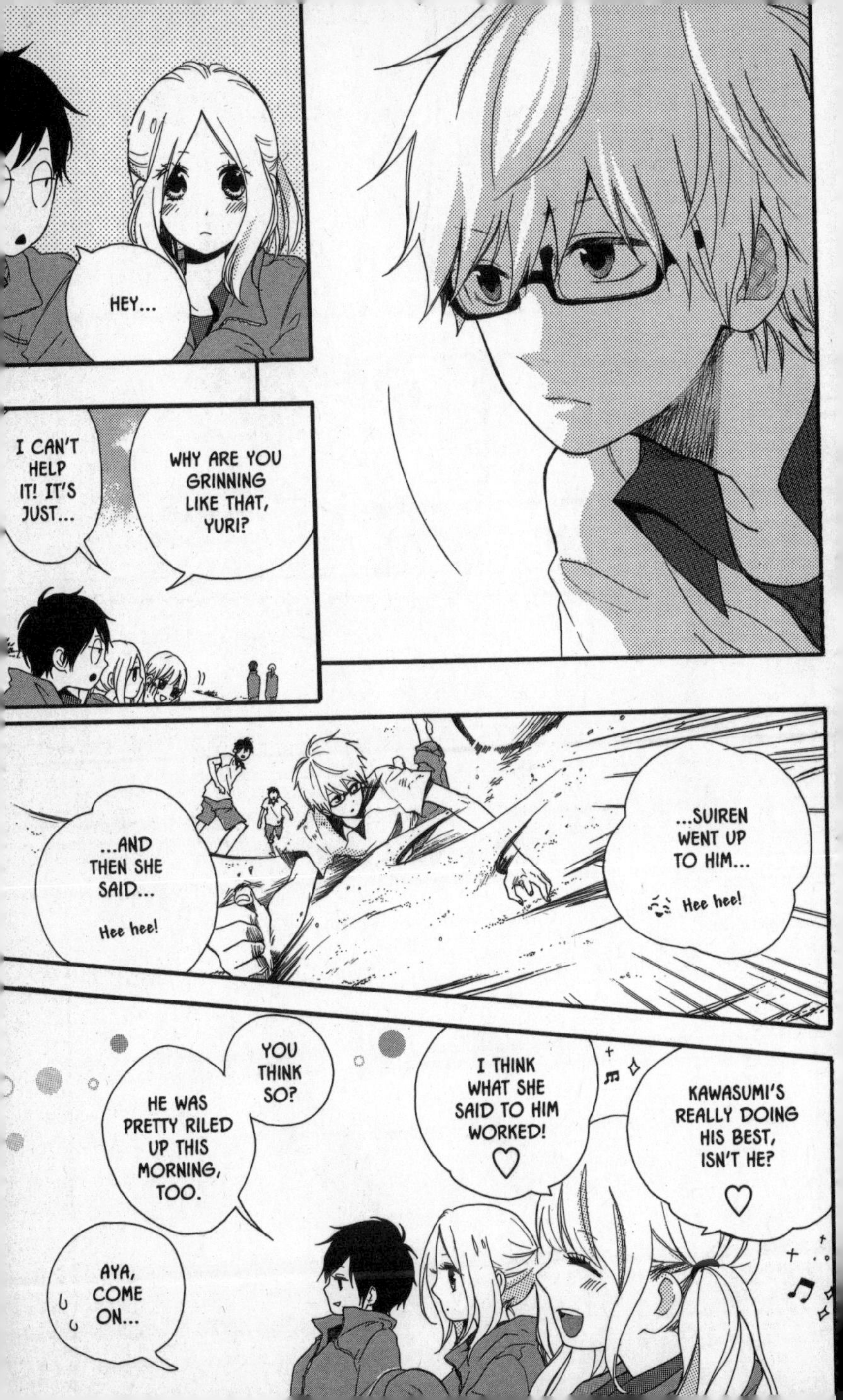
HEY...
WHY ARE YOU GRINNING LIKE THAT, YURI?
I CAN'T HELP IT! IT'S JUST...
...SUIREN WENT UP TO HIM... Hee hee!
...AND THEN SHE SAID... Hee hee!
KAWASUMI'S REALLY DOING HIS BEST, ISN'T HE? ♡
I THINK WHAT SHE SAID TO HIM WORKED! ♡
YOU THINK SO?
HE WAS PRETTY RILED UP THIS MORNING, TOO.
AYA, COME ON...

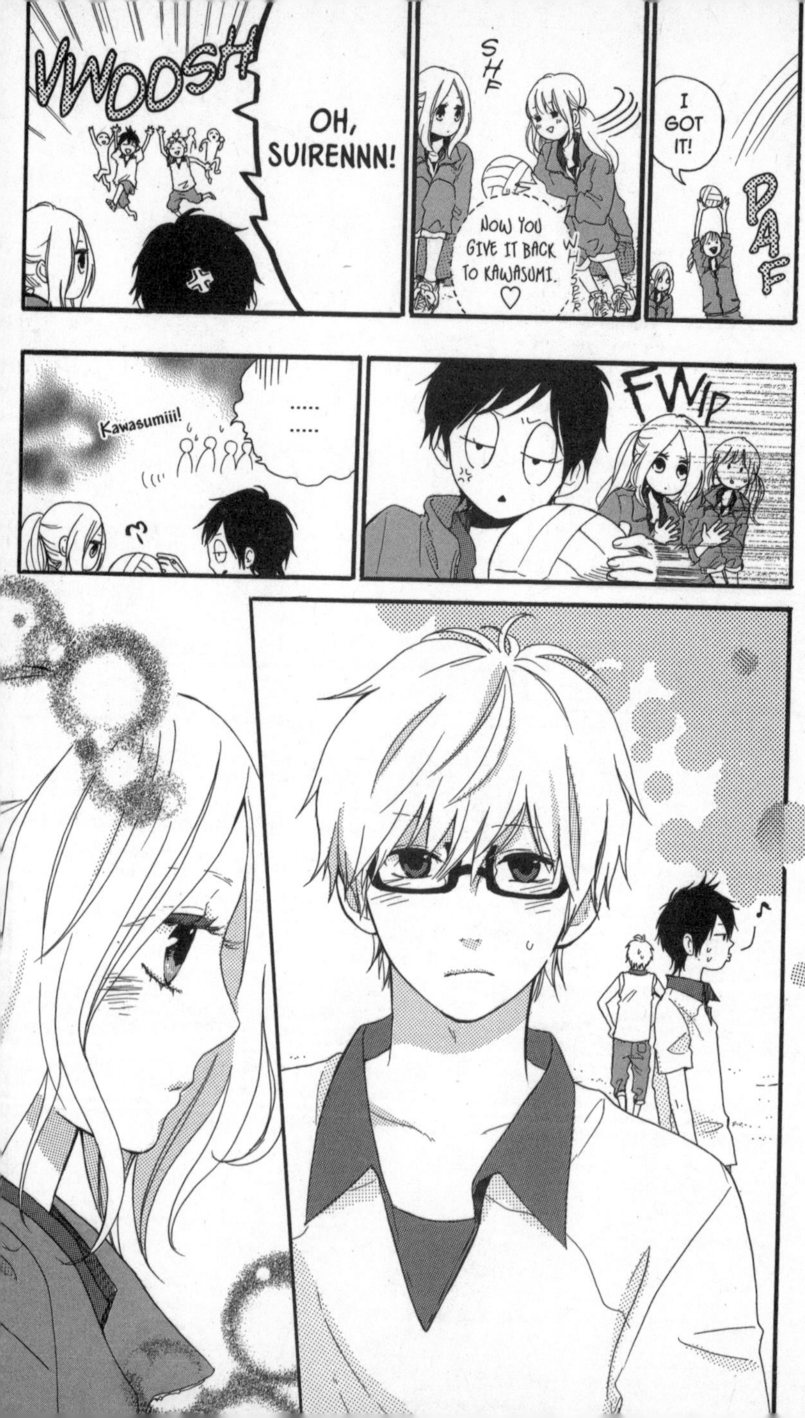
I GOT IT!
DAF
SHF
NOW YOU GIVE IT BACK TO KAWASUMI. ♡
WHISPER
VWOOSH
OH, SUIRENNN!
FWIP
......
......
Kawasumiii!

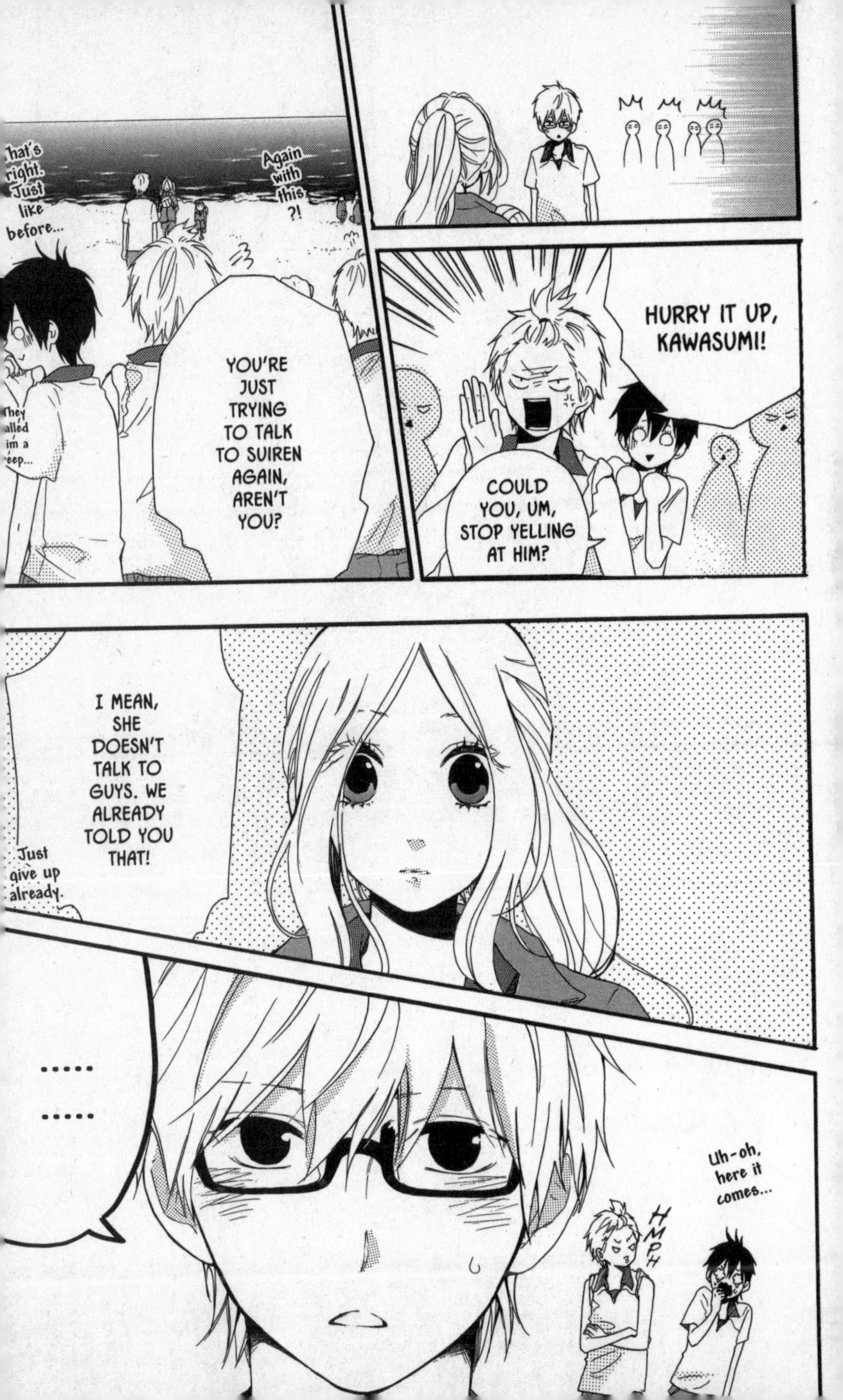
HURRY IT UP, KAWASUMI!
COULD YOU, UM, STOP YELLING AT HIM?
Again with this?!
YOU'RE JUST TRYING TO TALK TO SUIREN AGAIN, AREN'T YOU?
hat's right. Just like before...
hey alled im a eep...
I MEAN, SHE DOESN'T TALK TO GUYS. WE ALREADY TOLD YOU THAT!
Just give up already.
Uh-oh, here it comes...
HMPH
.....
.....

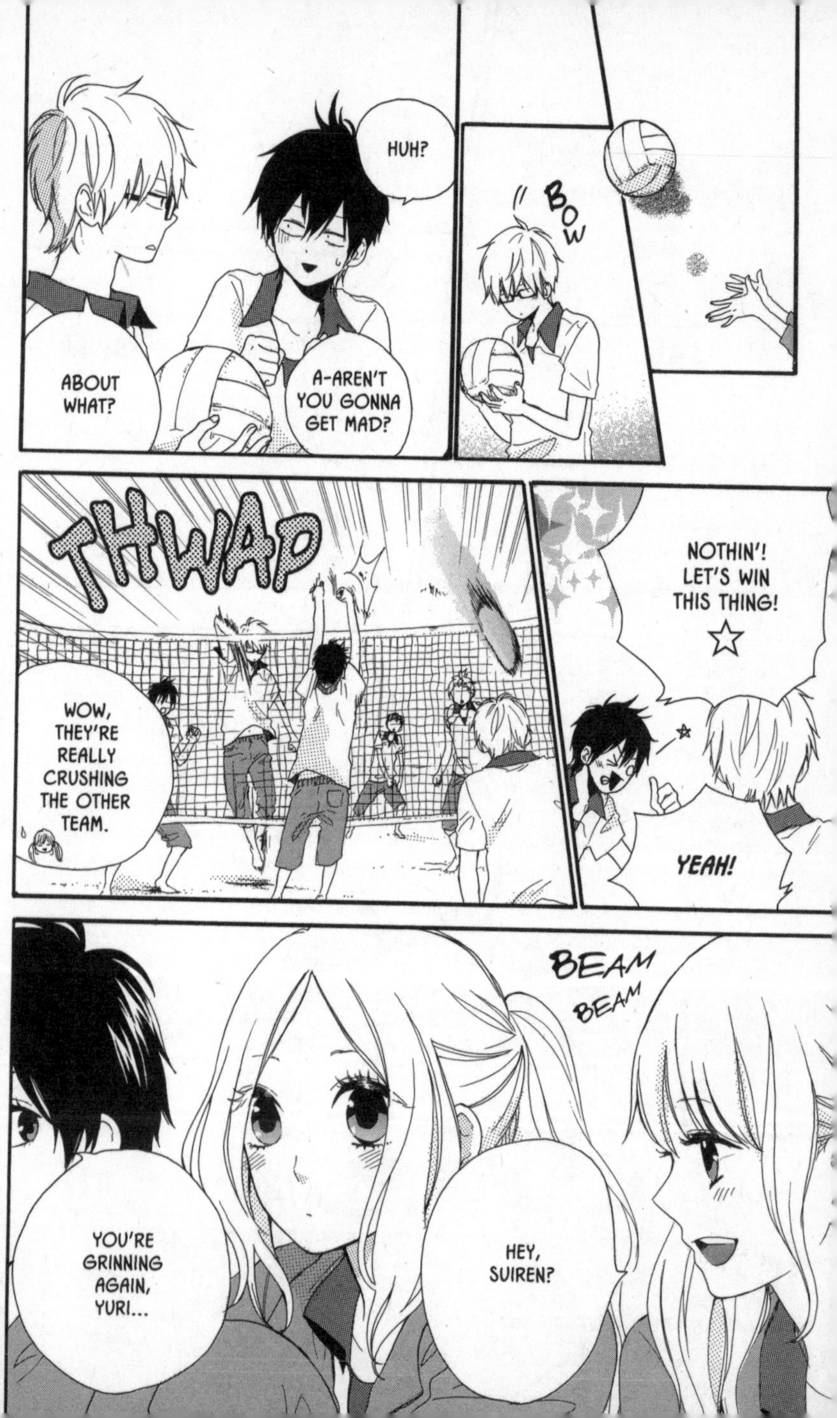
BOW
HUH?
A-AREN'T YOU GONNA GET MAD?
ABOUT WHAT?
NOTHIN'! LET'S WIN THIS THING! ☆
YEAH!
THWAP
WOW, THEY'RE REALLY CRUSHING THE OTHER TEAM.
BEAM BEAM
HEY, SUIREN?
YOU'RE GRINNING AGAIN, YURI...

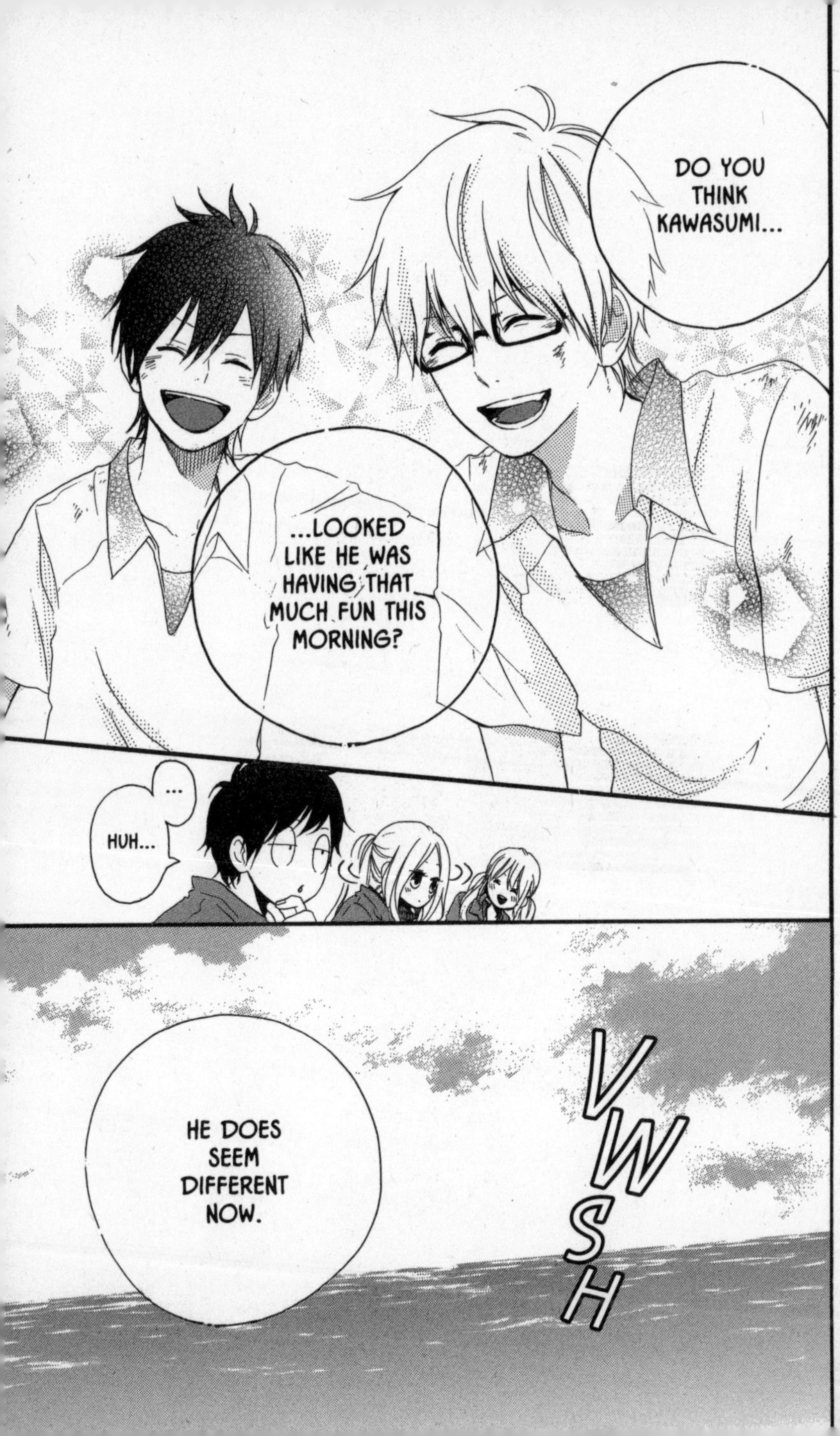
DO YOU THINK KAWASUMI...
...LOOKED LIKE HE WAS HAVING THAT MUCH FUN THIS MORNING?
...
HUH...
VWSH
HE DOES SEEM DIFFERENT NOW.

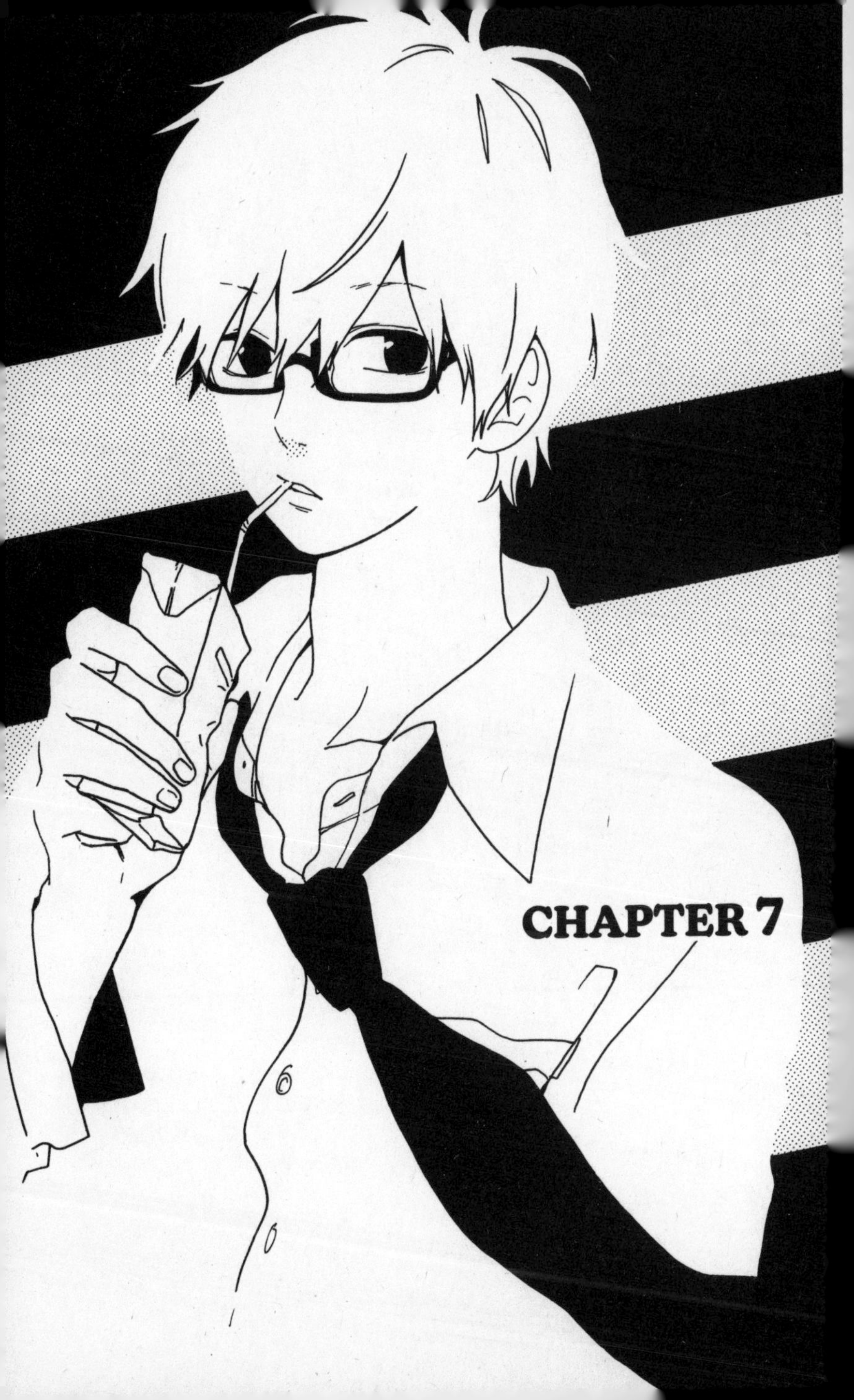
CHAPTER 7

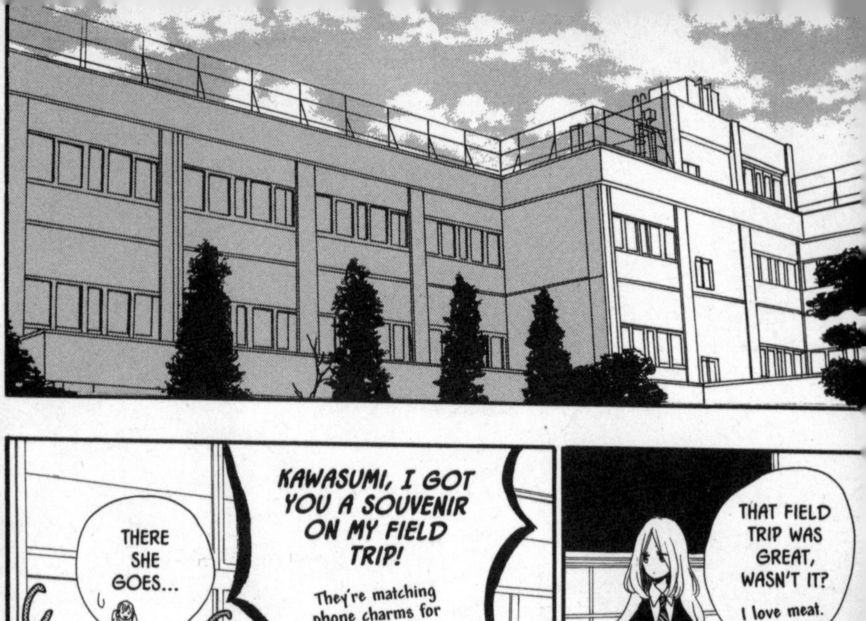
THAT FIELD TRIP WAS GREAT, WASN'T IT?
I love meat.
I CAN'T BELIEVE WE HAVE TO GO BACK TO CLASS TODAY. I DON'T WANT TO DO ANYTHING.
KAWASUMI, I GOT YOU A SOUVENIR ON MY FIELD TRIP!
They're matching phone charms for both of us!
THERE SHE GOES...
CLOMP
CLOMP
CLOMP
IT'S WAY TOO EARLY FOR THIS, I SWEAR.
So annoy-ing.

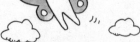

I'M SO HAPPY THAT I WAS ABLE TO PUBLISH MY FIRST MANGA SERIES. I COULDN'T HAVE DONE IT WITHOUT THE SUPPORT OF SO MANY PEOPLE.

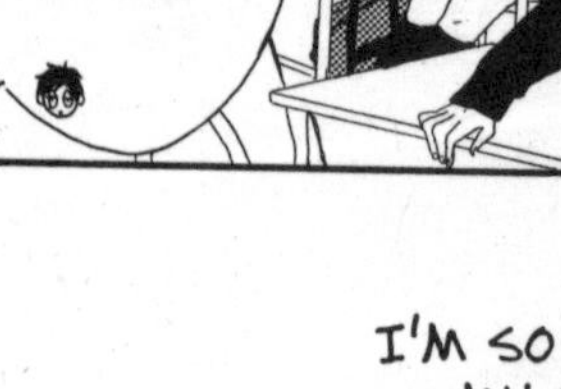

I APPRECIATE EVERYONE WHO'S READ THIS FAR.

THANK YOU VERY MUCH.

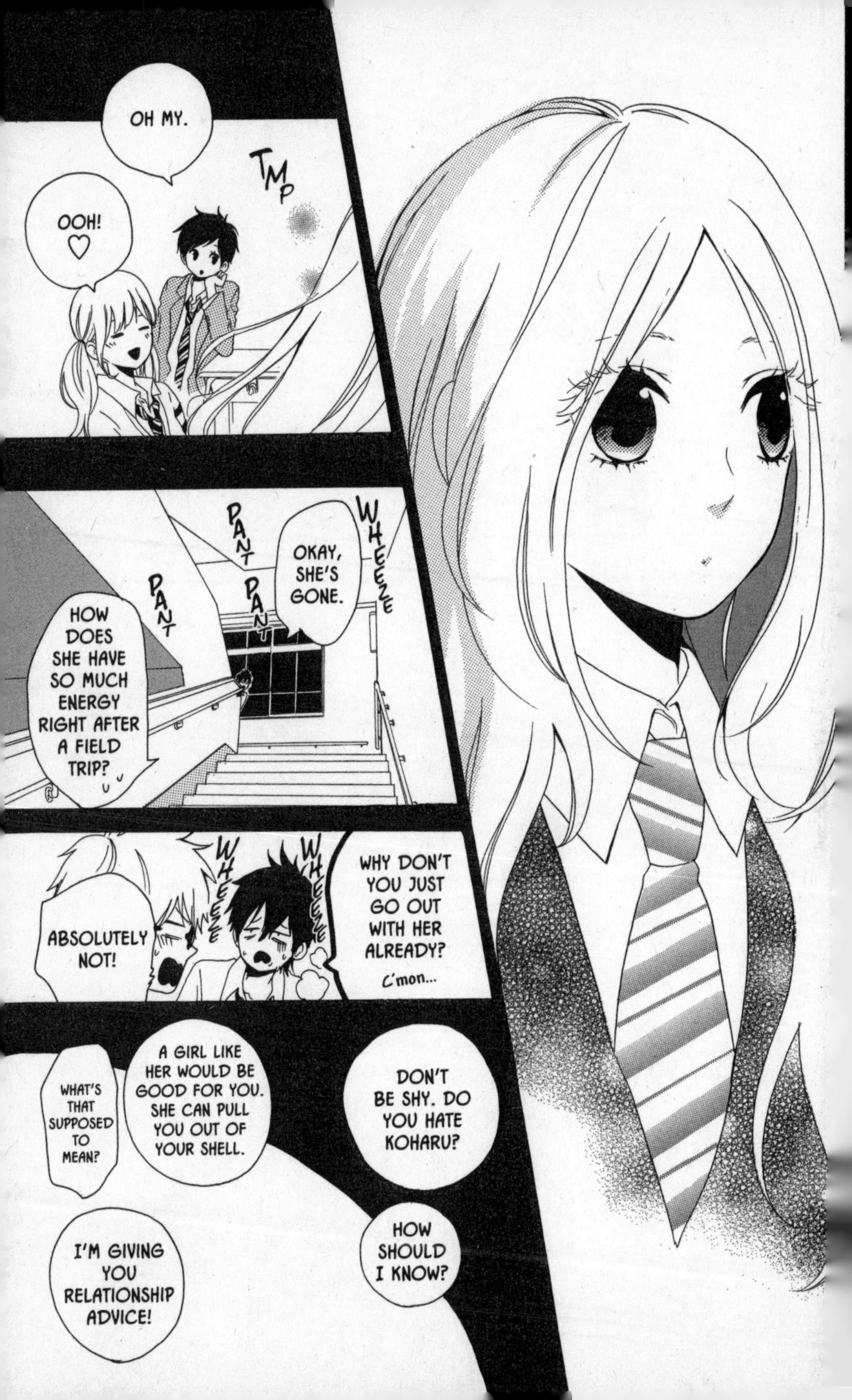
OH MY.
TMP
OOH! ♥
WHEEZE
OKAY, SHE'S GONE.
PANT PANT
PANT
HOW DOES SHE HAVE SO MUCH ENERGY RIGHT AFTER A FIELD TRIP?
WHY DON'T YOU JUST GO OUT WITH HER ALREADY?
C'mon...
WHEEZE
WHEEZE
ABSOLUTELY NOT!
DON'T BE SHY. DO YOU HATE KOHARU?
HOW SHOULD I KNOW?
A GIRL LIKE HER WOULD BE GOOD FOR YOU. SHE CAN PULL YOU OUT OF YOUR SHELL.
WHAT'S THAT SUPPOSED TO MEAN?
I'M GIVING YOU RELATIONSHIP ADVICE!

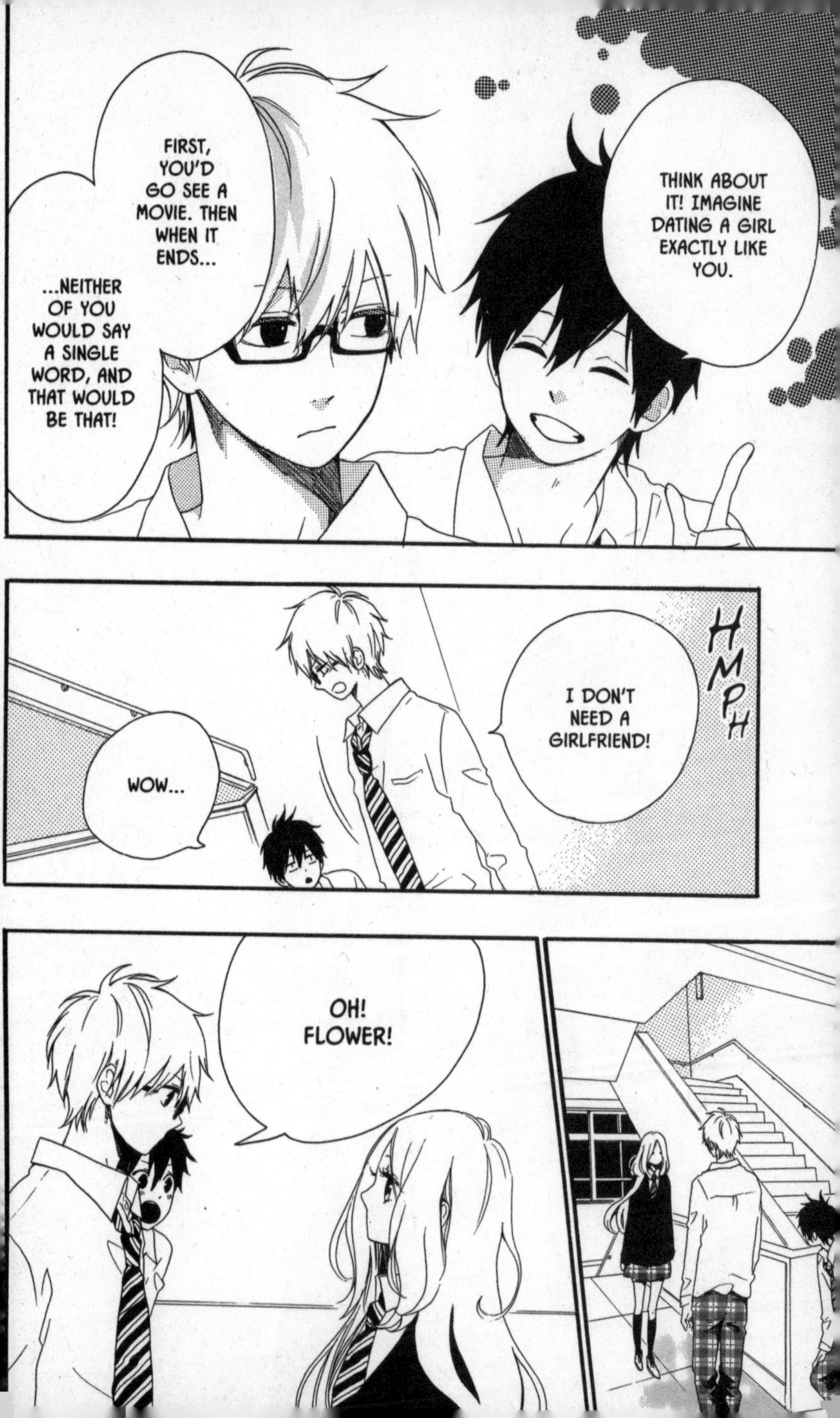
THINK ABOUT IT! IMAGINE DATING A GIRL EXACTLY LIKE YOU.
FIRST, YOU'D GO SEE A MOVIE. THEN WHEN IT ENDS...
...NEITHER OF YOU WOULD SAY A SINGLE WORD, AND THAT WOULD BE THAT!
HMPH
I DON'T NEED A GIRLFRIEND!
WOW...
OH! FLOWER!

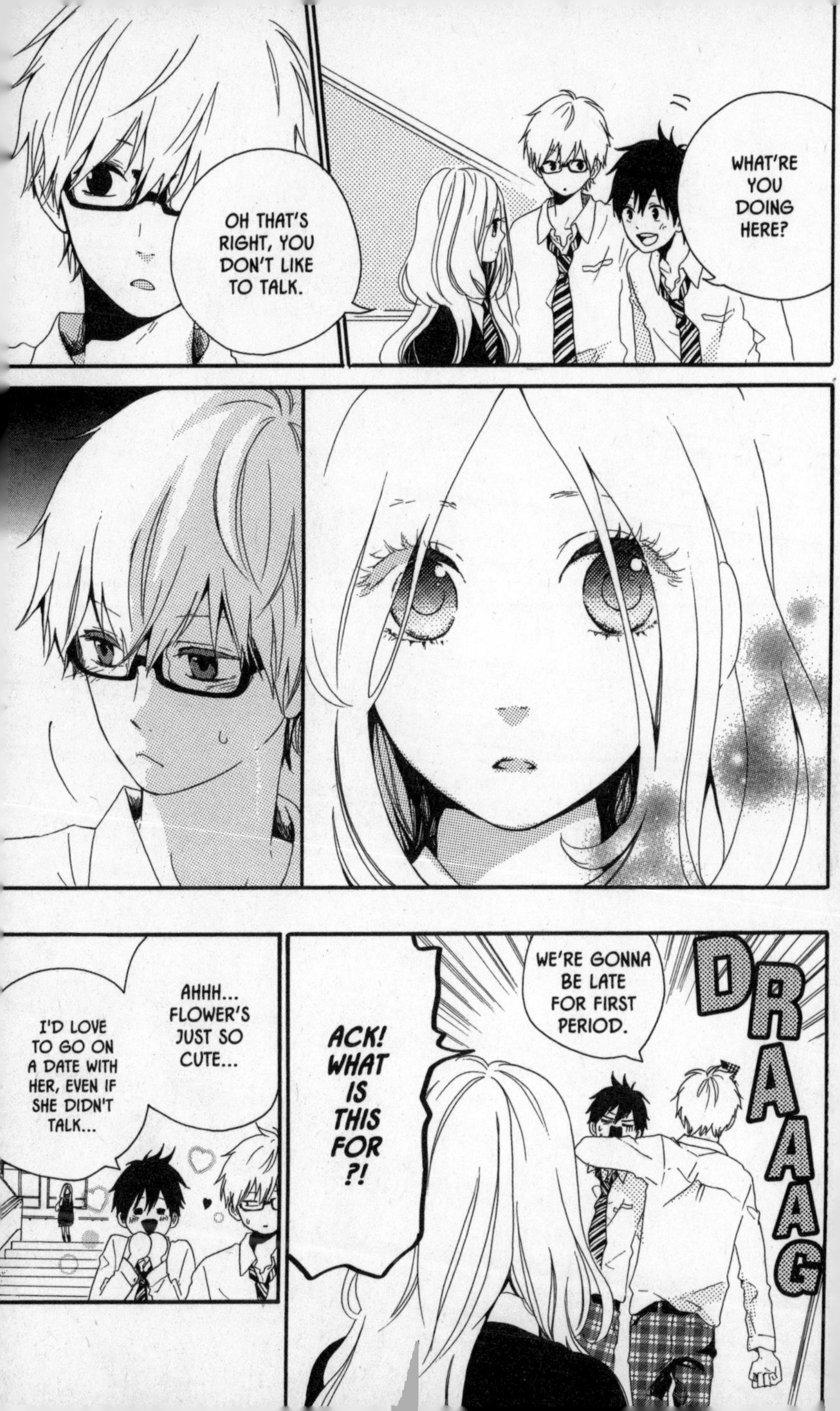
WHAT'RE YOU DOING HERE?
OH THAT'S RIGHT, YOU DON'T LIKE TO TALK.
DRAAAG
WE'RE GONNA BE LATE FOR FIRST PERIOD.
ACK! WHAT IS THIS FOR?!
AHHH... FLOWER'S JUST SO CUTE...
I'D LOVE TO GO ON A DATE WITH HER, EVEN IF SHE DIDN'T TALK...

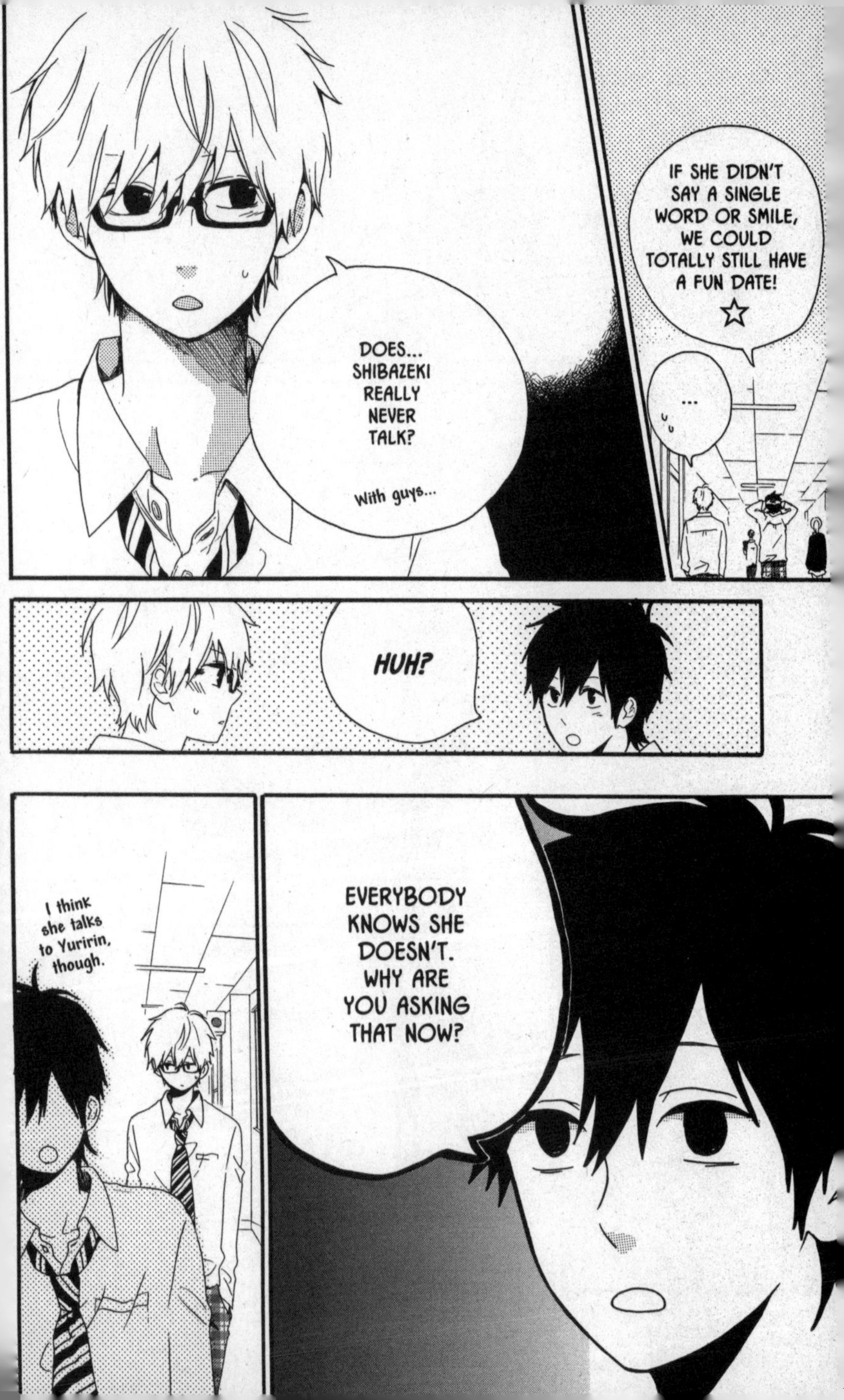
IF SHE DIDN'T SAY A SINGLE WORD OR SMILE, WE COULD TOTALLY STILL HAVE A FUN DATE! ☆
...
DOES... SHIBAZEKI REALLY NEVER TALK?
With guys...
HUH?
EVERYBODY KNOWS SHE DOESN'T. WHY ARE YOU ASKING THAT NOW?
I think she talks to Yuririn, though.

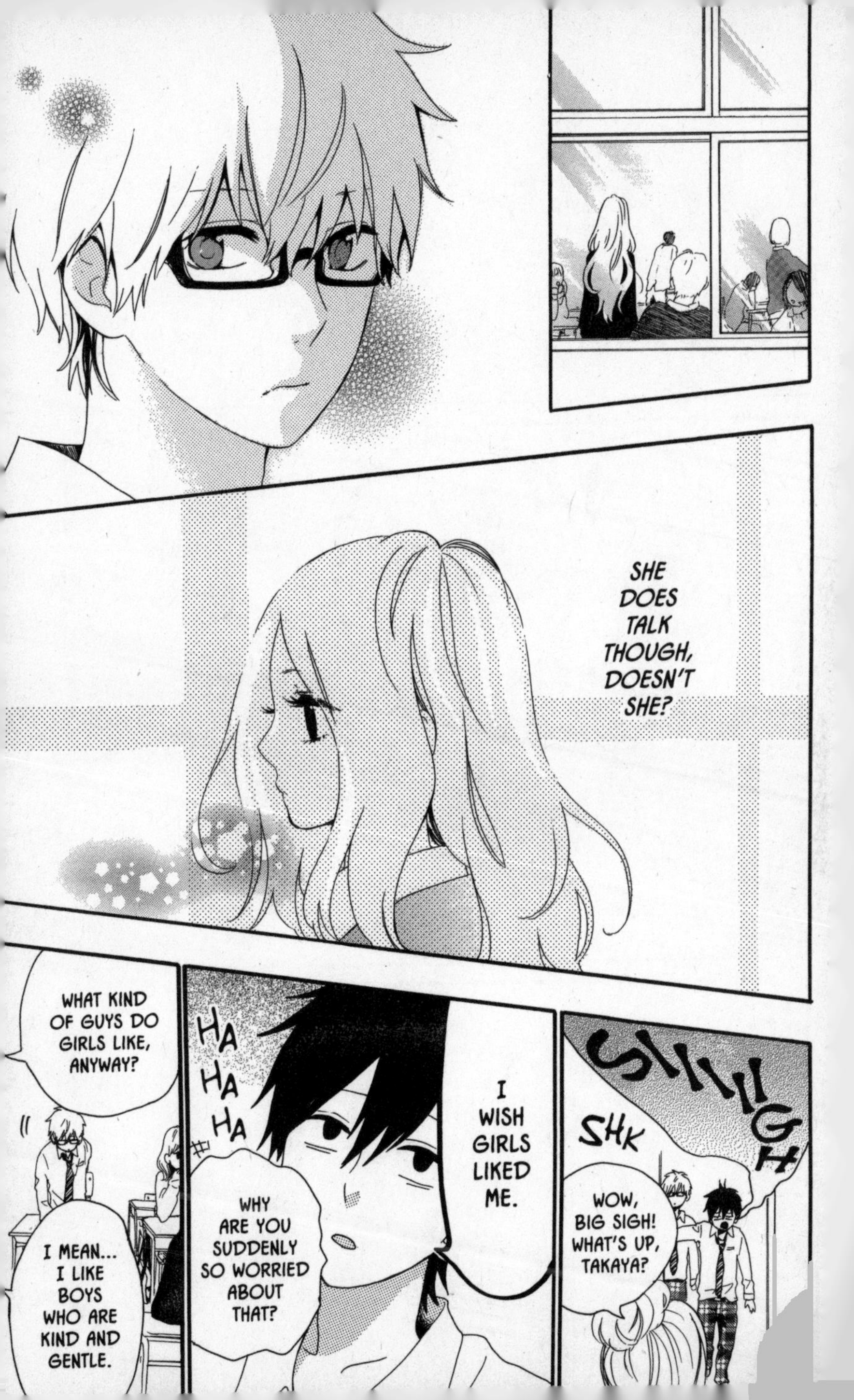
SHE DOES TALK THOUGH, DOESN'T SHE?
SIIIIGH
SHK
WOW, BIG SIGH! WHAT'S UP, TAKAYA?
I WISH GIRLS LIKED ME.
HA HA HA
WHY ARE YOU SUDDENLY SO WORRIED ABOUT THAT?
WHAT KIND OF GUYS DO GIRLS LIKE, ANYWAY?
I MEAN... I LIKE BOYS WHO ARE KIND AND GENTLE.

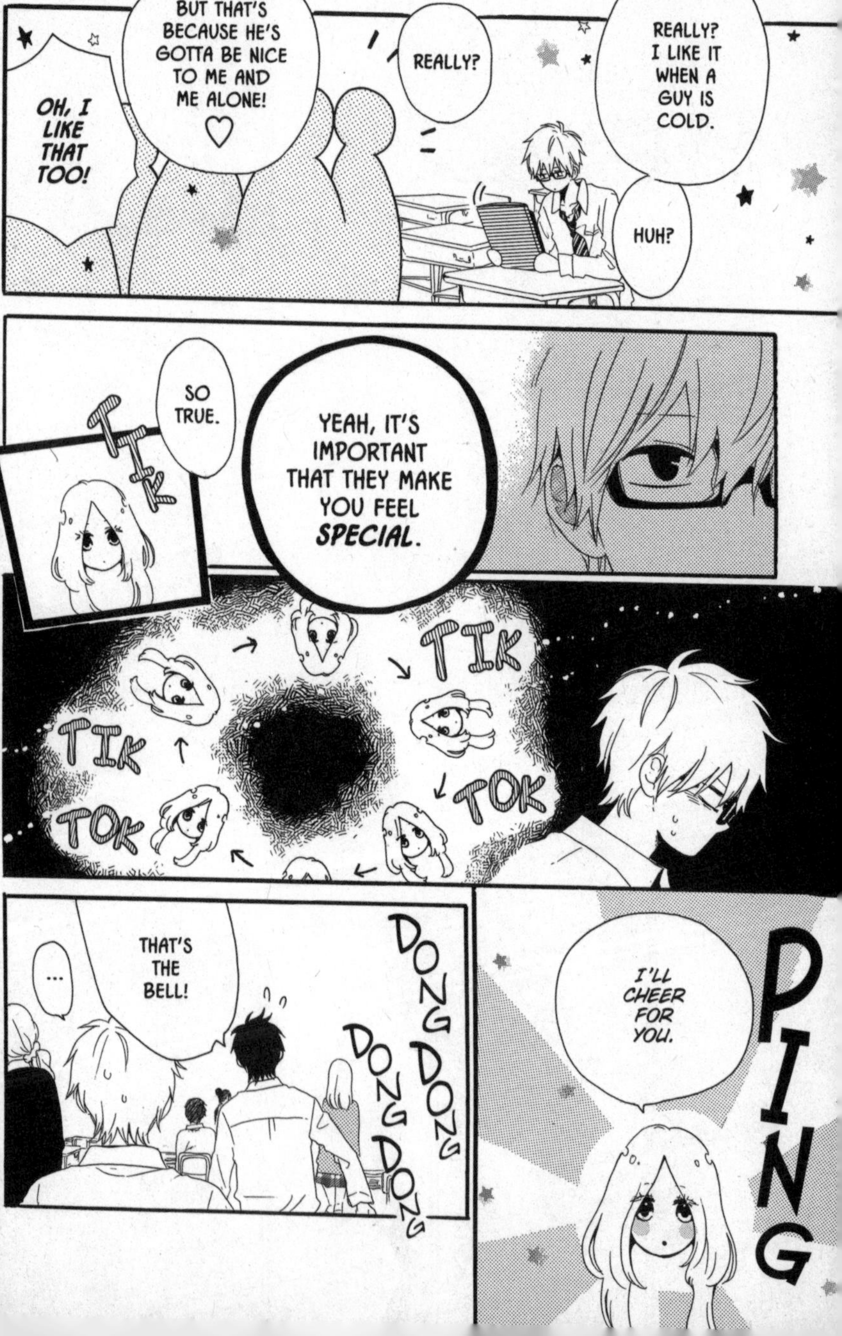
REALLY? I LIKE IT WHEN A GUY IS COLD.
HUH?
REALLY?
BUT THAT'S BECAUSE HE'S GOTTA BE NICE TO ME AND ME ALONE! ♡
OH, I LIKE THAT TOO!
YEAH, IT'S IMPORTANT THAT THEY MAKE YOU FEEL SPECIAL.
SO TRUE.
TIK
TIK
TOK
TOK
TIK
PING
I'LL CHEER FOR YOU.
DONG DONG
DONG DONG
THAT'S THE BELL!
...

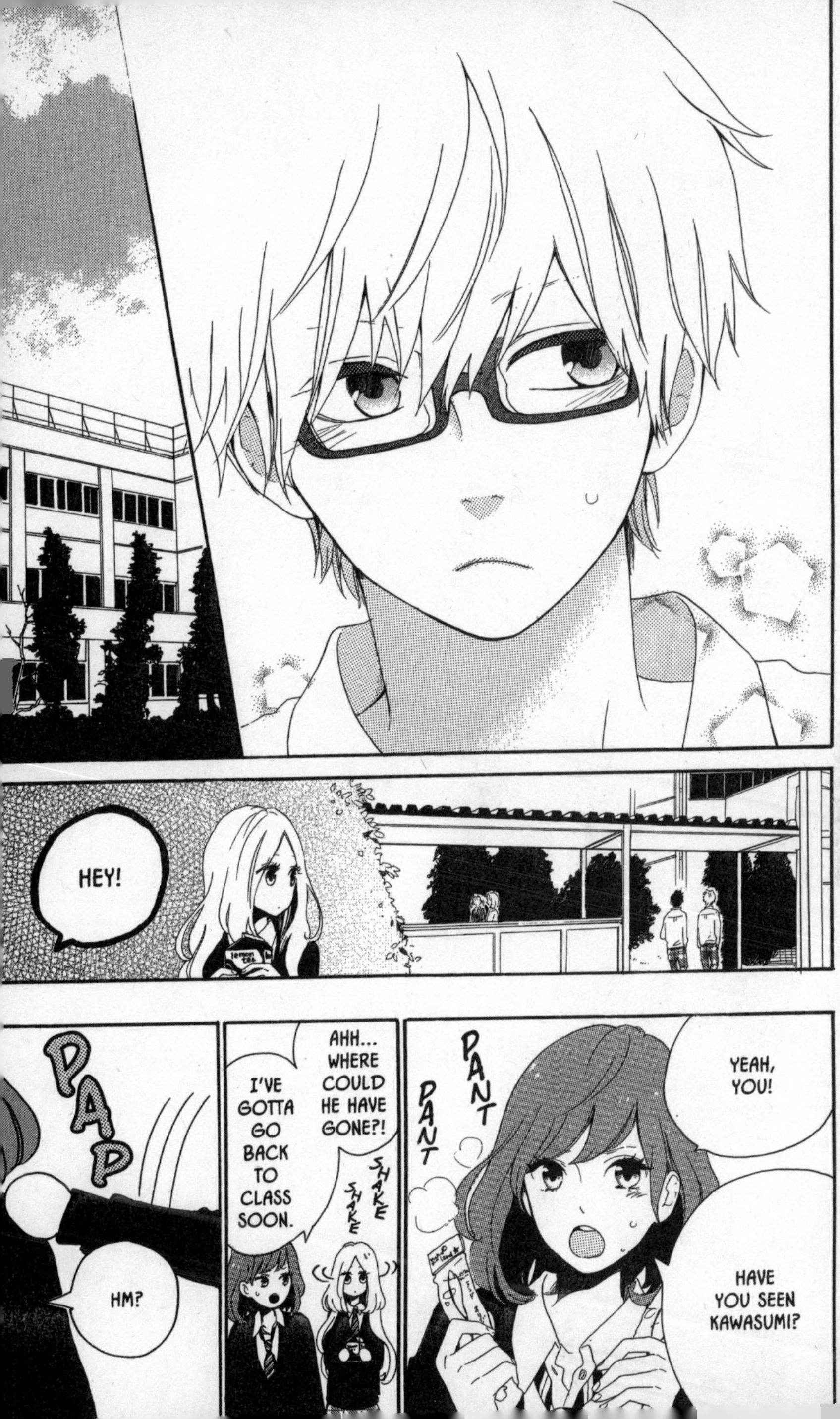
HEY!
YEAH, YOU!
PANT PANT
HAVE YOU SEEN KAWASUMI?
AHH... WHERE COULD HE HAVE GONE?!
I'VE GOTTA GO BACK TO CLASS SOON.
SHAKE SHAKE
PAP
HM?

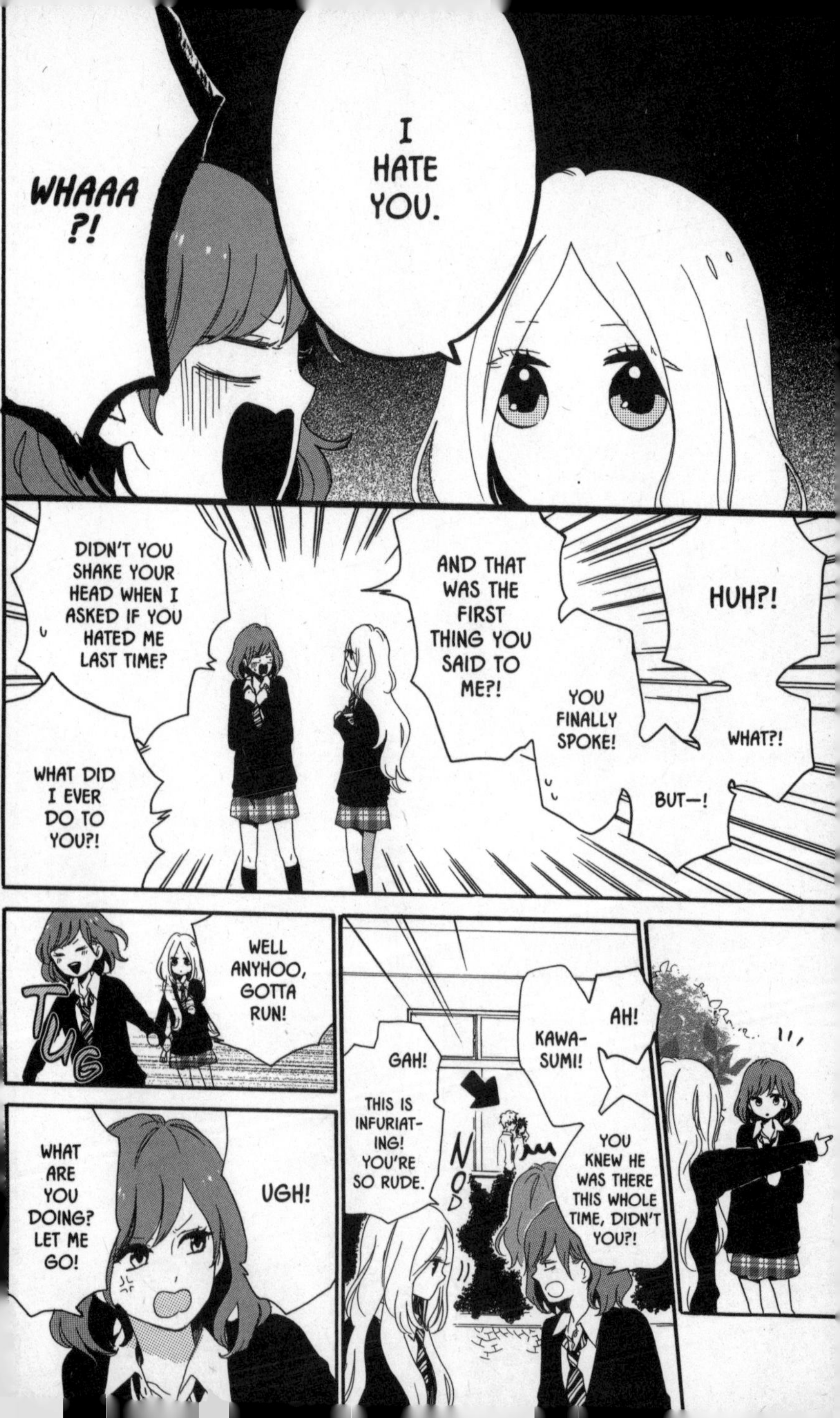
I HATE YOU.
WHAAA ?!
HUH?!
WHAT?!
BUT—!
YOU FINALLY SPOKE!
AND THAT WAS THE FIRST THING YOU SAID TO ME?!
DIDN'T YOU SHAKE YOUR HEAD WHEN I ASKED IF YOU HATED ME LAST TIME?
WHAT DID I EVER DO TO YOU?!
AH!
KAWA-SUMI!
NOD
YOU KNEW HE WAS THERE THIS WHOLE TIME, DIDN'T YOU?!
GAH!
THIS IS INFURIAT-ING! YOU'RE SO RUDE.
WELL ANYHOO, GOTTA RUN!
TUG
UGH!
WHAT ARE YOU DOING? LET ME GO!

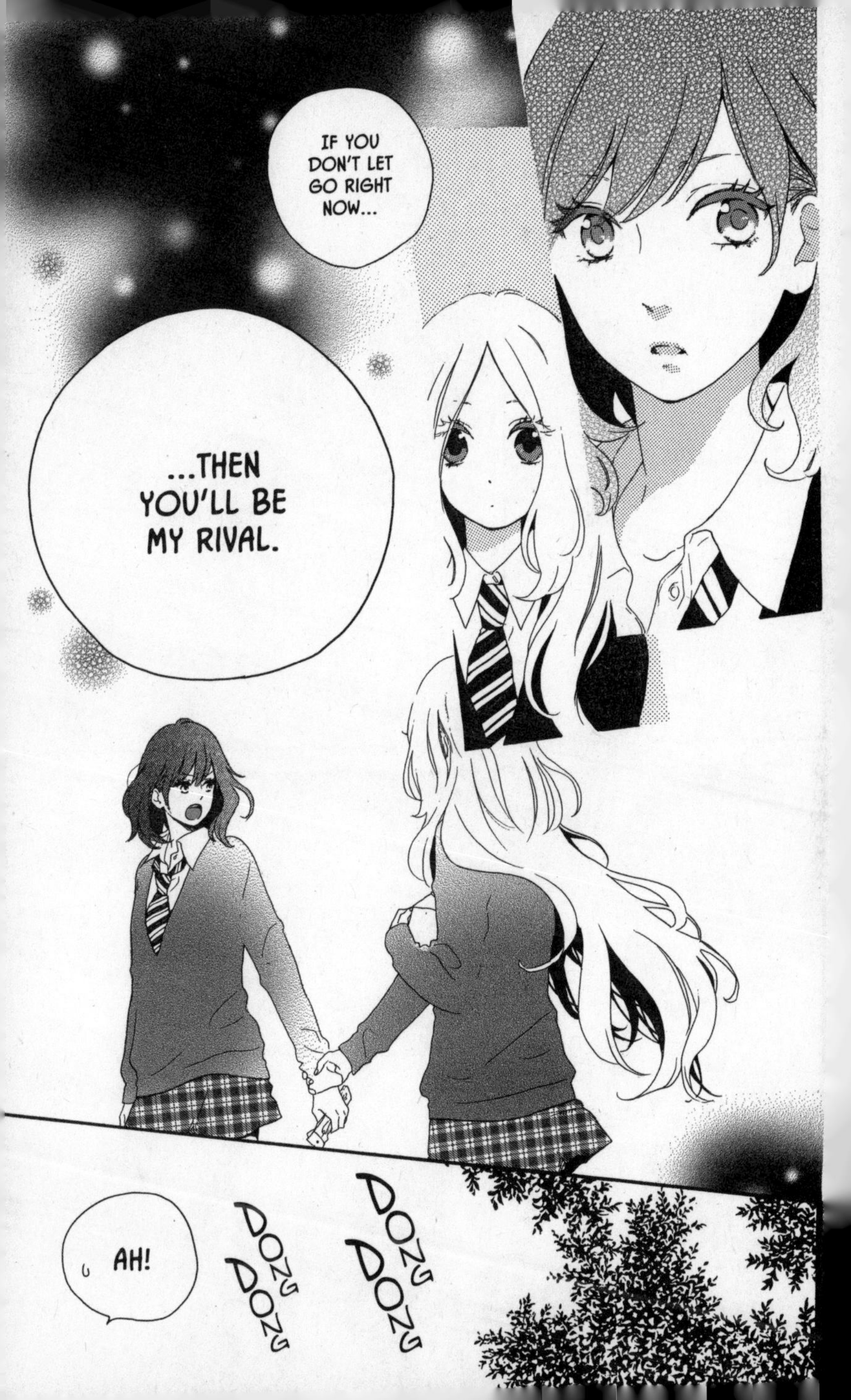
IF YOU DON'T LET GO RIGHT NOW...
...THEN YOU'LL BE MY RIVAL.
DONG DONG
DONG DONG
AH!

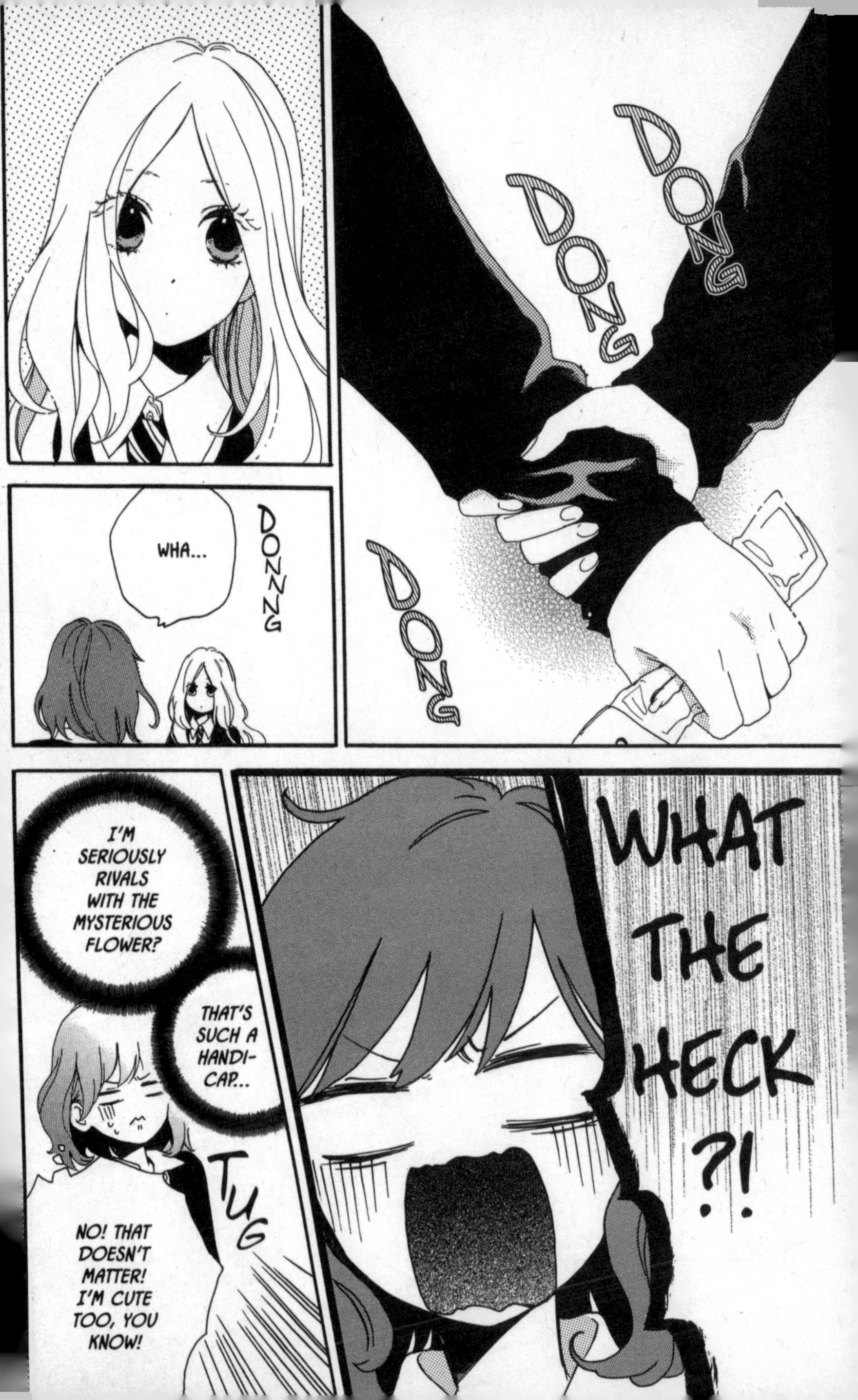
DONG
DONG
DONG
WHA...
DONNNG
WHAT THE HECK?!
I'M SERIOUSLY RIVALS WITH THE MYSTERIOUS FLOWER?
THAT'S SUCH A HANDI-CAP...
TUG
NO! THAT DOESN'T MATTER! I'M CUTE TOO, YOU KNOW!

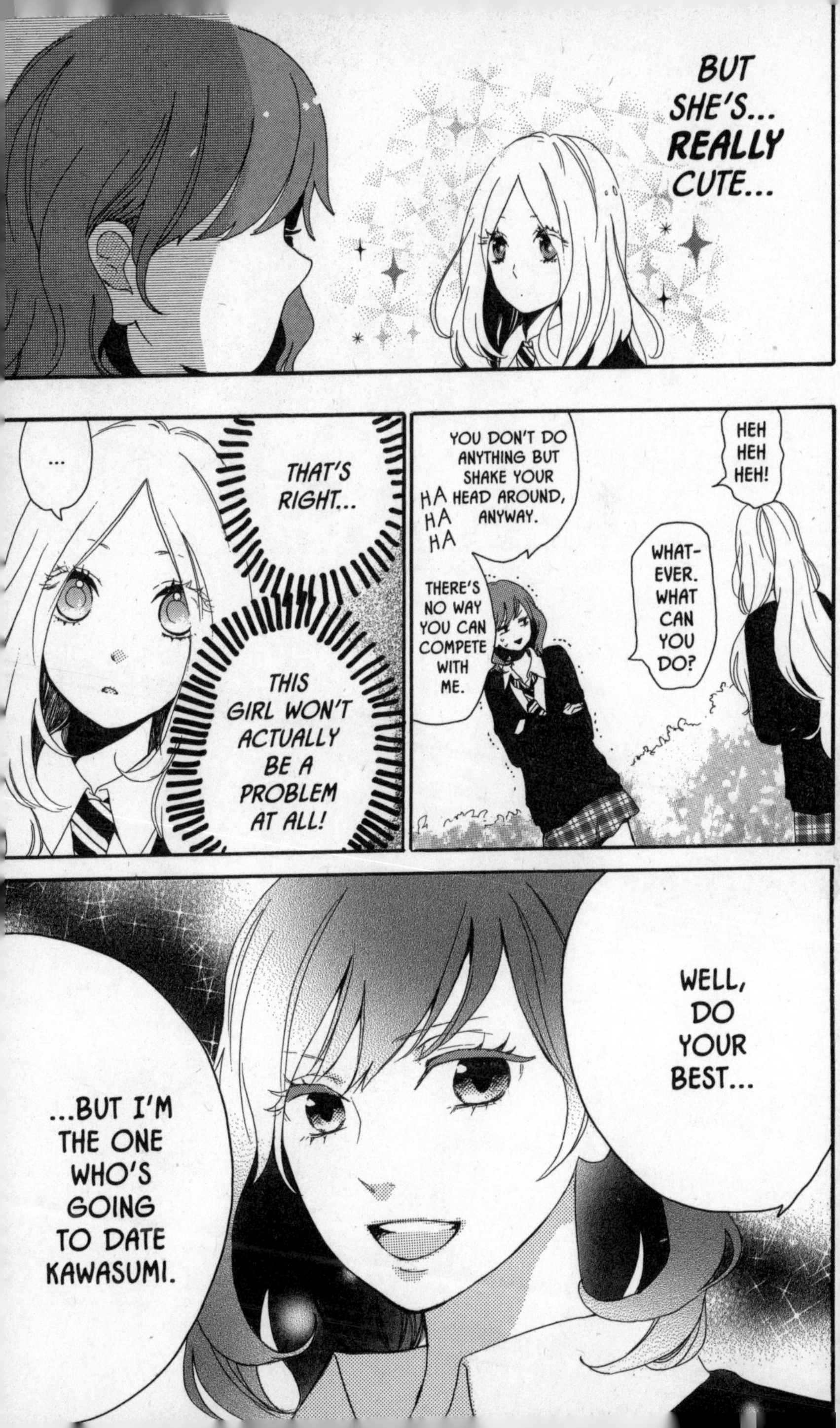
BUT SHE'S... REALLY CUTE...
HEH HEH HEH!
WHAT-EVER. WHAT CAN YOU DO?
YOU DON'T DO ANYTHING BUT SHAKE YOUR HEAD AROUND, ANYWAY.
HA HA HA
THERE'S NO WAY YOU CAN COMPETE WITH ME.
THAT'S RIGHT...
...
THIS GIRL WON'T ACTUALLY BE A PROBLEM AT ALL!
WELL, DO YOUR BEST...
...BUT I'M THE ONE WHO'S GOING TO DATE KAWASUMI.

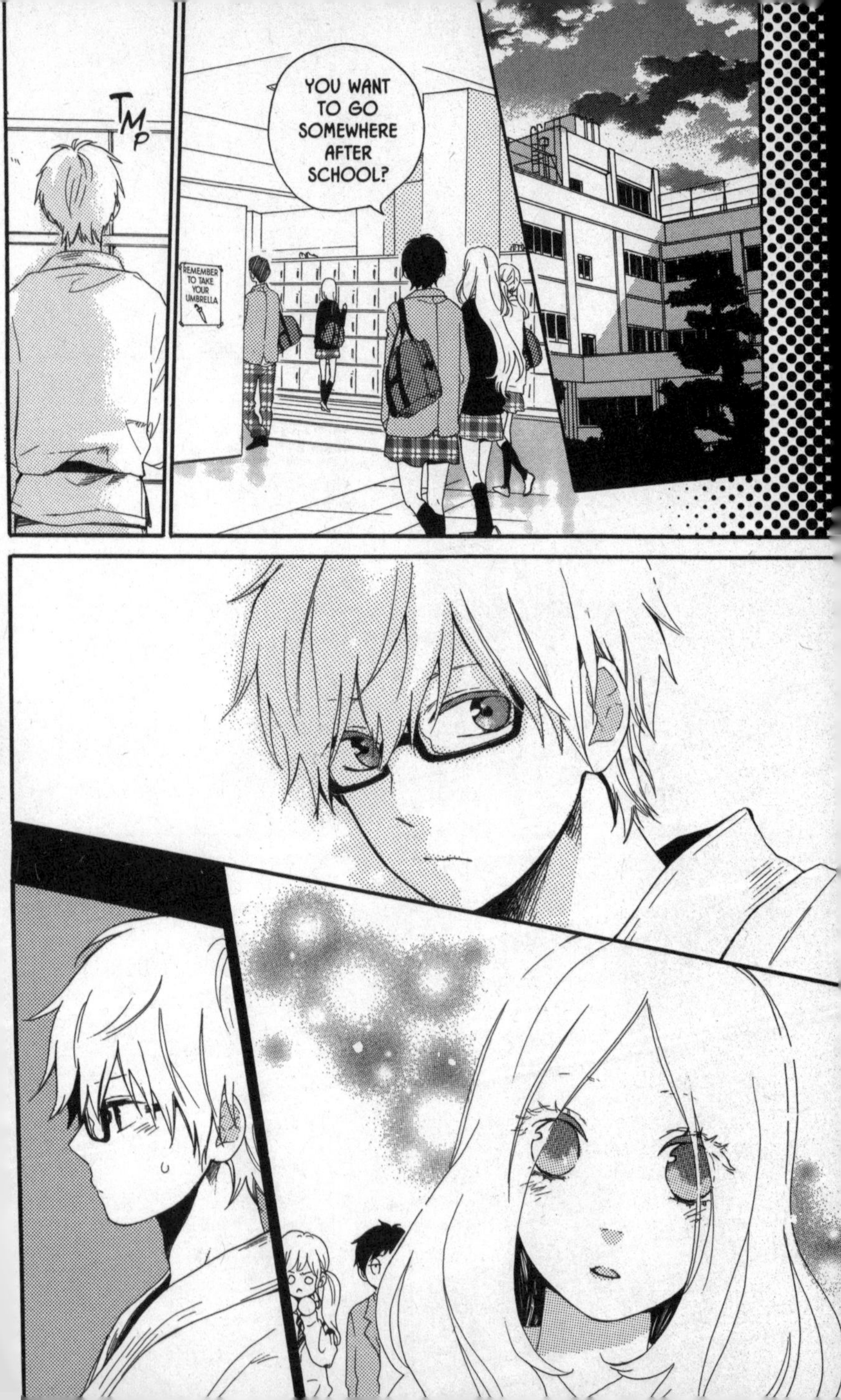
YOU WANT TO GO SOMEWHERE AFTER SCHOOL?
REMEMBER TO TAKE YOUR UMBRELLA
TMP

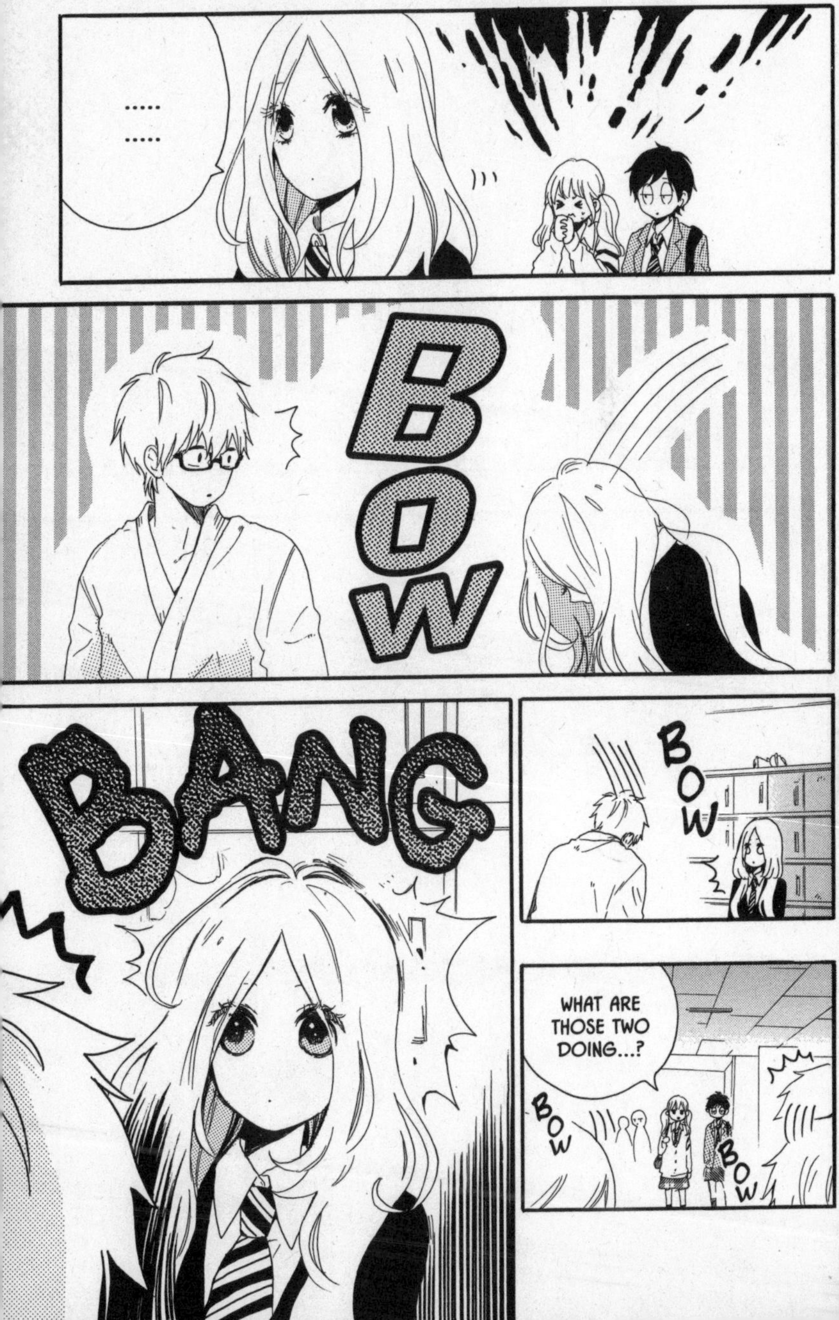
......
......
BOW
BOW
WHAT ARE THOSE TWO DOING...?
BOW
BOW
BANG

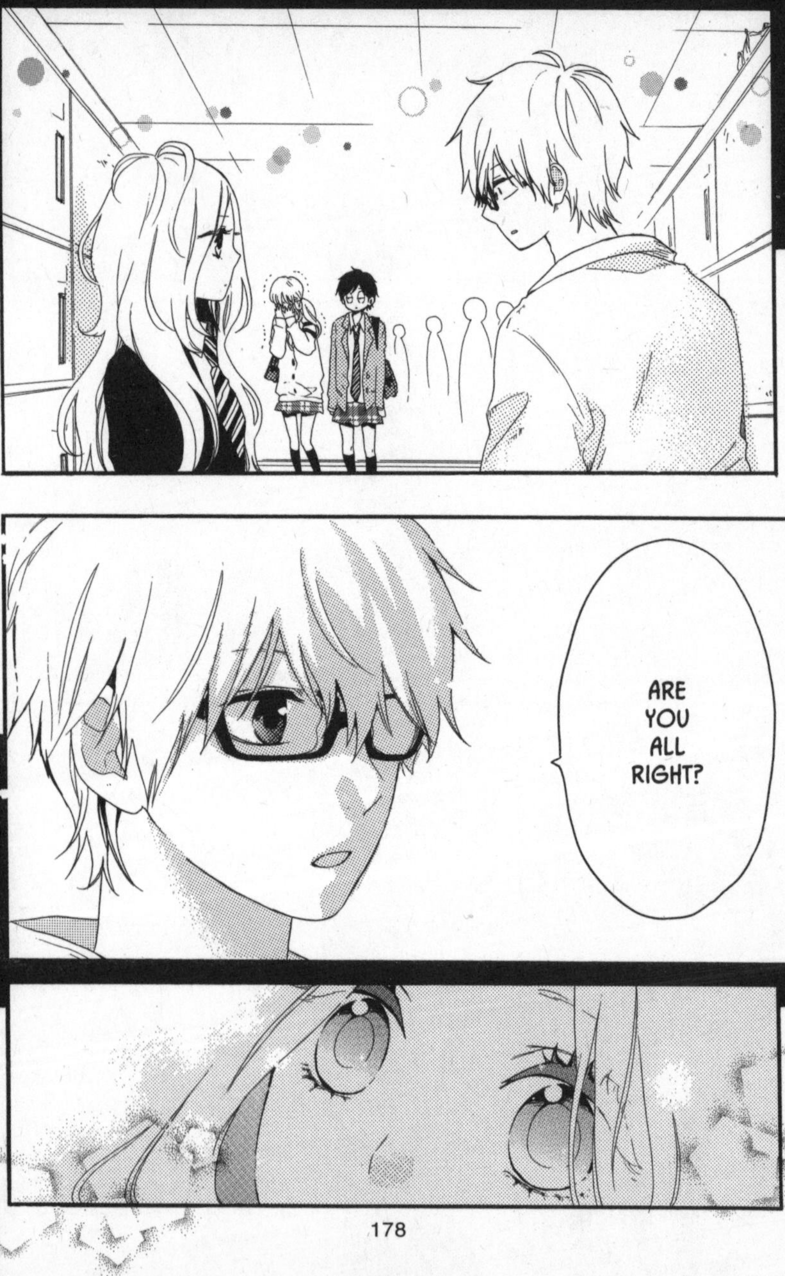
ARE YOU ALL RIGHT?

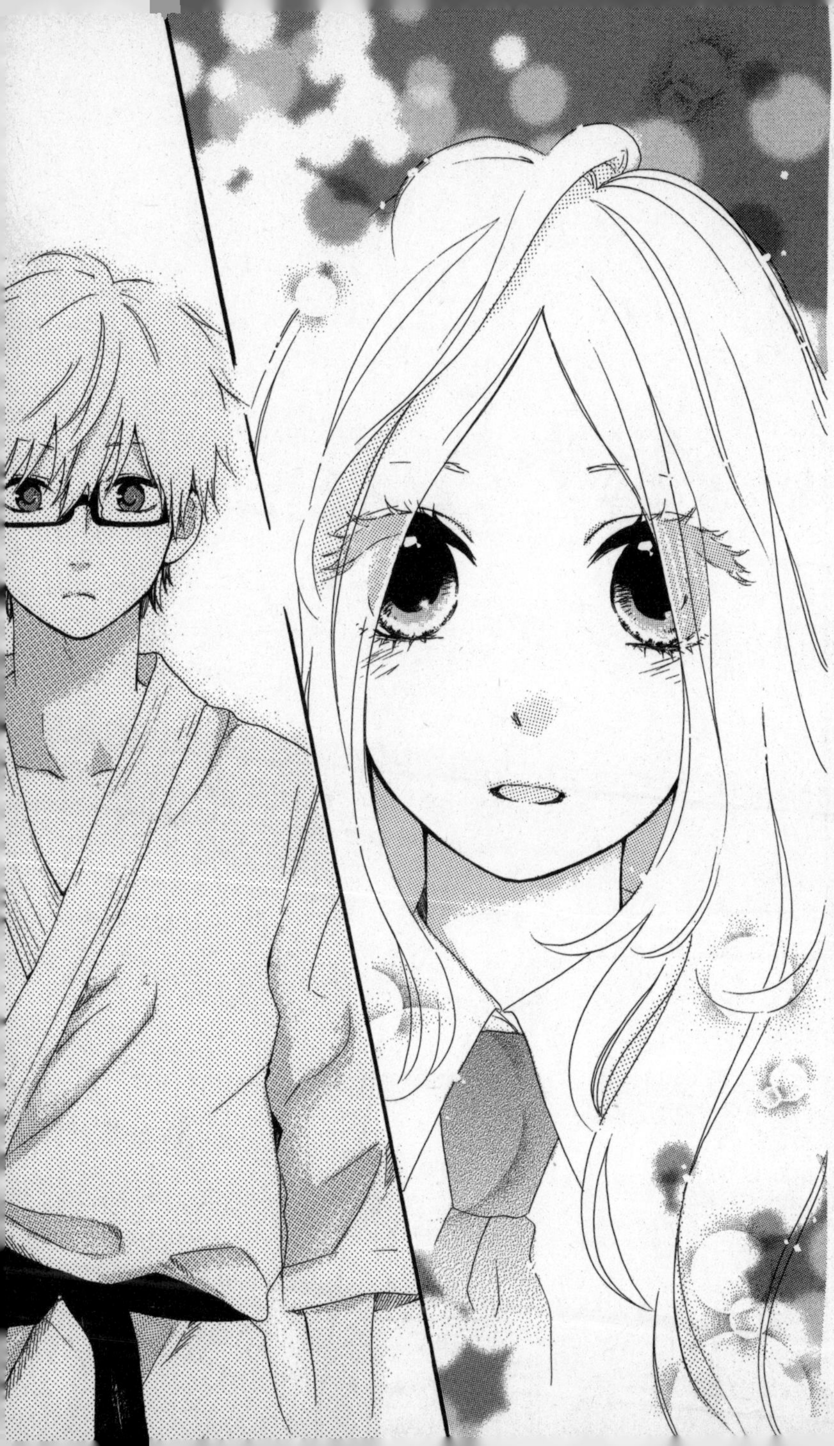

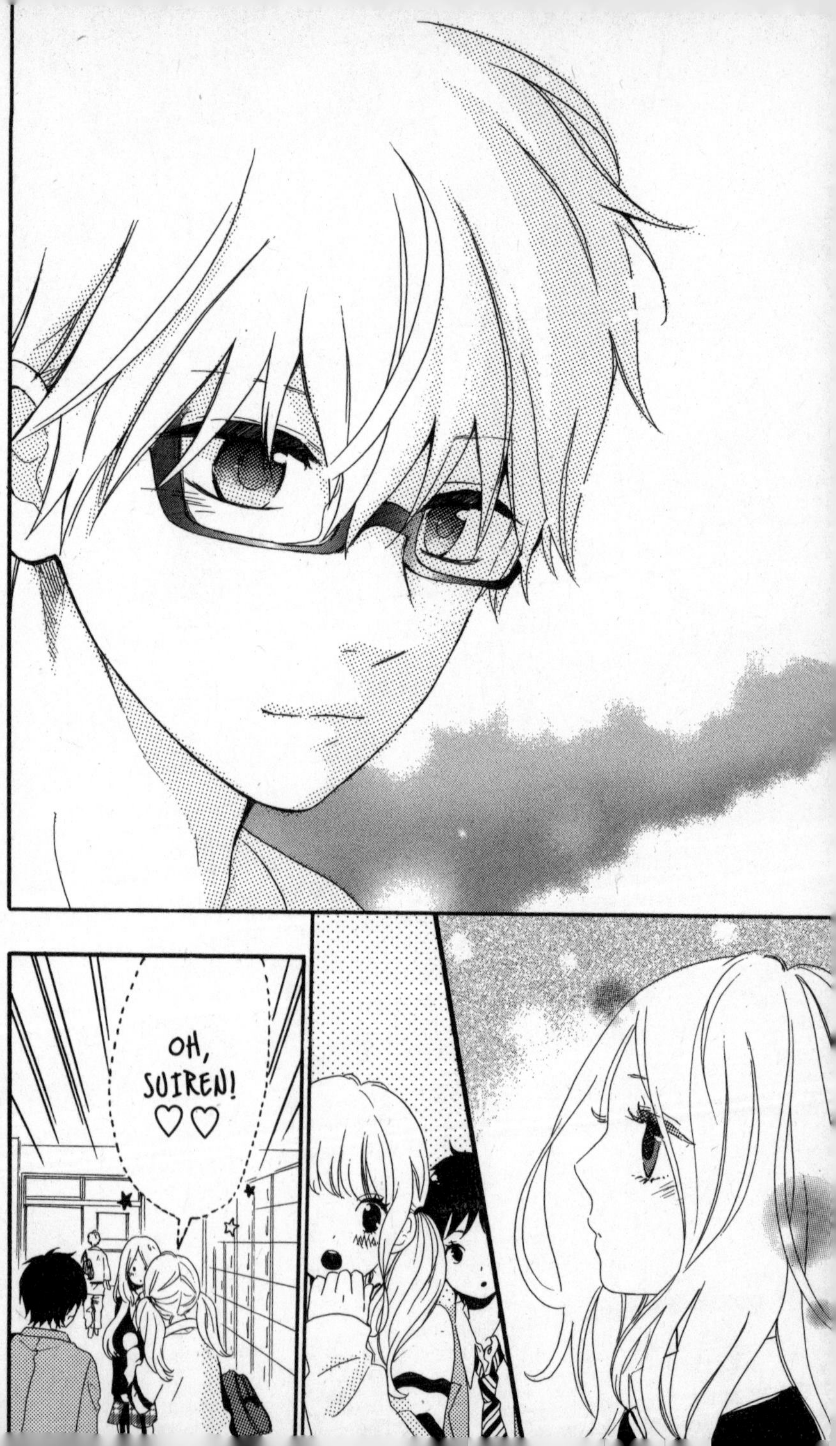
OH, SUIREN! ♡♡

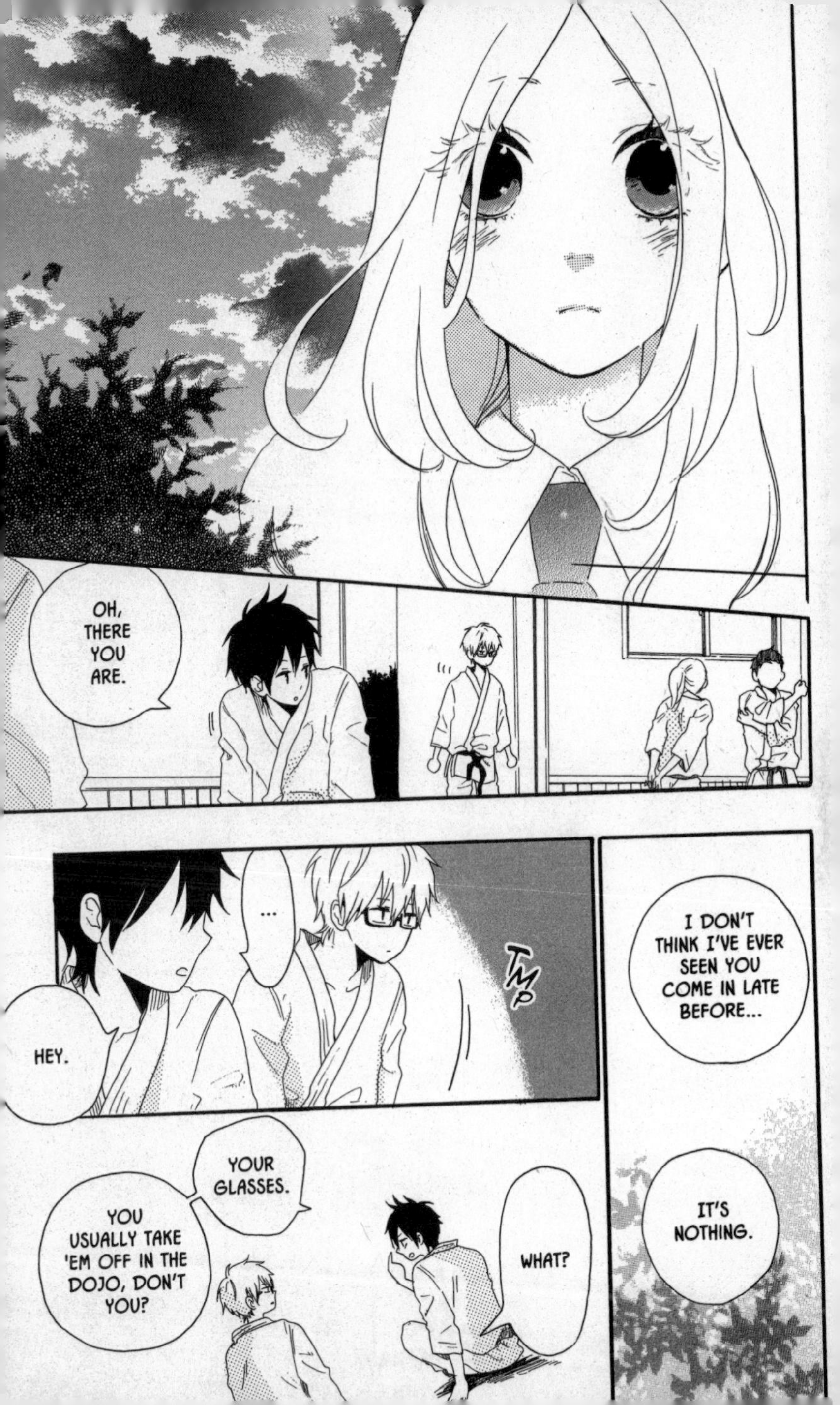
OH, THERE YOU ARE.
I DON'T THINK I'VE EVER SEEN YOU COME IN LATE BEFORE...
IT'S NOTHING.
TMP
...
HEY.
WHAT?
YOUR GLASSES.
YOU USUALLY TAKE 'EM OFF IN THE DOJO, DON'T YOU?

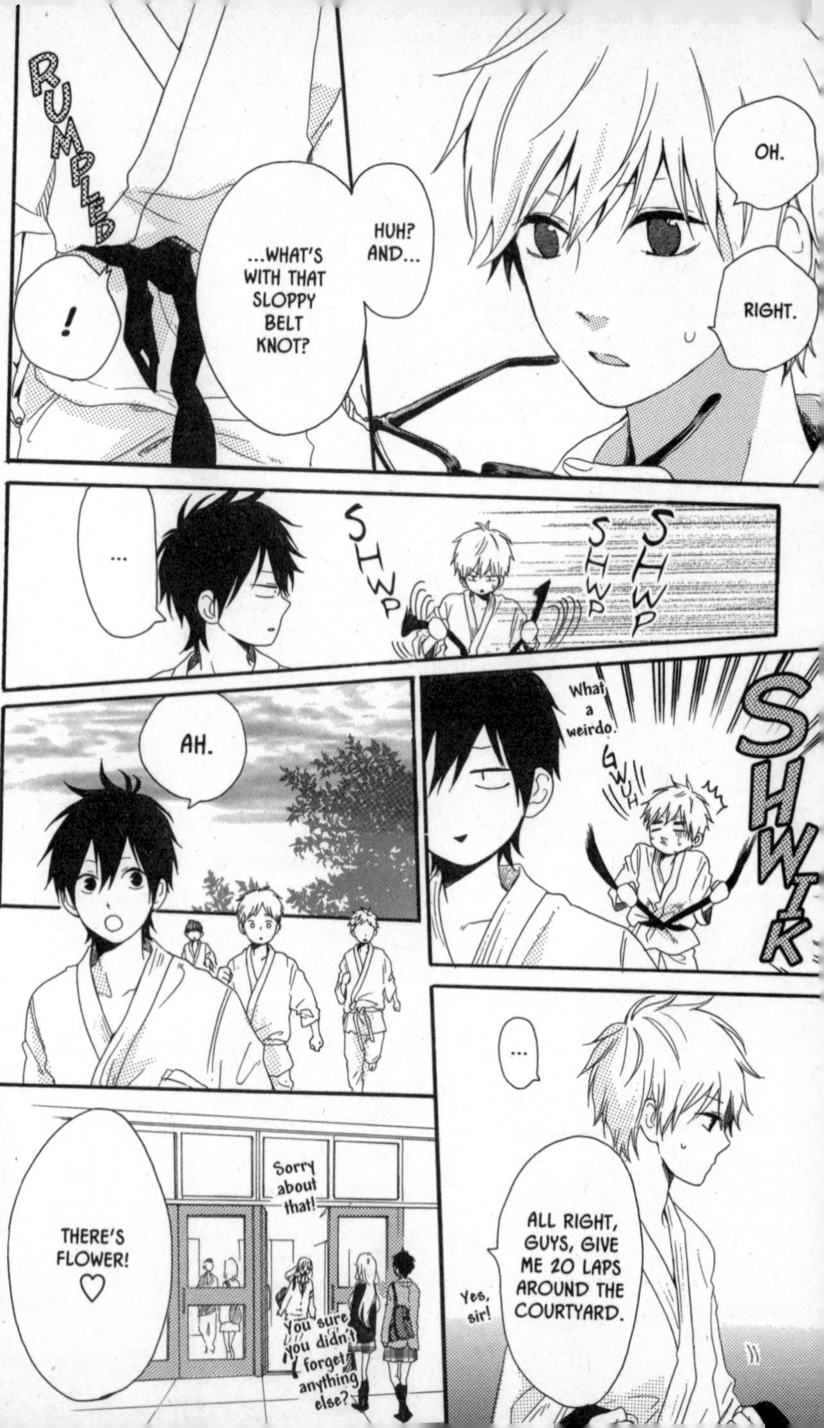
OH.
RIGHT.
HUH? AND...
...WHAT'S WITH THAT SLOPPY BELT KNOT?
RUMPLED
!
SHWP SHWP
SHWP SHWP
SHWP
...
SHWIK
What a weirdo.
GWUH
AH.
...
ALL RIGHT, GUYS, GIVE ME 20 LAPS AROUND THE COURTYARD.
Yes, sir!
Sorry about that!
THERE'S FLOWER! ♡
You sure you didn't forget anything else?

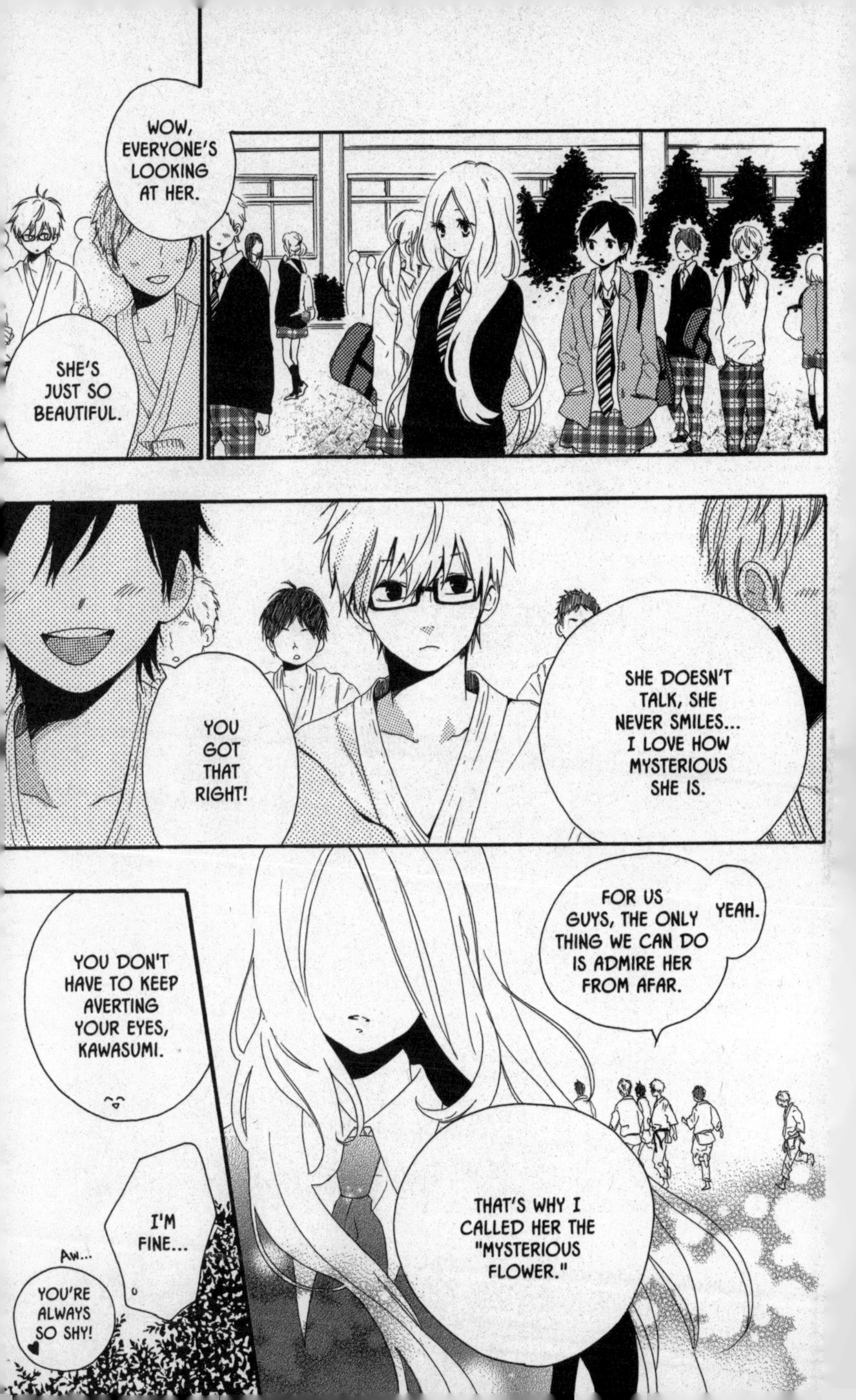
WOW, EVERYONE'S LOOKING AT HER.
SHE'S JUST SO BEAUTIFUL.
SHE DOESN'T TALK, SHE NEVER SMILES... I LOVE HOW MYSTERIOUS SHE IS.
YOU GOT THAT RIGHT!
YEAH.
FOR US GUYS, THE ONLY THING WE CAN DO IS ADMIRE HER FROM AFAR.
THAT'S WHY I CALLED HER THE "MYSTERIOUS FLOWER."
YOU DON'T HAVE TO KEEP AVERTING YOUR EYES, KAWASUMI.
I'M FINE...
AW...
YOU'RE ALWAYS SO SHY!

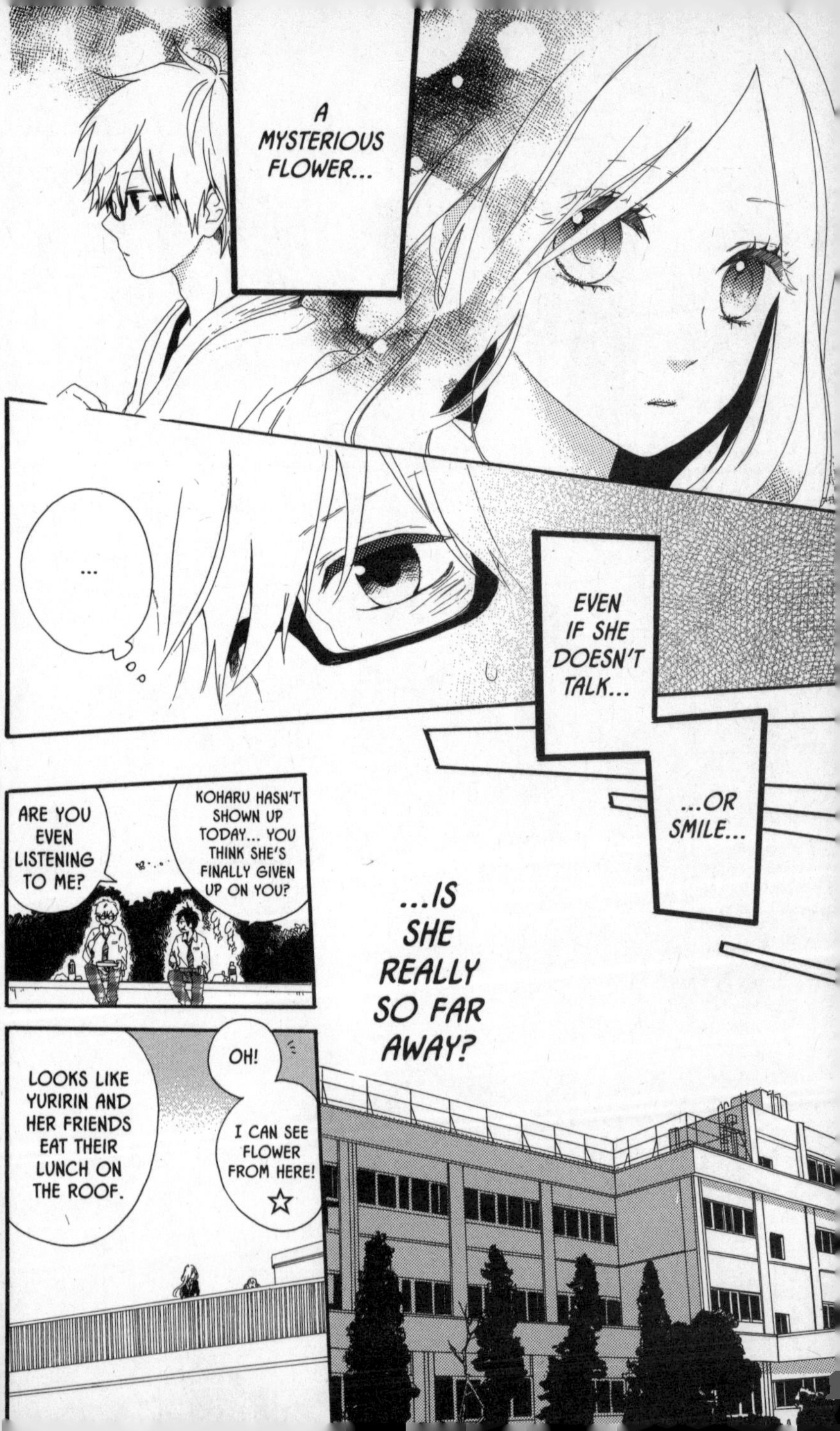
A MYSTERIOUS FLOWER...
EVEN IF SHE DOESN'T TALK...
...
...OR SMILE...
...IS SHE REALLY SO FAR AWAY?
KOHARU HASN'T SHOWN UP TODAY... YOU THINK SHE'S FINALLY GIVEN UP ON YOU?
ARE YOU EVEN LISTENING TO ME?
OH!
I CAN SEE FLOWER FROM HERE! ☆
LOOKS LIKE YURIRIN AND HER FRIENDS EAT THEIR LUNCH ON THE ROOF.

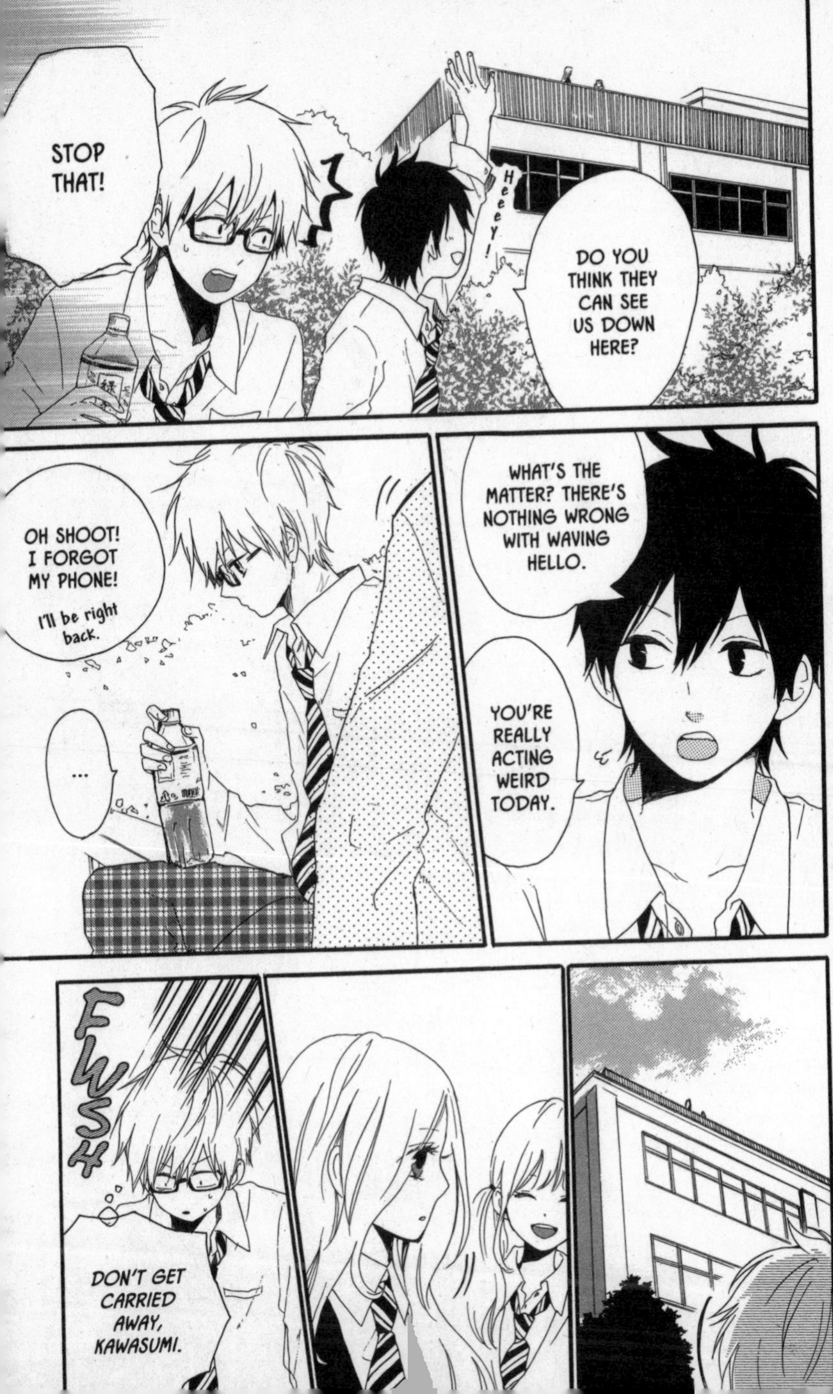
DO YOU THINK THEY CAN SEE US DOWN HERE?
Heeey!
STOP THAT!
WHAT'S THE MATTER? THERE'S NOTHING WRONG WITH WAVING HELLO.
YOU'RE REALLY ACTING WEIRD TODAY.
OH SHOOT! I FORGOT MY PHONE!
I'll be right back.
...
FWSH
DON'T GET CARRIED AWAY, KAWASUMI.

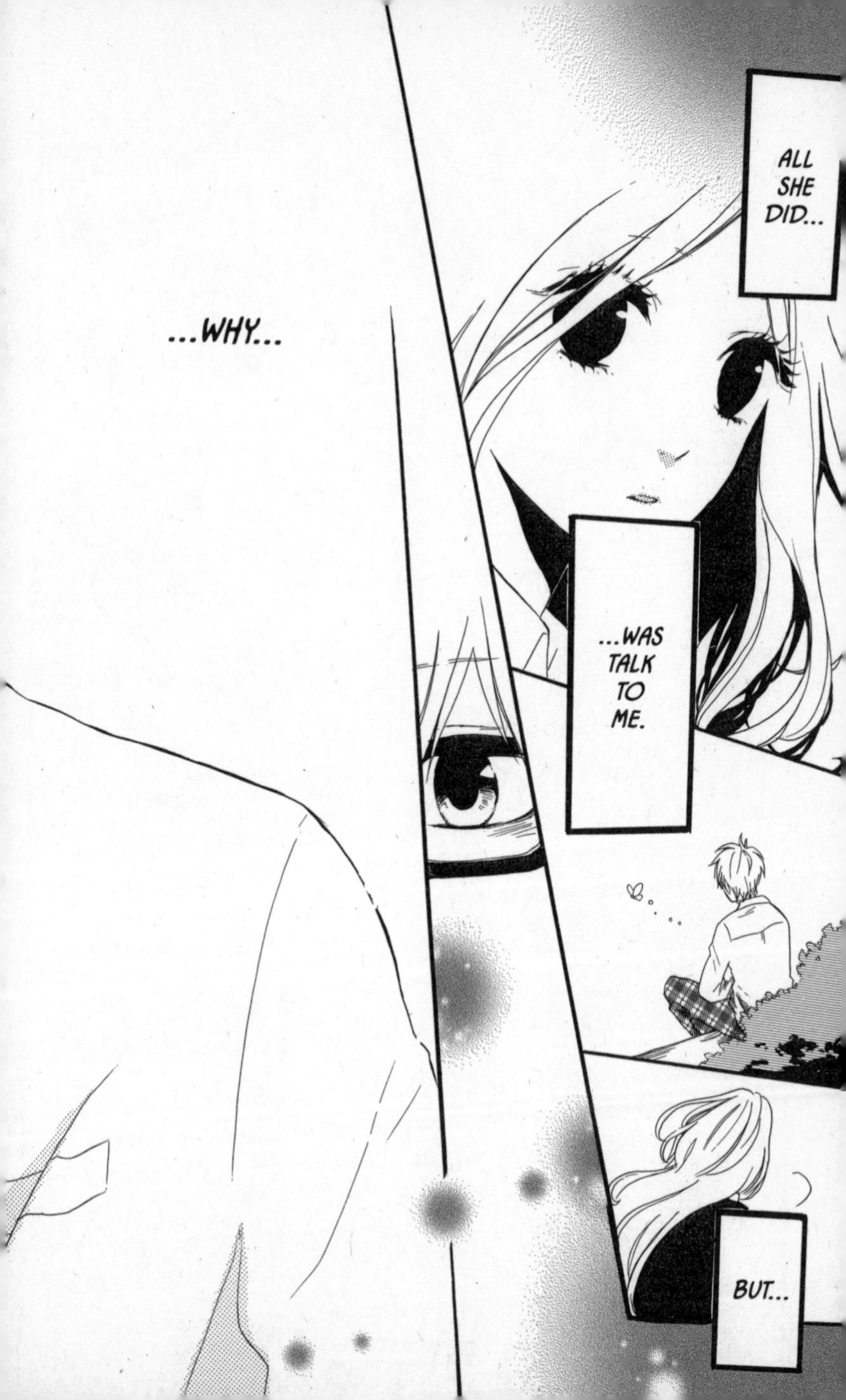
ALL SHE DID...
...WAS TALK TO ME.
BUT...
...WHY...

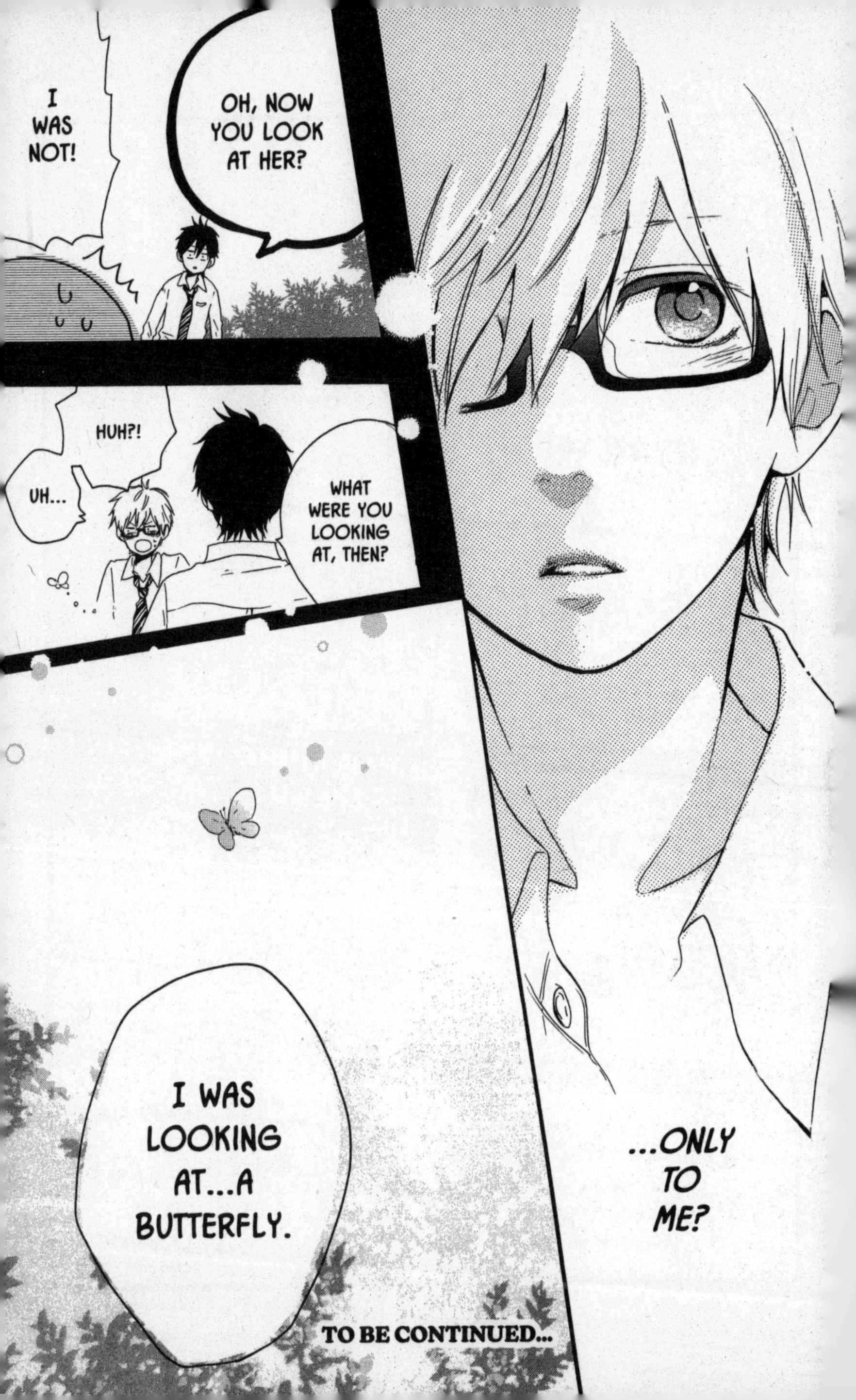
OH, NOW YOU LOOK AT HER?
I WAS NOT!
WHAT WERE YOU LOOKING AT, THEN?
HUH?!
UH...
I WAS LOOKING AT...A BUTTERFLY.
...ONLY TO ME?
TO BE CONTINUED...

SPECIAL THANKS

- MY EDITOR
- EVERYONE IN EDITORIAL AT MARGARET
- THE GRAPHIC DESIGNER
- MY ASSISTANT, HAMAGUCHI YOSHI-CHAN FOR FINISHING TOUCHES

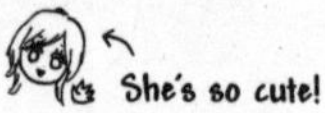
She's so cute!

EVERYONE WHO READ THIS MANGA.

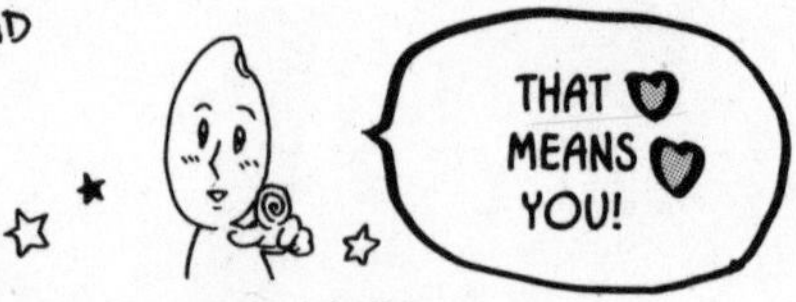
THAT ♥ MEANS ♥ YOU!

Thank you very much!!

THIS IS WHAT THINGS HAVE FELT LIKE SO FAR. →

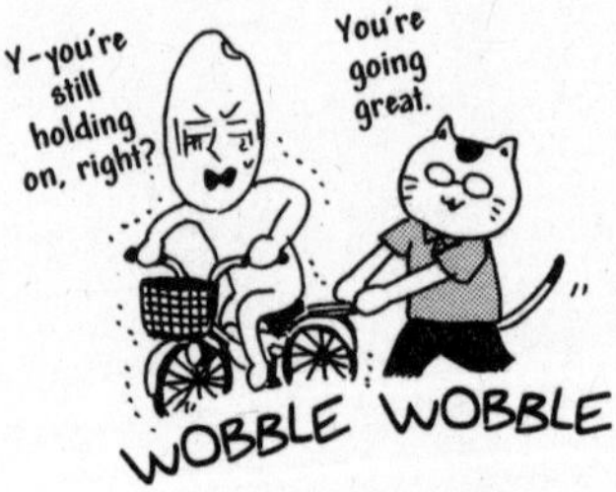
You're going great.
Y-you're still holding on, right?
WOBBLE WOBBLE

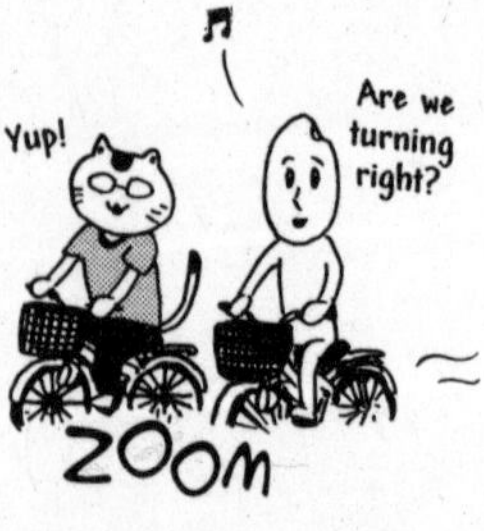
Are we turning right?
Yup!
ZOOM

NOW, I'M WORKING TO MAKE IT A LITTLE MORE LIKE THIS.

I GET REALLY FIRED UP BY LETTERS. PLEASE SEND ALONG YOUR INPUT AS WELL. I WOULD EVEN BE HAPPY WITH A POSTCARD.

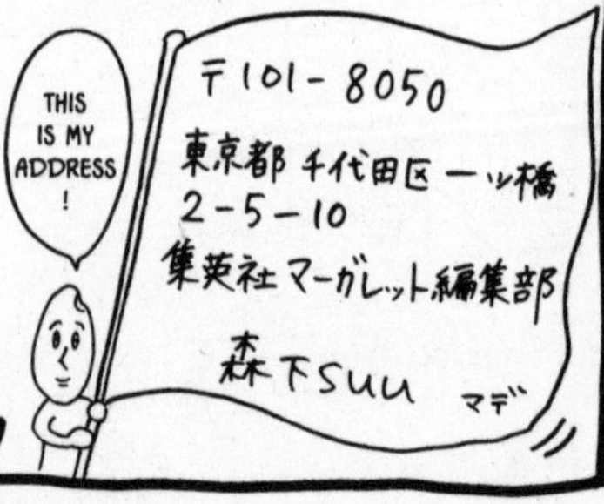
THIS IS MY ADDRESS!
〒101-8050
東京都千代田区一ツ橋
2-5-10
集英社マーガレット編集部
森下SUU マデ

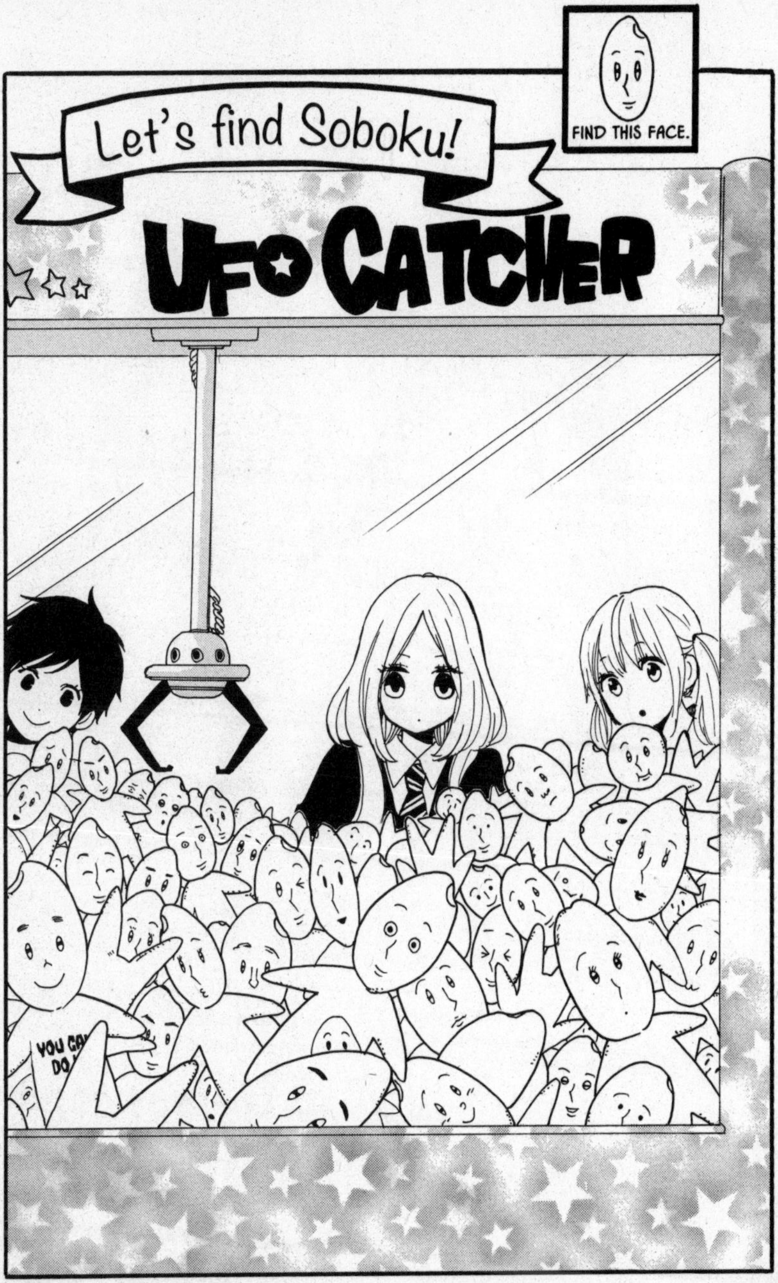
Let's find Soboku!
FIND THIS FACE.
UFO CATCHER

suu Morishita is a creator duo.
The story is by Makiro, and the art is by Nachiyan.
In 2010 they debuted with the one-shot
"Anote Konote." Their works include
Like a Butterfly and *Shortcake Cake*.

Like a
Butterfly

Volume 1 • Shojo Beat Edition

Story and Art by **suu Morishita**

TRANSLATION + ADAPTATION **Abby Lehrke**
TOUCH-UP ART + LETTERING **Monaliza de Asis**
DESIGN **Shawn Carrico**
EDITOR **Holly Fisher**

HIBI CHOCHO © 2012 by Suu Morishita
All rights reserved.
First published in Japan in 2012 by SHUEISHA Inc., Tokyo.
English translation arranged by SHUEISHA Inc.

The stories, characters, and incidents mentioned
in this publication are entirely fictional.

Printed in the U.S.A.

Published by VIZ Media, LLC
P.O. Box 77010
San Francisco, CA 94107

10 9 8 7 6 5 4 3 2 1
First printing, July 2023

VIZ MEDIA
viz.com

Shojo Beat
shojobeat.com

Like a Butterfly

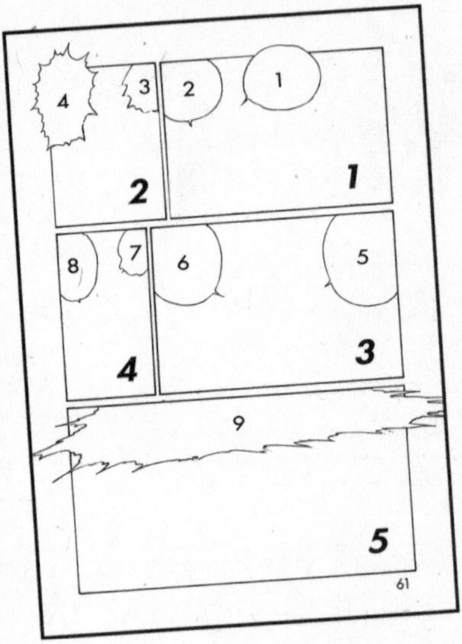

1
2
1
3
4
2
5
6
3
7
8
4
9
5
61

THIS IS THE LAST PAGE.

In keeping with the original Japanese comic format, this book reads from right to left—so action, sound effects, and word balloons are completely reversed. This preserves the orientation of the original artwork. Check out the diagram shown here to get the hang of things, and then turn to the other side of the book to get started!

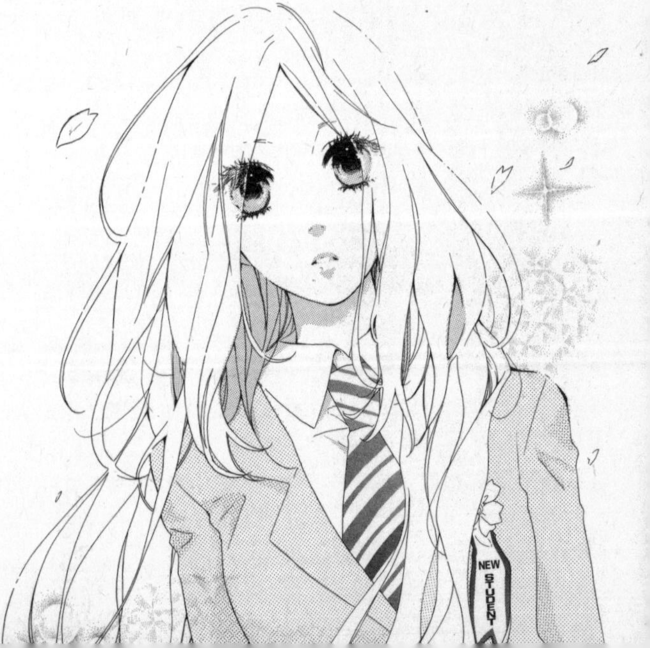

NEW STUDENT